D0225603

DATE DUE

DEMCO 38-296

WHITE LAKE TOWNSHIP LIBRARY
7527 E. HIGHLAND RD.
WHITE LAKE, MI 48383   #73
(248) 698-4942
AUG 3 1 2009

TERM PAPER RESOURCE GUIDE TO AMERICAN INDIAN HISTORY

TERM PAPER RESOURCE GUIDE TO AMERICAN INDIAN HISTORY

Patrick Russell LeBeau

Greenwood Press
Westport, Connecticut • London

Library of Congress Cataloging-in-Publication Data

LeBeau, Patrick Russell, 1958–
    Term paper resource guide to American Indian history / Patrick LeBeau.
        p. cm.
    Includes bibliographical references and index.
        ISBN 978–0–313–35271–3 (alk. paper)
1.   Indians of North America—History—Study and teaching—Activity programs. 2.   Indians of
North America—History—Bibliography. 3.   Report writing—Handbooks, manuals, etc.   I. Title.
E76.6.L334 2009
973.004'97—dc22   2008047683

British Library Cataloguing in Publication Data is available.

Copyright © 2009 by Patrick Russell LeBeau

All rights reserved. No portion of this book may be
reproduced, by any process or technique, without the
express written consent of the publisher.

Library of Congress Catalog Card Number: 2008047683
ISBN: 978–0–313–35271–3

First published in 2009

Greenwood Press, 88 Post Road West, Westport, CT 06881
An imprint of Greenwood Publishing Group, Inc.
www.greenwood.com

Printed in the United States of America

The paper used in this book complies with the
Permanent Paper Standard issued by the National
Information Standards Organization (Z39.48–1984).

10 9 8 7 6 5 4 3 2 1

Jennifer A. Cuthbert deserves special acknowledgment for her wit and clever advice at key moments and for her caring and loving support.

Contents

Introduction

The extensive primary, secondary, Web, and multimedia sources that can be found on American Indians show that Indians have been and continue to be a fascinating subject of study and interest, an interest attributable to the rich and dramatic story the whole of Indian history tells. The earliest European explorer told a story of a new land inhabited by a savage people. The scientific historian tells a story of devastating loss of life among Indians due to pandemic and epidemic diseases brought by European explorers, settlers, and adventurers. The military historian tells a story of hundreds of years of Indian wars and conflicts, while the political and diplomatic historians tell a story of diplomacy, treaties, and the taking of Indian land and natural resources. The social historian tells a story of how Indians rediscover lost customs and practices, and the cultural historian tells a story of the richness of Indian languages, arts, and oral literary traditions. The Indians tell their own stories of tribal history, of cultural revitalization and of the survival of Indian people and tribes in a modern world. American Indian history is a vast and, at times, complicated story.

The goal of *Term Paper Resource Guide to American Indian History* is to provide 100 of the most significant topics in American Indian history, from first contact to recent years, and to have those topics serve as signposts to point and lead students to a greater and richer knowledge of the story of American Indians, rather than to tell the complete story.

To give an idea of the limitation of selecting 100 topics is to point to the more than 550 federally recognized American Indian tribes living within the boundaries of the United States in 2008 and to know that many more Indian tribes existed in the historic past. Each one of these tribes has a story to tell, and a selection of 100 topics cannot possibly tell them all. For that reason, the guide focuses on those American Indian tribes that share a special status with the U.S. government, one that is legal and political and is derived from treaties and other agreements with the U.S. government. In this way, a story told about one tribe is most often a story told about them all, despite time or geography. Each event, though often focused on one region and tribe, and sometimes, one individual, shares a commonality with all tribes and Indian people.

Further, to avoid confusion, the term "American Indian" is used as a consistent way of referencing American Indians as a whole and will at times be interchangeable with "Native American." For the most part, "American Indian" is the legal and preferred term, but even the U.S. Congress shifted to "Native American" in 1990. The U.S. Constitution and most treaties and agreements use "Indian" but will often attach a prefix, such as "Sioux," to indicate tribal distinctions. One tribe can have numerous names from many different sources including names they give themselves. For example, the Oglala Lakota, a name they give themselves, are also known as the Sioux, which is a name of French origin and the common designation found in most history books. The official U.S. name for the tribe is "The Oglala Sioux Indian Tribe," but in recent years the Oglalas have dropped the "Indian" from that title. The indigenous peoples of Alaska and Hawaii are referred to as Native Alaskans and Native Hawaiians, respectively.

When writing about Indians, use the name the tribes have for themselves, such as Oglala Lakota or Menominee, whenever possible and use the term "American Indian" (or "Alaskan Native" or "Hawaiian Native") when writing on general themes and issues. Because Indians have been objectified and used as foils or scapegoats in many books, be sensitive to tribal identities and avoid the pitfalls of stereotyping. The book *So You Want to Write About American Indians?: A Guide for Writers, Student and Scholars* (Edwards Brothers, Inc., 2005), by Devon Abbott Mihesuah, offers good advice.

Term Paper Resource Guide to American Indian History targets high school and undergraduate college students seeking ideas for research papers as well as those librarians and teachers situated to help them. Each selection begins with a descriptive title and short summary of the event, followed by *Term Paper Suggestions* and *Alternative Term Paper Suggestions* sections. The cited primary, secondary, World Wide Web, and multimedia sources have been selected for their availability in most libraries and from online retail stores like Amazon.com and Barnes and Noble. In the secondary sources, the articles, most of them scholarly, are available from JSTOR or MUSE databases, which most schools and libraries have access and permission to view, download, and print. Each source has a descriptive annotation that will help students make selections of source materials, while the term paper and alternative term paper suggestions provide an entrance into the complex study of the American Indian. The suggestions are meant to guide the student to subjects or ideas worth writing about and to encourage the student to have an agenda, goal, or objective.

The term paper suggestions are also designed to encourage student researchers to consider the Indian side of the story and the Indian point of view, which have been so often ignored in the bulk of books written about Indians, in an effort to avoid ethnocentric thinking and impressionism. In recent years, scholars and other experts have collected data and have written books to recognize the importance of Indian oral traditions and an Indian way of recounting history. Even in the areas of linguistics, archeology, and ethnography, new interpretations from Indian points of view are being written and shared with the scholarly community in an effort to provide balanced analysis and interpretation. The suggestions make use of the many sources of information on Indian cultural traditions as well as new ways of interpreting Indian artifacts and material culture.

Though the Indian war stories receive the most scholarly attention, the selection of federal Indian policy and opinions of the U.S. Supreme Court on Indian cases, though at first glance technical and complex, are often the most interesting and far-reaching events in American Indian history. These events are the ones that have the most lasting and controversial social/cultural impact on the lives of Indian people and tribes. Unlike the romance of the Indian war story, which tends to focus on battle tactics and strategies, the study of federal Indian policy and judicial rulings reveals a deeper and more meaningful story of Indian history, because many of the concerns of Indian people and tribes, past and present, are revealed.

USING THE GUIDE

Each selection in the guide follows an eight-part format: event title, narrative summary, term paper suggestions, and alternative paper suggestions, followed by primary, secondary, World Wide Web, and multimedia sources. The title and summary explain the topic and its importance in

American Indian history. The term paper suggestions, which often contain questions, are designed as critical-thinking exercises as well as serving to provide ideas for research papers. The alternative paper suggestions guide the student researcher to other possible modes of expression, such as the use of Indian oral traditions in audio form or staging a mock trial, and encourages the use of electronic media, such as Microsoft Power-Point, iMovie, or Web sites. Alternative paper suggestions might also encourage the creative arts, such as poetry, journal writing, and letter writing. A brief description of the four categories of the source materials follows:

Primary Sources—Whenever possible, easily accessible online sources are cited. Though actual treaties and congressional acts are often cited, firsthand historical narratives or books written by principle participants are cited as well. Two universal primary sources are: *Indian Affairs: Law and Treaties,* http://digital.library.okstate.edu/kappler/index.htm and *Indian Land Cessions,* http://www.usgwarchives.org/maps/cessions/.

Secondary Sources—These are the most recent and, in some cases, the only texts on the topic. The scholarly articles are available through JSTOR or MUSE databases. The standard secondary reference work to American Indian history is the 20-volume *Handbook of the North American Indians,* edited by William C. Sturtevant, http://anthropology.si.edu/handbook.htm.

World Wide Web—Although most of the Web sites serve as a brief introduction to the topics, some are detailed and comprehensive. In several cases, the Web sources supplement the primary sources. A good general site is the "Index of Native American Resources on the Internet," http://www.hanksville.org/NAresources/.

Multimedia Sources—Most are documentary films. A standard general documentary is *500 Nations* (Warner Video, 1994, 372 minutes), which has 8 episodes in 4 DVDs, plus 1 CD-ROM of archival and primary source materials, and is available from Amazon.com.

1. Smallpox Epidemics (1530s–1880s)

Originating from Europe and transmitted via explorers, traders, fishermen, and colonists, many forms of infectious diseases have ravaged American Indian populations since first contact. Smallpox is the most documented and understood of them all, and its long-term demographic destruction has been observed and recorded by early explorers, such as Hernando De Soto in the 1530s, and by U.S. ethnographers of American Indians, such as James Mooney in the 1880s. Smallpox devastated American Indian communities for hundreds of years. Current studies have demonstrated that American Indian communities suffered biological, social, and economic devastation due to pandemics and epidemics like smallpox and influenza. Coinciding with first contact with Europeans, smallpox is estimated to have killed 30 percent of the American Indian population in the New World, due to American Indians' lack of biological defenses to fight new infectious diseases imported from Europe. Many historians think this devastating loss of life facilitated European conquest and settlement to a larger extent than was previously thought. Of particular interest is how, over time, Indian cultures were changed by such devastating loss of life and what parts of Indian cultures have persisted despite these losses. Some historians have discovered credible evidence that during the French and Indian War and Pontiac's Rebellion, colonial leaders and military officers deliberately used blankets infected with the smallpox pathogen to infect and harm American Indian combatants and tribal communities.

TERM PAPER SUGGESTIONS

1. According to scholars of early European colonization of North and South America, the conquest of Indian tribal communities could not have been possible without the help of diseases brought over from Europe, and smallpox, variola major, was the most virulent. Using the theories of these scholars and the known mortality rates of those people infected with smallpox, write a paper that demonstrates the effectiveness of smallpox as an "unknowing" weapon of conquest.

2. Later in U.S. history, scholars discovered evidence of smallpox used as a "knowing" weapon of conquest, but this is hotly disputed. Examine

both sides of the argument and write an essay that presents your findings. What is the strongest argument? What are the moral, ethical considerations?

3. Smallpox epidemics have caused Indians to retaliate against neighboring Euro-Americans with violence and retribution. Write an essay that provides reasons why Indians would do so.

4. Pandemics like smallpox changed Indian culture. In the documented case of the Mandan, Hidatsa, and Arickara, smallpox killed many during the winter of 1837–1838. Write an essay that shows how these tribes changed after they were devastated by smallpox. How much of their culture survived, and how much of their culture was destroyed?

5. Trade with Indians started long before significant European settlements and trade of material goods penetrated deeper into regions where Indian people had very little contact with and knowledge of European civilizations. This trade also brought contagions, like the virulent form of smallpox, which had a devastating impact on Indian tribes of the interior. Watch the short film *Ikwe* (NFB, 1986) and study a few secondary sources for this connection between trade and the spread of disease. Write an essay that explores the way Indian populations could be greatly reduced by the spread of disease and how this would influence the speed and ease of European settlement of Indian lands.

6. Because the United States discontinued smallpox vaccinations in 1972 for a number of good reasons (for example, because the vaccine itself poses a potential health risk), many Americans would not necessarily be able to combat the disease if an outbreak occurred today. Because several governments around the world have kept virulent smallpox strains for potential use as biological weapons, the possibility of an accidental or deliberate outbreak of the disease worries many health professionals and governmental officials. Write an essay that outlines the arguments for and against a renewal of the U.S. vaccination policy and program, and use your knowledge of the effect of smallpox among American Indians to bolster your findings.

ALTERNATIVE TERM PAPER SUGGESTIONS

1. Some historians have characterized the result of pandemics and epidemics as creating a "widowed land" as opposed to a "virgin land." Using readily available online maps of North America, and create before and after maps that support the "widowed land" theory by color coding and showing the demographics of pre-contact American Indian populations and then a second map showing the decrease in population due to ravages and the importation of new infectious diseases from Europe shortly after contact.

2. Identify five Indian tribes from the early United States, circa 1780, to the end of the Indian wars, circa 1880, that evidence indicates were destroyed or nearly so by smallpox. Graph the rate of death over a period of time, usually very short, for each tribe and place them in a larger time line chronology, which includes treaties and agreements with the United States, to show how smallpox moves westward as Americans move westward and to demonstrate that Indian tribes are usually weakened militarily, economically, socially, and culturally by the time they sign land cession treaties or agreements with the United States.

SUGGESTED SOURCES

Primary Sources

D'Errico, Peter. "Jeffrey Amherst and Smallpox Blankets." *NativeWeb*. http://www .nativeweb.org/pages/legal/amherst/lord_jeff.html. A well-documented Web site that includes the best images of a series of letters written by British soldiers and officials discussing and approving a plan to distribute blankets infected with smallpox to Indians in 1763.

Mooney, James. *The Ghost-Dance Religion and the Sioux Outbreak of 1890.* 1896. Reprint, Lincoln, NE: Bison Books, 1991, 743–44. An eyewitness account of a trained observer and chronicler of American Indian cultures and societies who observed the devastating impact of smallpox on Indian people.

Secondary Sources

Cook, David Noble. *Born to Die: Disease and New World Conquest, 1492–1650.* Cambridge, UK: Cambridge University Press, 1998. Takes the position that pandemic and epidemic disease had more to do with the conquest of the New World than warfare or economics.

Cook, David Noble, and W. G. Lovell, eds. *Secret Judgments of God: Old World Disease in Colonial Spanish America.* Norman, OK: University of Oklahoma Press, 1992. An interdisciplinary group of historians, geographers, and anthropologists offers a series of case studies of how diseases destroyed American Indian populations in Spanish America.

Crosby, Alfred W. *The Columbian Exchange: Biological and Cultural Consequences of 1492.* Westport, CT: Greenwood Press, 1972. The first complete study of how biological forces played an overwhelming role in the conquest of the New World.

DeVoto, Bernard. *Across the Wide Missouri.* Boston: Houghton Mifflin, 1947. Reprint, 1975. Chapter 11 provides a well-written and easily readable account of a smallpox epidemic among Indian tribes along the Missouri River in 1837.

Dobyns, H. F. *Their Number Become Thinned: Native American Population Dynamics in Eastern North America.* Knoxville, TN: University of Tennessee Press, 1983. Dobyns's research and findings started the debate on the original population of American Indians before the transmission of infectious diseases, which he estimated as much larger than originally thought.

Robertson, R. G. *Rotting Face: Smallpox and the American Indian.* Caldwell, ID: Caxton Press, 2001. Details the smallpox epidemic of 1837–1838 that almost destroyed the Mandan, Hidatsa, Arickara, and Blackfeet and how this devastation changed the political and social structure of these tribes. Interwoven in the text are chapters on the history of smallpox in America and essays on prevention, technology, and change.

Stannard, D. E. *American Holocaust: Columbus and the Conquest of the New World.* Oxford, UK: Oxford University Press, 1992. Explores the connection between disease, depredation, enslavement, and massacre and between racism and genocide in the New World. An easily readable, well-documented text that challenges age-old theories and arguments.

Thornton, R. *American Indian Holocaust and Survival: A Population History Since 1492.* Norman, OK: University of Oklahoma Press, 1987. Compares the population estimates of pre-contact American Indians and the impacts of disease and war to reduce that population.

World Wide Web

Barquet, Nicolau, MD, and Pere Domingo, MD. "Smallpox: The Triumph over the Most Terrible of the Ministers of Death." http://www.annals.org/cgi/content/full/127/8_Part_1/635. Describes how smallpox cruelly attacks the human organism and tells how a vaccine was developed to eradicate future outbreaks and epidemics.

Gill, Harold B. "Colonial Germ Warfare." http://www.earlyamerica.us/Foundation/journal/Spring04/warfare.cfm. Describes the plot of British soldiers to infect the Indians besieging Fort Pitt during Pontiac's War (1763) with smallpox, an early example of "germ" warfare.

"History of Bio-Warfare." http://www.pbs.org/wgbh/nova/bioterror/hist_nf.html. Provides a brief history of the use of disease as a war weapon.

"Kids' Connection." http://kidsnet.org/sfkc/. Scroll under "Topics" to find the link "Culture and Health" to information and activities to explore the "power of germs."

Lewy, Guenter. "Were American Indians the Victims of Genocide?" http://hnn.us/articles/7302.html. Examines the death rate inflicted by pandemic/epidemic disease on Indian populations and examines the Pequot War, Sand Creek, and Wounded Knee 1890 to determine whether

diseases and wars were a conscious act of genocide, a claim that has been
hotly debated by historians and other experts.

"Smallpox and the Cherokee." http://www.merceronline.com/Native/
native03.htm. A short description on the effects of smallpox on one
specific tribal community.

Smith, Susanna. "Old Tactics, New Threat: What Is Today's Risk of Smallpox?"
http://virtualmentor.ama-assn.org/2002/09/mhst1-0209.html. An
important question to consider and explore.

Multimedia Source

Ikwe. Dir. Norman Bailey. National Film Board of Canada, 1986. DVD.
57 minutes. Set in 1770, a young Chippewa girl marries a Scottish fur
trader, and this serves as the source of dramatic conflict. At the very
end of the film, smallpox kills many of her Chippewa tribe and is
presumably brought by the fur traders.

2. Early Explorers and Early Conquest (1535–1540)

From 1535 to 1540, European explores Jacques Cartier, Hernando De Soto,
and Francisco Vasquez de Coronado were the first to explore the North
American interior and the first to encounter Indians. Along with trade
goods, these same explorers also brought Old World diseases, such as small-
pox. In 1535, Frenchman Jacques Cartier mapped and explored the
St. Lawrence River Valley and Seaway in the northeast to the Great Lakes.
He named the land "the Country of Canada." The St. Lawrence offered
the French access to people and lands in the very heart of North America.
This access allowed trade, especially the fur trade, to flourish and expand.
In 1540, Hernando De Soto explored southeastern lands of the United
States from Florida to both banks of the Mississippi River. His journey led
to increased Spanish claim to lands east of the Mississippi and west of Span-
ish Florida. In the same year, 1540, Francisco Vasquez de Coronado
explored the area of New Mexico and other parts of the American southwest.
He is most remembered for his conquest of the Hawikuh Pueblo in New
Mexico in 1540. Both De Soto and Coronado found land but failed to find
mineral wealth. However, in an interesting moment of cultural exchange,
the two Spanish explorers and conquistadors brought horses to North
American Indians, horses that were lost, stolen, or that escaped. Though

gold and other riches were not found, these three explorers furthered French and Spanish claim to a large portion of North America from the Atlantic to the Pacific oceans, which would become a source of frustration for English, and later, American expansion.

TERM PAPER SUGGESTIONS

1. Cartier's discovery of the St. Lawrence River for France opened the door for French trade and colonization. Investigate and report how this river, which flows into the Atlantic Ocean, could be so important to trade and settlement. What geographical features of the river basin and valley help to accommodate colonization as well as trade?

2. Coronado and De Soto came to North America to conquer and to find gold and other precious minerals. Investigate how the search for mineral riches could motivate explorers to take risks and to seek out American Indian villages despite the risks.

3. Write a paper that compares the explorers' views and understandings of American Indians. What were their descriptions and what do these descriptions reveal?

4. Spanish conquistadors unwittingly brought the horse to North American Indians. Investigate how the horse changed the culture and lifestyle of Plains Indians from Texas to the Dakotas.

5. Explorers planted flags to claim land occupied by Indians and designated Indian lands with their own names. Write an essay that explores the "rite of discovery." What was the purpose of claiming land that was not physically occupied or conquered?

6. The Spanish seemed to explore to conquer and to possess whereas the French explored to establish trade relations. Write a comparison that explores the difference between French and Spanish goals of exploration and what this difference would mean to American Indians.

ALTERNATIVE TERM PAPER SUGGESTIONS

1. Assume you were an ordinary member of a European expedition to explore North America in the 1500s. From that perspective write a travel log or travel blog of your experiences and encounters with American Indians. Include how you might feel about the goals and demands of your leaders. Include images of people and places.

2. Assume you are an early European explorer of North America in the 1500s, and one of your goals is to draft a map of your discoveries. Create an

imaginative sketch of a map from the perspective of what early explorers would know and what they were able to see from the ground they stood on, rather than from the global and informative knowledge of modern maps, even road maps. How would an Indian village be depicted?

SUGGESTED SOURCES

Primary Sources

Cartier, Jacques. "Shorte and Briefe Narration, 1535–1536." http://www .americanjourneys.org/aj-027/index.asp. Firsthand account of the explorer's second voyage.

Castañeda de Nájera, Pedro de. "Journey of Coronado, 1540–1542." http://www .americanjourneys.org/aj-086/index.asp. The account of the expedition of Cibola, 1540, where Pedro de Castañeda of Nájera describes the Cibola people, ceremonies, customs, and settlement.

Oviedo y Valdés, Gonzalo Fernández de. "Narrative of De Soto's Expedition Based on the Diary of Rodrigo Ranjel, His Private Secretary." http://www .americanjourneys.org/aj-023/index.asp. Follows the expedition up to the point of De Soto's death.

Secondary Sources

Allen, J. L. "From Cabot to Cartier: The Early Exploration of Eastern North America, 1497–1543." *Annals of the Association of American Geographers* 82, no. 3 (1992): 500–521. Short descriptive essay on early North American exploration by the French.

Boissonnault, Réal. *Jacques Cartier: Explorer and Navigator.* Ottawa, ON, Canada: Environment Canada, Parks, 1987. This book looks at the impact that Cartier had on American Indians and the conflicts his expedition endured on his journey.

Cook, Ramsey. *The Voyages of Jacques Cartier.* Toronto, ON, Canada: University of Toronto Press, 1993. A definitive and complete work on the French explorer and his three historic voyages.

Day, Grove A. *Coronado and the Discovery of the Southwest.* New York: Meredith Press, 1967. Maps and important dates are included as well as an index, glossary, and resources for additional information.

Eccles, W. J. *The Canadian Frontier 1534–1760.* Albuquerque, NM: University of New Mexico, 1983. Includes maps and early history of Canada.

Fritz, Ronald H. *New Worlds: The Great Voyages of Discovery 1400–1600.* A well-appreciated compilation and synthesis of discovery and exploration in narrative form, a monumental standard reference text.

Hammond, George Peter. *Coronado's Seven Cities.* Albuquerque, NM: United States Coronado Exposition Commission, 1940. The search for the seven cities of gold is the motivation to endure starvation and hostile American Indians.

Jacob, Yves. *Jacques Cartier: de Saint-Malo au Saint-Laurent.* Paris, France: Editions Ouest-France, 1992. Desire, dreams, and discovery were the motivations to explore unknown lands despite the potential risks of death, deprivation, and disease.

Lavender, David Sievert. *De Soto, Coronado, Cabrillo: Explorers of the Northern Mystery.* Washington, DC: Division of Publications, National Park Service, U.S. Dept. of the Interior, 1992. This book focuses on the unique contributions Hispanics have made in the United States, from the earliest Spanish explorers to the present day.

Leacock, Stephen. *The Mariner of St. Malo: A Chronicle of the Voyages of Jacques Cartier.* Toronto, ON, Canada: Glasgow, Brook & Co., 1915. This book includes letters, maps, and a diary that Cartier produced during and after his adventure.

Mountjoy, Shane. *Francisco Coronado and the Seven Cities of Gold.* Philadelphia, PA: Chelsea House, 2006. A short (140 page) life-and-accomplishments of the famous conquistador and explorer.

World Wide Web

Avellaneda, Ignacio. *Los Sobrevivientes de la Florida: The Survivors of the De Soto Expedition.* http://www.nps.gov/history/history/online_books/deso/contents.htm. From primary sources this online book explores the geographic, economic, and religious reasons for De Soto's explorations.

"The DeSoto Chronicles." http://www.nps.gov/archive/deso/chronicles/index.htm. An interactive Web site that not only provides written summaries but historical and visual data as well.

"Hernando de Soto." http://www.newadvent.org/cathen/04753a.htm. Brief summary of the explorations of Hernando De Soto.

"Historical Maps of the United States." http://www.lib.utexas.edu/maps/histus.html-exploration.html. Provides links to maps useful for visually understanding geographical location. Shows many of the early explorations of North America.

"Jacques Cartier: Explorer of the St. Lawrence." http://www.ubishops.ca/ccc/div/soc/esg/stlaur/hist/hi_cartier.htm. A student-friendly site with easy-to-read summaries that provides links to all three of his voyages, a map, short essays, and a bibliography.

"Jacques Cartier: Explorer of the St. Lawrence River." http://www
.publicbookshelf.com/public_html/The_Great_Republic_By_the_Master
_Historians_Vol_I/jacquesca_bi.html. A short excerpt from Hubert
Bancroft's *The Great Republic by Master Historians* that describes Cartier's
exploration in a detailed but concise manner.

"Primary Sources." http://www.win.tue.nl/~engels/discovery/primary.html. This
site has many explorers' names as hyperlinks that lead to hard-to-find
primary sources.

Multimedia Sources

Conquest of America. Dir. Tony Bacon et al. A&E Television Networks, 2005.
2 DVDs. 180 minutes. Four-part series covering North America in four
geographical regions (Northeast, Northwest, Southeast, and Southwest).

Conquistadors. Dir. Michael Wood. Public Broadcasting Service Home Video,
2000. DVD. 240 minutes. Provides a detailed account of the manner
in which the Spanish explored and conquered the New World.

3. First European Settlements and Indian Revolt (1565–1598)

From 1565 to 1598, the first European settlements were established in
Florida, North Carolina, and New Mexico, and they constituted the first
contact points between Europeans and American Indians. In 1565, after
70 years of Spanish exploration, a Spanish admiral named Pedro Menén-
dez de Aviles landed in Florida and founded St. Augustine, the first permanent European colony, near the villages of the Timucua Indians.
Because of Spanish successes in Florida, Queen Elizabeth commissioned
Sir Walter Raleigh to colonize North America, and in 1585 he founded
the English colony at Roanoke Island, Virginia, but it was abandoned in
1586. In 1587, in a second attempt, John White and another group
colonized Roanoke Island, and after the colony was established White
returned to England for supplies. When he returned to Roanoke in
1590, he found little trace of the settlement; the settlers had simply
vanished, which has sparked speculation of their fate ever since. Regardless of the Roanoke mystery, in their initial attempts, the English failed
to create a permanent colony in North America. In 1598, Don Juan de
Oñate Salazar (known as Oñate) brought Spanish settlers to Texas and
New Mexico and established several permanent settlements near the

Pueblo Indians of the southwest. A long-remembered event happened shortly after Oñate's arrival, when the Acoma Pueblos allegedly refused to help the Spanish with supplies. Oñate retaliated by killing 800 Acoma, enslaving many more, and amputating the left foot of several Acoma males over the age of 25.

TERM PAPER SUGGESTIONS

1. Write a report on the oldest settlement in North America, St. Augustine. Include the role of American Indians, the role of the Spanish quest for riches and great mysteries, and the role of the settlers themselves.

2. In the late 1500s, England and Spain fought over the religious policies of Queen Elizabeth I; their fighting ended with the defeat of the Spanish Armada in 1589. Study and report on how the English and Spanish transferred their Old World hostilities to the New World. Because this was the time of Sir Francis Drake, explain how pirates or privateers were involved. How were American Indians involved?

3. Write an essay comparing the many theories that explain the mysterious disappearance of the English settlers at Roanoke Island. What theory is the most plausible? Why?

4. Based on source material, write a comparative essay on the treatment of American Indians living near the St. Augustine and Roanoke settlements. How did Indians respond to this treatment? Was this treatment always negative? What did the Europeans expect from the local Indian populations?

5. Write an essay on Oñate's cruel treatment of Indians and his own Spanish settlers. How does his treatment of the Acoma resonate to this very day? For example, in recent times, a statue honoring Oñate's explorations and discoveries has its left foot broken off, presumably by protesters. Why would they remove this part of the anatomy of the statue?

6. Write a paper about the first successful colonies in North America. Of the three early European colonies, only the Spanish colonies of Sante Fe and St. Augustine survived early hardships to maintain a continuous existence to this very day. What was the secret of their success? What was the problem with Roanoke, the English settlement? Why did it not survive?

ALTERNATIVE TERM PAPER SUGGESTIONS

1. Make a time line tracing St. Augustine, Florida and Santa Fe, New Mexico from their foundings to the present day. In an oral presentation, use this time

line as a powerful source of evidence to prove that Hispanics have had a longer settled presence in North America than English or French people.

2. The parts of New Mexico and Texas that Don Juan de Oñate explored and settled is called El Camino Real. Create a travel brochure using the Web site http://education.nmsu.edu/webquest/wq/camino/camino.html.

SUGGESTED SOURCES

Primary Sources

Barlowe, Arthur. "Captain Arthur Barlowe's Narrative of the First Voyage to the Coasts of America." http://www.americanjourneys.org/aj-034/index.asp. One of the earliest English accounts of Virginia and Roanoke.

Belval, Brian. *A Primary Source History of the Lost Colony of Roanoke.* New York: The Rosen Publishing Group, 2006. This is a collection of the most relevant sources.

Oñate, Juan de. "True Account of the Expedition of Oñate toward the East." http://www.americanjourneys.org/aj-014/index.asp. Further explorations of El Camino Real.

Pardo, Juan. "Account of Florida, 1566–1568." http://www.americanjourneys.org/aj-139/index.asp. An early description of Florida from the perspective of a Spanish explorer.

"Trial of the Indians of Acoma, 1598." http://www.americanjourneys.org/aj-104/index.asp. The narrative of the trial of the Acoma Pueblos who were accused of insurrection.

Secondary Sources

Durant, David N. *Raleigh's Lost Colony.* New York: Atheneum, 1981. This is a narrative story of the Roanoke mystery and the role of Sir Walter Raleigh.

Eterovich, Adam S. *Croatia and Croatians at the Lost Colony, 1585–1590.* San Carlos, CA: Ragusan Press, 2003. A new theory on the lost colony which suggests "Croatians" may have been involved; it has a lot to say about the development of triracial communities in North America (American Indians, black slaves, and white Europeans).

Kupperman, Karen Ordahl. *Roanoke, 2nd Edition: The Abandoned Colony.* Savage, MD: Rowman and Littlefield Publishers, 2007. Well-researched narrative history with an epilogue that explores the nature of a successful colonization.

Manucy, Albert C. *Menendez: Pedro Menendez De Aviles, Captain General of the Ocean Sea.* Sarasota, FL: Pineapple Press, 1992. A readable biography of Pedro Menendez, a Spanish captain general, governor of Cuba, and the founder of St. Augustine (the first permanent European settlement in North America) in Florida.

McGeagh, Robert. *Juan De Oñate's Colony in the Wilderness: An Early History of the American Southwest.* Santa Fe, NM: Sunstone Press, 1990. A brief but comprehensive narrative of the early history of El Camino Real, the American southwest.

Middleton, Richard. *Colonial America, 1565–1776.* 3rd ed. Malden, MA: Blackwell, 2002. A good general work on early colonization that includes Spanish and French settlements in North America.

Miller, Lee. *Roanoke: Solving the Mystery of the Lost Colony.* New York: Penguin, 2002. The mystery of Roanoke is investigated in the style of a law enforcement detective.

Simmons, Marc. *The Last Conquistador: Juan De Oñate and the Settling of the Far Southwest.* Norman, OK: University of Oklahoma Press, 1993. This easy-to-read and accessible biography explores the hostile tension between the Pueblo people of the southwest and Spanish/Hispanic conquerors.

Stanley, George Edward. *The European Settlement of North America: 1492–1763 (A Primary Source History of the United States).* Milwaukee, WI: World Almanac Library, 2005. A collection of primary source documents, including documents of the early explorers' settlements of Jamestown, Roanoke, Plymouth, Massachusetts Bay, Quebec, and Georgia.

Villagrá, Gaspar Pérez de. *Historia de la Nueva México, 1610: A Critical and Annotated Spanish/English Edition.* Albuquerque, NM: University of New Mexico Press, 2004. An epic poem and travel journal in 34 cantos that documents Oñate's founding of New Mexico in 1598.

World Wide Web

Adams, Don, and Teresa A. Kendrick. "Don Juan de Oñate and the First Thanksgiving." http://historicaltextarchive.com/sections.php?op=viewarticle&artid=736. A well-written, researched, footnoted, and readable narrative of the "first Thanksgiving" as a Spanish and Pueblo first rather than an English pilgrim and Powhatan first. It includes a time line of the Oñate expedition.

"Kid Info." http://www.kidinfo.com/SchoolSubjects.html. Click on the "Roanoke" link. This site includes links to scholarly works and is very comprehensive.

"Lost Colony of Roanoke Mini Unit Study." http://www.learningthroughhistory.com/newsletter/archives/022004.php. This site is a comprehensive lesson plan with reading links to primary and secondary sources, a multimedia quiz, maps, and a writing project.

"Roanoke Revisited." Heritage Education Program. Fort Raleigh National Historic Site. http://www.nps.gov/archive/fora/search.htm. Short and concise summary of the "lost colony."

St. Augustine Links and Educational Resources for Students and Teachers. http://www.staugustinelinks.com/st-augustine-links.asp. Includes links to archeological excavations of St. Augustine, historical debates, and photographs of historic sites.

"Stereotype of the Month." http://www.bluecorncomics.com/stype214.htm. A collection of newspaper articles chronicles the protests and opposition by American Indians of the building of a statue honoring the Spanish explorer Oñate.

Multimedia Sources

Conquistadors. Dir. Michael Wood. Public Broadcasting Service Home Video, 2000. DVD. 240 minutes. Provides a detailed account of the manner in which the Spanish explored and conquered the New World.

Green, Paul. *The Lost Colony: A Symphonic Drama of American History (1937).* Chapel Hill, NC: University of North Carolina Press, 2001. This is the text of an outdoor drama that includes song and dance. It runs every summer at the Waterside Theater, Manteo, North Carolina.

4. First Significant English and French Settlements (1607–1620)

Jamestown, Plymouth, and Quebec were the first colonial settlements established by the French and English that had any long-term success. In 1607, with the help of wealthy nobles with direct connections to King James I, the Virginia Company of London founded and successfully maintained the settlement of Jamestown, Virginia. Founded to make its investors money, Jamestown's commercialism would be a hallmark of its character and relations with Indians. Contrastingly, in 1620, fleeing religious persecution, first from England and then from Holland, Puritan pilgrims established the settlement of Plymouth, Massachusetts, as a separatist religious colony in America. They created Plymouth to be able to practice their religion freely and to build a community based on their own religious ideals. They, too, would create a distinct character based on their religious beliefs, and these beliefs would influence how they treated Indians. In 1608, led by explorer and adventurer Samuel de

Champlain, the French founded Quebec, Canada, but their purpose was to trade with the Indians, especially in the lucrative fur trade. In contrast to the English practice of keeping a clear separation between what was Indian and what was English, the French method of interaction with Indians penetrated Indian communities to a greater extent than the English or, later, Americans ever would.

TERM PAPER SUGGESTIONS

1. Write about the differences in relations and interactions between American Indians and the early European colonists by geographical region and by nationality.

2. Using Francis Jennings's book and the histories describing the founding of Jamestown, Plymouth, and Quebec, explore the issue of "discovery" and the "founding" of new lands and nations.

3. Was war inevitable between Indians and colonists? If so, why? What were the justifications for war and were they valid? Was total war necessary? (Total war is defined as the killing of not only combatants but of women and children and the destruction of homes and food sources.)

4. Examine the contributions of Indians to the survival of the early colonial settlements. What were they, and how did they contribute to the long-term survival and wealth of the colony? How does the myth of the first Thanksgiving play a role in the common knowledge of Indian contributions?

5. Compare the differing language that French explorer Samuel Champlain, adventurer John Smith, and governor William Bradford used to describe American Indians.

6. Study the role of conversion and education as early techniques to assimilate Indian people into the greater Euro-American civilization. What were the limitations to these early efforts, and what were the benefits to Indian people?

ALTERNATIVE TERM PAPER SUGGESTIONS

1. From the perspective of a colonial leader, write a "jeremiad," a form of early American religious oratory, that justifies the settlement of Indian lands and warfare with Indians. Usually the American version of the jeremiad recited a gloomy future if direct action was not taken to secure land and resources from Indians and to destroy the military capabilities of Indian nations.

2. From the perspective of an Indian leader, write an oration designed to evoke war against the Europeans due to their insatiable desire of Indian land and resources.

SUGGESTED SOURCES

Primary Sources

Bradford, William. *Of Plimoth Plantation.* http://www.americanjourneys.org/ aj-025/. Describes the Mayflower voyage and the establishment of the pilgrim settlement at Plymouth.

Champlain, Samuel de. *Voyage of Samuel de Champlain, 1604–1608.* http://www .americanjourneys.org/aj-115/. An excerpt of an account of Champlain's exploration and settlement of the St. Lawrence Seaway.

"The Plymouth Colony Archive Project." http://www.histarch.uiuc.edu/plymouth/ . A Web site documenting the archeological excavation of the Plymouth site and providing searchable primary and secondary sources and texts.

The Second Charter of Virginia May 23, 1609. http://www.yale.edu/lawweb/ avalon/states/va02.htm. Full text of the charter.

Smith, John. *A True Relation by Captain John Smith, 1608.* Madison, WI: Wisconsin Historical Society, 2003. http://www.americanjourneys.org/ aj-074/. Describes the first landing, battles, interactions with and capture of/escape by Indians, as well as explorations of the neighboring lands.

Secondary Sources

Billings, Warren M. *Jamestown and the Founding of a Nation.* Gettysburg, PA: Thomas Publications, 1991. The history of Jamestown from the first landing, 1607, to the American Revolution.

Deetz, James, and Patricia Scott Deetz. *The Times of Their Lives: Life, Love, and Death in Plymouth Colony.* New York: W.H. Freeman, 2000. Chapter two, "I Will Harry Them Out of the Land," is of particular interest regarding the colony's relations with neighboring Indian tribes.

Douglas, James. *Old France in the New World: Quebec in the Seventeenth Century.* Cleveland: Burrows Brothers, 1906. Reprint, Google Books, 2007. The first book to explore cross-cultural influences between the French and Indian people in the New World.

Jennings, Francis. *The Founders of America: From the Earliest Migrations to the Present.* New York: Norton, 1994. Shows how the American Indians "founded" and "discovered" America, a wise counter perspective to colonial mythologies. This is a very useful general history of major pre-Columbian and early European American Indian civilizations.

Kupperman, Karen Ordahl. *Indians and English: Facing Off in Early America.* Ithaca, NY: Cornell University Press, 2000. Describes how Indians and the English interacted at Jamestown in 1607 and how this interaction influenced the relations between them between 1607 and 1622.

Le Moine, J. M. *Quebec, Past and Present: A History of Quebec 1608–1876.* A well-documented text that is written in two voices, the author's and Champlain's. The two voices describe the socioeconomic relations between the French and the local Indians, and these relations are compared to the relations between the English and local Indians in the British colonies.

Philbrick, Nathaniel. *Mayflower.* New York: Viking Penguin, 2006. Part IV, entitled "War," describes the brutality of colonial wars with Indians despite the Thanksgiving mythology of friendly relations.

Stratton, Eugene Aubrey. *Plymouth Colony: Its History and People.* Salt Lake City, UT: Ancestry Publishing, 1986. Divided into two parts: "Chronological Histories" and "Topical Narratives." The latter explores the political and social structure of the colony and includes narratives of everyday life.

Szasz, Margaret Connell. *Indian Education in the American Colonies, 1607–1783.* Albuquerque, NM: University of New Mexico Press, 1988. Lincoln, NE: Bison Books, 2007. A general history of the efforts of the colonists to "civilize" and educate Indian children.

World Wide Web

"History of Canada." http://www.linksnorth.com/canada-history/. Has information about early events and present situations in Canada where the Quebec Colony was. It also describes the issues with native Indians at that time.

"Jamestown." http://www.kidinfo.com/American_History/Colonization_Jamestown.html. This site includes links to scholarly works. Very comprehensive.

Jamestown Rediscovery. http://www.apva.org/jr.html. Jamestown Rediscovery is investigating the remains of 1607–1698 Jamestown on Jamestown Island, Virginia and reporting its findings on this site. Contains historical summaries, a time line, biographies, and description of the official archeological findings at Jamestown.

"Mayflower History." http://www.mayflowerhistory.com/PrimarySources/primarysources.php. Contains scans of interesting primary sources and documents of the sixteenth century.

"Native American History." http://www.lib.washington.edu/subject/history/tm/native.html. Has excellent links to resources regarding American Indian history.

"Plymouth." http://www.kidinfo.com/American_History/Colonization _Plymouth.html. This site includes links to scholarly works. Very comprehensive.

"The Plymouth Colony Archive Project." http://www.histarch.uiuc.edu/plymouth/. A Web site documenting the archeological excavation of the Plymouth site and providing searchable primary and secondary sources and texts. The "search" hyperlink takes you to the "Search the Archive" page, which links to many primary and secondary sources, including the First Peace Treaty, maps, laws, and lesson plans.

Virtual Jamestown. http://www.virtualjamestown.org/page2.html. Includes many reliable primary, secondary, and interactive sources including maps, time lines, 3D recreations of an Indian village, and educational materials designed for teachers and students. Includes the complete works of John Smith.

Multimedia Source

The New World: Nightmare in Jamestown. Dir. Charles Poe. NGHT, 2005. DVD. 50 minutes. National Geographic documentary on the Jamestown colony with interactive maps and a section on John Smith's voyage.

5. Pocahontas Helps the English Settlers (1607)

Pocahontas sparks the imagination of historians and the ordinary person with equal passion and unending curiosity, due to her interaction with Jamestown men and the romantic mythology that interaction has generated. She was the daughter of Powhatan, the powerful chief of an Algonquian Indian tribe of the Tidewater region of Virginia, and the niece of Opechancanough. Opechancanough succeeded Powhatan after his death and the English thereafter called the tribe Powhatans. However, her fame emerges from her alleged romance with Captain John Smith and her documented marriage to John Rolfe. Her possible rescue of John Smith from Powhatan, who was intent on killing him; the political, military, and economic reasons to arrange a marriage to Rolfe; and the speculation over her role and purpose in American history have all been debated since 1607. The existence of a sparse yet complex set of historical facts, combined with a bevy of suggestive primary sources, such as portraits and the writings of John Smith and John Rolfe, have been the fuel to perpetuate a diverse set of interpretative narratives on Pocahontas, not to mention Hollywood and Disney interpretations. What is undisputed is that Pocahontas is often presented as a mythic ideal of the cooperative Indian woman and as a stereotypical representation of the Indian princess. Yet the very fact that she is remembered and revered to this day indicates she has been a powerful force of human achievement despite the numerous romantic and shallow representations that plague her historical legacy.

TERM PAPER SUGGESTIONS

1. Captain John Smith first mentions the rescue by Pocahontas in his book *General Historie of Virginia,* which was published in 1624, but not in his earlier history, *True Relation,* which was published in 1608. Some believe Smith's story about the rescue despite the earlier omission, and some do not. Write a comparison of the pro and con arguments presented to support or challenge the veracity of Captain John Smith's claim.

2. Write an essay that examines the reasons behind John Rolfe's desire to marry Pocahontas. Why would he be hesitant and why would he eventually marry her? Their marriage produced two children. What were the racial implications of this union for the future?

3. Along with the primary sources cited here and the many primary sources found at the Virtual Jamestown Web site, search out written descriptions of Pocahontas and write a general portrait of how the early Jamestown colonists saw Pocahontas, including her demeanor and inner character.

4. Write on the leadership qualities of Pocahontas and how her actions could be construed as being on behalf of her people's welfare and to promote peace and friendship. How does she ameliorate the relations between the English settlers and the Powhatan Indians?

5. Write on the mythic and heroic qualities of Pocahontas. Describe those qualities that go beyond what can be proven from the primary sources to create a larger-than-life portrait of her persona. Many have embraced her as a mythic ideal of American Indian womanhood.

6. Examine and write on the subject of Pocahontas as a stereotype and false representation of Indian women. How can stereotypes be harmful to an accurate portrayal of Indian women in the past as well as in the present?

ALTERNATIVE TERM PAPER SUGGESTIONS

1. Search for and collect images of Pocahontas on the World Wide Web. During Halloween, search (on the Web and/or in the local community) for Pocahontas costumes or actual people dressed as Pocahontas and take digital snapshots. Finally, search for advertisements or actual products of Pocahontas dolls and digitally record them. Using Microsoft PowerPoint, create a slide show of the collected images or, alternatively, create a digital collage of the images. Compare these images with the historical Pocahontas and report on the differences and likenesses.

2. Capture still images of Pocahontas from the various films and video games (animated or otherwise) that exist in order to show a chronological sequence of images of Pocahontas from these forms of media entertainment. Visit the Internet Movie Database (www.imdb.com) and search for Pocahontas films for a complete list of available titles. The goal is to capture snippets for purpose of comparison. Create a digital movie to show examples of how Pocahontas has been rendered and imagined by filmmakers.

SUGGESTED SOURCES

Primary Sources

Rolfe, John. *Letter of John Rolfe.* http://www.americanjourneys.org/aj-079/. This is a letter written to Sir Thomas Dale explaining why he, John Rolfe, a devout Christian, wanted to marry Pocahontas for the good of the colony.

Smith, John. *A True Relation by Captain John Smith, 1608.* http://www.americanjourneys.org/aj-074/. Describes the first landing, battles, interactions with and capture of/escape by Indians, as well as explorations of the neighboring lands.

Smith, John. *General Historie of Virginia by Captain John Smith; the Fourth Booke.* http://www.americanjourneys.org/aj-082/. Smith compiled writings from the colonists to write this history.

Secondary Sources

Allen, Paula Gunn. *Pocahontas: Medicine Woman, Spy, Entrepreneur, Diplomat.* New York: HarperCollins, 2003. This is an alternative mythology-building narrative that reinterprets the Pocahontas story from a feminist and New Age perspective.

Bruchac, Joseph. *Pocahontas.* Orlando, FL: Harcourt, 2003. A novel from an acclaimed American Indian writer that draws on John Smith's own writings and the storytelling qualities of Pocahontas's people to tell a story from both sides.

Grizzard, Frank E. *Jamestown Colony: A Political, Social, and Cultural History*, Santa Barbara, CA: ABC-CLIO, 2007. A good overall reference to primary and secondary sources on Jamestown's history and information on individuals, groups, places, and incidents.

Kupperman, Karen Ordahl. *The Jamestown Project*. Cambridge, MA: Belknap Press, 2007. Very detailed and meticulous history of Jamestown and its English settlers.

Lemay, J. A. Leo. *Did Pocahontas Save Captain Smith?* Athens, GA: University of Georgia Press, 1992. A case study designed to investigate the validity of the Pocahontas rescue of Captain Smith.

Rountree, Helen C. *Pocahontas, Powhatan, Opechancanough: Three Indian Lives Changed by Jamestown*. Charlottesville, VA: University of Virginia Press, 2005. A triple biography of three major American Indians: Pocahontas; her father, Chief Powhatan; and her uncle, Chief Opechancanough, who ruled after her father's death.

Rountree, Helen C. *Pocahontas's People: The Powhatan Indians of Virginia through Four Centuries*. Norman, OK: University of Oklahoma Press, 1996. Starting with the earliest recorded histories of the Powhatan Indians of Virginia and proceeding to modern times, this book aims to demonstrate the cultural persistence and survival of Powhatan Indians, who are often thought of as historical relics.

Townsend, Camilla. *Pocahontas and the Powhatan Dilemma*. The American Portraits Series. New York: Hill and Wang, 2004. A new look at Pocahontas in narrative form that draws from ethnological sources as well as the myths surrounding Pocahontas and her life.

Woolley, Benjamin. *Savage Kingdom: The True Story of Jamestown, 1607*. New York: Harper Perennial, 2008. A very readable narrative history that includes all of the major characters and historical incidents.

World Wide Web

"Jamestown." http://www.kidinfo.com/American_History/Colonization_Jamestown.html. This site includes links to scholarly works. Very comprehensive.

Jamestown Rediscovery. http://www.apva.org/jr.html. Jamestown Rediscovery is investigating the remains of 1607–1698 Jamestown on Jamestown Island, Virginia and reporting its findings on this site. Contains historical summaries, a time line, biographies, and description of the official archeological findings made at Jamestown.

"John Smith Assumes Presidency of Jamestown." http://memory.loc.gov/ammem/today/sep10.html. A portal to many Library of Congress sources on Jamestown, Pocahontas, and John Smith.

"John Smith's Letter to Queen Anne Regarding Pocahontas." http://members.aol.com/mayflo1620/pocahontas.html. This is the 1616 letter in modern digital form and text.

"Pocahontas." http://www.apva.org/history/pocahont.html. Short biography and image of Pocahontas.

"Timeline History of Jamestown, Virginia." http://www.williamsburgprivatetours.com/Timeline%20%20Jamestown.htm. A complete time line from 1606 to 1699 of Jamestown, Virginia.

Virtual Jamestown. http://www.virtualjamestown.org/page2.html. Includes many reliable primary, secondary, and interactive sources including maps, time lines, 3D recreations of an Indian village, and educational materials designed for teachers and students. Includes the complete works of John Smith.

Multimedia Sources

The New World. Dir. Terrence Malick. New Line Cinema, 2005. DVD. 135 minutes. This movie tells the story of the founding of Jamestown, Virginia, beginning in 1607, with Pocahontas, John Smith, and John Rolfe taking center stage.

Pocahontas Revealed. Dir. Kirk Wolfinger. WGBH, 2007. DVD. 56 minutes. "Science examines an American Legend." The DVD includes printable materials for educators.

6. Massasoit, Pilgrims, and the First Peace Treaty (1621)

Arriving in late summer, the English pilgrims, who were also known as Separatists and Puritans, survived, albeit with great loss of life, the trans-Atlantic voyage of 1620. They hurriedly built the small village of Plymouth and endured the first hard winter, common to the coast of New England. They welcomed the end of winter and the spring of 1621 with some trepidation; but with the help of two Indians, Samoset and Squanto, and the neighboring Wampanoag Indians, they were able to accomplish a prodigious planting of crops and to secure enough meat and fish to preserve for the upcoming winter. Samoset, a Pemaquid, and

Squanto, a Patuxet, were emissaries of Chief Massasoit of the Wampanoags, a confederation of coastal Indian tribes which included the Pemaquid and Patuxet, and they served as interpreters and liaisons between local Indian tribes and the English colonists. Both had extensive exposure to English colonists (Squanto even traveled to England for a time), and both spoke English. With their successful and bountiful harvest, the pilgrims invited the Wampanoags and their leader, Massasoit, for a harvest feast that became known as the first Thanksgiving (although the Spanish and Acoma Pueblo dispute this claim). To have such a bountiful year would not have been possible without a formal agreement of peace between the Wampanoags and the pilgrims, and this was clearly the goal of Massasoit when he made overtures to the pilgrims in March of 1621. These actions led to a meeting between Governor John Carver and Massasoit where they negotiated seven terms of peace and friendship, which were recorded in *Mourt's Relation: A Journal of the Pilgrims at Plymouth, 1622, Part I.* The act of recording in writing the negotiations and terms between English colonists and neighboring Indians established a "treaty-making" precedent for all future encounters between American Indians and the English colonists and, later, the Americans.

TERM PAPER SUGGESTIONS

1. Study the process and details of negotiation. In brief, Squanto and Samoset told the pilgrims that Massasoit desired trade and peace between his tribe and the English colonists. A parley was arranged by Edward Winslow, a meeting took place between Massasoit and Governor Carver, and an agreement was reached. Write a report that examines the manner in which Massasoit and the Wampanoag controlled the process. What was their goal and what did their actions reveal?

2. Study the terms and language of the treaty. Analyze and report on the treaty's purpose, whether one side or the other had an advantage, and whether the terms were reasonable and easily honored by both parties.

3. Look for written accounts of Indians, such as Edward Winslow's description of Massasoit, to form the basis for an interpretation of how the Indians were understood and described by the pilgrims. What words did they use? What did the Wampanoags think of the pilgrims? The "Plymouth Colony Archive Project" Web site provides many such primary sources.

4. Write about the importance of Samoset and Squanto to the Plymouth Colony. What was their role and how did they help?

5. Why would the Wampanoag want to have peaceful relations with the pilgrims?

6. Edward Winslow described the first Thanksgiving and reported that about 90 Wampanoag warriors attended the feast. However, some have speculated that the warriors were not invited. Compare Winslow's account to other accounts of the first Thanksgiving. How do the accounts differ and how are they the same?

ALTERNATIVE TERM PAPER SUGGESTIONS

1. Using software programs, create an overview map of an early colonial settlement designed in the European fashion to accommodate 100 colonists. Based on source material and other archeological data, determine the amount of land needed for cultivation, the number of buildings required, other improvements that were needed, and how much time would be required to clear the land to accomplish all of your goals. Compare your plan with what is known about the neighboring American Indian settlements. Use this visual to report on the difficulty of early colonization efforts in U.S. Northeast.

2. According to popular myth, the first Thanksgiving took place in 1621 between the Wampanoag and the Plymouth pilgrims. Throughout U.S. history this event has been imagined in many ways through drawings, pictures, paintings, and sketches. Make digital scans and photographs of as many of these images that you can find, and also collect images from the World Wide Web. Even holiday cards celebrating Thanksgiving are good sources. Elementary school children often render images or construct costumes in honor of this national holiday. Create an electronic collage or slide show of these images in an effort to demonstrate common trends in the depiction of Indians. Are the images consistently stereotypical?

SUGGESTED SOURCES

Primary Sources

Bradford, William. *Bradford's History of Plimoth Plantation from the Original Manuscript.* Whitefish, MT: Kessinger Publishing, 2004. A facsimile of the original with an index.

Bradford, William. *Of Plimoth Plantation.* http://www.americanjourneys.org/aj-025/. Describes the Mayflower voyage and the establishment of the pilgrim settlement at Plymouth.

Secondary Sources

Deetz, James, and Patricia Scott Deetz. *The Times of Their Lives: Life, Love, and Death in Plymouth Colony.* New York: W.H. Freeman, 2000.

Chapter two, "I Will Harry Them Out of the Land," is of particular interest regarding the colony's relations with neighboring Indian tribes.

Doherty, Katherine, M. *The Wampanoag.* London: Franklin Watts, 1996. Brief overview of the Wampanoag Indians intended for a young readership.

Fixico, Donald, ed. *Treaties with American Indians: An Encyclopedia of Rights, Conflict and Sovereignty.* Santa Barbara, CA: ABC-CLIO, 2007. A comprehensive reference source.

Mills, Earl. *Son of Mashpee: Reflections of Chief Flying Eagle, A Wampanoag.* North Falmouth, MA: Word Studio, 1996. Written by a Wampanoag tribal historian, this work provides an internal view of Wampanoag worldview and culture.

Philbrick, Nathaniel. *Mayflower.* New York: Viking Penguin, 2006. Part IV, entitled "War," describes the brutality of colonial wars with Indians despite the Thanksgiving mythology of friendly relations. Not for the fainthearted.

Prucha, Francis Paul. *American Indian Treaties: The History of a Political Anomaly.* Berkeley, CA: University of California Press, 1994. A general history of United States and Indian treaty relationships.

Stratton, Eugene Aubrey. *Plymouth Colony: Its History and People.* Salt Lake City, UT: Ancestry Publishing, 1986. Divided into two parts: "Chronological Histories" and "Topical Narratives." The latter explores the political and social structure of the colony and includes narratives of everyday life.

Weeks, Alvin Gardner. *Massasoit of the Wampanoags with a Brief Commentary on Indian Character; and Sketches of Other Great Chiefs, Tribes and Nations.* Google Books, 2007. http://books.google.com/books?id=anBHAAAAIAAJ. An early history of the famous chief from the perspective of an admirer of Indian leadership and manhood. A reprint of the original 1919 Plimpton Press publication.

World Wide Web

"The Pilgrims and Plymouth Colony, 1620." http://www.rootsweb.ancestry.com/~mosmd/index.htm. An educational site for source materials for teachers, students, and the curious. Comprehensive and filled with relevant links to other sites.

"Plimoth Plantation." http://www.plimoth.org/flightpath/. An informative Web site with visual and text sources.

"Plymouth." http://www.kidinfo.com/American_History/Colonization_Plymouth.html. A comprehensive site that includes links for serious scholars.

"The Plymouth Colony Archive Project." http://www.histarch.uiuc.edu/plymouth/index.html. A Web site documenting the archeological excavation of the Plymouth site and providing searchable primary and secondary sources and texts. Includes a downloadable PDF of the First Peace Treaty and of the first Thanksgiving, entitled "The Pilgrims Sign a Peace Treaty with the Wampanoag," which are very useful.

"The Wampanoag/Pilgrim Treaty, 1621." http://www.rootsweb.ancestry.com/~mosmd/peacetreaty.htm. Narrative description with primary source quotations and the text of the treaty itself.

Multimedia Source

Dear America: A Journey to the New World: The Story of Remember Patience Whipple, Plymouth, Massachusetts, 1620. Dir. Don McCutcheon. Scholastic Productions, 1999. VHS. 30 minutes. A short docu-drama of the life and times of Patience Whipple; based on her diary entries which always began with, "Dear America."

7. Powhatan War in Virginia (1622–1644)

Chief Powhatan, of the dominant Indian tribe of the Chesapeake Bay area, the Powhatans, tried for many years to manipulate and control the English who had settled at Jamestown, Virginia in 1607. In an effort to establish a monopoly of trade with the English, he attempted to isolate the colony from other Indian tribes and to force the English to do his bidding in exchange for food and protection. Wisely, the English forged alliances with other Indian tribes of the region, such as the Chickahominy, Pamunkeys, and Matponi, but this created a fragile and at times hostile relationship between the Powhatan tribe and the Jamestown colonists. The marriage of Pocahontas, the famous Indian woman who allegedly saved Captain John Smith, to Englishman John Rolfe led to an uneasy peace until the death of Powhatan. When Opechancanough assumed the role of chief, he advocated a war policy against the English at Jamestown, and he led two campaigns, in 1622 and later in 1644, to oust them from the Chesapeake. In the 1622 attack, one third of the colonists were killed, but with the help of their Indian allies, the English survived and brutally retaliated by destroying Powhatan crops, towns, and villages. In 1644, Opechancanough tried again, and again he failed, in part due to Jamestown's Indian allies. However, after 1644 the English waged a war against all Indian tribes of the area, and by 1676, they succeeded in forcing Indian tribes to capitulate and to live on reservations.

TERM PAPER SUGGESTIONS

1. Write about diplomacy. Examine how the two dominant groups of the Chesapeake Bay, the Jamestown English and the Powhatan Indian tribe, were able to use diplomacy to exert their power in the region. What were other sources of diplomatic power, and how did they use them to their best advantage?

2. Explain why the Powhatans did not destroy the English at an early stage.

3. Discuss how the marriage of Pocahontas and John Rolfe could lead to peaceful relations.

4. Within the context of the 70 years it took the English to take control of Virginia, investigate and explain the concept of "just war" and the justification for "total war," which is the total destruction of a people, their way of life, and their ability to exist.

5. Investigate the methods of war. Was European technology decisive? Did the Europeans ever fight like Indians, and what does that mean?

6. The Virginia Colony established the first Indian reservations. Write about how treaties were negotiated and reservations established and how a foundation was created for future relations with Indians.

ALTERNATIVE TERM PAPER SUGGESTIONS

1. Assume you are the representative of an English colonial settlement, sent out to convince a neighboring Indian tribe to negotiate a treaty of peace with your governor. What would you propose and how would you handle the logistics? Your goal is to get tribal leaders to meet with your governor, negotiate in good faith, and to arrive at a formal agreement. Prepare a step-by-step "to do" list to achieve your goals as well as a list of treaty terms.

2. Prepare a speech in the manner of Powhatan or Opechancanough designed to influence your people to action. Choose diplomacy or war and write an oratory that provides the logic and purpose for either.

SUGGESTED SOURCES

Primary Sources

Smith, John. *General Historie of Virginia by Captain John Smith; the Fourth Booke.* http://www.americanjourneys.org/aj-082/. Smith compiled writings from the colonists to write this history.

Spellman, Henry. *Relation of Virginia.* http://www.americanjourneys.org/aj-136/. This document describes the early years of the Jamestown colony and settlement.

Secondary Sources

Gleach, Frederic W. *Powhatan's World and Colonial Virginia: A Conflict of Cultures.* Lincoln, NE: University of Nebraska Press, 1997. Gleach uses the latest historical and archeological evidence to offer a balanced and complete accounting of the tumultuous early years of the Jamestown colony.

Grizzard, Frank E. *Jamestown Colony: A Political, Social, and Cultural History.* Santa Barbara, CA: ABC-CLIO, 2007. A good overall reference to primary and secondary sources on Jamestown's history, as well as information on individuals, groups, places, and incidents.

Horn, James P. *A Land as God Made It: Jamestown and the Birth of America.* New York: Basic Books, 2005. Detailed history of the first 18 years of the Jamestown colony and settlement; focuses on the relationship between the settlers and Tidewater Indians.

Kelso, William M. *Jamestown, the Buried Truth.* Charlottesville, VA: University of Virginia Press, 2006. Head archeologist at the Jamestown Rediscovery project reveals what has been found at the archeological site.

Kupperman, Karen Ordahl. *The Jamestown Project.* Cambridge, MA: Belknap Press, 2007. Very detailed and meticulous history of Jamestown and its English settlers.

Rountree, Helen C. *Before and After Jamestown: Virginia's Powhatan and Their Predecessors.* Gainesville, FL: University Press of Florida, 2002. A look at the Indians of Virginia's coastal plains from a thousand years ago to the present day, presented in a readable and accessible manner; includes hundreds of photographs, maps, and drawings.

Rountree, Helen C. *Pocahontas, Powhatan, Opechancanough: Three Indian Lives Changed by Jamestown.* Charlottesville, VA: University of Virginia Press, 2005. A triple biography of three major American Indians: Pocahontas; her father, Chief Powhatan; and her uncle, Chief Opechancanough, who ruled after her father's death.

Rountree, Helen C. *Pocahontas's People: The Powhatan Indians of Virginia through Four Centuries.* Norman, OK: University of Oklahoma Press, 1996. Starting with the earliest recorded histories of the Powhatan Indians of Virginia and proceeding to modern times, this book aims to demonstrate the cultural persistence and survival of Powhatan Indians, who are often thought of as historical relics.

Rountree, Helen C. *The Powhatan Indians of Virginia: Their Traditional Culture.* Norman, OK: University of Oklahoma Press, 1992. Well-researched ethnological treatise of the culture and life ways of a people.

Woolley, Benjamin. *Savage Kingdom: The True Story of Jamestown, 1607.* New York: Harper Perennial, 2008. A very readable narrative history that includes all of the major characters and historical incidents.

World Wide Web

"The Anglo-Powhatan Wars." http://www.virginiaplaces.org/nativeamerican/ anglopowhatan.html. Describes the Anglo-Powhatan Wars and the 1622 attack. The focus is on maps and geography to explain the wars.

"Jamestown." http://www.kidinfo.com/American_History/Colonization _Jamestown.html. This site includes links to scholarly works. Very comprehensive.

Jamestown Rediscovery. http://www.apva.org/jr.html. Jamestown Rediscovery is investigating the remains of 1607–1698 Jamestown on Jamestown Island, Virginia and reporting its findings on this site. Contains historical summaries, a time line, biographies, and description of the official archeological findings made at Jamestown.

"John Smith Assumes Presidency of Jamestown." http://memory.loc.gov/ ammem/today/sep10.html. A portal to many Library of Congress sources on Jamestown, Pocahontas, and John Smith.

"Timeline History of Jamestown, Virginia." http://www.williamsburgprivatetours .com/Timeline%20%20Jamestown.htm. A complete time line from 1606 to 1699 of Jamestown, Virginia.

Virtual Jamestown. http://www.virtualjamestown.org/page2.html. Includes many reliable primary, secondary, and interactive sources including maps, time lines, 3D recreations of an Indian village, and educational materials designed for teachers and students. Includes the complete works of John Smith.

Multimedia Sources

"America in 1607: Jamestown and the Powhatan." http://ngm.nationalgeographic .com/ngm/jamestown/. An impressive interactive site which has an interactive graphic model of Jamestown and Werocomoco, the neighboring Powhatan village. The site includes interviews, other visual material, and a children's interactive game, "On the Trail of Captain John Smith, a Jamestown Adventure."

Jamestown Unearthed. Dir. Michael Durling. Williamsburg, VA: Colonial Williamsburg Foundation, 2007. VHS. 57 minutes. An educational look at the archeological excavation of the original Jamestown settlement.

The New World: Nightmare in Jamestown. Dir. Charles Poe. NGHT, 2005. DVD. 50 minutes. National Geographic documentary on the Jamestown colony with interactive maps and a section on John Smith's voyage.

8. Pequot War (1637)

In the 1630s within the vicinity of the Long Island Sound and the Connecticut River Valley, the Pequots, the Dutch, the English, and numerous other Indian tribes, such as the Narragansetts, quarreled over control of the lucrative fur trade and bickered over loose and fragile political/economic alliances. Finding success that approached a monopoly in the trade with the European colonists, the Pequots had to contend with jealous Indian neighbors and competing European rivals. Within this climate of hostility and mistrust, deadly action ensued: Pequots killed Narragansetts intent on trading with the Dutch; the Dutch retaliated by killing the Pequot sachem, Tatobem; the Pequots countered by killing Englishmen that they mistook for Dutch traders; and the English went to war. The English escalated the conflict to total war when they destroyed the Pequot settlement of Mystic by killing and burning warriors, women, children, and animals trapped inside Mystic and by hunting survivors with mastiff war dogs. To many historians war was inevitable, and the misunderstandings and skirmishes were a way of gaining power and justifying a war; however, historians also debate the methodologies that led the English to a war hovering on extermination. Some think the evidence shows that the systematic hunting and killing of Pequot survivors led to heightened colonial morale and the capitulation of numerous Indians tribes of the bay region. After this war, and for many years, the New England colonies were able to expand and thrive without serious economic or military threat.

TERM PAPER SUGGESTIONS

1. Examine how the fur trade could lead to intertribal hostilities and war with Europeans. Focus on the Pequot and the Mohegan tribes.
2. Compare the rationale of the English in waging war against the Indians and that of the Indians in waging war against the English.
3. Write an essay that demonstrates the power of alliances.

4. In terms of the Pequot settlement at Mystic, discuss the difference between a "battle" and a "massacre" and whether the English were on a mission to exterminate the Pequots.

5. Write on the concept of cultural change and persistence to explain the survival of the Pequots after the war and their ability to survive as a people to this day.

6. Explore why author Herman Melville would choose "Peqoud" as the name the whaling ship where most of the dramatic action takes place in his epic work, *Moby Dick*.

ALTERNATIVE TERM PAPER SUGGESTIONS

1. Write a narrative account from the perspective of a soldier in the Connecticut militia. Form a critical perspective of purpose, strategy, and tactics used to wage war against the Indians.

2. Assume you were a survivor of the attack and destruction of the settlement at Mystic. Write a description of your experience meant to be remembered by your ancestors.

SUGGESTED SOURCES

Primary Sources

Mason, John. *A Brief History of the Pequot War: Especially of the Memorable Taking of Their Fort at Mistick in Connecticut in 1637* (1736). http://digitalcommons.unl.edu/etas/42/. This history was believed to be written around 1670. This downloadable PDF document is a "corrected and annotated" edition of the account of the war from the pen of the Connecticut army captain warring against the Pequots in 1636–1637.

Vincent, Philip. *A True Relation of the Late Battell Fought in New England, Between the English, and the Salvages: With the Present State of Things There* (1637). http://digitalcommons.unl.edu/etas/35/. Downloadable PDF. Vincent describes the Mystic conflict as a battle; whereas, the Pequots have described the conflict as a massacre. Vincent wrote his account six months after the incident.

Secondary Sources

Axelrod, Alan. *Chronicle of the Indian Wars: From Colonial Times to Wounded Knee*. New York: Prentice Hall, 1993. A general survey of Indian wars; this work cites the Pequot War as one of the important ones.

Bonfanti, Leo. *The Pequot-Mohican War.* Danvers, MA: Old Saltbox Publishing, 1971. Short narrative of the war stressing its importance in New England history.

Cave, Alfred A. *The Pequot War.* Amherst, MA: University of Massachusetts Press, 1996. Comprehensive history of the cultural, economic, and military struggles of the early New England Puritans and neighboring Indian tribes, especially the Pequots.

Hall, David D., ed. *The Antinomian Controversy, 1636–1638: A Documentary History.* 2nd ed. Durham, NC: Duke University Press, 1990. Fully documents this theological crisis during the time of the Pequot War and reveals the mind of the Puritan through the writing of John Cotton and John Wheelwright and the through the trial of Anne Hutchinson.

Hauptman, Laurence M., and James D. Wherry, eds. *The Pequots in Southern New England: The Fall and Rise of an American Indian Nation.* Norman, OK: University of Oklahoma Press, 1993. A collection of essays exploring relations from early colonial contact to the 1990s.

Jennings, Francis. *The Invasion of America: Indians, Colonialism, and the Cant of Conquest.* New York: W.W. Norton, 1976. Explores the attitudes of the Puritans towards the Indians and their lands.

Salisbury, Neal. *Manitou and Providence: Indians, Europeans, and the Making of New England, 1500–1643.* Oxford, UK: Oxford University Press, 1982. Takes the perspective of the Indians of New England.

Vaughan, Alden T. *New England Frontier: Puritans and Indians, 1620–1675.* 3rd ed. Norman, OK: University of Oklahoma Press, 1965. Reprinted by the University of Oklahoma Press in 1995. Provides a general history of the region and the time period.

Wagner, David R. *Mystic Fiasco: How the Indian Won the Pequot War.* Google Books, 2003. http://books.google.com/books?id=-TufOXD9GmwC. Explores the role and importance of American Indian allies in the defeat of the Pequot, which the author suggests may mean these allies actually won the war.

World Wide Web

A Brief History of the Pequot War: Especially of the Memorable Taking of Their Fort at Mistick in Connecticut in 1637. Boston, 1736. *History of the Pequot War.* http://bc.barnard.columbia.edu/~rmccaugh/earlyAC/readings/pequot/pequot.htm. Link to a complete online scanned copy of John Mason's original narrative.

"Chronology of the Pequot War." http://bc.barnard.columbia.edu/~rmccaugh/earlyAC/pequottl.htm. Covers the period 1630–1638 with author notes and references.

"History of the Pequot Indians." http://www.colonialwarsct.org/1637_pequot _history.htm. A well-documented narrative history that includes language and geographical information.

Machantucket Pequot Museum and Research Center. http://www .pequotmuseum.org/. Has many online exhibits and essays, such as how to build a wigwam, under tabs entitled, "Native Lifeways," "Society and Culture," and "The Natural World."

"Mystic Voices: The Story of the Pequot War." http://www.pequotwar.com/. Provides objectives, themes, and creative approaches to the documentary *Mystic Voices.*

"The Pequot War." http://www.dowdgen.com/dowd/document/pequots.html. Though a genealogy site, it has a short historical narrative with very useful maps of the region.

"1637-Pequot War." http://www.colonialwarsct.org/1637.htm. Comprehensive narrative of the war with full references and links to other sites.

Multimedia Source

Mystic Voices: The Story of the Pequot War. Dir. Guy Perrotta and Charles Clemmons. Mystic Voices, 2004. DVD. A documentary of the Pequot War. http://www.pequotwar.com/.

9. Iroquois Wars (1638–1650)

The Iroquois Wars were a series of seventeenth-century conflicts involving the French, Dutch, Iroquois Five Nations (Cayuga, Mohawk, Oneida, Onondaga, and Seneca), Huron, Algonquian, Abenaki, Mi'kmaqs, and other Indian tribes. These wars centered on control of the fur trade and the diplomatic balance between contending nations. On one side were the French and their Indian allies, and on the other were the Five Nations of the Iroquois and the Dutch, who supplied the Iroquois with firearms. Many historians think the goal of the Iroquois was to destroy competing and rival Indian tribes engaged in the fur trade by raiding them and by destroying their military might. In this way, they could acquire control of more lands and people in an effort to keep favorable trade terms for their goods by squashing competition. By trading with the French,

Dutch, and English, the Iroquois were also able to bargain for lower prices of European goods by "playing off" one European group from the other. The pressure to control this trade led to the capitulation, destruction, and dispersal of numerous Indian tribes westward. The Huron tribe suffered almost total destruction. However, the Iroquois made lifelong enemies of the French, and their efforts did not stop French expansion into the Mississippi Valley and Illinois. Eventually, through military actions, the French were able to force the Iroquois into favorable treaty terms by 1701. Furthermore, the Iroquois were defeated by the Chippewa and Ottawa when the Iroquois encroached into Chippewa and Ottawa land, a defeat recalled to this day in Chippewa and Ottawa oral stories.

TERM PAPER SUGGESTIONS

1. Write an essay examining the role of beaver and other fur-bearing animals in the various wars. Why were pelts sought and valued by the Europeans?
2. Write a report on the military tactics of the time. Did the arming of Indians with European firearms make a difference? Were the tactics of the Iroquois superior to those of their Indian rivals?
3. Many historians write that the main reason for the Iroquois Wars was the desire for economic gain through control of the beaver trade. Discuss the economic benefits that the Iroquois gained through the fur trade.
4. Write about Iroquoian diplomacy. Some historians have argued that diplomacy was more important than warfare. Why did the Iroquois desire to keep the peace between England and France and between the various Indian tribes engaged in the fur trade?
5. Write about the French military and political responses to the Iroquois efforts to control the fur trade.
6. Examine the long-term effects of Indians fighting Indians. How did the English and, later, the Americans benefit from intertribal warfare?

ALTERNATIVE TERM PAPER SUGGESTIONS

1. Using Microsoft PowerPoint and graphing software, create slides and graphs to show how a monopoly over one trade good, such as beaver pelts, could drive the price of the good upward and how, if many traders were offering the same goods, the price would go downward.
2. Examine a number of electronic games where the Iroquois are represented as combatants (for example, *Age of Empires*, Microsoft, 2007) to determine their role and chance of winning the game.

SUGGESTED SOURCES

Primary Sources

Colden, Cadwallader. *History of the Five Nations.* London: Printed for T. Osborne, 1747. http://www.canadiana.org/ECO/mtq?doc=33241. This is the complete scanned text of Colden's history of the Iroquois (the Five Nations). The history first appeared in 1727; he wrote it based on information gathered from libraries, frontier settlers, and Indian elders.

Morgan, Henry Lewis. *League of the Ho-dé-no-sau-nee Or Iroquois.* New York: Dodd, Meade and Company, 1904. http://books.google.com/books?id=5usNAAAAIAAJ. Considered the first American anthropological/ethnological study of North American Indians.

"Three Accounts of the Iroquois Wars from the Jesuit Relations." *The Jesuit Relations and Allied Documents . . .* (excerpts). Cleveland, OH: Burrows Bros. Co., 1896–1901. http://www.wisconsinhistory.org/turningpoints/search.asp?id=9. Describes (in French) the retreat of the Huron, Ottawa, Sauk, Fox, Kickapoo, Pottawatomie, and other tribes into Wisconsin due to the Iroquoian wars.

Secondary Sources

Barr, Daniel P. *Unconquered: The Iroquois League at War in Colonial America.* Westport, CT: Praeger, 2006. This book provides Iroquois military history from the period of first contact with Europeans to the American Revolution.

Fenton, William N. *The Great Law and the Longhouse: A Political History of the Iroquois Confederacy.* Norman, OK: University of Oklahoma Press, 1998. More than warfare, the Iroquois relied on complicated yet effective politics and diplomacy to establish and maintain their power.

Hunt, George T. *Wars of the Iroquois: A Study in Intertribal Trade Relations.* 1940. Reprint, Madison, WI: University of Wisconsin Press, 2005. The classic history of the causes and effects of the "Beaver Wars" and the Iroquoian trade tactic of establishing and defending the "play-off" system.

Jennings, Francis. *The Ambiguous Iroquois Empire.* New York: W.W. Norton, 1990. Details the manner in which the Iroquois gained and maintained power in the early period of colonization.

Otterbein, Keith F. "Huron vs. Iroquois: A Case Study in Inter-Tribal Warfare." *Ethnohistory* 26, no. 2 (Spring 1979): 141–52. Describes how the Huron could have defeated the Iroquois if they had implemented better tactics.

Otterbein, Keith F. "Why the Iroquois Won: An Analysis of Iroquois Military Tactics." *Ethnohistory* 11, no. 1 (Winter 1964): 56–63. Explores the military tactics of the Iroquois as the deciding factor in the victories as opposed to other means, such as the availability of European firearms.

Richter, Daniel Karl. *The Ordeal of the Longhouse: The Peoples of the Iroquois League in the Era of European Colonization.* Chapel Hill, NC: University of North Carolina Press, 1992. A complete history of how the Iroquois adapted to changing economic and social conditions brought on by colonization and trade.

Schiavo, Anthony P., Jr., and Claudio R. Salvucci. *Iroquois Wars I: Extracts from the Jesuit Relations and Primary Sources from 1535–1650* and *Iroquois Wars II: Extracts from the Jesuit Relations, 1650–1675.* Merchantville, NJ: Evolution Publishing, 2003. Contain primary source excerpts of Jesuits, Jacques Cartier, Samuel de Champlain, and others; the authors interpret these writings to paint a portrait of the Iroquois Indians and wars during the early colonial period.

Shannon, Timothy. *Iroquois Diplomacy on the Early American Frontier.* New York: Viking Adult, 2008. A general history of the power of Iroquois diplomacy that tells how Iroquois diplomacy perpetuated peace between warring tribes and colonial powers.

Sherill, P. T. *The Great Peace of Montreal of 1701: French-Native Diplomacy in the Seventeenth Century.* Montreal, Quebec, Canada: McGill-Queen's University Press, 2001. Details the Iroquoian and "Beaver Wars" with the French and the resulting diplomatic negotiations that resulted in a treaty between the French, French Indian allies, including the Chippewas and Ottawas, and the Iroquois.

World Wide Web

"Iroquois Wars of the 17th Century." http://www.wisconsinhistory.org/turningpoints/tp-005/. A links page to a collection of digital primary sources covering the Iroquois and Beaver Wars of the seventeenth century.

"Iroquois Wars." http://www.thecanadianencyclopedia.com/index.cfm? PgNm=TCE&Params=A1ARTA0004062. A detailed narrative of the wars with historical drawings, paintings, images, and links to Web sites about the individual tribes of the Five Nations of the Iroquois and to the Iroquois destruction of the Huron Indians.

"Iroquois Wars of the 17th Century." http://www.wisconsinhistory.org/turningpoints/tp-005/?action=more_essay. Explains the origin of the Iroquois Wars and movement of Indian tribes during the warfare.

Multimedia Source

Four Directions Teachings. http://www.fourdirectionsteachings.com/index.html.
Elders tell a story of Indian participants in the Iroquois Wars, and they share a teaching from their cultural traditions in oral form through audio narration.

10. King Philip's War (1675–1676)

In 1675, within the vicinity of the Plymouth Bay and Massachusetts Bay colonies, King Philip's War broke out between the Wampanoag Confederation and the English colonists. Modern historians, using comparative statistical data, have called this war the "bloodiest war in America's history." Metacom was the son of Massasoit, the Wampanoag chief who negotiated the first treaty with the pilgrims and who attended the first Thanksgiving. Metacom was known by the name King Philip by the Puritans and he understood that his people were in decline due to disease and the ever-increasing pressure from the English for more Indian land and resources. Because of these frictions, many scholars believe war was inevitable and that the hostility of Metacom and his people was understandable. However, English encroachments led to an escalation of war with all Indians, including English allies, such as the Narragansett. Any English justification for war allowed the English an opportunity to take more Indian lands through force of arms. The end result was the almost-total destruction of the Wampanoag Confederation and the ascendancy of the New England colonies. This in and of itself has led to an incredible historical record of colonial justification and to scholarly investigation of the details of the conquest of North American Indian tribes.

TERM PAPER SUGGESTIONS

1. Examine the writing of Increase Mather, well known for his involvement in the Salem witch trials and an avid Indian hater, and report on the rhetorical form he uses to justify war against the Wampanoag Confederation. How effective was his exhortation, and how receptive were his listeners and readers?

2. Metacom's father, Massasoit, helped the pilgrims to survive and thrive during their formative years of settlement. Compare the differences between the time of Metacom and the time of Massasoit and suggest what would account for the increase in hostilities between the two peoples.

3. Write on the power of jurisdiction over Indian tribes by the English, using the murder of John Sassamon, a Christian Indian, as the representative example.

4. The trial, conviction, and execution of three Wampanoags for the murder of Sassamon were the final sparks to ignite the bloody King Philip's War. Write an essay that explores and examines other causes for the war.

5. Explore the role of alliances in the war. What were the benefits or the detriments of allying with one side or the other? Was it possible to stay neutral?

6. Write about Mary Rowlandson's description of Indians in her famous "captivity narrative." Does her description of Indians and her treatment by Indians support, refute, or not affect justifications of war against Indian people? Did it matter to her whether Indians were converted to Christianity?

ALTERNATIVE TERM PAPER SUGGESTIONS

1. In the manner of Increase Mather, write a "jeremiad" from the point of view of Metacom. An American jeremiad was a rhetorical and mournful, woe inspired complaint used often by colonial religious and political leaders to justify the killing of Indians and the taking of their land. Your audience is your tribe, and your purpose is to convince your people to act against the English colonists for their own benefit and survival.

2. Write a captivity narrative from the point of view of a Wampanoag captured by Puritans.

SUGGESTED SOURCES

Primary Sources

Calloway, Colin G., ed. *The World Turned Upside Down: Indian Voices from Early America.* Boston: Bedford/St. Martin's, 1994. Includes Indian speeches about the land hunger of the colonists and their unending encroachment upon Indian lands.

Mather, Increase. "A Brief History of the Warr with the Indians in New-England." 1676. Edited by Paul Royster. http://works.bepress.com/paul_royster/4. An account of the war from the perspective of one of New England's most influential leaders.

Mather, Increase. *An Earnest Exhortation to the Inhabitants of New-England.* (1676). http://digitalcommons.unl.edu/etas/31/. Downloadable PDF. In the rhetorical form of the American jeremiad, Mather uses biblical references to justify total war and wanton destruction against Metacom and his people as God's just punishment on them.

Rowlandson, Mary. *The Narrative of the Captivity and the Restoration of Mrs. Mary Rowlandson.* (1682). http://www.gutenberg.org/etext/851. Copyright-free downloadable e-book or read-online version of Rowlandson's narrative.

"Thaddeus Clark Letter on King Philip's War, 1676." http://www.mainememory .net/bin/Detail?ln=22345. A scan of the actual primary source.

Secondary Sources

Bourne, Russell. *Red King's Rebellion: Racial Politics in New England, 1675–1678.* Oxford, UK: Oxford University Press, 1991. Presents a complete and balanced history of King Philip's War.

Calloway, Colin, ed. *After King Philip's War: Presence and Persistence in Indian New England.* Hanover, NH: University Press of New England, 1997. Calloway shows how Indian people survived and persisted despite devastating loss of life and culture.

Cogley, Richard W. *John Eliot's Mission to the Indians before King Philip's War.* Cambridge, MA: Harvard University Press, 1999. Explores Puritan ideology and missionary activities, also exploring the motivations of Indians to consider conversion.

Drake, James David. *King Philip's War: Civil War in New England.* Amherst, MA: University of Massachusetts Press, 2000. Reinterprets King Philip's War as a civil war between Indians of which colonists took advantage.

Kawashima, Yasuhide. *Igniting King Philip's War: The John Sassamon Murder Trial.* Lawrence, KS: University Press of Kansas, 2001. Explores the causal connections between Sassamon's murder, the trial that led to the execution of three Wampanoags, and the war.

Lepore, Jill. *The Name of War: King Philip's War and the Origins of American Identity.* New York: Vintage, 1999. Explains that the barbarity and the horror of the wars between Indians and Whites was practiced and experienced by both sides and argues that the barbarity practiced by white Americans was integral to the formation of an American identity.

Schultz, Eric B., and Michael J. Tougias. *King Philip's War: The History and Legacy of America's Forgotten Conflict.* Woodstock, VT: Countryman Press, 2000. Describes King Philip's War, the geography of the regions where battles were fought, and offers eyewitness accounts and narratives.

Slotkin, Richard, and James K. Folsom. *So Dreadful a Judgment: Puritan Responses to King Philip's War.* Middletown, CT: Wesleyan University Press, 1978. Examines the Puritans' point of view through their own use of language.

World Wide Web

"Battles Between King Philip's Warriors and the English, 1675–1676." http://www
.bio.umass.edu/biology/conn.river/incident.html. Provides contemporary
photographs of major battle sites of King Philip's War with narrative
commentary and other relevant information.

Giersbach, Walter. "Philip's War: America's Most Devastating Conflict." http://www
.militaryhistoryonline.com/horsemusket/kingphilip/default.aspx. A very
well-documented online essay of the war.

"King Philip's War." http://www.pilgrimhall.org/philipwar.htm. Describes King
Philip's War in terms of three causes and two effects.

"King Philip's War, 1675–1676." *Joseph Dow's History of Hampton.* http://www
.hampton.lib.nh.us/hampton/HISTORY/dow/chap13/dow13_1.htm.
An online reproduction of the 1893 posthumously published history.

Tougias, Michael. *King Philip's War in New England: America's First Major Indian
War.* http://www.historyplace.com/specials/kingphilip.htm. A concise
summary of the war from an author of substantive secondary source history.

Multimedia Source

500 Nations. Dir. Ack Leustig. 500 Nations Productions, 2005. 4 DVDs.
8 episodes (49 minutes per episode). "Episode 4: Invasion of the Coast"
tells the story of Metacom's War.

11. Pueblo Revolt (1680)

Because the Pueblo Indians of the southwest maintained autonomy for
12 years after the Pueblo Revolt (Popé's Rebellion) of 1680, historians
say it was the most successful act of resistance by American Indians against
European colonization and conquest. After Juan de Oñate first brought
Spanish settlers to New Mexico in 1598, the Pueblo people suffered many
indignities and cruelties from the Spanish invaders. One, they were militarily suppressed and forced to capitulate to Spanish rule. Two, the
Franciscan missionaries tried to force the Pueblo to convert to Catholicism. Conversion was successful to some extent but was more successful
in driving traditional practices underground. Three, the Pueblos were
forced to work for the Spanish at the expense of their own families and
communities. Finally, epidemic diseases drastically reduced their populations. Over time, the indignities compelled the Pueblos to consider rebellion despite the potential harm such an action might cause. The Pueblos

believed they had to return to their old ways and traditional religious practices to stop their decline, but this provoked retaliation and repression by the Spanish army and the Franciscans. Pueblo religious leaders, Popé among them, were charged with witchcraft and sorcery. The people revolted on August 10th, and the combined Pueblo forces of Taos, Picuris, Tewa, and many others forcibly ousted the Spanish from New Mexico. The Spanish had to retreat to El Paso, Texas, where they stayed until they regained enough military strength to reconquer New Mexico 12 years later.

TERM PAPER SUGGESTIONS

1. Write on the reasons the Pueblo Revolt happened and how it was possible for the Pueblo people to gain an advantage over the Spanish.
2. Why would Popé and other religious leaders advocate the destruction of Catholicism, its material objects as well as its practices, such as Catholic marriage vows?
3. Examine the role of missionaries in the colonization efforts. Why were they important and how did they contribute? Why did they have to tolerate Pueblo religious practices to a certain extent?
4. Discuss the role of Popé in Pueblo society and the revolt. Was Popé a tyrant in the same manner as the Spaniards? Some historians argue that he was no better.
5. Write on cross-cultural exchange: how did the Pueblo change due to Spanish influences, and how did the Spanish change due to Pueblo influences?
6. How was it possible to unite the various, and often disparate, Pueblo villages to act in concert to rebel against colonial rule and occupation?

ALTERNATIVE TERM PAPER SUGGESTIONS

1. Compare collected images of Pueblo architecture to that of the Spanish. In some cases, these forms and structures merge into a style that people call "Southwestern." Show visually through slide show comparison the parts that are Spanish and the parts that are Pueblo Indian. Is one more dominant than the other? Can colonization and conquest be detected and shown?
2. What is "Mexican," "Southwestern," and "Pueblo Indian" cuisine? Again, can tension and dominance be demonstrated by cross-cultural fusion? Create two to four recipes of each cuisine and, using iMovie, film a short "cooking show" segment preparing the dishes and commenting on their history.

SUGGESTED SOURCES

Primary Sources

Espinosa, Manuel. *The Pueblo Indian Revolt of 1696 and the Franciscan Missions in New Mexico: Letters of the Missionaries and Related Documents.* Norman, OK: University of Oklahoma Press, 1988. Primary source documents collected under one cover with the author's editorial and interpretive commentaries and introduction.

Hackett, Charles Wilson, ed. *Revolt of the Pueblo Indians of New Mexico and Otermin's Attempted Reconquest, 1680–1682,* Volume 8—Excerpt. Translated by Charmion Clair Shelby. http://www.americanjourneys.org/aj-009a/. Spanish and Indian versions of the events from Don Antonio de Otermin's descriptions and from interviews with Pueblo Indians. A "B" version at the same site provided an additional excerpt.

"The Pueblo Revolt: Letter of the Governor and Captain-general, Don Antonio de Otermin, from New Mexico, in Which He Gives Him a Full Account of What Has Happened to Him Since the Day the Indians Surrounded Him." (September 8, 1680.) http://www.pbs.org/weta/thewest/resources/archives/one/pueblo.htm. A modern English facsimile of the original letter.

Secondary Sources

Baldwin, Louis. *Intruders Within: Pueblo Resistance to Spanish Rule and the Revolt of 1680.* London: Franklin Watts, 1995. "Young adults'" narrative of the revolt.

Bowden, Henry Warner. "Spanish Missions, Cultural Conflict and the Pueblo Revolt of 1680." *Church History* 44, no. 2 (June 1975): 217–28. A technical and anthropological examination of the Pueblo Revolt of 1680, a contrast and compliment to the many historical and anecdotal versions.

Folsom, Franklin. *Indian Uprising on the Rio Grande: The Pueblo Revolt of 1680.* (Originally published as *Red Power on the Rio Grande* in 1973). Albuquerque, NM: University of New Mexico Press, 1996. With the help of renowned Tewa Pueblo scholar and anthropologist Alfonso Ortiz, this work tells the story of the revolt from the Pueblo perspective.

Knaut, Andrew L. *The Pueblo Revolt of 1680: Conquest and Resistance in Seventeenth Century New Mexico.* Norman, OK: University of Oklahoma Press, 1995. Tries to retell the story of the revolt from the perspective of the Pueblo Indians.

Ortiz, Alfonso. *The Tewa World.* Chicago, IL: University of Chicago Press, 1969. An insider's view of Tewa Pueblo culture and society. A good way to begin an understanding of how the Pueblo people think and perceive the world that surrounds them.

Preucel Robert W., ed. *Archaeologies of the Pueblo Revolt: Identity, Meaning, and Renewal in the Pueblo World.* Albuquerque, NM: University of New Mexico Press, 2002. Interprets and explores how Pueblo architecture, ceramics, and rock art reveal Pueblo society, culture, and warfare.

Riley, Carroll L. *Rio del Norte: People of the Upper Rio Grande from Earliest Times to the Pueblo Revolt.* Salt Lake City, UT: University of Utah Press, 1995. Survey of the Indians of the Rio Grande, providing an excellent survey of Pueblo Indian culture.

Roberts, David. *The Pueblo Revolt: The Secret Rebellion That Drove the Spaniards Out of the Southwest.* New York: Simon & Schuster, 2004. A good general narrative account of the revolt and of the people, both Spanish and Pueblo.

Silverberg, Robert. *The Pueblo Revolt.* Lincoln, NE: University of Nebraska Press, 1994. General and concise history of the region, people, and revolt.

Wallace, Susan E. *The Land of the Pueblos.* New York: H.B. Alden, 1888. Reprint, Santa Fe, NM: Sunstone Press, 2006. Reprint of the narrative account of Wallace as she recorded her impressions and observations of the Pueblo Indians before modern times.

Weber, David J. *What Caused the Pueblo Revolt of 1680?* New York: Bedford/St. Martin's, 1999. A collection of five essays examining the Pueblo Revolt.

World Wide Web

Naranjo, Pedro. "Why They Burned the Images, Temples, Crosses, Rosaries and Things of Divine Worship." http://www.digitalhistory.uh.edu/native_voices/voices_display.cfm?id=21. Primary source excerpt from Hackett's *Revolt of the Pueblo Indians of New Mexico.*

Ponce, Pedro. *Trouble for the Spanish: The Pueblo Revolt of 1680.* http://www.neh.gov/news/humanities/2002-11/pueblorevolt.html. An essay that explores the reliability of secondary sources when the primary sources are problematic.

"Pueblo Rebellion." http://www.desertusa.com/ind1/P_rebellion.html. Has a modern photograph of Santa Fe's Governor's Palace, where the Pueblos laid siege to Spanish colonists in 1608 and which is the oldest continually-used government building in the United States.

"The Pueblo Revolt." http://iweb.tntech.edu/kosburn/history-444/Pueblo-Revolt.html. An informative outline of the Pueblo Revolt, including an introduction, circumstances leading up to the revolt, early attempts of the revolt, the events, and Pueblo society.

"The Pueblo Revolt." http://www.pbs.org/weta/thewest/resources/archives/one/
pueblo.htm. More of Hackett's translations: a letter of the governor and
captain-general, Don Antonio de Otermin.

Multimedia Sources

Po'pay, a True American Hero Leader of the First American Revolution. http://www
.nativeart.net/affilpopay.php. Promised documentary film to be released
in 2008; meanwhile the site has a short online video.
The West. Dir. Stephen Ives. Public Broadcasting Service, 1996. 4 DVDs.
750 minutes. "Episode One, To 1806" describes Popé and his rebellion.

12. Abenaki Wars in Maine (1675–1748)

More so than their Iroquois neighbors living to the west and south, the Abenaki
had to endure constant war, because they lived on the border region between the
French in Canada and the English in New England. Perpetual warfare on the
frontier between settlers and Indians began when the Iroquois vied for dominance in the fur trade and when European wars and squabbles spilled over into
the European New World. From 1675 to 1678, maintaining a confederation of
at least 12 Algonquian tribes occupying the territory of what is now known as
Maine, New Hampshire, Vermont, and southern Quebec, the Abenaki fought
wars against the English and English Indian allies because the English wanted
Abenaki lands. The Abenaki responded to this threat by siding with the French
and conducting a guerrilla war against the English until a treaty in 1678 stopped
the hostilities for a time. However, due to unending English encroachments, the
Abenaki confederation fought against the English colonists in King William's
War, 1689–1697; Queen Anne's War, 1702–1713; Dummer's War or the
Third Abenaki War, 1722–1727; King George's War, 1744–1748; and the
French and Indian War, 1754–1763. Sporadic and eventual peace between
the French and the English resulted in the withdrawal of French support at
the end of King George's War and abandonment at the end of the French and
Indian War. The on-and-off peace between European nations put the Abenaki
in a position of weakness that the English often exploited. In addition, the wars
of the Abenaki show how the constant pressure of European nations to acquire
Indian lands and European desire to solicit Indian service in colonial wars
tended to weaken and slowly destroy the ability of the Abenaki to resist white
expansion.

TERM PAPER SUGGESTIONS

1. Explore the reasons that the Abenaki would ally with the French rather than the British. Why were the British colonists considered enemies?

2. Examine the role of the French Jesuits in the various wars of the Abenaki. In the Third Abenaki War, Father Sebastian Rasles was deeply involved. What was his role and that of Catholicism?

3. Explore the incessant pressure of war on the Abenaki. What toll does constant warfare take on a people and their culture?

4. Using the rhetorical pattern of cause and effect, explore the causes that led up to each war that the Abenaki were involved in. Were the reasons similar? Or different?

5. Take a look at how the Abenaki social structure and the lives of women and children would be affected by the continual absence of men from the community due to war.

6. Examine the various treaties involving the Abenaki, the French, and the English. What were the terms and to whom were they favorable? Did the Abenaki have to make their own treaties, or were they included in the larger treaties with European nations?

ALTERNATIVE TERM PAPER SUGGESTIONS

1. Create a map of the Abenaki lands and settlement in North America during the period from 1675–1748. Include the positions of the French, English, and Iroquois, perhaps in distinct colors of expansion and encroachment. Using this map, discuss the propensity of the Abenaki to wage war beyond the stereotypical notion of savagery.

2. Create a diary in which you can choose to be an Englishman, a Frenchman, or an Abenaki Indian involved in the long period of the Abenaki Wars, 1675–1748. In this diary make sure to describe all aspects of the wars and personal thoughts and experiences you might have had based on the historical record.

SUGGESTED SOURCES

Primary Sources

Calloway, Colin G., ed. *The World Turned Upside Down: Indian Voices from Early America*. Boston, MA: Bedford/St. Martin's, 1994. Includes Indian speeches about the land hunger of the colonists and their unending encroachment upon Indian lands.

Kidder, Frederic. *The Abenaki Indians, Their Treaties of 1713 and 1717, and a Vocabulary, with a Historical Introduction*. Portland, OR: B. Thurston,

1859. Google Books, 2006. http://books.google.com/books?id
=0C70O72cDtUC. Not only includes the treaties of 1713 and 1717 but
provides a short narrative introduction and short essay on Abenaki language.

Treat, Joseph. *Wabanaki Homeland and the New State of Maine: The 1820 Journal
and Plans of Survey of Joseph Treat.* Amherst, MA: University of
Massachusetts Press, 2007. Reprint of the survey of Abenaki lands.

Secondary Sources

Bruchac, Joseph. *The Faithful Hunter: Abenaki Stories.* Greenfield Center, NY:
Greenfield Review Press, 1988. A renowned Abenaki author/publisher
shares traditional stories of his people.

Calloway, Colin G. *The Western Abenakis of Vermont, 1600–1800: War, Migration, and the Survival of an Indian People.* Norman, OK: University of
Oklahoma Press, 1990. Detailed history of the struggles of the Abenaki
people in Vermont during the times of war and displacement.

Haefeli, Evan. *Captors and Captives: The 1704 French and Indian Raid on
Deerfield.* Amherst, MA: University of Massachusetts Press, 2003. Parts
of this narrative include the role of the Abenaki in the 1704 raid on
Deerfield, Massachusetts, the most-raided colonial settlement, which
was/is centered on lands once held by the Indian allies of the Abenaki.

Haviland, William A., and Marjory W. Power. *The Original Vermonters: Inhabitants, Past and Present.* A detailed history of Indians in Vermont.

Kayworth, Alfred E., and Raymond G. Potvin. *Scalp Hunters: Abenaki Ambush at
Lovewell Pond, 1725.* An interesting balanced history of this tragic event
of the Third Abenaki War or Dummer's War, 1722–1727.

Landau, Elaine. *The Abenaki.* Danbury, CT: Franklin Watts, 1996.
A grade 3–6 reading-level history of the Abenaki that provides general
background history for adults as well.

Morrison, Kenneth M. *The Embattled Northeast: The Elusive Ideal of Alliance in
Abenaki-Euroamerican Relations.* Berkeley, CA: University of California
Press, 1984. Political and economic study of Abenaki and English/
French interactions.

Wiseman, Frederick Matthew. *The Voice of the Dawn: An Autohistory of the
Abenaki.* Hanover, NH: University Press of New England, 2001. Archeological evidence is used to tell a story of the Abenaki of Vermont.

World Wide Web

"Abenaki Nation." The St. Francis/Sokoki Band of Vermont. http://www
.abenakination.org/. Official tribal Web site that includes valuable information about the historical Abenaki.

"Abenakis Culture & History." http://www.avcnet.org/ne-do-ba/menu_his.shtml. Official tribal Web site that includes valuable information about the historical Abenaki.

"The Cowasuck Band of the Pennacook Abenaki People." http://www.cowasuck.org/. Official tribal Web site that includes valuable information about the historical Abenaki.

"Native Languages of the Americas: Abenaki (Abanaki, Abenakis, Alnôbak)." http://www.native-languages.org/abenaki.htm. A site with many useful links to information about Abenaki language, history, and culture.

Schoolcraft, Henry R. "The Merrimac Valley, and Abenaki Tribes." (*Handbook of American Indians, 1906*). http://www.accessgenealogy.com/native/tribes/abenaki/abenakihist2.htm. A short and concise account of the Abenaki tribes of the Merrimac Valley containing links to other pertinent information about the Abenaki.

Sultzman, Lee. "Abenaki History." http://www.tolatsga.org/aben.html. A concise but informative narrative history of the Abenaki.

"Wabanaki and Abenaki Internet Resources." http://www.geocities.com/CapitolHill/9118/wabanaki.html. A links page to many useful and informative Abenaki sites.

"Wabanaki Timeline: Resistance: Making War and Negotiating Peace." http://www.abbemuseum.org/t3.html. A time line with visual imagery pertinent to the Abenaki and links to other useful historical Web sites.

Multimedia Source

Gene Boy Come Home. Dir. Alanis Obomsawin. National Film Board of Canada, 2007. DVD, VHS. 24 minutes. From an acclaimed Abenaki filmmaker, the documentary explores an Abenaki warrior who served two years in Vietnam and his journey back home. Get an idea of how the Abenaki view and understand war.

13. Carolina Indian Wars (1711–1716)

Despite enduring enslavement, land fraud, greedy traders, and land-hungry squatters, the Tuscarora, who lived near the tidewater rivers of North Carolina, and the Yamassee, who lived along the coastal rivers of South Carolina as far south as present-day Georgia, lived in relative peace with the English colonists. This was the case until new immigrants and old colonists coveted more Indian lands and resources, which led to two short-lived but bloody conflicts where the Indians lost to overwhelming odds. Reflecting intentional strategy or not, these small wars typified a European method of fighting wars one tribe at a time until capitulation or outright destruction was achieved, often with the assistance of allied Indians who were neighbors and competitors of the target Indian group. In North Carolina, a newly immigrated group of Swiss settlers founded the village of New Bern at the confluence of the rivers Neuse and Trent, on a stretch of land already occupied by a Tuscarora village; the Swiss destroyed the village and drove the Tuscarora away. Retaliation by the Tuscarora was swift and decisive when they attacked New Bern and other settlements, killing and capturing many. With the help of the South Carolinian militia and their Yamassee Indian allies, and despite early setbacks, the English colonists were able to defeat the Tuscarora, killing and enslaving hundreds and driving most of the survivors out of the Carolinas. These survivors joined the Iroquois League as its sixth nation, albeit much depleted in numbers. Just as the Tuscarora War ended in 1715 with the signing of a peace treaty between the English and Chief Tom Blount, the leader of a small group of Tuscarora remaining in North Carolina, along with the Yamassee and their allies, attacked English settlements in South Carolina and Georgia. Some historians believe they attacked at the behest of the French. The response by the South Carolina militia, now enemies of the Yamassee but bolstered by Cherokee allies, was vicious and effective, forcing the Yamassee and some Tuscarora to flee to Spanish Florida as Indian people and villages were destroyed to the point of extinction.

TERM PAPER SUGGESTIONS

1. Explore the role of Indian allies to the English in the destruction of target Indians nations, like the Tuscarora and/or the Yamassee. Why would Indians help the English to destroy other Indians?

2. Investigate the causes of both wars to determine similarities or differences and to arrive at a reason for Indians to fight back against European colonization.

3. Using the Tuscarora and Yamassee as an illustrative example, discuss why the English always won or gained from war with neighboring Indian tribes, that, in many cases, were people friendly to European settlement and colonization. What changed?

4. By examining these wars, can you detect a pattern of successful conquest of Indian nations? Describe the process and use examples from these wars to demonstrate a methodology, if not a sanctioned policy, of conquest and subjugation.

5. Does morality play a role in conquest and colonization? What logic or reason did the English use to justify Indian killing, and how did these justifications compare to the national mythology of building a great nation?

6. The Tuscarora and other Indians would engage in barbaric practices of torture and killing that led many European observers to conclude that Indians were savages. However, when you compare Indian practices to European practices of torture, like drawing and quartering or the methods employed by the Spanish Inquisition, how could one be construed as more "civilized" than the other? Why was it important to condemn Indians as savages?

ALTERNATIVE TERM PAPER SUGGESTIONS

1. Write a pamphlet in the form and language of the times using a word processing program capable of using period fonts and capable of rendering a facsimile of the colonial broadside, the typical document nailed to posts or trees. Your subject: justification of war against the Tuscarora or Yamassee.

2. Using digital recording software (available on most computers), create and record in your own voice an oral appeal from the perspective of the Tuscarora or Yamassee to wage war against the English, designed to provoke as many warriors as possible to join your cause.

SUGGESTED SOURCES

Primary Sources

"Letter from Christopher Gale to [His Sibling], Including a Memorial Concerning Attacks by Native Americans." http://docsouth.unc.edu/csr/index.html/document/csr01-0441. Christopher Gale, 1679–1735, was a major in the North Carolina militia during the Carolina Indian wars and recorded his experiences in letters written to his brother. This and the next source are primary sources concerning the Tuscarora Indians, warfare, and torture. Many more firsthand accounts can be found by a keyword search on the main site, http://docsouth.unc.edu/csr/.

"Letter from Thomas Pollock to [Robert Hunter], March 06, 1713." Volume 2, Pages 23–25. http://docsouth.unc.edu/csr/index.html/document/csr02-0014. Thomas Pollock was a colonel in the North Carolinian militia. Robert Hunter was commanding general of the forces sent against the Tuscarora. This letter from Pollock explains that the Tuscarora Indians were the cause of the war.

Secondary Sources

Blumer, Thomas J. *Catawba Nation: Treasures in History.* Charleston, SC: History Press, 2007. Expansive general history of the Catawba Nation that includes chapters on the First and Second Tuscarora Wars, 1711–1712, and the Yamassee War of 1715–1716. Includes coverage of early treaties.

Edgell, D. J., and Thomas E. Ross. *American Indians in North Carolina: Geographic Interpretations.* Southern Pines, NC: Karow Hollow Press, 1999. Chapters one and two cover the historical period. Includes many maps.

Gallay, Alan. *The Indian Slave Trade: The Rise of the English Empire in the American South, 1670–1717.* New Haven, CT: Yale University Press, 2002. Covers the period of South Carolina's first settlement to the end of the Yamassee War, 1715–1717, where the Yamassee were destroyed and many of their people sold into slavery.

Haan, Richard L. "The 'Trade Do's Not Flourish as Formerly': The Ecological Origins of the Yamassee War of 1715." *Ethnohistory* 28, no. 4 (Autumn 1981): 341–58. Examines how the decline of deer herds and the rise of cattle and pig raising contributed to the outbreak of war.

Lee, E. Lawrence. *Indian Wars in North Carolina, 1663–1763.* Raleigh, NC: North Carolina Division of Archives and History, 1997. A brief history divided into separate chapters of the wars in the Carolinas, including the Tuscarora War, 1711–1715; the Yamassee and Cheraw Wars, 1715–1718; the French and Indian War, 1756–1763; and the Cherokee War, 1759–1761.

Lee, Wayne E. "Fortify, Fight, or Flee: Tuscarora and Cherokee Defensive Warfare and Military Culture Adaptation." *The Journal of Military History* 68, no. 3 (July 2004): 713–70. Examines how the Tuscarora and other Indians defended themselves against attack.

Oatis, Steven J. *A Colonial Complex: South Carolina's Frontiers in the Era of the Yamassee War.* Lincoln, NE: University of Nebraska Press, 2004. Describes the South Carolina frontiers, 1680–1730, and the many conflicts and wars that occurred in the region.

Ramsey, William L. *The Yamassee War: A Study of Culture, Economy and Conflict in the Colonial South.* Lincoln, NE: University of Nebraska Press, 2008. A full account of the war of 1715–1716 that includes the role of commerce and the Indian slave trade.

Weir, Robert M. *Colonial South Carolina: A History.* New York: KTO Press, 1983. Reprint, 1997. An excellent overview of the colonial period that covers the Yamassee War and other issues of White/Indian relations.

Wetmore, Ruth Y. *First on the Land: The North Carolina Indians.* Winston-Salem, NC: J. F. Blair, 1975. General history of the Carolina Indians.

World Wide Web

"Catechna and the Tuscarora War." http://statelibrary.dcr.state.nc.us/nc/ncsites/Tusca1.htm. A short descriptive online excerpt from E. L. Lee's *Indian Wars in North Carolina, 1663–1763.*

Edwards, Bonnie. "The Tuscarora Indian War." http://www.rootsweb.ancestry.com/~ncbertie/tscnews.htm. A brief online narrative of the war.

"The Way We Lived in North Carolina." http://www.waywelivednc.com/before-1770/tuscarora-war.htm. Online excerpts from the book of the same name by Joe A. Mobley, augmented with visual and other data.

"Yamassee War of 1715." http://ourgeorgiahistory.com/wars/Georgia_Wars/yamasee_war.html. A brief online description of the war.

Multimedia Source

Conquest of America. Dir. Tony Bacon et al. A&E Television Networks, 2005. 2 DVDs. 180 minutes. Four-part series covering North America in four geographical regions (Northeast, Northwest, Southeast, and Southwest).

14. Natchez Massacre (1729)

The Natchez uprising is not well known, and the details of the rebellion and French response are not generally understood because, generally, in U.S. history textbooks, the French and Indian War (1754–1763) and the Louisiana Purchase (1803) are more important historical events. From 1729 up until the Louisiana Purchase, the Mississippi Valley and Louisiana were under French claim, and the Natchez lived in peace with French colonists and tolerated their settlements because of mutually beneficial trade relations. However, the Natchez eventually rebelled against the French, because the French desired their rich agricultural lands and the mineral wealth within their demesnes. The Natchez response to French encroachments was bloody and devastating, but the French retaliation was even more deadly. Even so, the significance of this short-lived "war" was how the French used the rebellion as an opportunity to destroy the Natchez as a political entity, in order to open Natchez land to French exploitation without further "tribal" opposition or appeasement. By organizing several invasion forces out of New Orleans, the French were able to decisively defeat the Natchez in battle and to sell Natchez captives into the West Indian slave trade. Though landless and displaced, many of the Natchez people survived because, as historians believe, they were accepted into the Chickasaw Nation and other Indian tribes as refugees. However, Natchez political, tribal, and cultural organization was destroyed, and so the survivors became individual refugees and no longer members of a sovereign tribe.

TERM PAPER SUGGESTIONS

1. In 1683, Robert Cavelier de La Salle, French explorer, established a settlement near the Natchez and the Mississippi River, and he was welcomed by the Natchez and allowed to proceed with his settlement plans. Explore the relationship between La Salle and the Natchez leadership.

2. Over time the Natchez and the French squabbled and fought over many small matters. Write a report that details these squabbles and that shows how they could contribute to a breakout of hostilities.

3. Write on the direct causes of the rebellion and the reason that the Natchez fought against the French.

4. What is a "just war"? How did the French use writing as a way to justify the killing and extermination of the Natchez people and culture?

5. Explore the outcomes of the war. Who benefited and who lost out? How were Africans employed in the war effort?

6. What is the difference between a war or battle and a massacre? Were the French guilty of the latter?

ALTERNATIVE TERM PAPER SUGGESTIONS

1. The Natchez had a hierarchal social order. Create a graph that shows their social and class stratification. Use this graph to demonstrate how the French could exploit this structure to their economic and political advantage.

2. Create a Microsoft PowerPoint presentation that shows the triracial nature of the Louisianan and Mississippian cultures, which were composed of African, European, and Indian populations. What were the consequences of this triracial mixing?

SUGGESTED SOURCES

Primary Source

Pickett, Albert James. *History of Alabama and Incidentally of Georgia and Mississippi.* Charleston, SC: Walker and James, 1851. http://homepages.rootsweb.ancestry.com/~cmamcrk4/pktfm.html. Although this can be found as a Google digital facsimile, the pertinent text about the Natchez is provided as an easy-to-access online link that brings you to the table of contents. Chapters 8 and 9 describe the French colony of Louisiana and Mississippi. Chapter 11 is entitled, "The Terrible Massacre at Natchez."

Secondary Sources

Barnett, James F., Jr. *The Natchez Indians: A History to 1735.* Jackson, MS: University of Mississippi, 2007. A history of the Natchez tribe and how their conflicts with the French led to their extinction.

Brain, Jeffrey P. "Late Prehistoric Settlement Patterning in the Yazoo Basin and Natchez Bluffs Regions of the Lower Mississippi Valley." *Mississippian Settlement Patterns.* New York: Academic Press, 1978, 331–68. Brain vividly describes the Natchez Grand Village, its organization, and its geography.

Cushman, H. B. *History of the Choctaw, Chickasaw, and Natchez Indians.* Norman, OK: University of Oklahoma Press, 1999. History of the three Indian tribes who were involved in wars against the French.

Elliott, Jack D., Jr. *The Fort of Natchez and the Colonial Origins of Mississippi.* Atlanta, GA: Eastern National Parks and Monument Association, 1998. Anthropological survey of the early Natchez and French colonization.

Francois-Rene, Victome de Chateaubriand. *The Natchez: An Indian Tale.* 1827. New York: L. H. Fertig, 1978. The reprint of the famous fictional tale that justifies a war of destruction against the Natchez.

Oswalt, Wendall H., and Sharlotte Neely. "The Natchez: Sophisticated Farmers of the Deep South." *This Land Was Theirs.* 5th ed. Mountain View, CA: Mayfield Publishing, 1996, 467–91. Explores Natchez culture through farming techniques.

Sayre, Gordon M. *The Indian Chief as Tragic Hero: Native Resistance and the Literatures of America from Moctezuma to Tecumseh.* Chapel Hill, NC: University of North Carolina Press, 2006. Chapter six examines the myth building of French writers to justify the massacre of the Natchez.

Stern, Theodore C. "The Natchez." *Native Americans.* 2nd ed. Edited by Robert F. Spencer and Jesse D. Jennings. New York: Harper & Row, 1977, 414–24. Brief encyclopedic history of the Natchez.

Swanton, John R. *Indian Tribes of the Lower Mississippi Valley and Adjacent Coast of the Gulf of Mexico.* 1911. (*Bureau of American Ethnology Bulletin,* no. 43, Washington, DC). Reprint, Mineola, NY: Dover Press, 1998. Technical resource describing the various tribes of the region.

Usner, Daniel H. *American Indians in the Lower Mississippi Valley.* Lincoln, NE: University of Nebraska Press, 1988. Comprehensive history of the Indians of the region; the Natchez are covered in the first several chapters.

Woods, Patricia Dillon. *French-Indian Relation on the Southern Frontier.* Ann Arbor, MI: UMI Research Press, 1980. Detailed account of French and Indian relations that includes the Natchez.

World Wide Web

Barnett, Jim. "The Natchez Indians." http://mshistory.k12.ms.us/articles/4/the-natchez-indians. An online essay with visual and photographic data, as well as lesson plans.

"Grand Village of the Natchez Indians." http://mdah.state.ms.us/hprop/gvni.html. Includes directions, photo gallery, and background history of this preserved, recreated, and maintained National Historic Landmark.

Legleu, Stephanie. "Indians and Africans in Slave Society." http://www.loyno.edu/history/journal/Legleu.html. A very detailed description of how slavery was a part of the society, economy, and war between the Natchez and French.

"Natchez Indians." http://www.rootsweb.ancestry.com/~msalhn/NativeAmerican/natchezindians.htm. A brief history of the Natchez.

"Natchez Indian Tribe History." http://www.accessgenealogy.com/native/tribes/natchez/natchezhist.htm. A good online overview of the tribe and early history.

"Natchez Massacre 1729." http://www.rootsweb.ancestry.com/~msalhn/NativeAmerican/natchezmassacre.htm. A brief description of the war based on the writings of Charlevoix and Clairborne.

Multimedia Sources

Conquest of America. Dir. Tony Bacon et al. A&E Television Networks, 2005. 2 DVDs. 180 minutes. Four-part series covering North America in four geographical regions (Northeast, Northwest, Southeast, and Southwest).

"Massacre Nov. 28, 1729 at Fort Rosalie." http://www.flickr.com/photos/sunnybrook100/556969851/in/set-72157600373643051/. A painting of the

Natchez Indians killing the French during the Natchez massacre that occurred at Fort Rosalie on November 28, 1729.

15. Albany Congress and Albany Plan of Union (1754)

The brief, three-page document known as the "Albany Plan of Union" has sparked a debate over the extent of American Indian influences on the development of an American form of democracy. What is clear is that Benjamin Franklin and Thomas Hutchinson wrote the Plan of Union and that Franklin, after the Congress, published the "Join, or Die" political cartoon of a snake divided into parts, an image used before and during the American Revolution. What is unclear is how influential the Iroquois Confederacy and the Great Law of Peace, as well as the influences of other Indian forms of government, were in the writing of the Plan of Union, a document that most agree was the precursor to the Articles of Confederation and the U.S. Constitution. (The Great Law of Peace is what some have called the constitution of the Iroquois Confederacy preserved in a series of wampum belts in the protection of the Onondaga, one of the Iroquois Nations.) The Plan of Union was written during the Albany Congress. Representatives of seven American colonies met in Albany, New York, then a rugged frontier town, to negotiate a uniform and unified colonial Indian policy and to negotiate a treaty with the Iroquois. Also at the convention, the colonial American delegates articulated an understanding about the political and economic differences between them and the English crown. Further, they decided their relations with American Indians required a local, colonial expertise as opposed to a distant crown interpretation to be effective. In the Albany Plan of Union, the writers clearly used literary references to the Iroquois Great Law of Peace such as "Grand Council" to represent these differences. What has been debated for many years is the extent that these references and other anecdotal evidence have altered and augmented Western forms of law and governance to create what is known as an American democracy and government.

TERM PAPER SUGGESTIONS

1. Write about Indian influences on notions of American democracy, American identity, and separation from England and English forms of government.

Why is the "Indian" a symbol of unity and resistance? Why identify with the "Indian" with use of terms like "Grand Council"?

2. Examine the need for colonial governments to create a unified Indian policy of trade and peace. Why was unity of purpose and intent so important to Franklin and other colonial leaders?

3. Examine the evidence scholars use to connect the Great Law of Peace and the Iroquois Confederacy to the development of U.S. democracy and government.

4. Examine the counter argument to the "Iroquois influence thesis." What is the strongest evidence against such a claim of Iroquois influence?

5. Examine the participation of Indians at the Albany Congress. What were their motives for negotiating with the American colonists?

6. Examine why the debate over the "influence theory" is still alive and well today. What is each side of the argument trying to prove or substantiate?

ALTERNATIVE TERM PAPER SUGGESTIONS

1. Write out your own form of government in 900 to 1,000 words where you stress democracy and the rights of its people and the details of governance. When finished, compare it with the Albany Plan of Union and the Great Law of the Iroquois.

2. Rather than write a law or constitution for the form of government you come up with, represent it with symbols and creative characters like the ones found on the wampum belts of the Iroquois or the symbols reproduced in their material culture, like the Great Tree of Peace that appears in beadwork or wampum. See http://www.ratical.org/many_worlds/6Nations/. This is a site entitled, "The Six Nations: Oldest Living Participatory Democracy on Earth," which has links to many images of the "Tree of Peace" and to other writings.

SUGGESTED SOURCES

Primary Sources

"Albany Plan of Union." http://www.yale.edu/lawweb/avalon/amerdoc/albany.htm. An online facsimile of the original text document.

"Albany Plan of Union." http://www.constitution.org/bcp/albany.htm. Another online facsimile of this important document.

"A Plan for Colonial Union." http://www.constitution.org/bcp/colunion.htm. This is an online facsimile of the letters that Benjamin Franklin wrote in 1754 detailing a "Plan for Colonial Union," commonly known as the Albany Plan of Union.

"The Constitution of the Iroquois Nations: The Binding Law of Gayanasha-gowa." http://www.indigenouspeople.net/iroqcon.htm. An English reproduction of the Great Law of the Iroquois that some historians cite as the inspirational source of the U.S. Constitution.

"Ratified Treaty #5: The Albany Congress, and Treaty of 1754." http:// earlytreaties.unl.edu/treaty.00005.html. A digitized online facsimile of the records of the Congress and text of the treaty, including reference to the Plan of Union; there are also links to scanned images of the primary source (E. B. O'Callaghan, ed., *Document Relative to the Colonial History of the State of New York,* vol. 8. Albany, NY: Weed, Parson, and Co., 1857. 853–92).

Secondary Sources

Barreiro, Jose, ed. *Indian Roots of American Democracy.* Ithaca, NY: Awe:kon Press, 1992. A collection of essays that explore the influences of Indians on American democracy.

Grinde, Donald A. *Exemplar of Liberty: Native America and the Evolution of Democracy.* Berkeley, CA: University of California, 1991. Explores how the founders of the United States used American Indian democratic ideas.

Johansen, Bruce E., ed. *Debating Democracy: Native American Legacy of Freedom.* Sante Fe, NM: Clear Light Publishers, 1998. Indian influences on the U.S. Constitution and formation of the U.S. government.

Johansen, Bruce E. *Forgotten Founders: How the American Indian Helped to Shape Democracy.* Cambridge, MA: Harvard Common Press, 1987. Narrative history of the connection between the Iroquois Constitution and Great Law to the U.S. Constitution and American democratic principles.

Johansen, Bruce E. *Native America and the Evolution of Democracy.* Westport, CT: Greenwood Press, 1999. One thousand interdisciplinary entries centered on the scholarly debate over the connection to and influence of American Indians in the formation of the U.S. government.

Johansen, Bruce E., and Barbara Alice Mann, eds. *Encyclopedia of the Haudeno-saunee (Iroquois Confederacy).* Westport, CT: Greenwood Press, 2000. Comprehensively written group of short essays covering the history and culture of the Six Nations of the Iroquois.

Lutz, Donald S. "The Iroquois Confederation Constitution: An Analysis." *Publius* 28, no. 2 (Spring 1998): 99–127. Rejects the "Iroquois influence thesis" but shifts to the importance of the Iroquois Constitution as an important document in its own right.

Lyons, Oren. *Exiled in the Land of the Free: Democracy, Indian Nations and the U.S. Constitution.* Santa Fe, NM: Clear Light Publishers, 1992. Eight American Indian authors and scholars present evidence supporting a view that Indian people had a form of democracy that Americans readily adapted to their own needs.

Newbold, Robert C. *The Albany Congress and the Plan of Union of 1754.* New York: Vantage Press, 1955. A narrative of the political and diplomatic importance of this congress.

Payne, Samuel B., Jr. "The Iroquois League, the Articles of Confederation, and the Constitution." *The William and Mary Quarterly* 53, no. 3 (July 1996): 605–20. Disputes the "Iroquois influence thesis" as faulty and lacking credible and convincing evidence.

Shannon, Timothy J. *Crossroads of Empire: Indians, Colonists, and the Albany Congress of 1754.* Ithaca, NY: Cornell University Press, 2000. A counter argument to the "Iroquois influence theory" as well as a social history of the Albany Congress and the role of Indians.

Tooker, Elisabeth. "The United States Constitution and the Iroquois League." *Ethnohistory* 35, no. 4 (Autumn 1988): 305–36. Disputes the evidence that many have used to show the origins of the U.S. Constitution to be from Indians.

World Wide Web

"The Albany Congress." http://www.nysm.nysed.gov/albany/albanycongress.html. A well-written summary of the Congress with images and links to people, places, and events.

"Albany Plan of Union." http://www.state.gov/r/pa/ho/time/cp/90611.htm. A short summary of the plan on an official U.S. government-sponsored Web site.

Daly, Janet. "The Effect of the Iroquois Constitution on the United States Constitution." 1997. http://www.ipoaa.com/iroquois_constitution _united_states.htm. Evaluates the Plan of Union and Iroquois influences.

Grinde, Donald A. "The Iroquois and the Origins of American Democracy." http://www.believersweb.org/view.cfm?ID=173. Grinde continues to present new evidence to support his argument that the U.S. Constitution has antecedents in the Great Law of the Iroquois.

Multimedia Source

"Images of the Albany Congress, 1754." http://images.google.com/images? q=albany+congress&ie=UTF-8&oe=utf-8&rls=org.mozilla:en-US:official&client=firefox-a&um=1&sa=X&oi=image_result_group&resnum

=1&ct=title. Images created to depict the Albany Congress of 1754 and to depict the representatives' sentiments; the "Join, or Die" banner with Benjamin Franklin's segmented snake device is one of the most familiar next to depictions of his own likeness.

16. French and Indian War (1754–1763)

Part of the global war known as the Seven Years War, the French and Indian War, even though lasting nine years, was part of a continuum of wars between Indians and English/American colonists. Starting with George Washington's defeat of the French in the Ohio Valley in 1754, followed by his own surrender at Fort Necessity, the war exploded along the English/French colonial frontier, from the St. Lawrence to the Mississippi Valley, south to the Ohio River, and beyond to Georgia and Florida. The war involved almost every major Indian tribe and confederation as well as the French, Spanish, English, Canadians, and Americans, until it ended with the Peace of Paris in 1763. The reasons Indians were involved and allied with the French were the same as in earlier wars: they resisted and resented English/American expansion into their lands. This expansion made Indians willing French allies. With equal vigor motivated by necessity, the English cultivated Indian allies of their own, by providing firearms and gunpowder to, and negotiating favorable trade terms with, the Iroquois and Cherokee. However, as the Cherokee learned in 1758, when a group of Virginians killed and scalped 12 warriors, allying with the Americans intent on seizing their lands and resources was not in their best interests, so they rebelled. As in most cases with Indian wars, the Indians suffered from an all-out effort to destroy their villages, their crops, and their persons, so much so that they were often weakened and left in desperate conditions at the end of any war. At that point, through the treaty-making process, the English would force Indians to transfer more of their lands, resources, and rights to them as the victors.

TERM PAPER SUGGESTIONS

1. Write on George Washington's survey and exploration of the lands west of the boundaries of the colony of Virginia. How do they reflect the sentiments of most colonial Americans, and how would these sentiments anger or worry neighboring American Indians?

2. Write about the British Superintendent of Indian Affairs Sir William Johnson's relation with the Iroquois Indians, particularly the Mohawks. How would his relationship with the English crown and the Mohawks antagonize the French, French Indian allies, and even the American?

3. Study the accounts of scalping in the French and Indian War. All combatants practiced scalping. Why?

4. Despite the early successes of the French and their Indian allies, the English won the war. Why? And how did this result in unfavorable conditions for American Indians?

5. Compare English and French relationships to American Indians. How were they the same and how were they different?

6. Examine the reasons for the English to advocate peace and friendship with American Indian tribes, often to the bewilderment of the American colonists and military officers commissioned to fight the wars.

ALTERNATIVE TERM PAPER SUGGESTIONS

1. Using available graphic software, such as Adobe Photoshop, and computer hardware, such as a scanner, create a map of Indian land possessions before and after the war. Your goal is to demonstrate the slow but inevitable expansion of American land possessions.

2. Collect depictions of Indians involved in the French and Indian War from online and other sources. Create a collage using Adobe Photoshop, or a slide show using Microsoft PowerPoint, to reveal the general look or character of the Indian warrior as savage.

SUGGESTED SOURCES

Primary Sources

The Journal of Major George Washington, 1754. http://digitalcommons.unl.edu/etas/33/. Downloadable PDF. Two maps are available as well. Shows the desire for Indian land long before actual possession of such land, which explains Indian resistance to American colonial expansion and alliance with the French.

"The Papers of Sir William Johnson." Albany, NY: The University of the State of New York, 1965. New York State Digital Collections, 2008. http://purl.org/net/nysl/nysdocs/423659. Downloadable PDF and browse-enabled files of the famous British "Superintendent of Indian Affairs, 1755 to 1744." The papers include many interesting observations and views of Indians.

Todish, Timothy J. *The Annotated and Illustrated Journals of Major Robert Rogers.* Illustrated by Gary Zaboly. Fleischmanns, NY: Purple Mountain Press, 2002. The actual verbatim journals of Major Rogers, supplemented with informative annotations and period illustrations.

"William Trent's Journal at Fort Pitt, 1763." http://www.hsp.org/files/pagesfromwilliamtrentsjournal.pdf. William Trent was the commander of the Pittsburg Militia and was reported to have served with distinction and honor. The site contains a downloadable PDF of excerpts of Trent's journal.

Secondary Sources

Alden, John R. *John Stuart and the Southern Colonial Frontier: A Study of Indian Relations, War, Trade, and Land Problems in the Southern Wilderness 1754–1775.* Ann Arbor, MI: University of Michigan Press, 1944. John Stuart was the Indian superintendent for the Southern Colonies. This work gives the reasons for Indian involvement in wars with the Americans starting with the French and Indian War.

Anderson, Fred. *Crucible of War: The Seven Years' War and the Fate of Empire in British North America, 1754–1766.* New York: Alfred A. Knopf/Random House, 2000. Considered the best scholarly source for this war.

Anderson, Fred. *The War That Made America: A Short History of the French and Indian War.* New York: Viking, 2005. A scaled-down version of Anderson's *Crucible of War.*

Borneman, Walter R. *The French and Indian War: Deciding the Fate of North America.* New York: HarperCollins, 2006. A study of leadership and ethnocentrism where Indians were but tools or pawns for the goals and aspirations of others.

Brummuel, Stephen. *White Devil: A True Story of War, Savagery and Vengeance in Colonial America.* Cambridge, MA: Da Capo Press, 2004. Examines the life of the famed Robert Rogers, who created the first "American" special forces "Ranger" unit designed to operate behind enemy lines.

Parkman, Francis. *Musket & Tomahawk: A Military History of the French & Indian War, 1753–1760.* A scaled-down version of Parkman's *Montcalm and Wolfe,* which focuses on the brutality of the war and Indian involvement.

Pound, Arthur. *Johnson of the Mohawks: A Biography of Sir William Johnson, Irish Immigrant, Mohawk War Chief, American Soldier, Empire Builder.* Freeport, NY: Books for Libraries Press, 1971. Explores the life of the British Indian agent who worked to keep the Iroquois, especially the Mohawk, a staunch ally of the English crown.

Schwartz, Seymour I. *The French and Indian War, 1754–1763: The Imperial Struggle for North America.* New York: Simon and Schuster, 1994. Searches for causes of the war in America that had different goals than the one in Europe.

Stephenson, Scott, R. *Clash of Empires: The British, French & Indian War, 1754–1763.* Pittsburgh, PA: Senator John Heinz Pittsburgh Regional History Center, 2005. Discusses the two major empires that were confronted during the French and Indian War.

Waddell, Louis M. *The French and Indian War in Pennsylvania, 1753–1763.* Harrisburg, PA: Pennsylvania Historical and Museum Commission, 1996. Examines the role and battles of this pivotal region of the war.

Ward, Matthew C. *Breaking the Backcountry: Seven Years War in Virginia and Pennsylvania, 1754–1765.* Pittsburgh, PA: University of Pittsburgh Press, 2004. Studies the conflict where Indians, Americans, English, Canadians, and the French meet in a most savage way.

World Wide Web

Bray, George A., III. "Scalping During the French and Indian War." http://www.earlyamerica.com/review/1998/scalping.html. Explores this brutal practice performed by all combatants of the war.

Drew, Paul Redmond. "Sir William Johnson, Indian Superintendent: Colonial Development and Expansionism." http://www.earlyamerica.com/review/fall96/johnson.html. An essay examining the role of Johnson in managing the English expansion into Indian lands and his involvement of Indians in his machinations.

"Fighting for a Continent: Newspaper Coverage of the English and French War for Control of North America, 1754–1760." http://www.earlyamerica.com/review/spring97/newspapers.html. Copeland introduces a series of period newspaper links.

"The French and Indian War." http://www.frenchandindianwar250.org/. History and page with links to state and national historic sites specializing in the French and Indian War; short histories and time lines are a few of the interactive and written sources found.

"French and Indian War." http://www.ohiohistorycentral.org/entry.php?rec=498. Describes the battles that occurred in Ohio during the French and Indian War.

"Maps of the French and Indian War." http://www.masshist.org/maps/MapsHome/Home.htm. Fourteen pertinent and viewable maps of the war that can be enlarged.

"1755: The French and Indian War Webpage." http://web.syr.edu/~laroux/. Links to primary sources and also includes a list of primary and secondary resources.

Multimedia Source

The War That Made America: The Story of the French and Indian War. Dir. Eric Strange and Ben Loeterman. Public Broadcasting Service, 2005. 2 DVDs. 240 minutes. A comprehensive documentary of the war that is meant to accompany Anderson's *Short History,* listed in Secondary Sources.

17. Royal Proclamation and Line of 1763

In 1763, the British issued a royal decree that defined Indian rights and dictated colonial Indian policy without consultation or representation of the American colonists. The proclamation forbade further expansion of the American colonies westward, unless under the direct supervision of crown authorities. The proclamation acknowledged that American Indians owned the land they resided on, which the treaty-making process had always acknowledged. Even with this acknowledgment, the ease with which the restrictions were circumvented allowed for the steady acquisition of Indian lands and the displacement of Indian populations. This acquisition and displacement occurred even though the written intent of the law was to impede reckless and rapid settlement and encroachment onto Indian lands in favor of a more gradual process that would have the same intent. The proclamation was intended to avert expensive warfare with Indians, by creating a border line between Indian-held lands and that of the settled colonies; by preventing American settlers from uncontrolled and wanton expansion into Indian lands; by making the English crown the sole authority to negotiate land acquisition treaties; and by making the crown the sole regulator of trade with the Indians, an age-old policy that often had to be reiterated and enforced. The policy called for the building of forts along the line to put a "real" physical barrier between the colonies and the Indians, but the recognized immensity of the project allowed for immediate exploitation, and it also caused outright colonial resentment that such an act violated their own notions of freedom and English rights. Making matters worse, to pay for the expense of building forts and garrisoning them with soldiers, the English crown imposed a tax on tea and stamps—thus generating more animosity that is well understood, but obscuring the link to Indian relations as a cause of the American Revolution.

TERM PAPER SUGGESTIONS

1. Historians often refer to the Royal Proclamation and Line as a "well-intentioned" measure. Explore the failure and success of this measure.
2. On the surface Indians benefited from the Royal Proclamation of 1763. Why? What provisions of the proclamation supported such a benefit?
3. Explore how the proclamation regulated trade with Indians. Why would Americans resent such a regulation?
4. Examine the porous nature of the "line." Is it possible to enforce a line of such length, from Florida, along the Appalachian Mountains and north to Acadia, Maine?
5. What was more important to the English crown? Peace on the frontier or keeping taxes low for the colonists? Were frontier wars with the Indians expensive? Explore the underlying economics of the Royal Proclamation and Line.
6. Investigate the desire to draw lines and to form barriers, real or on paper, between Indians and Euro-Americans.

ALTERNATIVE TERM PAPER SUGGESTION

1. Create a relief map, using traditional art techniques such as paper maché or using modern mapmaking or graphic software, to demonstrate the natural mountainous barrier that the English crown used to draw their "Line of 1763," making the expense of managing such a line easier.

SUGGESTED SOURCES

Primary Sources

Brigham, Clarence S. *British Royal Proclamations Relating to America, 1603–1783*. Worcester, MA: The Society, 1911. Reprint, Malden, MA: Forbes Press, 2007. Reprint facsimile of the original 1911 publication.

"The Royal Proclamation—October 7, 1763." http://www.yale.edu/lawweb/avalon/proc1763.htm. Online facsimile of the original text of the proclamation from the Avalon Project.

Secondary Sources

Barr, Daniel P., ed. *The Boundaries Between Us: Natives and Newcomers Along the Frontiers of the Old Northwest Territory, 1750–1850*. Kent, OH: Kent State University Press, 2006. Examines the impact of a nonstop wave of settlers encroaching on Indian lands.

Calloway, Colin G. *The Scratch of a Pen: 1763 and the Transformation of North America*. New York: Oxford University Press, 2006. Covering the changes in colonial and Indian policy, which includes the Royal Proclamation and Line of 1763, this history is the first of its kind to link British Indian policy to the American Revolution.

De Vorsey, Louis, Jr. *The Indian Boundary in the Southern Colonies, 1763–1775*. Chapel Hill, NC: University of North Carolina Press, 1966. Examines how this line had a tendency to shift and how it played an important role in Indian-White relations, modifying the pace of American colonial westward expansion.

Dowd, Gregory E. *War Under Heaven: Pontiac, the Indian Nations & the British Empire*. Baltimore, MD: Johns Hopkins University Press, 2002. Shows how the new peace of 1763 actually provoked war.

Farrand, Max. "The Indian Boundary Line." *The American Historical Review* 10, no. 4 (July 1905): 782–91. Examines the lack of funds and effort to maintain and police this barrier between the Indians and the American colonists.

Humphreys, R. A. "Lord Shelburne and the Proclamation of 1763." *The English Historical Review* 49, no. 194 (April 1934): 241–64. Examines William Petty, earl of Shelburne and president of the Board of Trade, and his desire to use the Royal Proclamation to regulate and control American colonial expansion.

Komar, Roman N. *The Royal Proclamation of 1763: A Legal Inquiry into Indian Lands in Canada*. Washington, DC: Indian Claims Commission, 1971. Shows the power of Indian rights under these age-old laws and proclamations.

Marshall, Peter. "Colonial Protest and Imperial Retrenchment: Indian Policy, 1764–1768." *Journal of American Studies* 5 (1971): 1–17. Explores the building of forts on the frontier and the tightening of British Indian policy to control and to slow the expansion of the American colonies into Indian lands, which usually resulted in expensive Indian wars. Marshall also explores the protests and responses of the colonists to these new policies.

Stagg, Jack. *Anglo-Indian Relations in North America to 1763 and an Analysis of the Royal Proclamation of 7 October 1763*. Executive summary of a historical background report. Ottawa, Canada: Department of Indian and Northern Affairs, 1981.

World Wide Web

"The English Colonies before 1763." http://www.earlyamerica.com/earlyamerica/maps/english_colonies/. Shows a map of the colonies during the French and Indian War.

"Proclamation Line of 1763, Quebec Act of 1774, and Westward Expansion." http://www.state.gov/r/pa/ho/time/cp/91862.htm. Provides links and narrative information about the Proclamation Line of 1763.

"Proclamation of 1763." http://www.ohiohistorycentral.org/entry.php?rec=1443. Short narrative with links to pertinent sites.

"The Royal Proclamation of October 7, 1763." http://www.bloorstreet.com/200block/rp1763.htm. Provides the text, a map, and links.

"U.S. Territorial Map 1775." http://xroads.virginia.edu/~MAP/TERRITORY/1775map.html. Shows the Proclamation Line of 1763 in relation to British policy and concerns.

Multimedia Source

Tribal Nations: The Story of Federal Indian Law. Dir. Lisa Jaeger. Tanana Chiefs, 2006. DVD. 60 minutes. One of the most important first steps to understanding federal Indian law is to understand how the Proclamation Line divided Indians from Americans, leading to the concept of "separate" nations.

18. Pontiac's War (1763–1766)

After the Treaty of Paris, 1763, in response to a dramatic shift of economic, diplomatic, and military power toward the English due to the absence of the French, Pontiac (1720–1769), an Ottawa, led an uprising against the British policy of "no more powder" in the Great Lakes region. A coalition of Indian warriors besieged and stormed several English forts in Michigan, Ohio, and Pennsylvania, including Fort Detroit, Fort Michilimackinac, and Fort Pitt. Ottawa warriors took Fort Michilimackinac in 1763 by playing a lacrosse game at the fort's gate and thereby causing defenders to let their guard down. Pontiac was involved in the siege of Fort Detroit, which the British successfully defended. The Indians' unified effort, the first of its kind, almost pushed the British out of the

Great Lakes. The "war," however, was much more widespread and all-encompassing than the singular focus on one Indian leader or "chief" would suggest. For one, the Indian uprising involved a alliance of woodland Indian people (Delaware, Miami, Chippewa, and Shawnee, to name a few) with their traditional enemies, the Iroquois; this alliance was a unified effort to stop Anglo-American settlement and taking of Indian lands in the Great Lakes region, as well as an attempt to reestablish favorable trade relations that the defeat of the French in the French and Indian War had destroyed. The Indians were angry with the British for refusing to provide gifts and favorable trade terms, but this was because of the absence of French competition. To put the war into a larger cultural perspective is to recognize the role of Neolin, the Delaware Prophet, whose vision advocated armed resistance and whose vision put all Indians on the same side— against British expansion onto Indian land.

TERM PAPER SUGGESTIONS

1. From an Indian point of view, explore the motivations and reasoning behind the war, especially for former enemies to join together to fight the British, whom Neolin, the Delaware Prophet, called a common Indian foe.

2. Most of the books about this war or rebellion focus on Pontiac, a charismatic Indian warrior leader, or chief. However, as you read about the war, you will find that Pontiac was a participant in a very limited zone of the war. Research definitions of leadership and compare them to how historians write about Pontiac. After reading about Pontiac's role and the other participants, do you think he matched up to these definitions of leadership? Was he a different kind of leader?

3. Investigate the spiritual component that underlay the whole war. Read about Neolin's vision. What did it advocate and why? Why was vision so central to the unification of Indians from different tribes? Why did the vision make sense to them? Why was spirituality important to Indians?

4. Compare Anglo-American notions of land ownership to Indian notions of land ownership. How do they compare to Neolin's vision of land ownership and his advocacy to stop selling or trading land to Anglo-Americans?

5. Neolin preached temperance and the return to the "old ways," void of European influences, especially alcohol. How did alcohol play a role in trade, warfare, and land? Why did Neolin preach to Indians to stop abusing it?

6. Compare the way the many atrocities committed by both Indians and Anglo-Americans are described in various accounts of the war. Are the accounts similar or different? Do the publication date and when the author lived have

any influence on the way he or she describes these atrocities? Does the intended audience of the book play a role in how they are described?

ALTERNATIVE TERM PAPER SUGGESTIONS

1. Check out as many books on Pontiac as you can that have colorful book covers. Scan the book covers and print them on a color printer. Cut the images of Indian warriors, that is, Pontiac, and create a collage by pasting the cutouts on poster board, or rescan them to make a scanner collage suitable for Microsoft PowerPoint or some other slide show computer program. From that collage write an analysis of what you see, and share as an oral presentation your findings. What general theme emerges as you look at the images of Pontiac? Describe the demeanor, stance, and face of each Pontiac warrior image. What kind of clothes is he wearing, and is there any difference between the images? What do the clothes say about his occupation or preoccupation?

2. Type all of the titles of the various books and articles you can find on Pontiac and list them as separate slides on Microsoft PowerPoint or some other slide show computer program. Along with the titles, you should write definitions of the key words in the title. Some examples are "conquest," "conspiracy," "chief," "general," and "king." As an oral presentation, engage your listeners in discussion. How do these words influence thinking about Indian warriors or leaders? How do they perpetuate western definitions of leadership?

SUGGESTED SOURCES

Primary Sources

M'Cullough, John. "Recollection of the Delaware Prophecy (of 1760s) 1808." http://www.historytools.org/sources/delaware.html. An online facsimile of Neolin's prophecy from John M'Cullough, who was born in the colony of Delaware in about 1748, excerpted from his narrative first published in 1808.

Parkman, Francis. *The Conspiracy of Pontiac and the Indian War After the Conquest of Canada: Volume 1: To the Massacre at Michillimackinac and Volume 2: From the Spring of 1763 to the Death of Pontiac*, Lincoln, NE: University of Nebraska Press, 1994 (1851). An exhaustive and well-written narrative of the war in the fashion of its time with all of its bias and prejudicial treatment of American Indians involved in the "uprising." Michael McConnell's introductory essay places Parkman's bias in historical perspective and demonstrates the importance of Parkman's work as a primary source for its view of Indians in a historical period of manifest destiny (1851) where Indians are still a "military" threat to U.S. aspirations and expansion.

Todish, Timothy J. and illustrated by Gary Zaboly. *The Annotated and Illustrated Journals of Major Robert Rogers.* Fleischmanns, NY: Purple Mountain Press, 2002. The actual verbatim journals supplemented with informative annotations and period illustrations.

Secondary Sources

Barr, Daniel P., ed. *The Boundaries Between Us: Natives and Newcomers Along the Frontiers of the Old Northwest Territory, 1750–1850.* Kent, OH: Kent State University Press, 2006. Examines the impact of a nonstop wave of settlers encroaching on Indian lands.

Bland, Celia, and W. David Baird. *Pontiac: Ottawa Rebel (North American Indians of Achievement Series).* New York: Chelsea House Publishers, 1995. Bland writes a very concise and easy-to-read narrative of Pontiac's War, packed full of images, illustrations, maps, and portraits. Bland does a commendable job of summarizing the facts but tends to follow the "savagism."

Calloway, Colin G. *The Scratch of a Pen: 1763 and the Transformation of North America.* New York: Oxford University Press, 2006. Covering the changes in colonial and Indian policy, which includes the Royal Proclamation Line of 1763. This history is the first of its kind to link British Indian policy to the American Revolution.

Cave, Alfred A. *Prophets of the Great Spirit: Native American Revitalization Movements in Eastern North America.* Lincoln, NE: University of Nebraska Press, 2006. Starting with the Neolin, the Delaware Prophet, and ending with Tenskwatawa, the Shawnee Prophet, Cave chronicles the pan-Indian prophet movement through almost a hundred years of American history.

Dixon, David. *Never Come to Peace Again: Pontiac's Uprising and the Fate of the British Empire in North America.* Norman, OK: University of Oklahoma Press, 2005. Reexamines the uprising in terms of American colonial revolutionary sentiments due to the perceived ineffectiveness of the British to control Indians from afar.

Dowd, Gregory. *A Spirited Resistance: The North American Indian Struggle for Unity, 1745–1815.* Baltimore, MD: Johns Hopkins University Press, 1992. The first historical treatment of the overall Indian resistance efforts from 1745 to 1815 where Pontiac and Pontiac's War are placed within a larger historical movement of Indian spiritual and military resistance. Unity of disparate Indian tribes is achieved through the convergence of charismatic Indian warrior leaders and messianic Indian prophets, in this case, Neolin, who advocate the return to the "old" Indian ways by rejecting the religion and material culture of Anglo-Americans in order to prevent further destruction of traditional tribal cultures.

Dowd, Gregory E. *War Under Heaven: Pontiac, the Indian Nations & the British Empire.* Baltimore, MD: Johns Hopkins University Press, 2002. Another reinterpretation of the war that shows the war as a monumental struggle over social and political posturing and positioning, which makes calling it an "uprising" or "revolt" sophomoric.

Middleton, Richard. *Pontiac's War: Its Causes, Course, and Consequences.* New York: Routledge, 2007. Cause and effect analysis of the war, which shows how the shift of power to the British after the Peace of Paris, 1763 and the ending of the French and Indian War led to a break down in long-standing relations between Indians and colonists.

Nester, William R. *"Haughty Conquerors": Amherst and the Great Indian Uprising of 1763.* Westport, CT: Praeger, 2000. A well-researched and footnoted military history of the conflict in narrative form.

Peckham, Howard H. *Pontiac and the Indian Uprising.* Detroit, MI: Wayne State University Press, 1994 (1947). A biased but well-documented source of the Pontiac's War. In particular, Peckham downplays the role of Neolin, the Delaware Prophet, as insignificant if not a lunatic, which contradicts most contemporary sources. However, Peckham has value in that he is an example of the way historians before 1960 viewed Indians and how they incorporated them into their historical narratives.

Todish, Timothy J., and Todd E. Harburn. *"A Most Troublesome Situation": The British Military and the Pontiac Indian Uprising of 1763–1764.* Fleischmanns, NY: Purple Mountain Press, 2006. Tells the story from the perspective of the British officers and soldiers who fought in the war against the Indians. Many firsthand accounts and primary sources.

World Wide Web

"Neolin." http://www.ohiohistorycentral.org/entry.php?rec=285. Short biography that includes cited sources.

"Pontiac." http://www.ohiohistorycentral.org/entry.php?rec=306. Short biography that includes cited sources.

"Pontiac's Rebellion." http://www.ohiohistorycentral.org/entry.php?rec=539. A compact and detailed summary of the conflict and major issues.

Sultzman, Lee. "Delaware History" *First Nations Histories,* 2006. http://www.tolatsga.org/dela.html. A comprehensive short history of the Delaware.

"Treaty of Paris (1763)." http://www.ohiohistorycentral.org/entry.php?rec=1857. A brief description that includes a bibliography of suggested readings.

Multimedia Source

Frontier Legends of the Old Northwest. Dir. Gary Foreman. A&E, 1998. 2 DVDs. 200 minutes. Four episodes covering Roger's Rangers, Pontiac's Rebellion, Colonel George Rogers Clark's (the highest ranking U.S. officer in the Northwest Territory) victory at Vincennes, Indiana, in 1799 against Indians, and Tecumseh's efforts during the War of 1812.

19. Treaty of Fort Stanwix (1768)

When the Europeans and Indians met to negotiate treaties, the treaties that resulted have been seen to follow a distinct pattern with four negotiated components: peace, friendship, trade, and always with the British, a distinct British/Indian boundary, a roundabout way of acquiring Indian lands. Treaties also recognized that the agreements reached were between sovereign nations, where land ownership and hunting and fishing rights were never questioned. At the level of the English crown, the purpose of treaties was to assure American Indian tribes that the American colonists and traders would respect Indian rights and lands, as well as to check or forestall further reckless expansion and encroachments, which generally caused expensive wars. The first Treaty of Fort Stanwix in 1768 was the last of its kind, for after 1768 the treaty-making system was transformed into a one-sided land acquisition and unconditional surrender process in favor of white Americans. The American colonists resented the terms of the 1768 treaty, because the 1768 treaty was designed to stop further colonial encroachment into Indian-held lands in the same manner as the Royal Proclamation of 1763 by creating distinct boundary lines between Indian and colonial lands. On the other hand, in the Fort Stanwix Treaty of 1768, in order to encompass the lands acquired by Americans ignoring treaties and the Proclamation of 1763, the Iroquois gave up lands and even ceded the lands of other Indians to make this new accommodation for a British/Indian boundary. Within this social-political context, the treaty angered many Indians and fueled the anti-British sentiments of Americans who thought the British crown infringed on their rights to expand westward as they saw fit.

TERM PAPER SUGGESTIONS

1. Explore why the British sought to appease the Indians and the Americans with the same treaty. What are the terms of the treaty that support this compromise position?

2. Examine the role of Sir William Johnson, the British Superintendent of Indian Affairs, in the treaty-making process. Some suggest his land speculation projects influenced his goals of negotiating.

3. Explore the reasons behind the failure of the treaty. Why did the treaty generate so much animosity from Indians as well as Americans?

4. Explore the power of the Iroquois to negotiate beneficial terms. Why would they give land away? What did they get in exchange?

5. From a global perspective and for global diplomatic reasons, Johnson and the British crown attempted to create a buffer zone between the Indians and the Americans. How did they propose to form this buffer zone, and how did their own imperial presence get in the way of accomplishing this task?

6. Write an essay that demonstrates a connection between this treaty and the American Revolution, a connection some believe was as strong as "taxation without representation." Look to the "Fort Gower Resolutions" to get an idea of what the Americans, especially the frontiersmen, thought of British policy and the treaty.

ALTERNATIVE TERM PAPER SUGGESTIONS

1. From the perspective of an American frontiersperson, write a list of grievances against the Treaty of Fort Stanwix.

2. As a Shawnee or Cherokee or Miami of the Ohio Valley or of the New York frontier, what would be your grievances against the Treaty of Fort Stanwix? What might you want people to hear and understand?

SUGGESTED SOURCES

Primary Sources

Halsey, Francis Whiting. "Part 3, Chapter 2, The Fort Stanwix Deed, and Patents that Followed it, 1768–1770." (*The Old New York Frontier.* New York: Scribner's Sons, 1901, 99–105). http://en.wikisource.org/wiki/The_Old_New_York_Frontier/Part_3/Chapter_2. Contains a map that delineates the land cessions by the Iroquois that angered many other Indian tribes.

"Ratified Treaty #7: Treaty of Fort Stanwix, or the Grant from the Six Nations to the King and Agreement of Boundary—Six Nations. Shawnee, Delaware, Mingos of Ohio, 1768." http://earlytreaties.unl.edu/treaty.00007.html. A digitized online facsimile of the actual treaty with links to scanned images of the primary source (E. B. O'Callaghan, ed. *Document Relative to the Colonial History of the State of New York,* vol. 8. Albany, NY: Weed, Parson and Co., 1857, 111–37).

Secondary Sources

Barr, Daniel P., ed. *The Boundaries Between Us: Natives and Newcomers Along the Frontiers of the Old Northwest Territory, 1750–1850.* Kent, OH: Kent State University Press, 2006. Examines the impact of a nonstop wave of settlers encroaching on Indian lands and the legal and political issues of laws and treaties.

Bond, Beverley W., Jr. *The Foundations of Ohio.* Columbus, OH: Ohio State Archaeological and Historical Society, 1941. Covers the importance of the Treaty of Fort Stanwix in 1768.

Colden, Cadwallader. *The History of the Five Nations: Depending on the Province of New York in America.* Ithaca, NY: Cornell University Press, 1958. An original reprint of Colden's report to the King of England that covers the history of the Iroquois to 1689. Part II covers the period of the two treaties of Fort Stanwix, 1768 and 1784.

Halsey, Francis Whiting. *The Old New York Frontier: Its Wars with Indians and Tories, Its Missionary Schools, Pioneers and Land Titles, 1614–1800.* New York: Charles Scribner's Sons, 1901. Reprint, Whitefish, MT: Kessinger Publishing, 2007. Examines the conquest of Indians and the acquisition of Indian lands, especially through the two treaties of Fort Stanwix.

Jones, Dorothy V. *License for Empire: Colonialism by Treaty in Early America.* Chicago, IL: University of Chicago Press, 1982. Examines the period of 1763–1768, when the importance of the British form of treating with Indians came to an end.

Kammen, Michael. *Colonial New York: A History.* New York: Oxford University Press, 1996. A general history of the colony and city of New York.

Prucha, Francis Paul. *American Indian Treaties: The History of a Political Anomaly.* Berkeley, CA: University of California Press, 1994. An overview of treaties, policies, and laws as they pertain to American Indians.

Richter, Daniel K. *The Ordeal of the Longhouse: The Peoples of the Iroquois League in the Era of European Colonization.* Chapel Hill, NC: University of North Carolina Press, 1992. A history of the Iroquois based on primary source materials and documents.

Ricky, Donald B., ed. *Encyclopedia of Ohio Indians.* St. Clair Shores, MI: Somerset Publishers, 1998. A brief history of the Ohio Indians and their involvement in the signing of the Treaty of Fort Stanwix.

World Wide Web

"Fort Gower Resolutions." http://www.ohiohistorycentral.org/entry.php?rec=1486. Americans wrote down their resentment of British Indian policies, particularly the Proclamation Line of 1763 and the restrictions on

expanding into the lands of the Indians, revolutionary sentiments leading
to the Declaration of Independence and the American Revolution.

"Fort Stanwix." http://ublib.buffalo.edu/libraries/e-resources/ebooks/records/
efh4968.html. A downloadable brochure available at the national site
containing all the important events surrounding Fort Stanwix history,
including the Treaty of 1768.

"Fort Stanwix." http://www.nps.gov/fost/index.htm. This is the Web site for the
national monument and has photographs, as well as links to history and
culture and to interactive sites for teachers and students.

"Treaty of Fort Stanwix (1768)." http://www.ohiohistorycentral.org/entry.php?
rec=1421. Brief summary of the treaty with bibliographic references
and links.

Multimedia Source

Frontier Legends of the Old Northwest. Dir. Gary Foreman. A&E, 1998. 2 DVDs.
200 minutes. Four episodes covering Roger's Rangers, Pontiac's Rebellion, Colonel George Rogers Clark's (the highest ranking U.S. officer in
the Northwest Territory) victory at Vincennes, Indiana, in 1799 against
Indians, and Tecumseh's efforts during the War of 1812.

20. Quebec Act (1774)

To stop American expansion, especially into the Michigan territory and
the Ohio Valley region, and to appease the French still living in Canada
as promised in the Peace of Paris, 1763, the Quebec Act of 1774 was
passed by the British Parliament at the urging of the English crown; it
set aside Michigan-Ohio lands for French-Canadian expansion and settlement. There were three reasons for this: (1) the Indians were friendly with
the French remaining in America, and the expansion would be much
slower and easier to regulate; (2) the Canadians' natural geographical area
of expansion was into the rich and fertile regions of the Great Lakes and
Ohio Valley, rather than north of Lake Superior and then west into the
prairie lands; and (3) this policy would stop American colonial expansion
and prevent more costly Indian wars by the creation of a new "Quebec
Colony" that would, in theory, put an end to the American colonies'
coast-to-coast charters, which allowed most colonies an open and unending western border in which to expand. Therefore the Quebec Act called
for the reevaluation and reestablishment of boundaries between the old

French-claimed lands, Indian lands, and American lands from the beginning of French and Indian War, and it called to extend the western boundary of Quebec into the Michigan and Ohio territories, south to the Ohio River. This would then reestablish the boundaries set forth in the Proclamation of 1763. In some ways, the Quebec Act was the last straw in the pre-American Revolution period, as it caused much anger as being yet another "intolerable" imposition of English authority over "American" matters.

TERM PAPER SUGGESTIONS

1. Compare and contrast the strengths and weaknesses of the Quebec Act. In the short term, the benefit to Indians would be immense, but over the long term, the act still allowed for further expansion into Indian lands.

2. Explore the reasons why the British crown desired to control American expansion. Did England have valid reasons for a regulated and slow colonial expansion?

3. Examine how the Quebec Act was a continuation of long-standing British Indian policy. What were its antecedents? How was it different from individual colony negotiations with Indians, and when did a "unified" Indian policy become necessary?

4. Write on the connection between the Quebec Act and the American Revolution. Why was it included on the list of "Intolerable Acts"? Why would the Americans find the act so offensive and restrictive of their liberties?

5. Although, on the surface, this act seems peripheral and secondary, it is important to an overall understanding of English/American Indian policy. Why?

6. How did the tenants of the Quebec Act reverberate and find substance in postwar United States in the Old Northwest and in Ohio, leading up to the War of 1812?

ALTERNATIVE TERM PAPER SUGGESTIONS

1. Find a map that depicts the North American land holdings of the English, French, and Indians during the French and Indian War. Find a map that shows the Proclamation Line of 1763 and a map that shows the land distribution dictated by the 1768 Treaty of Fort Stanwix. Finally, find a map of the land encompassing the Quebec Act. Use these maps in chronological order in a visual presentation using slides or Microsoft PowerPoint slides to show

the development of English Indian policy leading up to the American Revolution.

2. Using the map made of the Quebec Act, show how the people of the Quebec Colony viewed and understood the Quebec Act to be their "declaration of independence." How did the Quebec Act uphold and strengthen the rights of French and Indian peoples?

SUGGESTED SOURCES

Primary Source

"Quebec Act: October 7, 1774." http://www.yale.edu/lawweb/avalon/amerrev/parliament/quebec_act_1774.htm. Full text and facsimile of the act, which extended the boundaries of the province of Quebec to the Ohio River on the south and to the Mississippi River on the west. The act also gave the French Canadians complete religious freedom and restored the French form of civil law.

Secondary Sources

Barr, Daniel P., ed. *The Boundaries Between Us: Natives and Newcomers Along the Frontiers of the Old Northwest Territory, 1750–1850.* Kent, OH: Kent State University Press, 2006. Examines the impact of a nonstop wave of settlers encroaching on Indian lands and the legal and political issues of laws and treaties.

Calloway, Colin G. *The Scratch of a Pen: 1763 and the Transformation of North America.* New York: Oxford University Press, 2006. Covers the changes in colonial and Indian policy, including the Royal Proclamation Line of 1763. This history is the first of its kind to link British Indian policy to the American Revolution.

Dunn, Walter S. *Choosing Sides on the Frontier in American History.* Westport, CT: Praeger, 2007. A history that claims land, including Indian land, was what the American Revolution was fought over. The Quebec Act is but one example of how Great Britain tried to prevent further land acquisition by the American colonists.

Jones, Dorothy V. *License for Empire: Colonialism by Treaty in Early America.* Chicago, IL: University of Chicago Press, 1982. Examines the period of 1763–1768, when the importance of the British form of treating with Indians came to an end.

Metzger, Charles H. *The Quebec Act: A Primary Cause of the American Revolution.* Philadelphia, PA: U.S. Catholic Historical Society, 1936. Describes the connection to the American Revolution.

Neatby, Hilda, and Michael Hayden. *The Quebec Act: Protest and Policy.* Upper Saddle River, NJ: Prentice-Hall, 1972. Discusses Canadian history, politics, Quebec separatism, and English–French relations.

World Wide Web

"Proclamation Line of 1763, Quebec Act of 1774, and Westward Expansion". http://www.state.gov/r/pa/ho/time/cp/91862.htm. Explores the relationship of the two acts to westward expansion and how the acts angered the Americans because they prevented westward expansion.

"Quebec Act." http://www.thecanadianencyclopedia.com/index.cfm?PgNm=TCE &Params=A1ARTA0006592. Short summary with images and links.

"The Royal Proclamation of 1763 and the Quebec Act of 1774. *Historical Narratives of Early Canada.* W. R. Wilson, 2004. http://www .uppercanadahistory.ca/pp/ppa.html. An excellent site that links the Royal Proclamation of 1763 to the Quebec Act of 1774 using images of primary source materials, relevant maps, and pictures of key individuals.

"1774 Quebec Act." http://www.encyclopedia.com/doc/1E1-QuebecAc.html. A site with short summaries as well as links and interactive sources; in particular, there is a detailed and important map of the intended boundaries of the new Quebec of 1774, which shows, graphically, why the Americans would feel confined by the provisions of the act.

Multimedia Source

500 Nations. Dir. Ack Leustig. 500 Nations Productions, 2005. 4 DVDs. 8 episodes (49 minutes per episode). "Episode 5: Cauldron of War" tells the story of tensions on the Quebec frontier before and during the American Revolution.

21. Lord Dunmore's War with the Shawnee (1774)

In 1774, Lord Dunmore, last Royal governor of Virginia, decided to ignore the Royal Proclamation of 1763 and the provisions of the Treaty of Fort Stanwix of 1768, by sending a survey team into the southern Ohio territory along the Ohio River and south of the river into the tribal lands of the Shawnee known as Kentucky, lands protected and reserved by the Fort Stanwix Treaty. Believing that royal decrees and treaties with Indians violated their colonial rights, the Virginians reasserted their claims to these western lands and their intention to survey and settle the lands, which, as everyone knew, would anger the Shawnee of southern Ohio and Kentucky. Chiefs Black Fish and Cornstalk attempted to stop the Virginian encroachment by giving fair warning and with deadly threats and diplomacy, but neither of their efforts worked: in the first case, despite a warning, Virginians crossed the line into Black Fish's territory, and a skirmish ensued where men on both sides were killed; in the second, Cornstalk and his party were ambushed as they traveled to negotiate peace, and his brother, Silverheels, was killed. As the hostilities escalated, Lord Dunmore used the moment to declare war on June 10, and he raised the Virginia militia. What followed was the October 10 Battle of Point Pleasant, where an estimated 700 Shawnee and Indian allies clashed with at least 2,000 Virginians. The battle was brutal, loses were heavy, and it continued until leaders of both sides quit the battlefield. A truce was negotiated on October 26, 1774, and hostilities ceased.

TERM PAPER SUGGESTIONS

1. Write on the motivations for the Virginians and Lord Dunmore to violate the proclamations and treaties of the English crown, and discuss how their actions could be construed as characteristic of revolution and rebellion.

2. Explore the frustrations of Black Fish and Cornstalk as they tried to prevent war with reasoned diplomatic measures. Why were they doomed to fail?

3. Investigate the plan of the British crown to prevent such frontier and border wars through policies, proclamations, and treaties. Why did these measures fail?

4. Search for and write on the reasons the British military did not participate in this short war. Why did they sit on the sidelines? What would have prevented their involvement?

5. Write on the leadership qualities of Lord Dunmore himself. Was he better at politics than generalship? What about diplomacy?

6. Only at the point of his sword was Lord Dunmore able to stop his Virginia militia from destructive vengeance against Shawnee villages. Why were the Americans so intent on destroying Indians? What generated such hatred?

ALTERNATIVE TERM PAPER SUGGESTIONS

1. Use graphic software, a scanner, and digital or print maps to create a period map of Lord Dunmore's War that shows the relative positions of the Shawnee, British, and Virginia forces, as well as the disputed lands. This map should demonstrate the significant geographical borders Dunmore proposed to cross and should demonstrate that his proposal was a significant change in policy.

2. Create a different map that depicts Virginia's coast-to-coast charter and western boundaries. How did Lord Dunmore's desire for western lands fit into this colonial claim to Indian lands?

SUGGESTED SOURCES

Primary Sources

Foster, Emily. *The Ohio Frontier: Anthology of Early Writings.* Lexington, KY: University Press of Kentucky, 2000. A primary source collection of writings covering many frontier-Indian conflicts and issues.

Thwaites, Reuben Gold, and Louise Phelps Kellogg, eds. *Documentary History of Dunmore's War, 1774.* Madison, WI: Wisconsin Historical Society, 1905. http://books.google.com/books?id=RQq3bpujDAsC. Contains many primary sources, such as the rosters of the various companies of soldiers and other statistical data.

Withers, Scot, et al. *Chronicles of Warfare, or, A History of the Settlement by Whites, of North-Western Virginia, and of the Indian Wars and Massacres in that Section of the State.* R. Clarke Company, 1895. http://books.google.com/books?id=sjjdU6akFQYC. A good source for information on atrocities committed by Indians and Americans.

Secondary Sources

Barr, Daniel P., ed. *The Boundaries Between Us: Natives and Newcomers Along the Frontiers of the Old Northwest Territory, 1750–1850.* Kent, OH: Kent State University Press, 2006. Examines the impact of a nonstop wave of settlers encroaching on Indian lands.

Calloway, Colin G. *The Shawnees and the War for America.* New York: Viking Press, 2007. Interesting general war history of the Shawnee that covers Dunmore's War.

Dowd, Gregory. *A Spirited Resistance: The North American Indian Struggle for Unity, 1745–1815.* Baltimore, MD: Johns Hopkins University Press, 1992. The first historical treatment of Indian resistance efforts to American expansion. Lord Dunmore's War was an early example of how the colonists responded to Indian resistance efforts.

Downes, Randolph. "Dunmore's War: An Interpretation." *The Mississippi Valley Historical Review* 21, no. 3 (December 1934): 311–30. After citing Richard Butler, who wrote an account of the war, Downes argues that the Shawnee were, indeed, very active in trying to prevent a bloody conflict and that the Americans were greedy for Shawnee lands.

Downes, Randolph C. *Council Fires on the Upper Ohio: A Narrative of Indian Affairs in the Upper Ohio Valley Until 1795.* Pittsburgh, PA: University of Pittsburgh Press, 1940. Reprint, 1969. Examines the conflicts between the Shawnee and the Americans in Western Pennsylvania.

Hintzen, William. *The Border Wars of the Upper Ohio Valley (1769–1794)*. Manchester, CT: Precision Shooting, 1999. Details the wars fought in these 25 years on the eastern frontier of West Virginia.

Hurt, R. Douglas. *The Ohio Frontier: Crucible of the Old Northwest, 1720–1830*. Bloomington, IN: Indiana University Press, 1998. A good overview of the frontier wars and the place Dunmore's War occupies in the chronology.

Quarles, Benjamin. "Lord Dunmore as Liberator." *The William and Mary Quarterly* 15, no. 4 (October 1958): 494–507. Examines the diplomatic and political history of Lord Dunmore.

Skidmore, Warren. *Lord Dunmore's Little War of 1774*. Bowie, MD: Heritage Books, 2002. A book of primary documents, short biographies of American participants, and other data.

World Wide Web

"Dunmore's War." http://www.ohiogenealogy.org/athens/dunmores_war.htm. A detailed account of the war with many quotations from primary sources.

"Lord Dunmore's War and the Battle of Pleasant." http://www.ohiohistorycentral.org/entry.php?rec=514. Short summary with valuable links and bibliography.

Willyard, Kyle. "Culpeper in Lord Dunmore's War." http://www.liming.org/nwta/culdunmore.html. Short history of the 40 men from Culpeper County, Virginia who served in the war as militia.

Multimedia Source

The War Against the Indians. Dir. Harry Rasky. Canadian Broadcast Company, 1998. 2 VHS tapes. 141 minutes. Explores 500 years of Indian wars from the perspective of American Indians.

22. Boston Tea Party, Mohawks, and Tammany (1773)

To understand the role of the image of the Indian in the creation of U.S. national identity and to understand the rise and persistence of American Indian stereotypes, the legacy of the Boston Tea Party of 1773 is good place to start. Members of the Sons of Liberty disguised themselves as Mohawk warriors to engage in an act of civil disobedience by throwing tea into the Boston Harbor. As "Mohawks," they directly associated themselves with the Albany Plan of Union, and by naming themselves "sons" of the Delaware chief, Tammany, whose name translates into "Liberty," they became Americans rather than British. The Sons of Liberty created the archetypal model of the invented, stereotypical Indian warrior by converting socially accepted secret organizations of European origin, such as the society of Free and Accepted Masons, into a uniquely American version. The image of the Indian served the American patriots well. Often, a weathervane fashioned in the form of an Indian archer identified a secret meeting place, usually a barn, where Sons of Liberty patriots would gather. They wore Indian warrior guises, sang Indian songs, and smoked an Indian pipe of their own invention. Tar and feathering, tomahawks embedded in entrance ways, and the menacing presence of Americans dressed as Indians at doorsteps signaled to their enemies their patriotic and serious intent. They acted in a controlled-savage manner against their English opponents, but they still believed in their civilized and European origins. Because they communicated an American identity rather than a Mohawk one, the Sons of Liberty sought to portray a generic, standard image of an Indian with very little relation to any existing Indian tribe.

TERM PAPER SUGGESTIONS

1. If not to disguise, for what other reasons would the Sons of Liberty use imagery of the American Indian in their public acts of protest, such as the Boston Tea Party?

2. Investigate and write about the use of Indian imagery as symbolic of America and American identity.

3. Besides those involved with the Boston Tea Party, what other "American" secret societies use the American Indian as a symbol or guise? Investigate and report. (Hint: look at the early history of the Boy Scouts of America.)

4. In Horton's *History of the Tammany Society*, he describes the mythical history of Chief Tammany, whose name means "Liberty" in English. Why did the Sons of Tammany or Liberty call themselves "Sons"? What did that imply and mean?

5. Investigate how the dressing up as an Indian signals and allows for antisocial behavior. Individuals dressed as Indians often perpetrated destruction, like the destruction of the hated tea, tar and feathering, and riotous behavior. Why?

6. Explore the role of Indian logos and mascots, especially at the end of the 1800s. How can they be compared to the Boston Tea Party Indians?

ALTERNATIVE TERM PAPER SUGGESTIONS

1. Create a collage of found objects or products that depict American Indians in any way. This collage can be created using a scanner and/or digital camera. Do the same with images of the Boston Tea Party. Collages of Indian images and objects demonstrate the importance of the Indian as an image in American history and consumer culture.

2. Using whatever materials are on hand (pencil and paper, software, construction paper, or cloth) design an Indian outfit, head to toe, without any references, pictures, or images of any sort. Use your memory. The goal is to compare what you have designed and imagined to images of Indians found in history books and children's literature and to contemplate the power of static and stereotypical images of Indians to influence thinking.

SUGGESTED SOURCES

Primary Sources

Hewes, George. "Take Your Tea and Shove It." Nashville, TN: Ibis Communications, 2008. http://www.eyewitnesstohistory.com/teaparty.htm. Around the middle of the page, after the brief description, Hewes, who participated in the Boston Tea Party, gives his account of it.

Horton, R. G. *History of the Tammany Society, or, Columbian Order.* New York: Tammany Society, 1865. Pages 849–56 provide an account of the life and history of the mythical Tammany.

Kilroe, Edwin P. *Saint Tammany and the Origin of the Society of Tammany: Or Columbian Order.* New York: M. B. Brown Printing and Binding, 1913. Google Books, 2008. http://books.google.com/books?id=tG5DAAAAIAAJ. Covers most of the same ground as Horton but has more on the history of Chief Tammany.

Secondary Sources

Bird, Elizabeth, S. *Dressing in Feathers: The Construction of the Indian in American Popular Culture.* Boulder, CO: Westview Press, 1996. Though not directly related to the Boston Tea Party Indians, this collection of essays does offer how that legacy plays out in popular culture.

Deloria, Phil. *Playing Indian.* New Haven: Yale University Press, 1998. A history of people, such as the Sons of Liberty, who dress up like Indians and the reason why.

Franks, Ray. *What's In a Nickname: Exploring the Jungle of College Athletic Mascots.* Amarillo, TX: Ray Franks Publishing Ranch, 1982. Considering that the Washington Redskins and the Atlanta Braves sports team were originally from Boston and that they were originally honoring the Boston Tea Party

Indians, this book on the logos and mascot of every college team is interesting in that more than half of the mascots depict Indians.

Fryatt, Norma R. *Boston and the Tea Riots.* Princeton, NJ: Auerbach Publications, 1972. Explores the causes, describes the events, and interprets the aftermath of the Boston Tea Party.

Grinde, Donald A. *Exemplar of Liberty: Native America and the Evolution of Democracy.* Berkeley, CA: University of California, 1991. Explores how the founders of the United States used American Indian democratic ideas.

Huhndorf, Shari, M. *Going Native: Indians in the American Cultural Imagination.* Ithaca, NY: Cornell University Press, 2001. General history of Americans identifying with Indians.

Labaree, Benjamin Wood. *The Boston Tea Party.* Holliston, MA: Northeastern, 1979. The standard authority on the event and its aftermath.

Preuss, Arthur. *A Dictionary of Secret and Other Societies.* London: B. Herder Book Co., 1924. Reprint, Whitefish, MT: Kessinger Publishing, 2007. Lists many of the societies where Indians play a role.

World Wide Web

"Boston Tea Party: Ships and Museum." http://www.bostonteapartyship.com/. The official site of the ships and museum located in Boston Harbor with many interesting links to historical information and interactive activities.

Jansen, Cassandra. "Boston Tea Party." http://www.let.rug.nl/~usa/E/teaparty/bostonxx.htm. Short summary with links and with an image of a commemorative stamp.

Kreamer, Todd Alan. "Sons of Liberty: Patriots or Terrorists?" http://www.earlyamerica.com/review/fall96/sons.html. A well-reasoned argument.

Multimedia Source

"Images of the Boston Tea Party." http://images.google.com/images?client=firefox-a&rls=org.mozilla:en-US:official&channel=s&hl=en&q=boston+tea+party,+1773&um=1&ie=UTF-8&sa=X&oi=image_result_group&resnum=1&ct=title. Links page to many interesting images from a variety of sites.

23. General John Sullivan's Destruction of the Iroquois (1779)

In 1779, Major General John Sullivan destroyed the Iroquois homeland of 40 villages, which resulted in almost total elimination of the Iroquois

Confederacy. His army celebrated their victory over a barrel of rum, and they donned Indian garb, smeared war paint on their faces, danced an Indian dance led by a captured Oneida sachem, and screamed an Indian war whoop in defiant celebration. The Americans' attack was motivated by the long-time alliance of the Iroquois with the British, especially the pro-British Mohawk, Cayuga, Seneca, and Onondaga, and their assistance in the Saratoga campaign to help the British in their attempt to drive the Americans out of the New York/Pennsylvania frontier. Further, the Iroquois participated in raids on the frontier settlements from Pennsylvania's Wyoming Valley to German Flatts, New York, a war-ravaged frontier town, fighting alongside the famed Butler's Rangers, British light troops. To counter these military alliances, Major General Sullivan was sent on an punitive expedition that turned into a frenzy of destruction. Crops and villages were torched and Iroquoian people killed, mostly women and children. The devastation was so extreme that it broke the power of the Iroquois to wage war or to resist American expansion from that point forward. The hostilities between the Iroquois and Americans continued until 1784, when the second Treaty of Fort Stanwix was signed by all representatives of the Six Nations of the Iroquois (Cayuga, Mohawk, Oneida, Onondaga, Seneca, and Tuscarora) whether or not they fought with the British. In the Treaty of Fort Stanwix of 1784, which was radically one-sided, the Iroquois surrendered large tracts of land and accepted American dominance.

TERM PAPER SUGGESTIONS

1. Why would most of the Iroquois ally themselves with the British, as opposed to the Americans? Why would many of them stay neutral?

2. Describe the relationship between the English and the Iroquois in military terms. What martial qualities did the Indians have that the British found useful in their war against the rebellious Americans?

3. Why would Sullivan and his army be willing to destroy the Iroquois completely? Explore the motivation to conduct total war, which meant killing women and children.

4. How did British Indian policy and Indian treaties, such as those with the Iroquois, factor into the starting of the American Revolution?

5. Explore whether the Iroquois had many options but to fight in the war. Could they have followed a strategy of peace?

6. Compare the first Treaty of Fort Stanwix, 1768, to the second Treaty of Fort Stanwix. Besides the switch of sovereign powers from the British to the United States, what were the significant differences? What terms remained the same?

ALTERNATIVE TERM PAPER SUGGESTIONS

1. Using a Microsoft PowerPoint presentation format, create a slide show depicting in graphic form Sullivan's campaign against the Iroquois. Superimpose the 40 villages of the Iroquois on a historical map of New York to illustrate the geographical extent of the campaign.

2. Create a Web site blog that records the negative sentiments of Americans toward the Iroquois, and invite others to counter or address those sentiments.

SUGGESTED SOURCES

Primary Sources

Abler, Thomas S., ed. *Chainbreaker: The Revolutionary War Memoirs of Governor Blacksnake as Told to Benjamin Williams.* Lincoln, NE: Bison Books, 2005. Recollections of Seneca chief Governor Blacksnake, or Chainbreaker, during the time of the American Revolution and Sullivan's campaign.

Hardenbergh, John L. *The Journal of Lieut. John L. Hardenbergh of the Second New York Continental Regiment, in General Sullivan's Campaign against the Western Indians.* 1879. Reprint, Whitefish, MT: Kessinger Publishing, 2007. A soldier's account of the Sullivan Campaign that has been often cited and referenced.

Willers, Diedrich, Jr. *The Centennial Celebration of General Sullivan's Campaign against the Iroquois In 1779.* Reprint, Whitefish, MT: Kessinger Publishing, 2007. An anniversary observance collection of essays that reprints many primary source documents and addresses.

Secondary Sources

Barr, Daniel P., ed. *The Boundaries Between Us: Natives and Newcomers Along the Frontiers of the Old Northwest Territory, 1750–1850.* Kent, OH: Kent State University Press, 2006. Examines the impact of a nonstop wave of settlers encroaching on Indian lands.

Barr, Daniel P. *Unconquered: The Iroquois League at War in Colonial America.* Westport, CT: Praeger, 2006. This book provides Iroquois military history from the period of first contact with Europeans to the American Revolution.

Fischer, Joseph R. *A Well-Executed Failure: The Sullivan Campaign against the Iroquois. July–September 1779.* Columbia, SC: University of South Carolina Press, 1997. Military history analysis of Sullivan's generalship and of his army.

Graymont, Barbara. *The Iroquois in the American Revolution.* Syracuse, NY: Syracuse University Press, 1975. Uses archeology, anthropology, and history to analyze the role of the Iroquois in the American Revolution. The book also has chapters devoted to Sullivan's campaign and the Fort Stanwix Treaty of 1784.

Nammach, Georgiana C. *Fraud, Politics and Dispossession of the Indians: The Iroquois Land Frontier in the Colonial Period.* Norman, OK: University of Oklahoma, 1969. Explores the methods Americans used to acquire Iroquois land, which explains the Indians' distrust of the colonists.

Nester, William R. *The Frontier War for American Independence.* Mechanicsburg, PA: Stackpole Books, 2004. Comprehensive examination of war with and against Indians in the various North American frontiers.

Norton, Tiffany. *History of Sullivan's Campaign against the Iroquois: Being a Full Account of That Epoch of the Revolution.* 1879. Reprint, Whitefish, MT: Kessinger Publishing, 2007. Google Books, 2008. http://books .google.com/books?id=96PCwz4JK2IC. A reliable examination due to its reliance on primary source documents and maps of the Sullivan Campaign. Norton attempts to separate fact from myth.

Prucha, Francis Paul. *American Indian Treaties: The History of a Political Anomaly.* Berkeley, CA: University of California Press, 1994. An overview of treaties, policies, and laws as they pertain to American Indians.

Richter, Daniel Karl. *The Ordeal of the Longhouse: The Peoples of the Iroquois League in the Era of European Colonization.* Chapel Hill, NC: University of North Carolina Press, 1992. A complete history of how the Iroquois adapted to changing economic and social conditions brought on by colonization and trade.

Richter, Daniel Karl, James H. Merrell, and Wilcomb E. Washburn. *Beyond the Covenant Chain, the Iroquois and Their Neighbors in Indian North America 1600–1800.* 1987. Reprint, Pennsylvania State University Press, 2003. A collection of essays exploring the power of the Iroquois in relation to other Indian tribes and Europeans.

Snow, Dean. *The Iroquois.* Oxford, UK: Blackwell, 1994. Organized around names of the Iroquoian calendar, Snow's book tells the story of the Iroquois from AD 900 to 2000. A good general history.

World Wide Web

"The Clinton-Sullivan Campaign of 1779." http://www.nps.gov/fost/historycul-
    ture/the-western-expedition-against-the-six-nations-1779.htm. A well-
    written summary from the national monument site of Fort Stanwix.
"The 1779 Sullivan Campaign." http://www.earlyamerica.com/review/1998/
    sullivan.html. A detailed short narrative of the campaign that is heavily
    footnoted and sourced.
"Treaty of Fort Stanwix (1784)." http://www.ohiohistorycentral.org/entry.php?
    rec=1420. A short description with links and a bibliography.

Multimedia Source

Four Directions Teachings. http://www.fourdirectionsteachings.com/index.html.
    Elders tell a story of Indian participants in the Iroquois Wars, and they
    share a teaching from their cultural traditions in oral form through audio
    narration.

24. Treaty of Greenville (1786–1795)

After the American Revolution, Americans swarmed into the Ohio Valley, south of Lake Erie and north of the Ohio River, and south into Kentucky. This provoked war with the Indians living in those regions. Little Turtle of the Miami and Blue Jacket of the Shawnee formed a resistance to the American invasion by sending war parties to raid frontier settlements. By 1788 and helped by the British in violation of the 1786 Treaty of Paris, Ottawas, Chippewas, Kickapoos, Pottawatomies, Chickamaugas, and Cherokees would join the Miami and Shawnee to wage war. Over several years and with the urging of American settlers who suffered the brunt of this war, the First American Regiment, the Legion of the United States and Kentucky and Ohio Militia, was organized to fight and to build protective forts. After Colonel Arthur St. Claire, first governor of the Northwest Territory and leader of the U.S. military forces in Ohio, resigned, Revolutionary leader "Mad Anthony" Wayne took charge and fought many battles against Little Turtle and Blue Jacket, culminating in the decisive battle of Fallen Timbers in 1794, where Blue Jacket was soundly defeated. With the refusal of their British allies to allow them refuge within British forts and the continued destruction of Indian towns by Wayne, the Indians were forced to capitulate, and Indian resistance was broken forever in the Ohio region. The Treaty of Greenville in 1795 ended all hostilities and conveyed to the United States, via unconditional surrender terms, lands north and west of the Ohio River—lands within the present-day boundaries of the state of Ohio. The treaty also created yet another "permanent" boundary line, close to the present-day boundary between Ohio and Indiana, that settlers were warned not to cross.

TERM PAPER SUGGESTIONS

1. Examine the journals of the American settlers to discover their views of Indians and to survey the risk and dangers involved in settling "a wild land," from their point view.

2. Explore how Indian wars lead to creation of new boundaries, especially of states, to the disadvantage of Indian tribes. Be sure to define "sovereign territory" in the context of boundaries and borders.

3. One Shawnee chief, Kekewepelletha, agreed to ceding the Miami River Valley, a portion of the Ohio region, to the United States, but every other Shawnee chief repudiated that agreement. How could this lead to confusion or exploitation?

4. Explore the many various Indian tribes of the Ohio region. How many and how diverse were they?

5. In terms of Indians, the Americans formed a unified stance; in contrast, individual Indian tribes tended to have changing policies toward the Americans. Why?

6. How did the Treaty of Greenville follow a pattern of peace and friendship, land acquisition, and creating a "border" or line between Americans and Indians? Is the inclusion of "peace and friendship" contradictory to the other characteristics of the treaty or must "peace and friendship" be a prerequisite to acquiring Indian land and resources?

ALTERNATIVE TERM PAPER SUGGESTIONS

1. Study old maps of the Ohio region included in Booth's text. Scan these maps to make a Microsoft PowerPoint slide show of the region and of the progression of American settlement.

2. Imagine you are an Indian of the time. Create a Web site that tries to logically argue against western expansion. Create a catchy name, reference maps and Indian policies, and use the promises of federal officials to warn against any further encroachment onto Indian lands.

SUGGESTED SOURCES

Primary Sources

Booth, Russell H. *The Tuscarawas Valley in Indian Days, 1750–1797: Original Journals and Old Maps.* Cambridge, OH: Gomber House Press, 1994. A primary source collection of eyewitness accounts of settlers of eastern Ohio, original survey maps showing Indian towns and white settlement patterns. A very useful source that documents how Americans settled and occupied Indian lands after wars and treaties.

Foster, Emily. *The Ohio Frontier: Anthology of Early Writings.* Lexington, KY: University Press of Kentucky, 2000. A primary source collection of writings covering many frontier-Indian conflicts and issues.

"The Paris Peace Treaty of 1783." http://www.law.ou.edu/ushistory/paris.shtml. Article 2 details the new boundaries of the United States that include the Ohio region.

"The Treaty of Greenville." http://www.earlyamerica.com/earlyamerica/ milestones/greenville/. A page with a brief introduction and link to a photo facsimile of the original treaty.

Secondary Sources

Barr, Daniel P., ed. *The Boundaries Between Us: Natives and Newcomers Along the Frontiers of the Old Northwest Territory, 1750–1850.* Kent, OH: Kent State University Press, 2006. Examines the impact of a nonstop wave of settlers encroaching on Indian lands.

Calloway, Colin G. *The Shawnees and the War for America.* New York: Viking, 2007. General history that examines, in depth, the Ohio Indian wars.

Clayton, Andrew R. L. *Frontier Indiana.* Bloomington, IN: Indiana University Press, 1996. Describes the history of the Miami Indians and of Little Turtle.

Dowd, Gregory. *A Spirited Resistance: The North American Indian Struggle for Unity, 1745–1815.* Baltimore, MD: Johns Hopkins University Press, 1992. The first historical treatment of Indian resistance efforts to American expansion that includes Dunmore's War.

Downes, Randolph C. *Council Fires on the Upper Ohio: A Narrative of Indian Affairs in the Upper Ohio Valley until 1795.* Pittsburgh, PA: University of Pittsburgh Press, 1940. Reprint, 1969. Examines the conflicts between the Shawnee and the Americans in Western Pennsylvania.

Eckert, Allan. *Blue Jacket: War Chief of the Shawnee.* Ashland, KY: Jesse Stuart Foundation, 2003. Though not a scholarly work, it does try to provide a Shawnee perspective.

Edel, Wilbur. *Kekionga!: The Worst Defeat in the History of the U.S. Army.* Westport, CT: Greenwood, 1997. Documents the battle of Kekionga where the army of the fledgling United States suffered a humiliating defeat by a band of Ohio Indians.

Gaff, Alan D. *Bayonets in the Wilderness: Anthony Wayne's Legion in the Old Northwest.* Norman, OK: University of Oklahoma Press, 2004. A military history of the U.S. Army's first major war and victory after the American Revolution.

Hintzen, William. *The Border Wars of the Upper Ohio Valley (1769–1794).* Manchester, CT: Precision Shooting, 1999. Details the wars fought during 25 years on the frontier of Ohio, Pennsylvania, and Virginia.

Hurt, R. Douglas. *The Ohio Frontier: Crucible of the Old Northwest, 1720–1830.* Bloomington, IN: Indiana University Press, 1998. A good overview of the frontier wars and the place Dunmore's War occupies in the chronology.

Sugden, John. *Blue Jacket: Warrior of the Shawnees.* Lincoln, NE: University of Nebraska Press, 2003. Examines the leadership qualities of Blue Jacket and his role in the war of Ohio.

World Wide Web

Battin, Richard. "'Mad Anthony' Wayne at Fallen Timbers." http://www.earlyamerica.com/review/fall96/anthony.html. Concise history of this significant battle.

"Michikinikwa, Also Known as Little Turtle." http://www.ohiohistorycentral.org/entry.php?rec=240. Brief summary with images and links.

"Treaty of Greenville 1795." http://www.yale.edu/lawweb/avalon/greenvil.htm. A modern English facsimile of the treaty from the Avalon Project.

Multimedia Source

"Blue Jacket Drama." Custom Site & Sound, 2005. http://www.bluejacketdrama.com/. Link to an annual outdoor theatrical performance of Ohio's Indians.

25. Indians and the Northwest Ordinance of 1787

The Northwest Ordinance of 1787, drafted by Thomas Jefferson and approved by Congress in 1787, demonstrated a desire for federal government to acquire Indian lands and to systematically incorporate those lands into the domain and boundaries of the United States in the form of new states—states with the same powers and privileges of the original thirteen. The Ordinance of 1787 has been celebrated for its democratic principles and its sophisticated organizational plan of settlement, which provided for education and reasonably segmented portions of land for settlement and governance. However, these plans predated and precluded actual legal possession of the land from Indian tribes, revealing a government-sanctioned policy of conquest and land acquisition. Passed under the Articles of Confederation while the Constitutional Convention debated, the ordinance addressed land east of the Mississippi River, south of Lake Superior, and north and east of the Ohio River. The part mentioning Indians proclaims: "the utmost good faith shall always be observed towards Indians, in their lands and property shall never be taken from them without their consent; and in their property, rights and liberty, they never shall be invaded or disturbed, unless in just and lawful wars authorized by congress; but laws founded in justice and humanity shall from time to time be made, for preventing wrongs being done to them, and for preserving peace and friendship with them." Recognized as one of the four most important documents of the fledging United States, the intent of the ordinance, despite claiming "fairness" to Indians, was to occupy and possess Indian lands.

TERM PAPER SUGGESTIONS

1. Write on the intent of the Northwest Ordinance as reasonable and fair to Indians.

2. As the author of the ordinance, was Thomas Jefferson thinking about the future of Indians or the future of his newly created country and his countrymen?

3. Explore the term "good faith" to determine whether the United States practiced this concept with Indians in the aftermath of the passage of the ordinance. Was land taken from Indians without their consent?

4. Investigate the power of the federal government over American Indians with the passage of the Northwest Ordinance. How were Indians rendered powerless over the process, whether they were powerless or not, militarily?

5. Identify and categorize the various Indian tribes within the boundaries of the Northwest Territory and use that data to show the difficulty of not "taking" Indian lands without their consent.

6. When the ordinance states that "laws founded in justice and humanity shall from time to time be made," does that imply a plenary or paternalistic relationship with Indian tribes? Explain. How does this relate to the U.S. Constitution?

ALTERNATIVE TERM PAPER SUGGESTIONS

1. Create an electronic slide show of the various historical maps depicting the plan, implementation, and the goal of the Northwest Ordinance to organize settlement and governance of the area. Then superimpose the major American Indian settlements and land possessions to show the ethical and geographical difficulties of implementing such a plan.

2. In the same map, show where Indians would be placed, assuming they were cooperative and willing to be placed. You are creating reservations within proposed states.

SUGGESTED SOURCES

Primary Sources

"An Ordinance for the Government of the Territory of the United States North West of the River Ohio." http://www.loc.gov/rr/program/bib/ourdocs/ northwest.html. A mega site with a multitude of primary sources on the Northwest Ordinance that are briefly explained; links to the actual digital facsimiles of the documents are provided and, in some cases, the scanned images of the originals are included as well.

"Text of the Northwest Ordinance." http://www.earlyamerica.com/earlyamerica/ milestones/ordinance/text.html. Modern English digital reproduction of the ordinance.

Secondary Sources

Barr, Daniel P., ed. *The Boundaries Between Us: Natives and Newcomers Along the Frontiers of the Old Northwest Territory, 1750–1850.* Kent, OH: Kent State University Press, 2006. Examines the impact of a nonstop wave of settlers encroaching on Indian lands.

Duffey, Denis P. "The Northwest Ordinance as a Constitutional Document." *Columbia Law Review* 95, no. 4 (May 1995): 929–68. The author aligns the importance of the Northwest Ordinance next to the Declaration of Independence and the Articles of Confederation.

Onuf, Peter S. *Statehood and Union: A History of the Northwest Ordinance.* Bloomington, IN: Indiana University Press, 1987. A standard reference to the ordinance, implementation, and aftermath.

Prucha, Francis Paul. *Documents of United States Indian Policy.* 3rd ed. Lincoln, NE: University of Nebraska Press, 2000. Provides only the parts pertinent to Indians and Indian tribes. See item 8, page 9, for the "Northwest Ordinance."

Williams, Frederick D. *The Northwest Ordinance: Essays on Its Formulation, Provisions, and Legacy.* East Lansing, MI: Michigan State University Press, 1989. Focuses on securing the land, peopling the land, and educating the people once settled.

World Wide Web

"The Northwest and the Ordinances, 1783–1858." http://memory.loc.gov/ ammem/umhtml/umessay5.html. This site is valuable for its series of maps showing a comparison of land boundaries and organization from 1784 to 1818. Click on "Page Image Viewer" to view them individually and with more focus.

"Northwest Ordinance." http://www.jmu.edu/madison/center/main_pages/ madison_archives/constit_confed/confederation/northwest/northwest _ord.htm. A site with just a brief "Background and Explanation" and a digital facsimile of the document.

"Northwest Ordinance." http://www.ohiohistorycentral.org/entry.php? rec=1747. A brief summary with an early map and bibliographical references.

Multimedia Source

Frontier Legends of the Old Northwest. Dir. Gary Foreman. A&E, 1998. 2 DVDs. 200 minutes. Four episodes covering Roger's Rangers, Pontiac's Rebellion, Colonel George Rogers Clark's (the highest ranking U.S. officer in the Northwest Territory) victory at Vincennes, Indiana, in 1799 against Indians, and Tecumseh's efforts during the War of 1812.

26. American Indians and the U.S. Constitution (1787)

The relationship between Indians and the United States Constitution is complex and threefold: (1) Article I, Section 2, " . . . excluding Indians not taxed," challenges the jurisdiction states have over Indians and recognizes limited tribal sovereignty; (2) Article I, Section 8, "Congress shall have power . . . to regulate commerce with foreign nations, and among the several states, and with the Indian tribes," recognizes the power Congress has over Indians, but to list "Indian tribes" next to "foreign nations" and "states" affirms tribal sovereignty; and (3) Article VI, Paragraph II, "all treaties made . . . shall be the Supreme law of the land," protects and guarantees, on its surface, ratified treaties between Indian tribes and the federal government—and, because treaties are negotiated between nations, this is a powerful argument for tribal sovereignty. The U.S. Constitution recognizes tribal governments and land held in common, and the rights, money, and privileges guaranteed in treaties for the exchange of Indian land are protected and honored by the U.S. Constitution. State governments and the legislative and executive branches of the U.S. government, have, over the years, challenged Indian treaties and have passed laws limiting or extinguishing rights written in those treaties as promises and payments for land. Indians have often had to sue these governments in federal court to get these rights back. Constitutional principles can be explored by looking at select federal and state court cases where the validity and legality of Indian treaties and sovereignty have often been debated and decided.

TERM PAPER SUGGESTIONS

1. Examine Article I, Section 2, " . . . excluding Indians not taxed," in court cases where this section is used to support or deny Indian treaty rights and sovereignty.
2. Examine Indian tribal status in Article I, Section 8, "Congress shall have power . . . to regulate commerce with foreign nations, and among the several states, and with the Indian tribes," relative to Congress's powers as they pertain to foreign nations and states. You will have to define and explain the "trust" relationship between the federal government and federally recognized Indian tribes.
3. Examine how Indian tribes use Article VI, Paragraph II, "all treaties made . . . shall be the Supreme law of the land," often referred to as the "Supremacy Clause," to uphold rights and privileges guaranteed in ratified treaties.
4. Define a federally-recognized Indian tribe and explore how the U.S. Constitution allows these tribes to have and operate their own governments in the same manner as states, counties, and cities.
5. Explore how the U.S. Constitution creates a special status for federally recognized tribal governments and tribal members. What makes tribal members different from any other member of minority or ethnic groups?
6. Investigate the reason Indian tribes can own and operate casino gambling operations, own communal land, and live free from federal and, in most cases, state taxes. What is the role of the U.S. Constitution in upholding these rights?

ALTERNATIVE TERM PAPER SUGGESTIONS

1. Using a Microsoft PowerPoint presentation format, create a five-point argument for or against the establishment of gambling operations on Indian tribal lands. How would state-operated casinos, like those in Nevada, or other state-sanctioned gambling operations, like bingo or lottery, factor into the argument?

2. Create posters (or slides) of the sections in the Constitution where Indians are mentioned so that they can be isolated. Color-code the pertinent words and subdivide the sections into "Citizenship," "Commerce Clause," and "Supremacy Clause." The goal is to show how Indian tribes are incorporated into the very fabric of the U.S. Constitution.

SUGGESTED SOURCES

Primary Source

The United States Constitution. http://www.law.cornell.edu/constitution/index.html. The value of this site is that it allows the user with keyword search to locate, for example, "Indian law," "Indian sovereignty," and "Indian treaty rights," in hundreds of U.S. Supreme Court opinions and their relation to the U.S. Constitution.

Secondary Sources

Ball, Milner S. "Constitution, Court, Indian Tribes." *American Bar Foundation Research Journal* 12, no. 1 (Winter 1987): 1–140. Archival Database, 2008. Online facsimile. http://www3.interscience.wiley.com/journal/119480851/abstract?CRETRY=1&SRETRY=0 A six-chapter monograph that outlines and defines and then explains many of the important issues surrounding the U.S. Constitution and Indian tribes.

Clinton, Robert N., and Rebecca Tsosie. *American Indian Law: Native Nations and the Federal System: Cases and Materials.* Newark, NJ: LexisNexis Matthew Bender, 2007. A bevy of source materials.

Corntassel, Jeff, and Richard C. Witmer. *Forced Federalism: Contemporary Challenges to Indigenous Nationhood.* Norman, OK: University of Oklahoma Press, 2008. Explores contemporary issues of taxation and gaming from a state and local level, as well as the way those entities have used an image of the "rich Indian" to challenge tribal sovereignty within a 20-year period (1988 to 2008).

Deloria, Vine, Jr., and David E. Wilkins. *Tribes, Treaties, and Constitutional Tribulations.* Austin, TX: University of Texas Press, 2000. Explores the relationship between the U.S. Constitution and Indian tribes.

Dutha, N. Bruce, and Colin Calloway. *American Indians and the Law*. New York: Viking, 2008. Defines and clarifies sovereignty as it applies to federally recognized tribes since 1787.

Harring, Sidney L. *Crow Dog's Case: American Indian Sovereignty, Tribal Law, and United States Law in the Nineteenth Century*. New York: Cambridge University Press, 1994. Case study of Indian sovereignty and justice from a social-historical perspective.

LeBeau, Patrick Russell. "Lesson the Third: Indian Treaties and the U.S. Constitution." *Rethinking Michigan Indian History*. East Lansing, MI: Michigan State University Press, 2005. Activities and resources augment this chapter that explores how the U.S. Constitution affirms and protects Indian treaties.

Luna-Firebaugh, Eileen. *Tribal Policing: Asserting Sovereignty, Seeking Justice*. Tucson, AZ: University of Arizona Press, 2007. As an extension of sovereignty, Indian tribes have developed their own police departments, and this work examines the complexities inherent in issues of jurisdiction and enforcement.

Miller, Mark Edwin. *Forgotten Tribes: Unrecognized Indians and the Federal Acknowledgment Process*. Lincoln, NE: University of Nebraska Press, 2004. Investigates how the legal process of determining federally recognized "Indians" leaves many legitimate Indians without legal standing.

Rosen, Deborah A. *American Indians and State Law: Sovereignty, Race and Citizenship, 1790–1880*. Lincoln, NE: University of Nebraska Press, 2007. From the perspective of states and territories, this work shows how states exerted authority over Indian tribes residing within state/territory boundaries.

Wilkins, David E. *Uneven Ground: American Indian Sovereignty and Federal Law*. Norman, OK: University of Oklahoma Press, 2001. Investigates the manner in which Indian sovereignty has eroded since the 1787 U.S. Constitution.

World Wide Web

"American Indian Law and Overview." http://topics.law.cornell.edu/wex/american_indian_law. General database for a multitude of issues pertaining to Indian law, constitutional rights, and sovereignty.

"American Indian Tribal Sovereignty Primer." http://www.airpi.org/pubs/indinsov.html. Short answers to pertinent questions, such as "What is Tribal Sovereignty?"

"Indian and Native Peoples Law: Primary Materials—Laws and Government Documents." http://www.findlaw.com/01topics/21indian/

gov_laws.html. Includes links to all the constitutional references, U.S. Code, select court cases, select treaties, tribal constitutions, select tribal constitutions, and other pertinent sources.

Miller, Robert. "American Indians & the United States Constitution." http://www.flashpointmag.com/amindus.htm. Presents how European invaders acquired the land and cheated Native Americans through several formal "government to government" treaties and other documents.

Washburn, Kevin. "Introduction to American Indian Law and the Constitution." http://local.law.umn.edu/constitutionallaw/washburn01.html. A scholarly and documented essay on Indian law and the Constitution.

Multimedia Source

History of the Constitution. Dir. Ron Myer. Center Communications, 2005. DVD. 8-part series, 224 minutes. Explores how the Constitution originated and how it has protected citizens from abuses of power.

27. Treaty of New York (1790)

The Treaty of New York with the Creeks was the first Indian treaty negotiated under the U.S. Constitution of 1787, with George Washington and Henry Knox, Secretary of War under the Articles of Confederation and under President Washington's presidency, active in the negotiations and prominent signatories. The treaty of 1790 is important in that it calls for the Creeks to surrender any Indian to the United States who committed a capital crime against a U.S. citizen and for that Indian to be held and tried under U.S. laws and courts rather than Creek. The treaty set a precedent for all future treaties with Indians that would erode tribal sovereignty and jurisdictional rights. The treaty of 1790 marked the beginning of new era of U.S. power to dictate treaty terms to weakened Indian tribes and to force their capitulation and transfer of land more efficiently. Instead of focusing on trade and peace, even though these were still minor terms, the terms of Indian treaties henceforth would shift to acquiring Indian lands, forcing Indians into smaller tracts of land, and placing Indian rights and sovereignty under the overall protection and sovereignty of the United States. In 1796, due to pressure from Georgia and representatives from other southern states, the treaty was renegotiated and rewritten to favor the states in further land cessions and to repudiate Article VI. Article VI forfeited United States protection of those Americans settling illegally on Indians lands and allowed the Creeks to punish those American squatters.

TERM PAPER SUGGESTIONS

1. Explore the differences between treaties made with the British and those made under the Articles of Confederation.
2. From the perspective of Creek chiefs and representatives, compare the treaty negotiation method and process with the British to the treaty negotiation method and process with the Americans.
3. Examine the diplomatic skills of Creek leader Alexander McGillivray and his ability to protect the rights of his people.
4. Compare the treaty of 1790 to that of 1796. Be sure to examine the congressional debates and letters of McGillivray.
5. Examine the changes the Creeks endured as a result of the transfer of power from the British to the Americans.
6. Write on the reasoning behind the inclusion of "secret articles" in the treaty of 1790.

ALTERNATIVE TERM PAPER SUGGESTIONS

1. Design a short play about a treaty negotiation between representatives of the United States and representatives of an Indian tribe. Make the goals reflective of the results achieved by both sides in the New York Treaty of 1790, even if "secret" articles are necessary.
2. Create a simplified treaty that represents the most common articles and provisions of British treaties with Indians, and create another one between Americans and Indians (for example, include sections such as "Peace and Friendship," "Land Acquisition," "Payments and Annuities," and "Reserved Rights"). Make a Microsoft PowerPoint slide show to explore the differences visually.

SUGGESTED SOURCES

Primary Sources

Caughey, John Walton. *McGillivray of the Creeks.* 1939. Reprint, Columbia, SC: University of South Carolina Press, 2007. Diplomatic history of the Creek leader, serving as a primary source due the inclusion of 214 letters between McGillivray and Spanish and U.S. officials.

"The Treaty of New York." http://www.gwu.edu/~ffcp/exhibit/p9/p9_6 Large.jpg. Photo facsimile of the 1790 treaty.

"Treaty with Creeks, 1790." http://www.tngennet.org/cessions/17900807.html. A digital facsimile of the treaty, with links to pertinent paragraphs.

"Treaty with the Creeks, 1796." http://www.tngenweb.org/cessions/17960629. html. Full facsimile of the treaty with hyperlinks to pertinent paragraphs.

United States Congress. *Abridgment of the Debates of Congress, from 1789 to 1856.* http://books.google.com/books?id=jcUQAAAAYAAJ. Includes congressional debates on the 1790 Creek Treaty of New York.

Secondary Sources

Deloria, Vine, Jr., and David E. Wilkins. *Tribes, Treaties, and Constitutional Tribulations.* Austin, TX: University of Texas Press, 2000. Explores the relationship between the U.S. Constitution and Indian tribes.

Ethridge, Robbie Franklin. *Creek Country: Creek Indians and Their World, 1796–1816.* Chapel Hill, NC: University of North Carolina Press, 2003. Examines the Creek people in transition after the American Revolution and increased interaction with Blacks and Whites.

Piker, Joshua. *Okfuskee: A Creek Indian Town in Colonial America.* Cambridge, MA: Harvard University Press, 2004. Although ending at the eve of the American Revolution, this narrowly focused study is useful to get a perspective on the local life of one Indian town that is a member of a larger tribal confederation.

Prucha, Francis Paul. *American Indian Treaties: The History of a Political Anomaly.* Berkeley, CA: University of California Press, 1994. An overview of treaties, policies, and laws as they pertain to American Indians.

Saunt, Claudio. *A New Order of Things: Property, Power and the Transformation of the Creek Indians, 1733–1816.* Cambridge, UK: Cambridge University Press, 1999. Explores, in particular, the transition wrought on the Creek Indians after the American Revolution and War of 1812. "Part II" covers the period of McGillivray and the Treaty of New York.

Swanton, John R. *Early History of Creek Indians and Their Neighbors, Bureau of American Ethnology Bulletin 73.* Washington, DC: U.S. Government Printing Office, 1922. A report to the Bureau of American Ethnology on the state and condition of the Creek Confederacy completed in December of 1918 and published in 1922.

Williams, Robert, Jr. *Linking Arms Together: American Indian Treaty Visions of Law and Peace, 1600–1800.* New York: Routledge, 1999. Investigates the manner in which American Indians, including the Creeks, negotiated with Americans and Unites States officials; provides an interesting perspective of treaties from the American Indian point of view.

World Wide Web

"Alexander McGillivray (ca. 1750–1793)." http://www.newgeorgiaencyclopedia.org/
nge/Article.jsp?id=h-690&pid=s-42. A detailed short biography with
references.

"American Indian Land Cessions in Georgia." http://ngeorgia.com/history/
indianla.html. Chronology of U.S. Indian treaties that gained Indian
land in Georgia.

Forman, Carolyn Thomas. "Alexander McGillivray, Emperor of the Creeks."
http://digital.library.okstate.edu/Chronicles/v007/v007p106.html.
Reprint of the 1929 article; explores the statesmanship and leadership
qualities of McGillivray.

Hayden, Joseph Ralston. *The Senate and Treaties, 1789–1817.* New York: Macmillan,
1920. http://books.google.com/books?id=DfwMAAAAYAAJ. Discusses
the controversies and issues surrounding both early treaties with the
Creeks.

"Secret Articles of the Treaty of New York." http://www.johnhorse.com/trail/00/
bg/24.1.htm. Explains the secret articles of the 1790 treaty, which
concerned the return of runaway slaves, bribes paid from the
U.S. Treasury, and the rank of brigadier general conveyed to McGillivray.

Multimedia Source

Lost Worlds of Georgia, an Interactive Exhibit. http://www.lostworlds.org/
georgia.html. Shows how the Creeks might have looked physically and
might have acted at the time of early treaties and in ancient times. Other
DVDs and video resources are also available from this site.

28. Indian Trade and Intercourse Act(s) (1790–1834)

The Indian Trade and Intercourse Act(s) were a series of acts first set in place
in 1790 then renewed every two years with expanded authority and powers
given to Congress over Indian affairs; a longer revised version was approved
and passed in 1834. The act gave exclusive power and sole authority to regulate "Trade and Intercourse" with Indian tribes residing in the Indian
Territory. The act also excluded individual U.S. citizens from trading with,
purchasing lands from, or even traveling within the lands recognized as
belonging to Indian tribes. Even though certain trading companies were
licensed to conduct trade, they were essentially government-regulated

commercial enterprises. The act was meant to enforce the orderly acquisition of Indian land through the treaty-making process; to standardize pricing for Indian trade goods, mostly fur, through a factory system; to stop individuals from interfering with Indian affairs; and thus, to stop costly wars brought on by land squatters and unscrupulous traders. Section 1 of the 1790 act states, "no person shall be permitted to carry on any trade . . . without a license," and Section 4 states, "no sale of lands made by any Indians . . . shall be valid to any persons, to any state . . . unless . . . made and duly executed at some public treaty, held under the authority of the United States." Stopping white traders and squatters from illegal trade for Indian goods and stopping the unsanctioned taking of Indian lands was problematic at best and in many cases impossible to enforce.

TERM PAPER SUGGESTIONS

1. Explore and report on the changes to the original 1790 act through 1834, which were a series of additional sections designed to address "new" problems not accounted for in the first. How well did the act fare in promoting peace?

2. Report on the success or lack thereof of the U.S. factory system. What were its strengths and weaknesses?

3. How did American Indians respond to these new regulations? Did they cooperate or did they, at times, circumvent the system for their purposes?

4. Investigate trade in alcohol, which was prohibited in later versions of the act. Did trade in alcohol cause additional problems or concerns for peace in the Indian Territory?

5. Individuals and companies could trade with Indians if they were duly licensed and followed the letter of the law. Investigate their performance and their activities. They also had to compete with government trading factories: how did that affect their trading practices?

6. Explore the role of boundaries, their definition, and their implementation in the enforcement of the act from 1790 to 1834. Did the shrinking of what was defined as the Indian Territory make enforcement easier? What role did states play in the defining of boundaries?

ALTERNATIVE TERM PAPER SUGGESTIONS

1. Assume you are a licensed Indian trader during the early 1800s. Determine and create a list, a "bill of laden," of the quantity and quality of trade goods you would need to get yourself started. For your investors, also prepare a report on the relative risks and profits if you included alcohol as part of your load.

2. As a representative of an Indian tribe, draw up a list of complaints in bulleted form opposing to the U.S. government's idea of regulating trade and intercourse within your tribal boundaries and of doing so without your input.

SUGGESTED SOURCES

Primary Sources

Adair, William Penn. *Protest of W. P. Adair, Chairman of Cherokee Delegation.* Washington, 1870. Adair protested against the rights claimed by the Unites States government to force adopted Cherokees (non-Indian) to procure licenses from the federal government, under the Intercourse Act of 1834, to trade in Indian Country.

"An Act to Regulate Trade and Intercourse with the Indian Tribes." http://www.yale.edu/lawweb/avalon/statutes/native/na024.htm. An online digital facsimile of the seven sections of the 1790 act.

"An Act to Regulate Trade and Intercourse with the Indian Tribes Statute II." http://www.tngenweb.org/tnland/intruders/17900722.html. An easy-to-navigate digital facsimile of the Trade and Intercourse Act of 1790.

"Andrew Jackson's Sixth Annual Message, December 1, 1834." http://www.synaptic.bc.ca/ejournal/JacksonSixthAnnualMessage.htm. Contains President Andrew Jackson's Sixth Annual Message to Congress on December 1, 1834. Scroll down, or use the link on the right side, to get to where he discusses the status of the Indian Trade and Intercourse Act.

Prucha, Francis Paul. *Documents of the United States Indian Policy: Third Edition.* Lincoln, NE: University of Nebraska Press, 2000. On page 14 is a copy of the Trade and Intercourse Act that was passed on July 22, 1790.

Secondary Sources

Barbour, Barton H. *Fort Union and Upper Missouri Fur Trade.* Norman, OK: University of Oklahoma Press, 2002. Micro history of the longest-lived trading post: a post that had to navigate the Trade and Intercourse Acts and still make a profit.

Miller, Robert J. *Native America, Discovered and Conquered.* Westport, CT: Greenwood Publishing Group, 2006. Explains that the Trade and Intercourse Act was the first federal Indian policy.

Peake, Ora Brooks. *A History of the United States Indian Factory System, 1795–1822.* Denver, CO: Sage Books, 1954. Reprint, Mansfield Centre, CT: Martino, 2007. Explores the development of the federal-sponsored "factory system," which was designed to compete with private Indian trading companies.

Prucha, Francis Paul. *American Indian Policy in the Formative Trade: The Indian Trade and Intercourse Acts 1790–1834.* Cambridge, MA: Harvard University Press, 1962. Gives a detailed description of the Indian trade and the laws of 1790 and 1834.

Rosen, Deborah A. *American Indians and State Law: Sovereignty, Race and Citizenship, 1790–1880.* Lincoln, NE: University of Nebraska Press, 2007. From the perspective of states and territories, this work shows how states exerted authority over Indian tribes residing within state/territory boundaries. Part One explores the influence of the Trade and Intercourse Act within the boundaries of state jurisdictions.

Stevens, Wayne E. *The Northwest Fur Trade, 1763–1800.* Urbana, IL: University of Illinois, 1928. A careful study of the fur trade, particularly after the 1790 act was passed.

Unrau, William E. *The Rise and Fall of Indian Country 1825–1855.* Lawrence, KS: University Press of Kansas, 2007. Focuses on Section 1 of the 1834 act, which established its boundaries between Indians and Whites, to show that this legislation was ineffectual from the beginning.

Unrau, William E. *White Man's Wicked Water: The Alcohol Trade and Prohibition in Indian Country, 1802–1892.* Lawrence, KS: University Press of Kansas, 1996. Examines how the alcohol trade flourished, even with the prohibitions imposed by the Trade and Intercourse Acts.

World Wide Web

"An Act to Regulate Trade and Intercourse with the Indian Tribes, and to Preserve Peace on the Frontiers." http://www.ohiohistorycentral.org/entry.php?rec=430. Further revision and expansion of the 1790 act, creating more complexities of law.

Hill, Luther. "Chapter VII: The Intercourse Act of 1834, and Progress of the Indian Tribes." *A History of the State of Okalahoma, 1908.* D. J. Coover, 2002. http://www.usgennet.org/usa/topic/historical/ok_10.htm. Early account of the progress of the 1834 act as it applied to Oklahoma.

"Indian Territorial Map of 1834." http://images.google.com/imgres?imgurl=http://www.rootsweb.ancestry.com/~itgenweb/itprojects/map-images/it-1834_small.gif&imgrefurl=http://www.rootsweb.ancestry.com/~itgenweb/itprojects/timeline-maps.htm&h=65&w=100&sz=3&hl=en&start=2&um=1&tbnid=Gcrh8MXkSh. Has several maps showing and defining "Indian Territory" from the early 1700s to 1889; very useful to get an idea of the (shrinking) boundaries mentioned in the Trade and Intercourse Acts and British/U.S. treaties.

Multimedia Source

The West. Dir. Stephen Ives. Public Broadcasting Service, 1996. 4 DVDs. 750 minutes. "Episode Two, 1806 to 1848" covers fur trade.

29. Treaty of Canandaigua (1794–1795)

The Treaty of Canandaigua, also known as the Pickering Treaty or the George Washington Covenant, was the second Indian treaty negotiated under the U.S. Constitution of 1787 and was made with the Six Nations of the Iroquois (Cayuga, Mohawk, Onondaga, Oneida, Seneca, and Tuscarora) in 1794. The importance of treaty was not only to establish peace and friendship and to affirm the sovereignty of Six Nations but also to recognize tribal land ownership that Articles II, III, and IV make clear. Further, the treaty serves as an exemplar of what U.S. treaties mean to American Indians and how they serve an important role in upholding the rights and sovereignty of Indian people and tribes. Like the U.S. Constitution, an Indian treaty is a living document that transcends time and has meaning and resonance for each generation of Indians. The Treaty of Canandaigua is a case in point, as each year since 1794, the U.S. government has delivered a "treaty cloth" and an annuity to the Six Nations in the fall as part of its treaty obligations. The treaty is used to argue or settle many injustices and disputes, such as the 1999 land claims of the Cayuga and Oneida, which were upheld by the U.S. Supreme Court, or the exercise of sovereignty that the Six Nations practice by issuing their own international passports. From an Iroquois perspective, the power and role of traditional oratory practiced by Cornplanter and Red Jacket in the negotiations of the treaty are significant signifiers of Six Nation tribal and cultural identity, and they should not be overlooked by researchers who strive to understand American Indian diplomacy.

TERM PAPER SUGGESTIONS

1. Explore Indian land rights as they are defined in U.S. Indian treaties like the Treaty of Canandaigua. Why does the Supreme Court respect Indian treaties and at times rule in favor of Indian land claims?
2. Write on Indian sovereignty. What is the significance of a tribe issuing its own passports?

3. Explore and report on the "aliveness" of Indian treaties. How do they survive as living and breathing documents like the U.S. Constitution? How are they tied to the U.S. Constitution? Use the Treaty of Canandaigua as a representative and illustrative example.

4. Some historians say that the Treaty of Canandaigua was concluded and ratified too quickly and with too many concessions to the Six Nations. They say this happened because George Washington felt an urgency to exert jurisdictional sovereignty over an Indian tribe but also over the newly federalized states. Rebut or support this argument.

5. Explore the power of Six Nation political and diplomatic oratory to argue successfully for their rights and to assert their sovereignty.

ALTERNATIVE TERM PAPER SUGGESTIONS

1. Prepare an oration in the manner of Cornplanter or Red Jacket to support your sense of identity and free will, and give this oration before a live audience. Some modern day business and public addresses have used Indian oratory as an illustrative model for persuasive arguments.

2. Create an Apple iMovie that shows the exchange of wampum and the treaty cloth to demonstrate the symbolic importance of this treaty ritual that is still honored to this day.

SUGGESTED SOURCES

Primary Sources

Canfield, William W. *The Legends of the Iroquois: Told by the Cornplanter*. A. Wessels Co., 1904. Reprint, Whitefish, MT: Kessinger Publishing, 2007. Also available from Google Books, 2008. http://books.google .com/books?id=E4xCAAAAIAAJ. Cultural history of the Seneca, including stories of the sachems and Handsome Lake.

Ganter, Granville, ed. *The Collected Speeches of Sagoyewatha, or Red Jacket*. Syracuse, NY: Syracuse University Press, 2006. Includes all of Red Jacket's authenticated and meaningful political and ceremonial speeches.

Jemison, G. Peter, (Seneca), and Anna M. Schein, eds. *Treaty of Canandaigua 1794: 200 Years of Treaty Relations between the Iroquois Confederacy and the United States*. Santa Fe, NM: Clear Light, 2000. A collection of essays covering the treaty over 200 years from a variety of legal, cultural, and historical positions, with an ample dose of oratory and tradition. Further, the "Appendix" includes many significant primary sources, such as correspondence between Chief Cornplanter and President Washington and the full text of the treaty itself.

"The 1794 Canandaigua Treaty." 1794. http://canandaigua-treaty.org/photo_copy_of_the_1794_treaty.html. A digital photo of the signed treaty.

Secondary Sources

Abler, Thomas S. *Cornplanter: Chief Warrior of the Allegany Seneca.* Syracuse, NY: Syracuse University Press, 2007. A scholarly biography that places Cornplanter at the center of Seneca diplomacy; the work also has chapters on the Treaty of Canandaigua and Handsome Lake.

Barr, Daniel P., ed. *The Boundaries Between Us: Natives and Newcomers Along the Frontiers of the Old Northwest Territory, 1750–1850.* Kent, OH: Kent State University Press, 2006. Examines the impact of a nonstop wave of settlers encroaching on Indian lands.

Densmore, Christopher. *Red Jacket: Iroquois Diplomat and Orator.* Syracuse, NY: Syracuse University Press, 1999. A scholarly biography that places Red Jacket at the center of Seneca diplomacy; includes appended primary sources, like the Treaties of Fort Stanwix, 1784 and the Treaty of Canandaigua.

Johansen, Bruce E., ed. *Enduring Legacies: Native American Treaties and Contemporary Controversies.* Westport, CT: Praeger, 2004. Examines and explores treaties' rights and controversies, including the Treaty of Canandaigua.

Nammach, Georgiana C. *Fraud, Politics and Dispossession of the Indians: The Iroquois Land Frontier in the Colonial Period.* Norman, OK: University of Oklahoma, 1969. Explores the methods Americans used to acquire Iroquois land, which explains the Indians' distrust of the colonists.

Parker, A. C., (Seneca). *The History of the Seneca Indians.* 1926. Reprint, Port Washington, NY: Ira Friedman, 1967. A history of the Seneca from one of their own descendants.

Parker, Arthur C., (Seneca). *Red Jacket, Seneca Chief.* Lincoln, NE: University of Nebraska Press, 1998. A biography of Red Jacket from one of his Seneca descendants, who explores Red Jacket's entire life, including his involvement in the Treaty of Canandaigua.

Richter, Daniel Karl. *The Ordeal of the Longhouse: The Peoples of the Iroquois League in the Era of European Colonization.* Chapel Hill, NC: University of North Carolina Press, 1992. A complete history of how the Iroquois adapted to changing economic and social conditions brought on by colonization and trade.

Wallace, A. F. *The Death and Rebirth of the Seneca.* New York: Vintage, 1972. A history of the revitalization of the Seneca inspired by the Seneca prophet Handsome Lake, a contemporary of the Treaty of Canandaigua, Cornplanter, and Red Jacket.

World Wide Web

Jemison, G. Peter, (Seneca). "The 1794 Treaty of Canandaigua." http://www
    .oswego.edu/library2/archives/digitized_collections/granger/canandaigua
    .html. An excellent overview of the treaty within a larger context of treaties
    with the Iroquois and Red Jacket's "Rust in the Chain" speech.
Koch, Robert G. "Red Jacket, Seneca Orator." http://crookedlakereview.com/
    articles/34_66/48mar1992/48koch.html. An article in praise of Red
    Jacket's oratory skills and the way his famous speeches reflected his life
    experiences.
"Red Jacket." http://www.oswego.edu/library2/archives/digitized_collections/
    granger/redJacket.html. Short biography with links.
"The Seneca Nation of Indians." Official Web site, 2008. http://www.sni.org/. Home
    page portal of the Seneca Nation with links to current and historical materials.
"1794 Canandaigua Treaty Commemoration Committee Site." http://www
    .canandaigua-treaty.org/. From the land of the Iroquois, a short descrip-
    tion of the treaty, maps, a digital photo facsimile of the treaty, photos
    of the 2005 commemoration, links to cultural sites, and explanation of
    the treaty-making process and the role of Red Jacket's "Rust in the
    Chain" speech are here at this Web site. Two little-known facts are that,
    to this day, the U.S. government sends a "treaty cloth" to keep the treaty
    binding and that the treaty has never been broken since 1794.
"Survey Map of Region and Buffalo Creek Reservation." http://www.oswego.edu/
    library2/archives/digitized_collections/granger/OldNY.jpg. Note: The
    Buffalo Creek Reservation is marked in extremely small letters directly
    above the words "ERIE C" on the survey map. The reservation lands were
    set aside for the Seneca in the 1794 Treaty of Canandaigua.

Multimedia Source

Catlin, George. "Seneca Chief, Red Jacket." http://www.nga.gov/fcgi-bin/timage
    _f?object=50412&image=11281&c=. The nineteenth-century artist's
    rendering of the great Indian chief/warrior.

30. Louisiana Purchase (1803–1830)

During his term in office, President Thomas Jefferson purchased the territory of Louisiana, a vast tract of land west of the Mississippi River and, by that purchase, nearly doubled the size of the United States. He also exponentially increased U.S. encounters with American Indians and all the difficulties of war, diplomacy, trade, and intercourse that entailed, not to mention the quagmire of Indian policies in which future legislators found themselves immersed. As explorers Meriwether Lewis and William Clark soon discovered on their epic journey to explore and map these new lands, numerous Indian tribes occupied the lands that Jefferson purchased. Establishing peace and friendship with these tribes and, more importantly, to exerting a symbolic sovereignty over them with the distribution of "peace medals," was an important mission of their exploration. Eventually, all of the tribes Lewis and Clark encountered would have to contend with American expansion, settlement, and encroachments; these would lead to war, land cession treaties, and the tribes' confinement to reservations. These tragic consequences of the Louisiana Purchase are often glossed over by an overemphasis on the young Indian guide Sacagawea and her friendship and assistance as a member of the Lewis and Clark Corps of Discovery. Despite her contributions and her role as a strong Indian woman, she was and is often romanticized and stereotyped. More important to American Indian history, President Jackson used the claimed lands of the Louisiana Purchase to implement his Indian Removal Act of 1830, because the newly purchased lands provided a removal destination. The Indian Territory, as it would be called, became the place to which eastern Indians were removed, even if western Indian tribes lived on the lands set aside by acts of Congress for eastern tribes to live.

TERM PAPER SUGGESTIONS

1. Explore the Louisiana Purchase as an event that increased the role of Indian Affairs in American history rather than as a doubling of the land base of the continental United States.

2. If French people and African people are considered with the American Indian populations, then show how the Louisiana Purchase created a multicultural nation that would eventually threaten the power base of Anglo-Saxon Americans.

3. Explore the number and variety of western Indian tribes that Lewis and Clark encountered on their journey.

4. Examine Indians' perceptions of Lewis and Clark and other Americans from the oral stories of American Indians that exist in the primary source records.

5. Write an essay that explicates the known facts about Sacagawea and compare those facts to a representative selection of biographies about Sacagawea.

6. What are the implications of the myriad biographies of Sacagawea that perpetuate a romantic stereotype? Does this affect the way young people understand American Indians?

7. Explain how the Louisiana Purchase could be used as lever and an incentive to pass and implement the Indian Removal Act of 1830.

ALTERNATIVE TERM PAPER SUGGESTIONS

1. Create a slide show presentation of visual imagery found in the sources that answer this question: Who were the Indians inhabiting the lands of the Louisiana territory purchased by President Jefferson?

2. After some research and study, write a week's worth of journal entries as if you were a member of Lewis and Clark's Corps of Discovery.

SUGGESTED SOURCES

Primary Sources

"The Journals of the Lewis and Clark Expedition." http://lewisandclarkjournals.unl
    .edu/. Digital facsimile of the complete journals.
"The Louisiana Purchase: A Heritage Explored." http://www.lib.lsu.edu/special/
    purchase/. A comprehensive Web site with pertinent links to primary
    sources, especially early views of Indians in the "purchased" lands, sum-
    marized in the overview under "The European View: A Sampling of
    Travelers' Accounts of Native Americans." Includes teachers' guides.
"The Louisiana Purchase Treaty." http://www.pbs.org/weta/thewest/resources/
    archives/one/louispur.htm. Digital facsimile of the treaty.
"Map of Indian Territory, 1836." http://images.google.com/imgres?
    imgurl=http://upload.wikimedia.org/wikipedia/commons/c/c7/Map
    _of_Indian_territory_1836.png&imgrefurl=http://commons.wikimedia
    .org/wiki/Image:Map_of_Indian_territory_1836.png&h=744&w=698
    &sz=655&hl=en&start=14&um=1&tbnid=Dqg. Shows the areas
    assigned to the "emigrant" Indians removed from their homelands east
    of the Mississippi River.

Secondary Sources

Ambrose, Stephen. *Undaunted Courage: Meriwether Lewis, Thomas Jefferson and
    the Opening of the American West.* New York: Simon & Schuster, 1997.
    Lively and readable historical narrative.

DeVoto, Bernard. *Across the Wide Missouri.* Boston, MA: Houghton Mifflin, 1947. Reprint, 1975. A good general history of Indians along the Missouri, 1833–1838.

Ewers, John C. *Indian Life on the Upper Missouri.* Norman, OK: University of Oklahoma Press, 1968. Reprint, 2000. Fifteen essays on the history of the Indians before, during, and after Lewis and Clark.

Fleming, Thomas. *The Louisiana Purchase.* Hoboken, NJ: Wiley, 2003. Concise narrative history.

Herbert, Janis. *Lewis and Clark for Kids: Their Journey of Discovery with 21 Activities.* Chicago, IL: Chicago Review Press, 2000. Although designed for grades 9–12, the book serves as an excellent general resource, and the activities can be adapted for older students as well.

Kastor, Peter J. *The Nation's Crucible: The Louisiana Purchase and the Creation of America.* Yale University Press, 2004. Comprehensive historical treatise that explores the consequence of bringing into the borders of the United States large populations of American Indians.

McLoughlin, William G. *After the Trail of Tears: The Cherokees' Struggle for Sovereignty, 1839–1880.* Chapel Hill, NC: University of North Carolina Press, 1993. Tells the effects of forced removal and the trauma of establishing sovereignty after the Cherokee reached Oklahoma.

Remini, Robert V. *The Legacy of Andrew Jackson: Essays on Democracy, Indian Removal and Slavery.* Baton Rouge, LA: Louisiana State University Press, 1988. Chapter two covers Indian removal and places it within other of Jackson's "accomplishments."

Summitt, April R. *Sacagawea: A Biography.* Westport, CT: Greenwood Press, 2008. Counters the romantic and stereotypical portrayal of Sacagawea biographies often found in K–12 classrooms.

Wallace, Anthony F. C. *The Long Bitter Trail: Andrew Jackson and the Indians.* New York: Hill and Wang, 1993. Chapter three is devoted to the Removal Act, appended with the text of the act and an excerpt of Jackson's December 8, 1829 Message to Congress.

World Wide Web

"Discovering Lewis and Clark." http://www.lewis-clark.org/. A comprehensive "hyperhistory" with numerous links to scholarly and primary source materials, including an impressive section on "Native Nations."

"Lewis & Clark." http://www.pbs.org/lewisandclark/. Comprehensive Web site with many primary sources, including maps, information on Native

Americans, and classroom resources; has three lessons on "Lewis & Clark and Native Americans."

"Louisiana Purchase." http://www.nps.gov/archive/jeff/LewisClark2/Circa1804/Heritage/LouisianaPurchase/LouisianaPurchase.htm. Describes the complicated process of executing the purchase. The site has beautiful period maps that can be enlarged.

"Sacagawea." http://www.nps.gov/archive/jeff/LewisClark2/CorpsOfDiscovery/TheOthers/Civilians/Sacagawea.htm. A short biography that answers some questions, like "Slave or Adopted?"

"Sacagawea." http://www.pbs.org/lewisandclark/inside/saca.html. Fact-based biography that addresses many of the myths surrounding Sacagawea's life, including the spelling of her name and participation in the corps.

"Sacagawea Biography (1788?–1812)." http://www.biography.com/search/article.do?id=9468731. Short biography.

Wilson, Gaye. "The Louisiana Purchase." http://www.monticello.org/jefferson/lewisandclark/louisiana.html. An essay describing the diplomacy involved in the purchase that includes visual material, including a photo of the first page of the Louisiana Purchase Treaty.

Multimedia Sources

Lewis & Clark: The Journey of the Corps of Discovery. Dir. Ken Burns. American Lives Film Project, 1997. 2 DVDs. 240 minutes. Comprehensive documentary.

The Spirit of Sacajawea. Dir. Beverly Penninger and Alyson Young. Naka Productions, 2007. DVD. 73 minutes. A documentary reexamining the myths and truths surrounding the life and person of Sacagawea that challenges the romanticized misinterpretations.

31. Tenskwatawa and the Battle of Tippecanoe (1811)

Although the Battle of Tippecanoe in 1811 bolstered the spirits of the U.S. Army and forged a nickname and slogan for William Henry Harrison, who would forever be known as "Old Tippecanoe" (he would sweep into the White House many years later with the ditty "Tippecanoe and Tyler too," only to die shortly after), the battle demonstrated the fear Americans had of a general Indian uprising on the frontier due to the spiritual power of Tenskwatawa, the Shawnee Prophet. In 1805, comparable to and reminiscent of Neolin, the Delaware Prophet, and Handsome Lake, the Seneca Prophet, Tenskwatawa had a vision of two paths for American Indians: one a terrible, hellish path and the other a path of happiness, if only Indians abandoned alcohol and the materialism of Euro-American culture and returned to traditional Indian cultural practices. His vision, like those of the other prophets, resonated beyond his own people and had the effect of creating a pan-Indian response to American expansion and aggression. The response was so overwhelming that he and his brother, Tecumseh, were able to create a loose confederation of Indians who gathered at Prophet's Town, Indiana. This concentration caused Indiana settlers became fearful and demand protection; they got it in the form of a federal army commanded by Harrison, who gathered his forces a short distance from Prophet's Town. In the absence of his brother and spurred on by a vision, Tenskwatawa unwisely attacked Harrison's encampment and he and his forces were soundly defeated.

TERM PAPER SUGGESTIONS

1. Explore the general advance of the "frontier" line into Indiana territory and how that might have been an additional motivation for armed and hostile resistance to American expansion.

2. Investigate the rise of Indian prophets and their visions. How were they able to unify disparate Indian people into a viable military and diplomatic force able to resist American expansion? Why was Tenskwatawa more militant?

3. Look at Tenskwatawa's vision. Why would it appeal to American Indians?

4. Tell the story of the American settlers and their fear of somebody like Tenskwatawa. Why would they distrust, fear, and desire to retaliate against such a figure?

5. Many historians think that Tenskwatawa was not up to the level of his brother, Tecumseh, as a military tactician. They have suggested that Tenskwatawa's sudden attack on Harrison's encampment was to boost his stature and prowess. Refute or agree with this military assessment.

6. Was Harrison trying to create a reputation as an Indian fighter, or was he just carrying out U.S. Indian policies to protect American citizens and to advance U.S. interests in destroying the military might of American Indians?

ALTERNATIVE TERM PAPER SUGGESTIONS

1. Create an electronic annotated time line of the events leading up the Battle of Tippecanoe, with hyperlinks to relevant Web sites.

2. Pretend you are Tecumseh and you are intent on recruiting Indian people, not necessarily of your tribe, to make a stand against further selling of Indian land. Create an audio file of a speech you have prepared to persuade disparate Indian people to join your cause; use the vision and prophecy of your brother Tenskwatawa to help in the preparation of it.

SUGGESTED SOURCES

Primary Source

"Part of William Henry Harrison's Account of the Battle of Tippecanoe." http://tippecanoe.tripod.com/whh.html. Online portion of "Young Tippecanoe's" account of the battle.

Secondary Sources

Antal, Sandy. *A Wampum Denied: Procter's War of 1812.* East Lansing, MI: Michigan State University Press, 1997. Military history that focuses on Indian participation.

Barr, ed., Daniel P. *The Boundaries Between Us: Natives and Newcomers Along the Frontiers of the Old Northwest Territory, 1750–1850.* Kent, OH: Kent State University Press, 2006. Examines the impact of a nonstop wave of settlers encroaching on Indian lands.

Calloway, Colin G. *The Shawnees and the War for America.* New York: Viking, 2007. A general history with several chapters devoted to Tenskwatawa, Tecumseh, and the War of 1812.

Cave, Alfred A. *Prophets of the Great Spirit: Native American Revitalization Movements in Eastern North America.* Lincoln, NE: University of Nebraska Press, 2006. Explains the various Indian prophet movements of the period between 1744 and 1835, starting with Neolin and ending with Tenskwatawa.

Cayton, Andrew R. L. *Frontier Indiana.* Bloomington, IN: Indiana University Press, 1996. General history that places Tenskwatawa and Tecumseh into a larger social/political context.

Clark, Jerry E. Clark. *The Shawnee.* Lexington, KY: University Press of Kentucky, 1993. A general history.

Dowd, Gregory. *A Spirited Resistance: The North American Indian Struggle for Unity, 1745–1815.* Baltimore, MD: Johns Hopkins University Press, 1992. The first historical treatment of the overall Indian resistance efforts from 1745 to 1815, where Tenskwatawa is the center of focus due to his spiritual message, rather than Tecumseh due to his military prowess.

Drake, Benjamin. *Life of Tecumseh and His Brother the Prophet* 1841.http://www
.gutenberg.org/etext/15581. Download the PDF or read the online digital facsimile of the text.

Edmunds, R. David. *The Shawnee Prophet.* Lincoln, NE: University of Nebraska
Press, 1983. A easy-to-read narrative account of the role of Tenskwatawa
in the pan-Indian resistance to American expansion.

Eggleston, Edward, and Elizabeth Eggleston. *Tecumseh and the Shawnee
Prophet.* New York: Dodd, Mead and Company, 1878. http://books
.google.com/books?id=H0e9uoEOaVgC. History of Tecumseh and
Tenskwatawa based on the historical record. Chapter 12, "The Battle of
Tippecanoe," gives an early historical analysis of the battle and defeat of
Tenskwatawa.

Heckewelder, John Gottlieb, and William Cornelius Reichel Ernestus. *History,
Manners, and Customs of the Indian Nations.* The Historical Society of
Pennsylvania, 1876. Google Books, 2008. http://books.google.com
/books?id=EoqFU50BYaAC. With a word search, you can isolate the
pages pertaining to Tecumseh and Tenskwatawa (use keywords
"Tecumseh" or "The Prophet").

Owens, Robert M. *Mr. Jefferson's Hammer: William Henry Harrison and the
Origins of American Indian Policy.* Norman, OK: University of Oklahoma
Press, 2007. Examines the importance of Harrison, not as a president,
but as pivotal force in the development of U.S. Indian policy.

Sugden, John. *Blue Jacket: Warrior of the Shawnees.* Lincoln, NE: University of
Nebraska Press, 2003. Examines the leadership qualities of Blue Jacket
and his role in the war of Ohio and his mentorship of Tecumseh and
Tenskwatawa.

Van Meter, Jan R. *Tippecanoe and Tyler Too: Famous Slogans and Catchphrases in
American History.* Chicago, IL: University of Chicago Press, 2008.
A new and interesting book of famous slogans.

World Wide Web

"Battle of Tippecanoe." http://www.ohiohistorycentral.org/entry.php?rec=482.
Short summary of the battle and of Tenskwatawa's role.

"Plan of Tippecanoe Camp and Battle." http://www.galafilm.com/1812/e/maps/
map205.html. Shows the camp of Harrison's army before Tenskwatawa's attack.

"Shawnee Reservation Website." http://www.geocities.com/southbeach/cove/
8286/firstpg.html. Some useful links to Tenskwatawa and Tecumseh,
including text of Tenskwatawa's vision.

"Tenskwatawa." http://www.ohiohistorycentral.org/entry.php?rec=312. Short
biography with links to other entries.

"Tippecanoe Battlefield." http://www.tcha.mus.in.us/battlefield.htm. Web site for the historic site; includes link to "Tippecanoe Battlefield History."

Multimedia Sources

Battle of the Thames (Dorival, 1813), *The Death of Tecumseh, Battle of the Thames* (Currier, 1847), and the *Battle of Tippecanoe* (Kurtz and Allison, 1889). http://www.loc.gov/rr/print/list/picamer/paMiliHist.html. Famous lithographs and paintings.

Catlin, George. *Ten-squat-a-way, The Open Door, Known as The Prophet, Brother of Tecumseh* 1830. http://siris-artinventories.si.edu/ipac20/ipac.jsp?uri =full=3100001~!249255!0#focus. The nineteenth-century artist's rendering of the great Indian spiritual leader. Use Catlin or Ten-squat-a-way in the search window under "artist" or "title," respectively, to find the digital image.

Frontier Legends of the Old Northwest. Dir. Gary Foreman. A&E, 1998. 2 DVDs. 200 minutes. Four episodes covering Roger's Rangers, Pontiac's Rebellion, Colonel George Rogers Clark's (the highest ranking U.S. officer in the Northwest Territory) victory at Vincennes, Indiana, in 1799 against Indians, and Tecumseh's efforts during the War of 1812.

32. Death of Tecumseh and the Battle of Thames (October 5, 1813)

As the leader of a coalition of Indians allied with the British on the northwest frontier, Tecumseh had enjoyed several victories against American attempts to invade Canada from 1812 to 1813; most notable was his defeat of General William Hull and the surrender of Detroit in 1812. By 1813, Tecumseh was involved in the siege of Fort Meigs, where he criticized British General Henry Proctor for allowing Indians to scalp American prisoners; this echoed similar atrocities at the Battle of Frenchtown on January 22, 1813, where General Proctor earned the nickname "the Butcher." Tecumseh was not present at the Battle of Frenchtown, and he did not approve of such atrocities. What he did approve of was a staunch stance against further American progress toward an invasion of Canada. However, with the defeat of the British squadron of ships in the Battle of Lake Erie by American Commodore Oliver Perry and with Proctor's retreat from and abandonment of Detroit, Tecumseh was forced to join the retreating British forces until Proctor decided to make a stand at Moraviantown. Moraviantown was a settlement of Christian Delaware

Indians near the river Thames in Ontario, Canada. There, after a vicious battle, Tecumseh was killed and so with him the dream of a unified Indian front against further American expansion into the Indian lands of the northwest frontier. The legacy of Tecumseh would take many forms, from the alleged skinning of his body by Kentucky soldiers to his killing being attributed to Colonel Richard Johnson; his status as the "greatest American Indian" is a legacy that builds and lives on to this very day.

TERM PAPER SUGGESTIONS

1. Explore the reasons Tecumseh made every effort to build a coalition of Indian tribes to fight against American expansion. What were his triumphs and what were his weaknesses?

2. Investigate Tecumseh's skill as a military tactician and the Battle of Thames itself. What were the advantages and disadvantages of the tactical position in which Tecumseh was placed?

3. Examine the relationship between Tecumseh and Proctor. After many squabbles and face-offs, did Tecumseh think that his dream of stanching, if not pushing back, the tide of American expansion was doomed to failure due to British malfeasance? Why did he need the British? How did Proctor serve as an exemplar of British attitudes about American Indians?

4. Before he was killed in battle, Tecumseh was the most feared American Indian alive. Why?

5. Study the role of racism. Atrocities occurred on both sides, but Indians are often blamed for most of them. Why? How does the alleged "skinning" of Tecumseh's body play a role?

6. Look at the role of Indian fighting in the election of former soldiers to government positions. Elected to the presidency in 1840, William Henry Harrison commanded part of the army that defeated Tecumseh, plus he took sole credit for defeating Tecumseh's brother at Tippecanoe, with his slogan, "Tippecanoe and Tyler Too." Elected as vice president in 1836 in Martin Van Buren's successful campaign, Colonel Richard Johnson's war hero status helped: "Rumpsey Dumpsey, Rumpsey Dumpsey, Colonel Johnson killed Tecumseh."

ALTERNATIVE TERM PAPER SUGGESTIONS

1. Oratorical speeches are important modes of communication in American Indian societies. Create and digitally record an oratory response of Tecumseh's admonitions against Proctor for retreating from the Fort Meigs siege and from Detroit.

2. Create a board game of the 1813 advance of the Americans from Fort Meigs in Ohio to Detroit in Michigan and then into Ontario, Canada. Because chance was a factor in the historical situation, be sure to make provisions for Tecumseh and the British to win.

SUGGESTED SOURCES

Primary Source

Brunson, Alfred. "Death of Tecumseh at the Battle of the Thames in 1813." *Collections of the State Historical Society of Wisconsin.* Vol. 4: 1857–1858. The Society, 1859, 369–74. http://books.google.com/books?id =Rzd26j2taBYC. Go to "Read This Book" and click on "Brunson on the Death of Tecumseh" to access this brief account.

Secondary Sources

Antal, Sandy. *A Wampum Denied: Procter's War of 1812.* East Lansing, MI: Michigan State University Press, 1997. Military history that focuses on Indian participation.

Barr, ed., Daniel P. *The Boundaries Between Us: Natives and Newcomers Along the Frontiers of the Old Northwest Territory, 1750–1850.* Kent, OH: Kent State University Press, 2006. Examines the impact of a nonstop wave of settlers encroaching on Indian lands.

Berton, Pierre. *The Death of Tecumseh.* Toronto, Canada: McClelland and Steward, 1994. A group of adventure narratives for young readers; the narratives are based on the historical record and serve as an accessible introduction.

Calloway, Colin G. *The Shawnees and the War for America.* New York: Viking, 2007. A general history with several chapters devoted to Tenskwatawa, Tecumseh, and the War of 1812.

Drake, Benjamin. *Life of Tecumseh and His Brother the Prophet.* 1841. http://www .gutenberg.org/etext/15581. Download the PDF or read the online digital facsimile of the text.

Edmunds, R. David. *Tecumseh and the Quest for Indian Leadership.* New York: Pearson Longman, 2007. Focuses on the efforts and difficulties of Tecumseh in building a united Indian front against American expansion. This new edition includes a "Study and Discussion Questions" section for classroom or study group use.

Eggleston, Edward, and Elizabeth Eggleston. *Tecumseh and the Shawnee Prophet.* New York: Dodd, Mead and Company, 1878. http://books.google.com/ books?id=H0e9uoEOaVgC. History of Tecumseh and Tenskwatawa based on the historical record. Chapter 34, "Battle of the Thames—

Death of Tecumseh" gives an early historical analysis of the battle and death of Tecumseh.

Emmons, Richard. *Tecumseh: Or, The Battle of the Thames, a National Drama, in Five Acts.* New York: Elton & Harrison, 1836. A popular play performed in New York City in 1836 and thereafter for a few years that supported the claim that Colonel Richard Johnson killed Tecumseh.

Kingston, John T. "Death of Tecumseh." *Collections of the State Historical Society of Wisconsin.* Vol. 4: 1857–1858. The Society, 1859. 375–76. http:// books.google.com/books?id=Rzd26j2taBYC. Go to "Read This Book" and click on "Kingston on the Death of Tecumseh" to access this brief account.

Klinck, Carl F. *Tecumseh: Fact and Fiction in Early Records.* Upper Saddle River, NJ: Prentice Hall, 1961. An analysis of early letters, descriptions, and narratives of Tecumseh; this assessment is important due to the legendary and mythic qualities often attributed to the famous Shawnee leader.

Owens, Robert M. *Mr. Jefferson's Hammer: William Henry Harrison and the Origins of American Indian Policy.* Norman, OK: University of Oklahoma Press, 2007. Examines the importance of Harrison, not as a president, but as pivotal force in the development of U.S. Indian policy.

St-Denis, Guy. *Tecumseh's Bones.* Montreal, QC, Canada: McGill-Queen's University Press, 2005. Explores the mystery and fate of Tecumseh's remains after his death; draws on a wealth of Canadian archival sources.

Sugden, John. *Tecumseh's Last Stand.* Norman, OK: University of Oklahoma Press, 1985. Concise history of the battles and events of August to October 1813, leading to Tecumseh's death on October 5.

Tucker, Glenn. *Tecumseh: A Vision of Glory.* Old Chelsea Station, NY: Cosimo, 2005. Most recent biography of Tecumseh; includes six maps, one of which is of the Battle of Thames.

World Wide Web

"Battle of Thames." http://www.forttours.com/pages/thames.asp. Description of the battle with many famous paintings and lithographs depicting Tecumseh's death.

Freehoff, William Francis. "War of 1812: Battle of the Thames." http://www .historynet.com/war-of-1812-battle-of-the-thames.htm. An online scholarly essay on the battle.

King, Alan. "Tecumseh: Xenia Township's Most Famous Native." http:// shopxenia.com/XeniaTwp/Tecumseh.html. A good, brief, and descriptive biography of Tecumseh.

"Map of the Battle of the Thames." http://www.galafilm.com/1812/e/maps/ map554.html. Depicts the military deployment of the opposing sides and indicates where the Indians were situated.

"Panther-Across-The-Sky." http://www.ratical.org/ratville/Tecumseh.html. Links the power of Tecumseh and his skills as a speaker to his ability to take advantage of natural phenomena, like the New Madrid Earthquake.

"Tecumseh." http://www.ohiohistorycentral.org/entry.php?rec=373. Short biography with links to other entries.

"Tecumseh's Last Stand." http://www.military.com/Content/MoreContent ?file=PRthames2. Military historical description with J. Dorival's 1833 lithograph of the battle.

Multimedia Sources

Battle of the Thames (Dorival, 1813), *The Death of Tecumseh, Battle of the Thames* (Currier, 1847), and the *Battle of Tippecanoe* (Kurtz and Allison, 1889). http://www.loc.gov/rr/print/list/picamer/paMiliHist.html. Famous lithographs and paintings.

"Tecumseh!: The Ultimate Outdoor Drama Experience." http://www .tecumsehdrama.com/. Promotional Web site for information and tickets to attend this outdoor drama now in its 36th season.

33. Creek War (1813–1814)

In the Deep South, especially along the Gulf Coast, the Creek (or Red Stick) War of 1813–1814 started as a civil war among Creeks, but it soon escalated into a war with the Americans. The civil war started when Little Warrior and his followers, on their way home from the Battle of Frenchtown, where they allegedly participated in the massacre of American prisoners, killed and raided settlers. As a Red Stick, an upper towns' faction who advocated a return to traditional ways and who pledged to stop further American encroachments into Creek lands, Little Warrior and his band were themselves taken captive and subsequently executed by Big Warrior, a "White Stick," a lower towns' faction who advocated appeasement and cooperation with Americans as a way of guaranteeing the survival of the Creek Nation. Generally, Red Sticks lived in the clan villages upstream of the Mobile and Tombigby Rivers and the Whitesticks lived in clan villages downstream, which led to the names upper and lower villages. The Red Sticks opposed American expansion and assimilation whereas the White Sticks favored assimilation and cooperation with the Americans. The Red Sticks resented the unending desire of the Americans for their land, and they hated the civilizing efforts put into practice by Indian Agent Benjamin Hawkins. With the execution of Little Warrior, the Red Sticks rebelled and started to kill and take possession of the lower towns of the Creek Nation. They also destroyed the material items procured from Euro-Americans, except for firearms and powder, which would soon be supplemented by the Spanish authorities of Florida. The Red Sticks' desire to sever relations with white culture and white efforts to civilize the Creek led to confrontations with the American military which resulted in the battles of the Burnt Corn and the massacre at Fort Mims. Alarmed and fearful, the militia was mobilized under the command of Colonel Andrew Jackson. He led a campaign to destroy the Red Sticks. By the end of summer, 1814, he had forced the Creeks to sign the Treaty of Fort Jackson, near Hickory Ground—the heart of the Creek Nation—where the Creeks ceded 23 million acres to the U.S. government.

TERM PAPER SUGGESTIONS

1. Explain the great divide within the Creek Nation. Why did they have to choose to resist or to cooperate with American expansion? What are the strengths and weaknesses of each argument—Red Stick and White Stick?

2. Explore whether the United States took advantage of the Red Stick/White Stick civil war to destroy the Creek Nation.

3. After the atrocity at Fort Mims, the strategy of Jackson after victories was to completely destroy Red Stick towns. Why? What was his purpose and what was the end result?

4. Study and describe the Battle of Horseshoe Bend. Hopelessly outnumbered and outgunned, the Creeks were destroyed at the battle of Horseshoe Bend, which forced their capitulation.

5. Study the treaty terms of the Fort Jackson Treaty. Even though the White Sticks and the Cherokees helped Jackson to take his victory, they also were damaged by the land cession. Why?

ALTERNATIVE TERM PAPER SUGGESTIONS

1. Create a debate between Red Sticks and White Sticks where they advance their arguments for defiance or cooperation.

2. Create a Web site of images of the Creek Wars. For example, the Canoe Battle has been depicted in graphic form. The purpose is to show how images of Indians work to mollify the killing of Indian people and the taking of Indian land by making Indians the aggressors and the Americans the victims.

SUGGESTED SOURCES

Primary Sources

"The Canoe Battle." http://www.archives.state.al.us/teacher/creekwar/lesson1/doc1.html. A description of a short and bloody skirmish.

"The Creek Documents: Being a Collection of Letters, Depositions, Claims, and Other Papers." http://homepages.rootsweb.ancestry.com/~cmamcrk4/crkdxndx.html. A links page to many primary sources involving the Creek War and other useful information as well.

"Harry Toulmin, Letter." http://www.archives.state.al.us/teacher/creekwar/lesson1/doc5.html. A letter describing the Creek Indians being supplied with arms and making threats against the local American population.

"Treaty of Fort Jackson." http://www.humanitiesweb.org/human.php?s=h&p=d&a=i&ID=103. This is the full text of the treaty that ended the war between the Creek Nation and the United States.

Secondary Sources

Ethridge, Robbie Franklin. *Creek Country: Creek Indians and Their World, 1796–1816.* Chapel Hill, NC: University of North Carolina Press, 2003. Examines the Creek people in transition after the American Revolution and increased interaction with Blacks and Whites.

Griffith, Benjamin W. *McIntosh and Weatherford, Creek Indian Leaders.* Tuscaloosa, AL: University of Alabama Press, 1988. Includes bibliographical references of Indian leaders. A brother-against-brother story of two Creek leader, not brothers, who fought against one another, one for the White Sticks and one for the Red Sticks.

Halbert, Henry S., and T. H. Ball. *The Creek War of 1813 and 1815.* 1895. Rootsweb, 2008. http://homepages.rootsweb.ancestry.com/~cmamcrk4/hbtoc.html. A links page to 1895 history.

Holland, James Wendell. *Andrew Jackson and the Creek War: Victory at the Horseshoe.* Tuscaloosa, AL: University of Alabama Press, 1968. A historical narrative describing the victory of Andrew Jackson and his army over the Creek Nation at Horseshoe Bend, Alabama.

O'Brian, Sean Michael. *In Bitterness and in Tears: Andrew Jackson's Destruction of the Creeks and Seminoles.* Guilford, CT: Lyons Press, 2005. Discusses the Creek War of 1813 and the Seminole War of 1818 and the forced removal of these tribes in the aftermath.

Owsley, Frank Lawrence. *Struggle for the Gulf Borderlands: The Creek War and the Battle of New Orleans, 1812–1815.* Gainesville, FL: University Presses of Florida, 1981. Places the Creek War into a larger War of 1812 between England and the United States and tries to show how victories against the Creek Nation and the British at New Orleans tipped the balance in favor of the Americans.

Remini, Robert Vincent. *Andrew Jackson and His Indian Wars.* New York: Viking, 2001. Reprint, Baton Rouge, LA: LSU Press, 2003. Takes the position that despite the cruelty of President Jackson's Indian policies, he may have saved many of the eastern Indians, like the Creek Nation, from a more sinister and devastating fate.

Saunt, Claudio. *A New Order of Things: Property, Power and the Transformation of the Creek Indians, 1733–1816.* Cambridge, UK: Cambridge University Press, 1999. Explores, in particular, the transition wrought on the Creek Indians after the American Revolution and War of 1812. "Part II" covers the period of McGillivray and the Treaty of New York.

Waselkov, Gregory A. *Conquering Spirit: Fort Mims and the Redstick War of 1813–1814.* Tuscaloosa, AL: University of Alabama Press, 2006. Cross-disciplinary examination of the Fort Mims massacre, which had the effect of rallying Americans to destroy the Creek Nation and of making Andrew Jackson famous.

World Wide Web

"Among the Creeks: A Study of the Peoples of the Creek Tribes of Southeastern America & Those Who Lived Amongst Them." http://homepages.rootsweb.ancestry.com/~cmamcrk4/. A mega site with primary to secondary sources and links, including information on the Creek War.

"The Battle of Horseshoe Bend: Collision of Cultures." http://www.nps.gov/history/nr/twhp/wwwlps/lessons/54horseshoe/54horseshoe.htm. A lesson plan and links page with maps (Creek Country, 1777–1814, and Horseshoe Bend), factual readings, visual evidence, activities, and resources.

"The Creek War, 1813–1814." http://www.let.rug.nl/usa/P/aj7/about/bio/jack06.htm. Brief history of Andrew Jackson's involvement in the Creek War, 1813–1814, and the recognition and fame he gained due to that involvement.

"Dale's Canoe Fight." http://www.archives.state.al.us/teacher/creekwar/lesson1/doc2.html. Shows a pen and ink drawing.

"Life of Margaret Ervin Austill." http://www.archives.state.al.us/teacher/ creekwar/lesson1/doc3-1.html. Primary source: an eyewitness account of bloody scenes of the Creek War of 1813–1814.

Multimedia Source

Lost Worlds of Georgia, an Interactive Exhibit. http://www.lostworlds.org/ georgia.html. Shows how the Creeks might have looked at the time of early treaties and in ancient times. Other DVDs and video resources are also available from this site.

34. Sequoyah's Syllabary (1821)

Although the Cherokee Sequoyah was exposed to the concept of writing via his association with Americans and as an enlisted soldier in Andrew Jackson's army sent to fight the English and Creek in the War of 1812 and the Creek War of 1813–1814, he never leaned to write in English. When he returned home from the war, inspired by the abilities of his American allies to write letters home or to record events, Sequoyah tinkered with a writing system for the Cherokee people based on symbols that represented word-sounds or phrases of his own Cherokee language. After 12 years of work that included reducing thousands of symbolic "letters" down to 85 symbols, he and his daughter, who helped him as a test subject and assistant, introduced the syllabary to his people in 1821. In a matter of months, thousands of people became literate due to the ease with which they could interpret the symbol-letters as part of their own oral language. In 1825, because of this success, the Cherokee Nation accepted Sequoyah's syllabary as the official written language of the Cherokee people. The rate at which Cherokees, even adults, could learn to read and write in Cherokee was and is much faster than an ordinary child in America learns to read and write in English, which can take several years. Sequoyah's achievement is remarkable considering nowhere in recorded history has a people become literate within their own language and culture in so little time.

TERM PAPER SUGGESTIONS

1. How was Sequoyah's syllabary a simultaneous recognition of what the Americans had to offer and a celebration of his own people's culture?

2. Rather than totally assimilate, the Cherokees emulated western civilization but remained steadfast in preserving their own traditional ways. Why? How is Sequoyah's achievement an illustrative example?

3. Examine how the lives of the Cherokee changed after the introduction of a written language.

4. Explain how the Cherokees' written language is an example of cultural change and cultural persistence, a way of making the society greater without losing its cultural identity.

5. What is Cherokee about Sequoyah's syllabary? Some of the symbols resemble the English alphabet or even Arabic numbers. How then are they "Cherokee"?

6. How does a written language preserve an oral one? Is there a relation between the losses of Indian oral languages due to the lack of written forms? Investigate the issue of American Indian language preservation.

ALTERNATIVE TERM PAPER SUGGESTIONS

1. Make a Microsoft PowerPoint slide show presentation of each symbol of Sequoyah's syllabary, and share it with people who are interested in Cherokee language.

2. Try making a syllabary of your own in very simple terms, and make Microsoft PowerPoint slides of each symbol, followed by some simple combinations to form words, phrases, or sentences. For example, rebuses, a mode of expressing words or phrases by pictures or objects, could be used to illustrate how difficult creating an alphabet is and how drawing on your own language and culture can produce some interesting results. (For example, you might use a picture of a can of beans followed by a picture of a knot to get "cannot." See the usHistory.org Web site for a rebus game from 1777 that illustrates this point: http://www.ushistory.org/March/games/rebus.htm. 2008.)

SUGGESTED SOURCES

Primary Sources

Kilpatrick, Jack F., and Anna Gritts Kilpatrick. *The Shadow of Sequoyah: Social Document of the Cherokees, 1862–1964.* Norman, OK: University of Oklahoma Press, 1965. A large and varied selection of 81 letters, notes, songs, and prayers written in Cherokee, though translated into English.

"Sequoyah's Original Syllabary." http://www.intertribal.net/NAT/Cherokee/ WebPgCC1/Original.htm. A digital facsimile of the original document with a link to Sequoyah's numerals and the "Cherokee Companion Home Page."

Secondary Sources

Bender, Margaret C. *Signs of Cherokee Culture: Sequoyah's Syllabary in Eastern Cherokee Life.* Chapel Hill, NC: University of North Carolina Press, 2002. Scholarly examination of the current use of the syllabary.

Brannon, Frank. *Cherokee Phoenix, Advent of a Newspaper: The Print Shop of the Cherokee Nation 1828–1834, with a Chronology.* Dillsboro, NC: Speak-easy Press, 2005. A history of the *Cherokee Phoenix* and of the Cherokee Indians.

Cwiklik, Robert. *Sequoyah and the Cherokee Alphabet.* Littleton, CO: Sonlight Curriculum, 2000. Another in a long line of acceptable introductory biographies of Sequoyah.

Foreman, Grant. *Sequoyah.* 1938. Norman, OK: University of Oklahoma Press, 1970. A 90-page sketch of Sequoyah, the "Indian Cadmus."

Hoig, Stan. *Sequoyah: The Cherokee Genius.* Oklahoma City: Oklahoma Historical Society, 1995. A much-cited biography.

Klausneer, Janet. *Sequoyah's Gift: A Portrait of the Cherokee Leader.* New York: HarperCollins, 1993. A readable short biography.

Perdue, Theda. *Rising From the Ashes: The Cherokee Phoenix as an Ethno Historical Source.* Durham, NC: Duke University Press, 1977. Provides analysis of the newspaper, its content, contributors, and circulation.

Rumford, James. *Sequoyah: The Cherokee Man Who Gave His People Writing.* New York: Houghton Mifflin, 2004. Although meant for a young audience, the book is useful for adults due to its use of the Cherokee language and the inclusion of a readable chart of the syllabary and time line of Sequoyah's life.

Walker, Willard, and James Sarbaugh. "The Early History of the Cherokee Syllabary." *Ethnohistory* 40, no. 1 (Winter 1993): 70–94. Refutes the claim that white Americans had a role in creating Sequoyah's syllabary.

World Wide Web

"Cherokee Syllabary and Sound." http://www.cherokee.org/Extras/Downloads/syllabary.html. Provides the Cherokee syllabary and pronunciation guide. Links to sound recordings are also provided.

Davis, John B. "The Life and Work of Sequoyah." *Chronicles of Oklahoma* 8, no. 2 (June 1930). http://digital.library.okstate.edu/chronicles/v008/

v008p149.html. A complete online scholarly biography of Sequoyah, fully referenced.

"English/Cherokee Dictionary." http://www.wehali.com/tsalagi/. English to Cherokee translator: type in a simple work, like "eagle," and it will be translated into Cherokee.

Parins, Jim. "The Genius of Sequoyah." http://anpa.ualr.edu/digital_library/ sequoyah/sequoyah.htm. A biographical essay that includes a listing of people who recognize Sequoyah's genius.

"Sequoyah." http://www.manataka.org/page81.html. A short biography that includes the Cherokee alphabet.

"Sequoyah's Talking Leaves." http://ngeorgia.com/history/alphabet.html. Short biography with links to other relevant entries.

Multimedia Source

The Sequoyah Birthplace Museum. http://www.sequoyahmuseum.org/. Includes an informative photo gallery of exhibits.

35. *Johnson v. M'Intosh* (1823)

In *Johnson v. M'Intosh,* the Supreme Court determined that the federal government had exclusive right to Indian lands via sale or "just war," and individuals or companies could not buy land from Indians privately. The antecedents for the case started in 1773 and 1775 when Thomas Johnson bought large tracts of land from the Piankeshaw Indian tribe of the Illinois territory. In 1818, William M'Intosh, the defendant, secured title of the same land from the United States. Thomas Johnson's descendants, who had inherited the land after Johnson had died, brought suit against M'Intosh and claimed they had original title. The Illinois district court ruled for M'Intosh, but the case was appealed to the Supreme Court. The major issue of this case was to decide whether Indian tribes possessed title to their own lands and whether the U.S. government recognized that Indians could sell their land to private citizens. Chief Justice John Marshall issued the opinion of the court on March 10, 1823: the court determined that the U.S. government had acquired title to Indian land based on the "discovery doctrine." This meant that European countries such as England, Spain, and France who had "discovered" North America had first claim to acquire lands from Indians before any individual or other nation-state. The Native Americans, he ruled, had to submit to the discovery doctrine, which meant they had to sell or cede their lands only to U.S. government and that they were only given the right of occupancy on their own lands.

TERM PAPER SUGGESTIONS

1. A "just war" is an explanation, either political or religious, that explains the need for war against an enemy, usually weaker militarily and smaller in population. What is a "just war" in the context of acquiring Indian land? Is it "conquest" or is it something else?

2. Define and report on the discovery doctrine. How do national boundaries play a role? Why rule that Indians can "occupy" land but the U.S. government actually owns it via purchase from Indian tribes or through "just war"?

3. Compare English Indian policy to American Indian policy as it pertains to Indian land. Why is it important for British or U.S. governments to be the sole authority over Indian affairs, especially the acquisition of land? How does *Johnson v. M'Intosh* end the confusion?

4. How are state governments, especially Georgia, involved in legal acquisition of Indian land? *Fletcher v. Peck* allowed Georgia to legally buy and/or "acquire" Indian land because it is a "government" under the authority of the larger federal government. How does *Johnson v. M'Intosh* change, add to, or amend *Fletcher v. Peck?*

5. Investigate the role of *Johnson v. M'Intosh* in U.S. property law.

6. Explore the erosion of tribal sovereignty due to judicial opinions on such cases as *Johnson v. M'Intosh.*

ALTERNATIVE TERM PAPER SUGGESTIONS

1. Using scans or photocopies of maps found in the legal and historical record, graphically show the land bought by Johnson within the boundaries of the state of Illinois and those of the lands acquired by Georgia a few years earlier to make comparison of the land acquisition process. Create a slide show for comparison purposes.

2. Create an electronic time line of the discovery doctrine from the time of Columbus to that of *Johnson v. M'Intosh* in 1823. You can do this with map images of lands claimed by Spain, England, Holland, and France, and later the United States, in 50-year increments.

SUGGESTED SOURCES

Primary Sources

"*Fletcher v. Peck*, 10 U.S. 87." http://www.utulsa.edu/law/classes/rice/ussct _cases/FLETCHER_V_PECK_1810.HTM. Online digital facsimile. Mentioned in the opinion rendered by Chief Justice Marshall as a precedent and similar case, except that the sale of land could be made to a state—the state of Georgia in this case.

Johnson, Herbert Alan. "John Marshall." *The Justices of the United States Supreme Court: Their Lives and Major Opinions.* Vol. 1. Leon Friedman and Fred L. Israel, eds. New York: Chelsea House, 1997, 181–99. Short biographies with select texts of major opinions.

"*Johnson v. M'Intosh.* 21 U.S. 543. U.S. Supr. Ct. (1823)." http://www .utulsa.edu/law/classes/rice/ussct_cases/JOHNSON_V_MCINTOSH _1823.HTM. Online digital facsimile of the case and of Chief Justice Marshall's opinion.

Secondary Sources

Banner, Stuart. "From Ownership to Occupancy." *How the Indians Lost Their Land: Law and Power on the Frontier.* Cambridge, MA: Harvard University Press, 2005, 150–90. Cites *Johnson v. M'Intosh* as the case that set the precedent that state and federal governments owned Indian land and that Indians merely occupied it.

Deloria, Vine, Jr., and David E. Wilkins. *Tribes, Treaties, and Constitutional Tribulations.* Austin, TX: University of Texas Press, 2000. Explores the relationship between the U.S. Constitution and the federal government and Indian tribes and their governments.

Kades, Eric. "The Dark Side of Efficiency: *Johnson v. M'Intosh* and the Expropriation of American Indian Lands." *University of Pennsylvania Law Review* 148, no. 4 (April 2000): 1065–1190. A very detailed history of case and background that includes maps and other statistical data.

Newcomb, Steven. *Pagans in the Promised Land: Decoding the Doctrine of Christian Discovery.* Golden, CO: Fulcrum, 2008. Argues that a "Christian" doctrine of discovery preceded and influenced the Chief Justice's opinion.

Norgen, Jill. *Cherokee Cases: Two Landmark Federal Decisions in the Fight for Sovereignty.* New York: McGraw-Hill, 1996. Reprint, Norman, OK: University of Oklahoma Press, 2003. Covers the two cases following *Johnson v. M'Intosh.*

Prucha, Francis Paul. *American Indian Treaties: The History of a Political Anomaly.* Berkeley, CA: University of California Press, 1994. A general history of United States and Indian treaty relationships.

Prucha, Francis Paul. *Documents of United States Indian Policy.* 3rd ed. Lincoln, NE: University of Nebraska Press, 2000. Provides only the parts pertinent to Indians and Indian tribes. See item 8, page 9, for the "Northwest Ordinance."

Robertson, Lindsay G. *Conquest by Law: How the Discovery of America Dispossessed Indigenous Peoples of Their Lands.* New York: Oxford University Press, 2005. *Johnson v. M'Intosh* is center stage, because it set the foundation by defining the "discovery doctrine," for the legal taking of Indian land.

Singer, Joseph William. *Property Law: Rules, Policies, and Practices.* 4th ed. Textbook. New York: Aspen Publishers, 2006. Puts *Johnson v. M'Intosh* within the context of property law and precedent.

Wilkins, David E. *American Indian Sovereignty and the U.S. Supreme Court: The Masking of Justice.* Austin, TX: University of Texas Press, 1997. Detailed analysis of 15 U.S. Supreme Court cases involving Native Americans, including *Johnson v. M'Intosh.*

Wilkins, David E. *Uneven Ground: American Indian Sovereignty and Federal Law.* Norman, OK: University of Oklahoma Press, 2001. A scholarly study of federal law and Supreme Court rulings, including the discovery doctrine.

Wunder, John R., ed. *Native American Law and Colonialism, Before 1776 to 1903.* New York: Garland Publishing, 1996. A collection of essays on Indian law, treaties, and the Supreme Court that includes much on the Cherokee cases.

World Wide Web

Engle, Patricia. "The Origins and Legacy of Justice Marshall's 'New Rule' of Conquest in *Johnson v. M'Intosh.*" http://digital.lib.lehigh.edu/trial/justification/court/essay/. Argues that the idea of conquest was first interjected in legal argument concerning Indian land in *Johnson v. M'Intosh.*

"*Johnson v. M'Intosh.*" http://law.jrank.org/pages/13664/Johnson-v-McIntosh .html. A comprehensive description and analysis of the significance and impact of the *Johnson v. M'Intosh* case and the discovery doctrine.

Kades, Eric. "History and Interpretation of the Great Case of *Johnson v. M'Intosh.*" http://www.historycooperative.org/journals/lhr/19.1/kades.html. A shorter version of the "Dark Side" monograph cited in the Secondary Sources.

Newcomb, Steven. "*Johnson v. M'Intosh:* The Christian Right of Colonization." http://www.kumeyaay.com/2008/01/johnson-v-mintosh-the-christian-right-of-colonization/. Argues that a "Christian" doctrine of discovery preceded and influenced Chief Justice's opinion.

Patenaude, Joel. "The Changing View of Indian Law by the U.S. Supreme Court." http://www.aaanativearts.com/article511.html. Shows how *Johnson v. M'Intosh* is the first of a long series of cases that eroded and defined American Indian sovereignty and rights.

Purdy, Jedediah S. "Property and Empire: The Law of Imperialism in *Johnson v. M'Intosh*." http://papers.ssrn.com/sol3/papers.cfm?abstract_id=942013. Downloadable PDF of an extensive scholarly article on the case and opinion.

Multimedia Sources

"*Johnson v. M'Intosh*: Supreme Court of the United States, 1823. 21 U.S. 543." http://www.audiocasefiles.com/cases/detail/case/8617/. Substantial sample clip from audio recording of the case file.

Tribal Nations: The Story of Federal Indian Law. Dir. Lisa Jaeger. Tanana Chiefs, 2006. DVD. 60 minutes. Introductory-level documentary of how federal Indian law has developed in the United States.

36. Bureau of Indian Affairs Created (1824)

Starting with the Continental Congress in 1775, the U.S. government determined it needed an agency to handle the complexities of the government's Indian affairs. In 1775, the first acts of Congress were to create three Departments of Indian Affairs to cover the north, central, and south sectors of the Indian frontier. Benjamin Franklin and Patrick Henry served as commissioners. As such, their major job during the Revolutionary War was to negotiate treaties of peace and neutrality with Indian tribes and, afterward, to regain control of orderly settlement and trade and acquisition of Indian land. In 1806, the War Department was established, and Indian Affairs was moved under its authority. In 1824 and still under the authority of the secretary of war, the "Office of Indian Affairs" was created after the collapse of the government-controlled Indian trading factories, but Secretary of War John C. Calhoun dubbed it the "Bureau of Indian Affairs." The confusion over "Office" or "Bureau" would not be settled until 1947, when "Bureau" won out. Meanwhile, the Office or Bureau was moved to the newly created Department of the Interior in 1849. Throughout its history the Bureau of Indian Affairs (BIA), the generic term for a branch of the government with many names, managed Indian affairs, which included handling Indian treaties rights, dispensing justice, distributing supplies and annuities, managing land, overseeing tribal governments, establishing jurisdiction, and handling untold hundreds of administrative duties as they related to Indian affairs. In 2008, the BIA was involved in a lawsuit, *Cobell v. Kempthorne,* which claims the BIA mismanaged trust funds. Because of this lawsuit, the BIA Web site, which was a valuable source of information on American Indians, has been streamlined if not virtually shut down.

TERM PAPER SUGGESTIONS

1. Why was it and is it necessary for the U.S. government to have an office or bureau to manage its Indian affairs? Is there an argument, historically or in the present, for the abolishment of this unique bureaucracy?
2. Examine the reasons for the "Office" of Indian Affairs to be placed within the War Department for a time.
3. Why move the "Office" to the newly created Department of the Interior in 1849? Were Indians less of a military threat?
4. How complex is the BIA? Explore the depth of its organization and the scope of its responsibilities.
5. Explore the attitude of Indians toward the BIA. Has it changed since the preferential hiring practices were imposed?
6. Investigate the relation the BIA has to Indian treaties and law.

ALTERNATIVE TERM PAPER SUGGESTION

1. Create a tree diagram using Microsoft PowerPoint templates to diagram the BIA bureaucracy at different times in U.S. history (for example, 1775, 1875, and 1975). The depth and scope of the complexities of the BIA should, in the early period, be simple and by 1975 be fairly complex as the number of Indian agents and superintendents increased.

SUGGESTED SOURCES

Primary Source

"Annual Report of the Commissioner of Indian Affairs to the Secretary of the Interior for the Year 1886." Washington, DC: Government Printing Office, 1886. http://books.google.com/books?id=nHAOT23PLUYC &printsec=frontcover&dq=bureau+of+indian+affairs. Historical report of agents and superintendents of schools and has a "Topics Discussed" table of contents, which can direct a reader to the "Peace Policy and its Economy," for instance.

Secondary Sources

Jackson, Curtis E., and Marcia J. Gall. *A History of the Bureau of Indian Affairs and Its Activities Among Indians.* San Francisco: R & E Research Associates, 1977. An objective summary that avoids making judgments.

Monette, Richard E. *Bureau of Indian Affairs: From Broken Treaties to Casinos.* Westport, CT: Greenwood Press, 2009. Comprehensive history of the BIA and detailed explanation of how the BIA works and functions in modern times.

Nickeson, Steve. "The Structure of the Bureau of Indian Affairs." *Law and Contemporary Problems* 40, no. 1. *The American Indian and the Law* (Winter 1976): 61–76. Historical analysis of the structure of the BIA.

Officer, James E. "The Bureau of Indian Affairs Since 1945: An Assessment." *Annals of the American Academy of Political and Social Science* 436 (March 1978): 61–72. General overview and assessment of the BIA in assisting American Indians.

Porter, Frank W. *The Bureau of Indian Affairs: Know Your Government.* New York: Chelsea House, 1988. Though meant for grades 6–9, the book surveys the history, describes its structure, and discusses its influence on American Indians as of 1988.

Prucha, Francis Paul. *The Great Father: The United States Government and the American Indians.* Lincoln, NE: University of Nebraska Press, 1984. An analysis of the history, the personalities, and issues involved in relation between the United States and Indians.

Stuart, Paul. *Nations Within: Historical Statistics of American Indians.* Westport, CT: Greenwood Press, 1987. Interesting statistics with many originating from BIA records.

Taylor, Theodore W. *The Bureau of Indian Affairs: Public Policies Toward Indian Citizens.* Boulder, CO: Westview Press, 1984. Mostly covers U.S. policy but covers the history of the BIA as well.

World Wide Web

Hensen. C. L. "From War to Self-Determination: A History of the Bureau of Indian Affairs." http://www.americansc.org.uk/online/indians.htm. Detailed history of the BIA.

"Indian Trust: *Cobell v. Kempthorne.*" http://www.indiantrust.com/. On the left of the page Eloise Cobell offers her "Government Myth-Weaving" essay, while to the right of the page and in the buttons in the header are a wealth of informational links, for example the case overview and the legal positions of both sides.

"Records of the BIA." http://www.archives.gov/research/guide-fed-records/groups/ 075.html. Although only a "Guide to Federal Records," it does help researchers to understand the scope and complexities of the federal record.

Multimedia Source

"Occupation of the Bureau of Indian Affairs in 1972." http://encarta.msn .com/media_701508412/occupation_of_the_bureau_of_indian _affairs_building.html. Photograph of American Indian Movement militants in the famous occupation of the Bureau of Indian Affairs building in Washington, D.C.

37. *Cherokee Phoenix* in Print (1828–1834)

The *Cherokee Phoenix* was the first American Indian newspaper and the first bilingual newspaper printed in Indian and English languages. In 1828, the first edition printed the Constitution of the Cherokee Nation, important laws, articles covering national and local events, Bible passages, and human-interest stories, along with advertisements and notices. For a little over a year, the newspaper would continue to publish in this vein. However, advocates for Cherokee removal soon caused the focus of the newspaper to change to one of resistance and opposition to their removal. By 1829, the name of the newspaper was changed to *Cherokee Phoenix and Indians' Advocate,* and the editor of the newspaper, Elias Boudinot, had accurately perceived the power of a newspaper to present the Cherokee case against removal. Very soon, the circulation rose and extended to Cherokee tribes in Virginia, North Carolina, and Alabama, as well as to a large non-Indian population, both national and international, and this wide readership learned of the Cherokees' plight. Within its pages, issues of Georgia's rights over Indian lands and Indian rights were debated and expounded on, but when President Andrew Jackson supported states' rights and refused to enforce the Supreme Court decision favoring the Cherokees' position, their removal was inevitable. Boudinot changed his position and resigned in 1832, and the newspaper printed its last paper in 1834. Because Georgian officials and pro-removal Cherokees knew the power of the newspaper to unify Cherokee opposition, the printing press and office were seized in 1835, and Cherokee removal, the Trail of Tears, soon followed.

TERM PAPER SUGGESTIONS

1. Explore the importance of newspapers in communities of the nineteenth century. In the absence of television and computers, why were papers so popular? Within the community of the Cherokee Nation, how would a new form of communication be an asset to older modes of news and communication?

2. Explain how the *Cherokee Phoenix* maintained a connection to and celebration of Cherokee culture and language. How did it celebrate national pride? Find examples in the primary sources.

3. Investigate how the *Cherokee Phoenix* was one example of many that proved the Cherokees were capable of creating a modern civilization on their own terms. Why was it important for the Cherokee to show "progress" to Americans, and why did they feel the importance of maintaining a sense of Cherokee identity at the same time?

4. Explore the "power of the press" in the case of the *Cherokee Phoenix.* How did this newspaper become a tool to unify Cherokee opposition to Indian removal? What was the importance of reaching a national and international non-Indian readership?

5. Why did the first editor, Elias Boudinot, change his mind about removal? Why was he refused a chance to debate the pros and cons of removal in the *Cherokee Phoenix?*

6. Explore the reasons that the federal government, the state of Georgia, and pro-removal Cherokees first shut the press down and then seized the printing press and office. Why shut down the press on the eve of the Cherokee removal that would later be known as the Trail of Tears? Is it according to democratic principle to seize a printing press?

ALTERNATIVE TERM PAPER SUGGESTIONS

1. Create a Microsoft PowerPoint time line of the short run of the *Cherokee Phoenix,* leading up to and including its demise.

2. Collect images and screenshots of the actual *Cherokee Phoenix.* Focus on collecting several articles covering a similar theme (that is, advertisements, human interest, language, politics, or the like) and make a Microsoft PowerPoint slide show to demonstrate the sophistication of the newspaper.

SUGGESTED SOURCES

Primary Sources

"Cherokee Phoenix Archives." http://onlinebooks.library.upenn.edu/webbin/serial?id=cherokeephoenix. Has three levels of source materials on the *Cherokee Phoenix* newspaper, 1828–1834: photo facsimiles of the original papers, English language articles organized by topic, and selection of transcriptions organized by subject.

"The Cherokee Phoenix from Hunter Library." http://library.wcu.edu/CherokeePhoenix/. English language articles from the *Cherokee Phoenix* newspaper, 1828–1834.

Secondary Sources

Bass, Althea. *Cherokee Messenger.* Norman, OK: University of Oklahoma Press, 1996. Describes the Cherokee Indians and the *Cherokee Phoenix* from 1830 to 1840.

Brannon, Frank. *Cherokee Phoenix, Advent of a Newspaper: The Print Shop of the Cherokee Nation 1828–1834, with a Chronology.* Dillsboro, NC: Speak-easy Press, 2005. A history of the *Cherokee Phoenix* and of the Cherokee Indians.

Carlton, Andrew Doyal. *The Cherokee Phoenix and Indian Advocate: Its Response to Arguments for Cherokee Removal.* Atlanta: Georgia State University, 1996. Micro-study of the paper when the editorial focus changed to the debate over Cherokee removal.

Hoig, Stan. *Sequoyah: The Cherokee Genius.* Oklahoma City: Oklahoma Historical Society, 1995. A much-cited biography.

Hutton, Frankie, and Barbara S. Reed. *Outsider in 19th-Century Press History: Multicultural Perspectives.* Madison, WI: University of Wisconsin Press, 2002, 115–44. Places the *Cherokee Phoenix* within a greater U.S. press history context and explains how it reached readers beyond the border of the Cherokee Nation.

Landini, Ann Lackey. *The Cherokee Phoenix: The Voice of the Cherokee Nation.* Knoxville, TN: University of Tennessee, 1990. Provides roles of the *Cherokee Phoenix* among Cherokee Indians from 1828 to 1834.

Perdue, Theda, ed. *Cherokee Editor: The Writings of Elias Boudinot.* Athens, GA: University of Georgia Press, 1996. Collection of editorials of the famous editor who advocated for voluntary removal to the Indian Territory.

Perdue, Theda. *Rising From the Ashes: The Cherokee Phoenix as an Ethno Historical Source.* Durham, NC: Duke University Press, 1977. Provides analysis of the newspaper, its content, contributors, and circulation.

Riley, Sam G. "The Cherokee Phoenix: The Short, Unhappy Life of the First American Indian Newspaper." *Journalism Quarterly* 53, 1976. Discusses tribal problems and white harassment, which combined to end the weekly publication in 1834.

World Wide Web

Awtrey, Hugh R. "New Echota: Birthplace of the American Indian Press, 1940." *The Regional Review* IV, no. 3 (March 1940). http://www.nps.gov/history/history/online_books/regional_review/vol4-3i.htm. Including footnotes and photos, a National Park Service (NPS) official pays homage to the "smallest and most obscure" national monuments administered by the NPS.

"Cherokee." http://www.nativeamericans.com/Cherokee.htm. A wealth of information and links.

"Cherokee Phoenix." http://www.cherokeephoenix.org/. Web site of the online version of the modern Cherokee newspaper as of 2008.

"Elias Boudinot's Editorials in the Cherokee Phoenix." http://www.cerritos.edu/soliver/Student%20Activites/Trail%20of%20Tears/web/boudinot.htm. Provides a short introduction of Elias Boudinot's editorials (1829 and 1831) and then provides several examples. The content is centered on the forced or voluntary removal.

Pulley, Angela F. "Cherokee Phoenix." http://www.georgiaencyclopedia.org/nge/Article.jsp?id=h-611. Short scholarly history of the paper, its growth, and its role in the "removal" debates.

Worthy, Larry. "The Cherokee Phoenix (and Indian Advocate)." http://ngeorgia.com/history/phoenix.html. A short history that includes a photograph of the printing office.

Multimedia Source

"Indian Land Cessions in the American Southeast." http://www.tngenweb.org/cessions/cherokee.html. A links page to maps of lands ceded by or taken from Indian tribes in Georgia and other southern states east of the Mississippi.

38. Indian Removal Act (1830)

In 1830, President Andrew Jackson passed the Indian Removal Act, which called for the removal of Indians east of the Mississippi River to newly acquired western lands in roughly present-day Oklahoma and portions of Kansas and Nebraska. The act represented a continuance of the policy of separating Indians from Whites and of preventing large Indian settlements within state boundaries. The United States acquired western lands with the Louisiana Purchase of 1803, which was simply a transfer of discovery rights in exchange for money: many Indian tribes lived on these lands, as Lewis and Clark would discover. The Removal Act called for removal treaties to be signed by a majority of tribal members but a minority often signed the treaties. The removal treaties were designed to exchange land west of the Mississippi for land holdings east of the river, as well as to provide monies for improvements, transportation, and compensation. The process started in 1830 and ended in the mid-1840s and involved nearly every tribe east of the Mississippi River, particularly those tribes living in Georgia, Alabama, Mississippi, and Florida: the Choctaws, Chickasaws, Cherokees, Creeks, and Seminoles. One way or the other, despite legal efforts or downright recalcitrance, nearly 70 removal treaties were signed, and roughly 50,000 eastern Indians were removed. On the surface, the law required equitable treatment and fair compensation, but the actual implementation of the law was ruthless and cruel, especially to those tribal peoples who resisted. They were in many cases hunted down, rounded up, and forced out of their homes and onto the trail west, which soon became known as the Trail of Tears.

TERM PAPER SUGGESTIONS

1. Investigate what the Indian Removal Act of 1830 was trying to accomplish and why.
2. Compare *Johnson v. M'Intosh,* a judicial opinion, to the Indian Removal Act of 1830, an executive-sponsored legislative bill and act.
3. How did the Removal Act promote states' rights and the concept of separation between Whites and Indians?
4. Explore President Jackson's view and attitude toward Indians. Were his Indian policies part of a larger scheme to heighten the power of the executive branch of government, or did he truly hate Indians as some have proclaimed? Or both?
5. Explore the connection between President Thomas Jefferson's Louisiana Purchase and Indian removal. How did the extension of the western boundary under this purchase and the "discovery doctrine" make possible Indian removal?
6. Examine and report on the many arguments for and against Indian removal from the perspectives of Indians, politicians, judges, clergy, and the common people. Expose or report on the best argument.

ALTERNATIVE TERM PAPER SUGGESTIONS

1. Create a debate between Indians, lawmakers, and the president on the subject of Indian removal. Have each faction study the primary sources of their historical counterparts and have them fashion public arguments. Host a public forum and have them present their arguments for or against Indian removal.

2. Make a Web site of links to Indian responses to the Indian Removal Act and their reasons for their opposition. Many of these responses exist in English.

SUGGESTED SOURCES

Primary Sources

"Cherokee Indian Removal Debate: U.S. Senate, April 15–17, 1830." http://www
.cviog.uga.edu/Projects/gainfo/chdebate.htm. Speeches of Georgia Senator
John Forsyth, April 15, 1830, and Maine Senator Peleg Sprague, April 17,
1830.

Erbash, Jennifer. "The Cherokee Removal." http://lincoln.lib.niu.edu/teachers/
lesson5-cherokee.html. Lesson plan with links to primary sources:
Jackson's first and second annual messages, the debate speeches of Sena-
tors Forsyth and Sprague, the "Report of the Committee on Indian
Affairs and Speech of Robert Adams," and "Memorial of the Cherokee
Indians and Cherokee Address."

"Indian Removal Act." http://www.civics-online.org/library/formatted/texts/
indian_act.html. Full seven-section digital text of the act on one page.

"Indian Removal: Extract from Andrew Jackson's Seventh Annual Message to
Congress, December 7, 1835." http://www.pbs.org/weta/thewest/
resources/archives/two/removal.htm. President Jackson's justification for
Indian removal.

"Primary Document in American History: Indian Removal Act." http://www.loc.gov
/rr/program/bib/ourdocs/Indian.html. A Web guide with many relevant and
pertinent links on Indian removal: House and Senate Journals entries, maps,
nineteenth-century articles that debate the issues, and other links.

Ross, John. "Cherokee Letter Protesting the Treaty of New Echota." http://www
.pbs.org/wgbh/aia/part4/4h3083t.html. Chief John Ross's letter to the
Senate and House protesting the Cherokee Removal Treaty.

Secondary Sources

Banner, Stuart. "Removal." *How the Indians Lost Their Land: Law and Power on
the Frontier*. Cambridge, MA: Harvard University Press, 2005, 191–227.
Explores the role of "removal" in the loss of land.

Deloria, Vine, Jr., and David E. Wilkins. *Tribes, Treaties, and Constitutional Tribulations*. Austin, TX: University of Texas Press, 2000. Explores the relationship between the U.S. Constitution and the federal government and Indian tribes and their governments.

Foreman, Grant. *Indian Removal: The Emigration of the Five Civilized Tribes of Indians*. Norman, OK: University of Oklahoma Press, 1972. Five chapter essays covering the removal of the five major tribes: Choctaw, Creek, Chickasaw, Cherokee, and Seminole.

Garrison, Tim A. *The Legal Ideology of Removal: The Southern Judiciary and the Sovereignty of Native American Nations*. Athens, GA: University of Georgia Press, 2002. Examines the role of state courts in the Indian removal process to make a states' rights issue rather than a moral or ethical issue of sympathy for Indians.

Keller, Christian B. "Philanthropy Betrayed: Thomas Jefferson, the Louisiana Purchase, and the Origins of Federal Indian Removal Policy." *Proceedings of the American Philosophical Society* 144, no. 1 (March 2000): 39–66. Links the Louisiana Purchase to arguments for Indian removal east of the Mississippi because land became available for that purpose with the purchase.

Magliocca, Gerald N. *Andrew Jackson and the Constitution: The Rise and Fall of Generational Regimes*. Lawrence, KS: University of Press of Kansas, 2007. Places President Jackson's Indian policies within a larger context of efforts to increase the power of the executive branch.

Perdue, Theda, and Michael D. Green. *The Cherokee Removal: A Brief History with Documents*. New York: Bedford Books of St. Martin's Press, 1995. Many primary source documents are used to tell the story of Cherokee removal.

Remini, Robert V. *The Legacy of Andrew Jackson: Essays on Democracy, Indian Removal and Slavery*. Baton Rouge, LA: Louisiana State University Press, 1988. Chapter two covers Indian removal and places it within other of Jackson's "accomplishments."

Robertson, Lindsay G. *Conquest by Law: How the Discovery of America Dispossessed Indigenous Peoples of Their Lands*. New York: Oxford University Press, 2005. *Johnson v. M'Intosh* is center stage, because it set the foundation by defining the "discovery doctrine," for the legal taking of Indian land.

Satz, Ronald N. *American Indian Policy in the Jacksonian Era*. Norman, OK: University of Oklahoma Press, 2002. Although the book is relevant in all of its parts, chapters two through four are particularly so in terms of the Removal Act, policy and implementation.

Wallace, Anthony F. C. *The Long Bitter Trail: Andrew Jackson and the Indians*. HarperCollins *CanadaLLTD*, 1993. Chapter three is devoted to the

Removal Act, appended with the text of the act and an excerpt of
Jackson's December 8, 1829 Message to Congress.

Wilkins, David E. *Uneven Ground: American Indian Sovereignty and Federal Law.*
Norman, OK: University of Oklahoma Press, 2001. A scholarly study of
federal law and Supreme Court rulings, including the "Trust Doctrine,"
which Jackson used to support removal.

World Wide Web

"Andrew Jackson and the Indian Removal Act." http://www.historynet.com/
andrew-jackson-and-the-indian-removal-act.htm. Short historical
description.
"Indian Removal, 1814–1858." http://www.pbs.org/wgbh/aia/part4/4p2959.
html. Concise description and analysis of Indian removal.
"Indian Removal Act of 1830." http://www.conservapedia.com/Indian_Removal
_Act_of_1830. Full text of the act with an explanatory introduction.
"Indian Treaties and the Removal Act of 1830." http://www.state.gov/r/pa/ho/
time/dwe/16338.htm. General information and a legal statement on the
U.S. Indian Removal Policy.

Multimedia Source

The West. Dir. Stephen Ives. Public Broadcasting Service, 1996. 4 DVDs.
750 minutes. "Episode Two, 1806 to 1848" covers the Removal Act
and the Trail of Tears.

39. *Cherokee Nation v. Georgia* (1831)

The opinion of the Supreme Court in the case of *Cherokee Nation v.
Georgia,* 1831, ruled that Indians tribes were not equal to nations and
were "domestic dependent nations" residing within the boundaries of
the United States, that they would not be construed as "nations" in the
sense of France or England. Because President Andrew Jackson supported
and favored states' rights over Indian rights, the Cherokees had little
option but to take their case through the U.S. judicial system. In order
to impede the efforts to remove them, the Cherokee Nation brought an
injunction against Georgia to stop them from enforcing laws that would
destroy the Cherokee Nation. After the passage of the Indian Removal
Act of 1830, which the Cherokees disputed, they refused to remove themselves from Georgia and forced the United States to remove them forcibly.

Before the case reached the Supreme Court, the Cherokees were able to garner support from people like Davy Crockett, who opposed Georgia in their imposition of state law over Indian people, lands, and governments. The attorney for the Cherokees, William Writ, argued before the Supreme Court that the Cherokee were a foreign nation under the laws of the U.S. Constitution and thus were not subject to state law. The injunction was denied, and the matter of states' rights over Indian rights was set aside but not resolved. In the meantime, Georgia imposed its will over the Cherokee Nation and made the looming possibility of removal a near certainty, since the executive branch of the federal government, President Jackson, supported their states' rights cause.

TERM PAPER SUGGESTIONS

1. Explore the ramifications of tribal entities being defined as "domestic dependent nations." How was sovereignty affected and/or adjusted due to this ruling and characterization?

2. Investigate the role of states' rights in this court proceeding. How was state power enhanced, and how was Indian tribal power diminished?

3. What would be the overall problem of having large Indian nations, considered domestic or otherwise, within state boundaries?

4. Determine whether the discovery of gold and the hunger for Cherokee land and improvements on that land played a role in Georgia's desire to have the Cherokee removed.

5. Even though the Cherokee Nation in Georgia had a land base that was within national and state boundaries, they were still considered a foreign nation, albeit a domestic foreign nation, and therefore were legally not part of the United States but separate and within its boundaries. Explore the reasons for these legal distinctions.

6. What does military might have to do with the way power is exerted over an Indian nation that has long since lost its military power or even will? Did the Cherokees have much choice? Could they have won the legal battle if circumstances were different?

ALTERNATIVE TERM PAPER SUGGESTIONS

1. Imagine you are a tribal leader faced with removal. Write an appeal to the houses of Congress to end the pressure for your tribe's removal. What rhetorical forms (for example, an emotional appeal or angry argument) would you use, and what would be most effective?

2. Imagine you are an Indian in support of removal because you understand that the removal is inevitable and you know that early compliance would garner a less-dramatic socioeconomic hardship. How would you argue this point to your people, and where would you find a forum?

SUGGESTED SOURCES

Primary Sources

"*Cherokee Nation v. Georgia,* 30 U.S. (5 Pet.) 1. (1831)." http://www.pbs.org/ weta/thewest/resources/archives/two/cherokee.htm. A reader-friendly text of Chief Justice John Marshall's majority opinion of the case.

Erbash, Jennifer. "The Cherokee Removal." http://lincoln.lib.niu.edu/teachers/ lesson5-cherokee.html. Lesson plan with links to primary sources: Jackson's first and second annual messages, the debate speeches of Senators Forsyth and Sprague, the "Report of the Committee on Indian Affairs and Speech of Robert Adams," and "Memorial of the Cherokee Indians and Cherokee Address."

Peters, Richard. "The Case of the Cherokee Indians against the State of Georgia: Argued and Determined at the Supreme Court of the United States, January Term, 1831." http://neptune3.galib.uga.edu/ssp/cgi-bin/ tei-natamer-idx.pl?sessionid=7f000001&type=doc&tei2id=PAM016. Digital facsimile of Peters' explanation/interpretation of the ruling of *Cherokee Nation v. Georgia,* with links to photocopies of the actual pages.

Ross, John. "Cherokee Letter Protesting the Treaty of New Echota." http://www .pbs.org/wgbh/aia/part4/4h3083t.html. Chief John Ross's letter to the Senate and House protesting the Cherokee Removal Treaty.

Secondary Sources

Banner, Stuart. *How the Indians Lost Their Land: Law and Power on the Frontier.* Cambridge, MA: Harvard University Press, 2005. Explores all of the cases of the Cherokee to prevent removal and the loss of their ancestral lands.

Deloria, Vine, Jr., and David E. Wilkins. *Tribes, Treaties, and Constitutional Tribulations.* Austin, TX: University of Texas Press, 2000. Explores the relationship between the U.S. Constitution and the federal government and Indian tribes and their governments.

Garrison, Tim A. *The Legal Ideology of Removal: The Southern Judiciary and the Sovereignty of Native American Nations.* Athens, GA: University of Georgia Press, 2002. Examines the role of state courts in the Indian removal process to make a states' rights issue rather than a moral or ethical issue of sympathy for Indians.

Guttmann, Allen. *States' Rights and Indian Removal: The Cherokee Nation v. the State of Georgia.* Lexington, MA: D.C. Heath, 1965. Critical thinking text designed for high school classrooms; only 14 pages.

Keller, Christian B. "Philanthropy Betrayed: Thomas Jefferson, the Louisiana Purchase, and the Origins of Federal Indian Removal Policy." *Proceedings of the American Philosophical Society* 144, no. 1 (March 2000): 39–66. Links the Louisiana Purchase to arguments for Indian removal east of the Mississippi because land became available for that purpose with the purchase.

Norgen, Jill. *Cherokee Cases: Two Landmark Federal Decisions in the Fight for Sovereignty.* New York: McGraw-Hill, 1996. Reprint, Norman, OK: University of Oklahoma Press, 2003. Covers the two cases following *Johnson v. M'Intosh.*

Perdue, Theda, and Michael D. Green. *The Cherokee Removal: A Brief History with Documents.* New York: Bedford Books of St. Martin's Press, 1995. Many primary source documents are used to tell the story of Cherokee removal.

Prucha, Francis Paul. *American Indian Treaties: The History of a Political Anomaly.* Berkeley, CA: University of California Press, 1994. A general history of U.S. and Indian treaty relationships.

Prucha, Francis Paul. *Documents of United States Indian Policy.* 3rd ed. Lincoln, NE: University of Nebraska Press, 2000. Provides only the parts pertinent to Indians and Indian tribes. See item 8, page 9, for the "Northwest Ordinance."

Robertson, Lindsay G. *Conquest by Law: How the Discovery of America Dispossessed Indigenous Peoples of Their Lands.* New York: Oxford University Press, 2005. *Johnson v. M'Intosh* is center stage, because it set the foundation by defining the "discovery doctrine," for the legal taking of Indian land.

Sherrow, Victoria. *Cherokee Nation v. Georgia: Native American Rights.* Berkeley Heights, NJ: Enslow Publishers, 1997. Short summary meant for young readers.

Wilkins, David E. *American Indian Sovereignty and the U.S. Supreme Court: The Masking of Justice.* Austin, TX: University of Texas Press, 1997. Detailed analysis of 15 U.S. Supreme Court cases involving Native Americans, including *Johnson v. M'Intosh.*

Williams, David. *The Georgia Gold Rush: Twenty-Niners, Cherokees, and Gold Fever.* Columbia, SC: University of South Carolina Press, 2003. In part, explores the social/political impact on the Cherokees due to the Gold Rush of 1829.

World Wide Web

"Andrew Jackson and the Indian Removal Act." http://www.historynet.com/andrew-jackson-and-the-indian-removal-act.htm. Short historical description.

"The Marshall Cases." http://www.let.rug.nl/~usa/D/1801-1825/marshallcases/mar03.htm. Brief summary of the merits of the case and whether the Indian tribes meet the definition of foreign state.

Multimedia Source

The West. Dir. Stephen Ives. Public Broadcasting Service, 1996. 4 DVDs. 750 minutes. "Episode Two, 1806 to 1848" covers *Cherokee Nation v. Georgia.*

40. *Worcester v. Georgia* (1832)

In *Worcester v. Georgia,* Chief Justice John Marshall delivered an opinion that denied the state of Georgia authority and jurisdiction over the regulation of "trade and intercourse" between U.S. citizens and members of the Cherokee Nation because, according to the court, "treaties and laws of the United States contemplate the Indian territory as completely separated from that of the states; and provide that all intercourse with them shall be carried on exclusively by the government of the union." Further, Chief Justice Marshall ruled that the "the Cherokee Nation, then, is a distinct community occupying its own territory in which the laws of Georgia can have no force. The whole intercourse between the United States and this nation, is, by our constitution and laws, vested in the government of the United States." The Cherokee Nation was still ruled as a "domestic dependent nation," but the opinion placed them outside of the power of the states, at least in theory. More importantly, the court recognized and upheld tribal sovereignty, lands held in common, and self-determination, at least under the paternal oversight of the federal government. The case came before the Supreme Court in a "writ of error" and centered on Georgia's arrest of Samuel Worcester, a missionary to the Cherokee, for living and working in the Cherokee Nation without the state's permission—but the real reason was to stop Worcester from helping the Cherokees to resist removal and state law. The opinion was a major victory for the Cherokees, but it did not stop the Indian removal process. Unfortunately for the Cherokee, the executive branch of government favored states' rights and sent the army to help Georgians evict the Indians from the state under the authority of the Indian Removal Act of 1830. Very soon after, a minority faction of the Cherokee Nation signed the Cherokee removal treaty of New Echota, 1835.

TERM PAPER SUGGESTIONS

1. Compare the three court cases: *Johnson v. M'Intosh* (1823), *Cherokee Nation v. Georgia* (1831), and *Worcester v. Georgia* (1832).
2. Explain how *Worcester v. Georgia* was beneficial to American Indian tribes and tribal sovereignty.
3. How do states, such as Georgia, exert their power over Indian nations within their state borders? And how far can they go?
4. Study the struggle between the federal judicial, legislative, and executive branches of government in this court case. How can the president refuse to enforce the Supreme Court's ruling, and what recourse can the Supreme Court pursue? What was the role of the legislative branch in the overall controversy and debate over Indian affairs, laws, and treaties?
5. Write a paper that examines the aftermath of the *Worcester v. Georgia* opinion. Include the political tension and the removal of the Cherokee Indians.
6. Despite major setbacks and injustice, such as forced removal, *Worcester v. Georgia* has become the tool that American Indians have used to combat state and local intrusion on tribal sovereignty and self-determination. Why?

ALTERNATIVE TERM PAPER SUGGESTIONS

1. Create an electronic time line and cause-effect diagram of the various Supreme Court cases leading up to the removal of the Cherokee from Georgia.
2. As a member of the Cherokee Nation, write a letter to President Jackson urging his enforcement of the Supreme Court ruling in *Worcester v. Georgia* by using constitutional principles as the basis of your argument.

SUGGESTED SOURCES

Primary Sources

Ross, John. "Cherokee Letter Protesting the Treaty of New Echota." http://www.pbs.org/wgbh/aia/part4/4h3083t.html. Chief John Ross's letter to the Senate and House protesting the Cherokee Removal Treaty.

"*Worcester v. Georgia,* 31 U.S. (6 Pet.) 515, 8 L.Ed. 483 (1832)." http://www.utulsa.edu/law/classes/rice/ussct_cases/WORCESTER_V_GEORGIA_1832.HTM. Complete text of the complaint, the writ, and the opinions.

"*Worcester v. Georgia,* 1832." http://www.civics-online.org/library/formatted/texts/worcester.html. Digital facsimile of *Worcester v. Georgia,* 31 U.S. (6 Pet.) 515 (1832).

Secondary Sources

Banner, Stuart. *How the Indians Lost Their Land: Law and Power on the Frontier.* Cambridge, MA: Harvard University Press, 2005. Explores all of the cases of the Cherokee to prevent removal and the loss of their ancestral lands.

Deloria, Vine, Jr., and David E. Wilkins. *Tribes, Treaties, and Constitutional Tribulations.* Austin, TX: University of Texas Press, 2000. Explores the relationship between the U.S. Constitution and the federal government and Indian tribes and their governments.

Garrison, Tim A. *The Legal Ideology of Removal: The Southern Judiciary and the Sovereignty of Native American Nations.* Athens, GA: University of Georgia Press, 2002. Examines the role of state courts in the Indian removal process to make a states' rights issue rather than a moral or ethical issue of sympathy for Indians.

Gold, Susan Dudley. *Worcester v. Georgia: American Indian Rights.* New York: Benchmark Books, 2008. Short summary meant for young readers.

Guttmann, Allen. *States' Rights and Indian Removal: The Cherokee Nation v. the State of Georgia.* Lexington, MA: D.C. Heath, 1965. Critical thinking text designed for high school classrooms; only 14 pages.

Norgen, Jill. *Cherokee Cases: Two Landmark Federal Decisions in the Fight for Sovereignty.* New York: McGraw-Hill, 1996. Reprint, Norman, OK: University of Oklahoma Press, 2003. Covers the two cases following *Johnson v. M'Intosh.*

Perdue, Theda, and Michael D. Green. *The Cherokee Removal: A Brief History with Documents.* New York: Bedford Books of St. Martin's Press, 1995. Many primary source documents are used to tell the story of Cherokee removal.

Prucha, Francis Paul. *American Indian Treaties: The History of a Political Anomaly.* Berkeley, CA: University of California Press, 1994. A general history of United States and Indian treaty relationships.

Prucha, Francis Paul. *Documents of United States Indian Policy.* 3rd ed. Lincoln, NE: University of Nebraska Press, 2000. Provides only the parts pertinent to Indians and Indian tribes. See item 8, page 9, for the "Northwest Ordinance."

Wilkins, David E. *American Indian Sovereignty and the U.S. Supreme Court: The Masking of Justice.* Austin, TX: University of Texas Press, 1997. Detailed analysis of 15 U.S. Supreme Court cases involving Native Americans, including *Johnson v. M'Intosh.*

Williams, David. *The Georgia Gold Rush: Twenty-Niners, Cherokees, and Gold Fever.* Columbia, SC: University of South Carolina Press, 2003. In part, explores the social/political impact on the Cherokees due to the gold rush of 1829.

World Wide Web

"The Marshall Cases." http://www.let.rug.nl/~usa/D/1801-1825/marshallcases/mar03.htm. Brief summary of the merits of the case and whether the Indian tribes meet the definition of foreign state.

"*Worcester v. Georgia* (1832)." http://www.georgiaencyclopedia.org/nge/Article.jsp?id=h-2720. Short but well-documented summary of pertinent facts of the case.

"*Worcester v. Georgia,* 1832." http://www.oyez.org/cases/1792-1850/1832/1832_0/. Summary of the "facts of the case," the "question," and the "conclusion." Nice and concise.

Multimedia Source

The West. Dir. Stephen Ives. Public Broadcasting Service, 1996. 4 DVDs. 750 minutes. "Episode Two, 1806 to 1848" covers *Worcester v. Georgia.*

41. Black Hawk War (1832)

As the Indians of the southeast sought diplomatic and legal avenues of resistance, some of the Indians of Illinois and Wisconsin, under the leadership of Black Hawk, decided to resist militarily. At the time of the Treaty with the Sauk and Foxes of 1804, the treaty signers, including Black Hawk, had not understood they were ceding 50 million acres of land to the federal government, and they believed they were tricked into doing so. Angered by this misunderstanding, Black Hawk fought for the British in the War of 1812, and he became a staunch militant when Sac/Fox land was opened for public sale. The response from federal officials was to urge Indians to remove themselves and settle on the western bank of the Mississippi River. Around 1829, returning from a hunting trip, Black Hawk found a white family living in his lodge located on his ancestral land. White settlers often squatted on Indian land, even taking residence in the Indians' cabins and lodgings when the Indian land owners were hunting or traveling, which Indians often did during the summer and fall. By 1832, he and other militant Sac and Fox, known as the "British Band," decided to return to the village of White Cloud, as a sign of resistance and to join the followers of the Winnebago Prophet. The British Band's decision to join the Winnebago Prophet and their movement eastward started the Black Hawk War of 1832, which lasted until Black Hawk was defeated at the Battle of Wisconsin Heights. Soon after the battle and after a frantic retreat and betrayal, Black Hawk was captured on August 8 and was imprisoned. In the aftermath, the Sac and Fox were forced to sign a removal treaty and to cede even more land (Treaty with the Sauk and Foxes of 1832). Soon after, they were removed to lands west of the Mississippi, and after a year in prison, Black Hawk joined them.

TERM PAPER SUGGESTIONS

1. Examine the mistrust Black Hawk would have for the diplomatic and political avenue of recourse for grievances with the Americans.
2. Write an essay about young Abraham Lincoln's involvement in the Black Hawk War and his motives for joining the Illinois militia.
3. During the early eighteenth century, the U.S. government used treaties with Indians to accommodate the American settlers' desire for land. How could Indians endure such a policy of encroachment without reacting with violence? Use the Black Hawk War as an example.
4. How could an over reaction by Indians play into the goals of a policy such as that explained above? Remember that most Indian people, even the majority of Sauks and Foxes, were peaceful and tried to cooperate and accommodate, but they suffered the fate of militants.
5. Explore the effects of the war on Indian people of Illinois and Wisconsin.
6. Explore and report on Black Hawk's life after his release from prison and his celebrity and participation in Wild West shows. Why would Americans want to see him or meet him? What was the fascination?

ALTERNATIVE TERM PAPER SUGGESTIONS

1. Imagine yourself as Abraham Lincoln enlisting and fighting in the Black Hawk War of 1830. Write a diary that would reflect your Indian policies when you become president.

2. Make a Microsoft PowerPoint presentation with slides that include pictures and sketches of a *Wild West Show* featuring Black Hawk.

SUGGESTED SOURCES

Primary Sources

"Bibliography of Published Primary Sources on the Black Hawk War of 1832." http://lincoln.lib.niu.edu/blackhawk/bibliography.html. Eighty-seven primary source documents relevant and related to the Black Hawk War of 1832, including treaties, laws, and diaries and journals of firsthand accounts, with links to the digital facsimiles.

"The Black Hawk War: Original Documents and Other Primary Sources." http://www.wisconsinhistory.org/turningpoints/tp%2D012/. An easy-to-use site of primary sources, including "views" of battlefields.

Kennedy, Gerald, ed. *Life of Black Hawk.* London: Penguin Books, 2008. New edition of Black Hawk's autobiography with an introduction by Kennedy, suggestions for further reading, and a map of the war. The digital text of the original biography can be found in the above "Bibliography of Primary Sources," above.

Whitney, Ellen M., ed. *The Black Hawk War, 1831–1832.* 3 vols. Springfield, IL: State Historical Society, 1970. Collected primary sources on the Black Hawk War.

Secondary Sources

Hagan, William T. *The Sac and Fox Indians.* Norman, OK: University of Oklahoma Press, 1958. Describes the Black Hawk War, before and after.

Jackson, Donald, ed. *Black Hawk: An Autobiography.* Urbana, IL: University of Illinois Press, 1955. Readable biography with an informative introduction.

Jung, Patrick. J. *The Black Hawk War of 1832.* Norman, OK: University of Oklahoma Press, 2007. Explores the efforts of Black Hawk to form a pan-Indian alliance in the same manner as Tecumseh and with the same results.

Nichols, Roger L. *Black Hawk and the Warrior's Path.* Wheeling, IL: Harlan Davidson, Inc., 1992. Scholarly examination of Black Hawk and the Sauk and Fox.

Prucha, Francis Paul. *The Great Father: The United States Government and the American Indians.* 2 vols. Lincoln, NE: University of Nebraska Press, 1984. General summary of federal Indian policy.

Stark, William F. *Along the Black Hawk Trail.* Sheboygan, WI: Zimmerman Press, 1984. Examines the ground where major battle occurred.

Trask, Jerry A. *Black Hawk: The Battle for the Heart of America.* New York: Holt Paperbacks, 2007. A military cause and effect analysis of the war.

World Wide Web

"The Black Hawk War, 1832." Wisconsin Historical Society, 2008. http://www.wisconsinhistory.org/teachers/lessons/secondary/blackhawk.asp. Summary and lesson plan linked to short primary source excerpts of the accounts of Black Hawk, Henry Dodge, and General Atkinson.

"The Black Hawk War of 1832." http://lincoln.lib.niu.edu/blackhawk/. A mega site for information on the Black Hawk War.

Thwaites, Reuben Gold. "The Black Hawk War (1832)." http://www.multied.com/Documents/Blackhawk.html. A good general summary of the war.

Multimedia Source

"The Black Hawk War of 1832." http://lincoln.lib.niu.edu/blackhawk/video.html. Twenty-one short videos ("Real Player," "Media Player," or "QuickTime Player") of the Black Hawk War of 1832. This site also has an image gallery of significant personages and a detailed map of the Indian villages, forts, battles, and routes of armies.

42. Cherokee Trail of Tears (1838–1839)

In 1830, President Andrew Jackson signed the Indian Removal Act, which called for the removal of Indians from east of the Mississippi to lands west of the Mississippi set aside for that purpose. In response, the Cherokee Nation attempted, through the U.S. Supreme Court, to prevent Georgia from extinguishing title to their lands within the state and to prevent the federal government from removing them to lands west of the Mississippi. Despite rulings that upheld Cherokee title to their own land, their tribal sovereignty, and their treaty rights, and, despite many delays due to the court cases and other stratagems, the Cherokee were still removed, because of President Jackson's states' rights stance and his unwillingness to enforce the rulings of the Supreme Court. Still the president required the signing of a "removal treaty," which effectively split the Cherokee Nation into two factions: the minority pro-treaty faction, led by Stand Watie (a prominent Cherokee land owner and later a Brigadier General in the army of the Confederate States of America), Elias Boudinot (who led the party that signed the Cherokee removal Treaty of New Echota and was former editor of the *Cherokee Phoenix*), and Major Ridge (a prominent Cherokee land owner and father of Elias Boudinot), and the majority faction, who opposed removal, led by John Ross (the first elected leader of the Cherokee Nation). Jackson's treaty negotiators ignored the majority factions and opened discussion with the "treaty party," which led to the signing of the Treaty of New Echota, December 29, 1835. By 1838, many Cherokee people refused to be removed, so President Martin Van Buren, Jackson's handpicked successor, assigned General Winfield Scott the task of implementing their removal by force of arms; he accomplished this task by searching them out, confining them to "camps," and then marching them west. An estimated 15,000 Cherokees were marched 1,200 miles, by land and water, and because many hundreds of the Cherokees who died and suffered, these routes became known as the Trail of Tears.

TERM PAPER SUGGESTIONS

1. Examine Georgians' arguments for Cherokee removal. How did President Jackson support their cause? Did land and/or gold play a role?
2. Examine the anti-removal faction of the Cherokee Nation, presenting their best arguments for their case. Be sure to include the reasons they failed.
3. Detail the stance of the "treaty party" in their advocacy for removal. Why were they designated the "official" representatives of the Cherokee Nation, despite that they were a minority faction?
4. Explore the Treaty of New Echota, December 29, 1835. As compared to earlier English and U.S. treaties, what is different about this treaty and what is the same?
5. Investigate the role of General Scott and his military solution to the removal of the recalcitrant Cherokees.
6. Examine the voices of the Cherokee people who experienced the Trail of Tears.

ALTERNATIVE TERM PAPER SUGGESTIONS

1. Organize a mock debate between the pro-removal Cherokees and the anti-removal Cherokees.

2. Using the interactive maps available, the images of major Cherokee historical figures, and selected passages from eyewitness accounts, present a multimedia slide show or Web site of the hardships of forced removal.

SUGGESTED SOURCES

Primary Sources

"General Winfield Scott's Address to the Cherokee Nation (May 10, 1838)." http://www.cviog.uga.edu/Projects/gainfo/scottadd.htm. Digital facsimile of General Scott's address urging the Cherokee to cooperate before he and his army forced their removal.

"Indian Removal Act." http://www.civics-online.org/library/formatted/texts/indian_act.html. Full seven-section digital text of the act on one page.

Perdue, Theda, ed. *Cherokee Editor: The Writings of Elias Boudinot.* Athens, GA: University of Georgia Press, 1996. Collection of editorials of the famous editor who advocated for voluntary removal to the Indian Territory.

Ross, John. "Cherokee Letter Protesting the Treaty of New Echota." http://www.pbs.org/wgbh/aia/part4/4h3083t.html. Chief John Ross's letter to the Senate and House protesting the Cherokee Removal Treaty.

Rozema, Vicki. *Voices from the Trail of Tears.* Winston-Salem, NC: John F. Blair, 2003. A collection of primary sources describing the events leading up to, during, and after Indian removal.

"Treaty of New Echota, December, 29, 1835." http://www.cviog.uga.edu/Projects/gainfo/newechot.htm. Digital facsimile of the treaty.

Secondary Sources

Ehle, John. *Trail of Tears: The Rise and Fall of the Cherokee Nation.* New York: Anchor Books, 1988. Examines, some say in biased terms, the Boudinot, Ridge, and Watie faction or "treaty party," Cherokees who favored and advocated for removal.

Jahoda, Gloria. *Trail of Tears: The Story of the American Indian Removals, 1813–1855.* New York: Wing Books, 1995. A narrative overview of Indian removal of the Five Civilized Tribes, the name applied to the five tribes (Cherokee, Choctaw, Creek, Chickasaw, and Seminole) in the South who attempted assimilation into Western civilization and accommodation with neighboring white settlers in order to continue to live and thrive on their ancestral lands.

Johnston, Carolyn. *Cherokee Women in Crisis: Trail of Tears, Civil War, and Allotment, 1838–1907.* Tuscaloosa, AL: University of Alabama Press, 2003.

Examines the changing role and status of women in Cherokee women starting with removal.

McLoughlin, William G. *After the Trail of Tears: The Cherokees' Struggle for Sovereignty, 1839–1880.* Chapel Hill, NC: University of North Carolina Press, 1993. Tells the effects of forced removal and the trauma of establishing sovereignty after the Cherokee reached Oklahoma.

Perdue, Theda. *The Cherokee Nation and the Trail of Tears.* New York: Viking, 2007. Places Cherokee removal within a larger ethnographic and historical context of Cherokee history since first contact.

Perdue, Theda. *Rising From the Ashes: The Cherokee Phoenix as an Ethno Historical Source.* Durham, NC: Duke University Press, 1977. Provides analysis of the newspaper, its content, contributors, and circulation.

Perdue, Theda, and Michael D. Green. *The Cherokee Removal: A Brief History with Documents.* New York: Bedford Books of St. Martin's Press, 1995. Many primary source documents are used to tell the story of the Cherokee removal.

Wilkins, Thurman. *Cherokee Tragedy: The Ridge Family and the Decimation of a People.* Norman, OK: University of Oklahoma Press, 1986. Examines the role of this family as the leaders of the pro-removal (pro-treaty) faction and subsequent consequences.

World Wide Web

"Cherokee Removal—The Trail Where They Cried: *nu na hi du na tlo hi lu i.*" http://www.powersource.com/cocinc/history/trail.htm. Comprehensive summary of the story of the Trail of Tears, from early exploration to removal.

"The Trail of Tears." http://ngeorgia.com/history/nghisttt.html. Provides brief summary and links to relevant historical entries.

"Trail of Tears." http://www.42explore2.com/trailoftears.htm. Comprehensive links page of the most valuable Web sources on the Trail of Tears, including primary sources and teacher resources, grades 6–12.

"Trail of Tears." http://www.cherokeemuseum.org/html/collections_tot.html. Interactive map of Cherokee removal.

"Trail of Tears." http://www.nativeamericans.com/TrailofTears2.htm. Provides a sensitive summary and has many valuable links to relevant information.

"Trail of Tears." http://www.peaknet.net/~aardvark/. Summary and links page regarding Choctaw removal from the Choctaws' point of view.

"Trail of Tears National Historic Trail." http://www.nps.gov/trte/. Provides information, an interactive map, and research links.

Multimedia Sources

500 Nations. Columbia House, 1994. 4 DVDs. 49 minutes per episode in an eight-part documentary series. Volume 6, "Removal," is the relevant episode.

Martin, Ken. "Cherokee Images." 1996. http://cherokeehistory.com/image1a .html. Images and brief summaries of major Cherokee historical figures.

Trail of Tears: Cherokee Legacy. Rich-Heape Films, 2006. DVD. 120 minutes. Documentary telling the tragic story of the Cherokee removal.

43. Seminole Wars of 1817–1858

The First Seminole War involved General Andrew Jackson and the United States and the annexation and the pacification of Florida at the end of the War of 1812. With the power and the authority of the Indian Removal Act of 1839, a primary objective of the Second Seminole War was to remove the Seminole tribes residing in Florida to the Indian Territory. The Third Seminole War was a continuation of the Second War. In the First Seminole War, 1817–1818, Andrew Jackson's campaign destroyed Seminole villages near present-day Tallahassee and took St. Marks, a Spanish town and fort, despite Spanish sovereignty. When the Spanish ceded Florida to the United States, Jackson avoided an international diplomatic crisis, but his actions opened Florida to American settlers, forcing the Seminoles to seek refuge in the Florida Everglades. After 1830, the U.S. agents of the Indian Removal Act began to coerce the Seminole into signing a removal treaty, but most of the Seminole refused, killing those who favored signing. Osceola was named war chief, and the Second Seminole War, 1835–1842, became a seven-year armed resistance to removal that resulted in numerous skirmishes and small fights but no major battles. In the end, Osceola was betrayed and imprisoned at Fort Moultrie, South Carolina, where he died soon after. Despite this setback and the fact that many Seminoles were forcibly removed, Osceola's subordinates, Alligator and Chief Boleck, continued to resist, but the United States, due to the cost of the war, ceased military operations. The war broke out again seven years later when Chief Boleck, incited by American encroachments on his land, started to raid and skirmish until he acquiesced and negotiated a cash settlement, which ended with his removal and the end to the Third Seminole War, 1855–1858. However, many Seminole were never removed, and descendants remain in Florida to this day.

TERM PAPER SUGGESTIONS

1. Examine Andrew Jackson's campaign against the Seminole in the First War. Was his purpose greater than simply the pacification of the Seminole Indians?

2. Discuss why the Seminoles refused to move west even though they were promised money and lands. Why did they not want to leave Florida?

3. Analyze the economic impact that the Seminole Wars had on the U.S. Treasury. Why were Indian wars so expensive? Does this explain why the United States was always eager to negotiate monetary settlements with Indian people?

4. Explore Osceola's tactics. What were his military advantages and what were his military weaknesses? How did he make the best of his situation?

5. Discuss how the lives of Seminoles changed after the Seminole Wars and also how the U.S. government's point of view changed towards the Seminoles during the postwar period.

6. Why did the United States want to remove the Seminoles in the first place? What were the United States's purpose and goals?

ALTERNATIVE TERM PAPER SUGGESTIONS

1. Create a mock trial where Osceola is charged with an illegal war of aggression against the United States.

2. Create a mock trial where General and later President Jackson is charged with illegally forcing Seminoles to be removed to the Indian Territory and the needless death of many tribal members.

SUGGESTED SOURCES

Primary Sources

Bemrose, John. *Reminiscences of the Second Seminole War.* Tampa, FL: University of Tampa Press, 2001. Reprint of an eyewitness account of the war from the perspective of a U.S. Army soldier.

"Indian Removal: Extract from Andrew Jackson's Seventh Annual Message to Congress." http://www.pbs.org/weta/thewest/resources/archives/two/removal.htm. Digital facsimile regarding the necessity of Indian removal, 1835.

Letter Concerning the Outbreak of Hostilities in the Third Seminole War, 1856. (Governor, State Governors' Incoming Correspondence, 1857–1888, Series S 577) http://www.floridamemory.com/FloridaHighlights/Seminole_War/Seminole_War_text.cfm. Digital facsimile of the text of the letter with scanned images of the original.

Secondary Sources

Covington, James W. *The Seminoles of Florida.* Gainesville, FL: University of Florida Press, 1993. A comprehensive narrative cultural history of the Seminole tribe.

Elliott, Charles W. *Winfield Scott, the Soldier and the Man.* New York: MacMillan and Co., 1937. Reprint, Cranbury, NJ: Scholars Bookshelf, 2006. A biography of General Scott with detailed information on his campaign in Florida.

Hamilton, Holman. *Zachary Taylor, Soldier of the Republic.* New York: The Bobbs Merrill Co., 1941. Biography of Taylor's life and military career that provides detailed account of his battle at Lake Okeechobee and his command of the Florida theater.

Knetsch, Joe. *Florida's Seminole Wars.* Charleston, SC: Arcadia Publishing, 2003. General summary/overview of the three Seminole Wars.

MacCauley, Clay. *The Seminole Indians of Florida.* Charleston, SC: Bibliobazaar, 2008. A good general overview and history of the Seminole of Florida.

Mahon, John K. *History of the Second Seminole War, 1835–1842,* revised edition. Gainesville, FL: University of Florida Press, 1990. Detailed history of the Second Seminole War.

Meltzer, Milton. *Hunted like a Wolf: The Story of the Seminole War.* Sarasota, FL: Pineapple Press, 2004. A detailed narrative account that includes coverage of Black Seminoles, of the Second Seminole War.

Missall, John, and Mary Lou Missall. *The Seminole Wars: America's Longest Indian Conflict.* Gainesville, FL: University Press of Florida, 2004. Covers the wars 1817 to 1858, which includes the wars resisting removal.

Mulroy, Kevin. *The Seminole Freedmen.* Norman, OK: University of Oklahoma Press, 2007. Covers the history of the Black Seminole.

Walton, George H. *Fearless and Free: the Seminole Indian War, 1835–1842.* Indianapolis, IN: Bobbs-Merrill, 1977. Military history of the Seminole wars.

World Wide Web

Hawk, Robert. "The Second Seminole War, 1835–1842." http://www.floridaguard.army.mil/history/read.asp?did=1300. A concise and detailed summary of the war.

"Seminole Indian War." http://www.jupiter.fl.us/HistoryWeb/KidsHistory/Seminole-Indian-War.cfm. Excellent brief summary of the wars with expandable visual data of people and places.

"The Seminole Wars." http://fcit.usf.edu/FLORIDA/lessons/sem_war/sem_war1.htm. Brief overview of the three wars that includes a map.

"USA Seminole War 1835–1842." http://www.onwar.com/aced/data/sierra/seminole1835.htm. Statistical database covering combat forces, combat losses, and expenditures.

White, John C. "American Military Strategy in the Second Seminole War." http://www.globalsecurity.org/military/library/report/1995/WJC.htm. Entire digital essay of a master's thesis with extensive footnotes and bibliography.

Multimedia Source

Seminoles: Indians of the Southeast. New Dimension Media, 2004. VHS. 10 minutes. Explains why Chief Osceola and his followers fought against the U.S. Army to retain their lands. From the Great Native American Nations Classroom Series.

44. Stand Watie, Cherokee, Fights for the Confederacy in the Civil War (1861–1865)

Born into the Cherokee Nation of Georgia in 1806, Stand Watie, by the time he was a young man, had to contend with President Andrew Jackson's Indian Removal Act of 1830. Although Watie converted to Christianity and believed in assimilation, he advocated the signing of the Cherokee removal treaty of New Echota in 1835, because he knew that President Andrew Jackson and his white Georgian neighbors were determined at any cost to remove the Cherokees west to Indian Territory. By signing, he thought to prevent hostilities and to negotiate money for Georgian Cherokees' lands and property, for transportation, and to help them settle in Oklahoma. In addition to generating a blood feud where every leader of the "treaty party" was murdered except for Watie, the result of his advocacy was to split the Cherokee Nation into two factions: one that favored removal and one that opposed. Watie and his followers signed the removal treaty and went west, while the opponents to removal were forced westward in what would be called the Trail of Tears. By 1861, Watie and his faction were firm supporters of the Confederacy, while John Ross and faction were pro-Union. Watie soon signed an alliance with the Confederate States of America (CSA), and he organized the Cherokee Mounted Rifles, who would fight in many major trans-Mississippi Civil War battles, engagements, and skirmishes, such as Wilson's Creek and

Pea Ridge. Watie himself would rise to the rank of brigadier general in the CSA; he would not only have to fight Union soldiers but those Cherokees under Ross who had joined the Union side. Nearly three months after the signing of General Robert E. Lee's surrender at Appomattox Court House that ended the U.S. Civil War, Stand Watie surrendered in June of 1865, the last Confederate general to surrender.

TERM PAPER SUGGESTIONS

1. Explore why many Cherokees, like John Ross, would find Stand Watie and his friends traitors to the Cherokee Nation, and explore why the Watie faction believed they were not.
2. Write on the influences that Christianity and assimilation had on the Boudinot, Ridge, and Watie faction that they would favor removal and cooperation with southern Whites.
3. Examine the reasons why Stand Watie and his faction would side with the Confederacy.
4. Analyze the role that Stand Watie and his Confederate Indians served for the CSA and the reasons that the CSA would tolerate their participation. Were they not enemies at one time?
5. Explain the effects of the Civil War on the Cherokee Nation, regardless of side.
6. Explain why Stand Watie was the last Confederate general to surrender.

ALTERNATIVE TERM PAPER SUGGESTIONS

1. Simulate a trial with Microsoft PowerPoint where his own people charge Stand Watie with treason. Present both sides in slide form, including opening/ending arguments, witness testimony, and documents to support each argument.
2. Create a collage of the theme "Brother against Brother," but use images of Cherokee soldiers of the Civil War instead of the usual white Americans to illustrate an alternative view of Indian warriors and status.

SUGGESTED SOURCES

Primary Sources

"In Time & Place: The Cherokee Removal." http://www.intimeandplace.org/ cherokee/reading/removal.html. A comprehensive and interesting time line with links to primary sources.

"Report on a Letter by Stand Watie." http://books.google.com/books?id
    =rdcRAAAAYAAJ&pg=PA36&dq=stand+watie&lr=. Explains what
    Stand Watie and his "treaty party" wanted from the U.S. government.
"Treaty of New Echota, December 29, 1835." http://www.cviog.uga.edu/
    Projects/gainfo/newechot.htm. Digital facsimile of the treaty.

Secondary Sources

Abel, Annie Heloise. *The American Indian and the end of the Confederacy, 1863–
    1865.* 1925. Reprint, Lincoln, NE: University of Nebraska Press, 1993.
    Explores the plight of the Five Civilized Tribes (the Cherokees,
    Chickasaws, Choctaws, Creeks, and Seminoles) in the Indian Territory
    during the American Civil War.
Abel, Annie Heloise. *The American Indian in the Civil War, 1862–1865.* Lincoln,
    NE: University of Nebraska Press, 1992. Thorough military history of
    American Indians in the Civil War.
Confer, Clarissa W. *The Cherokee in the Civil War.* Norman, OK: University of
    Oklahoma Press, 2007. A scholarly examination of the effects of the Civil
    War on the Cherokee Nation regardless of the side individuals served.
Cottrell, Steve. *Civil War in the Indian Territory.* Gretna, LA: Pelican, 1995.
    A good detailed military history.
Cunningham, Frank. *General Stand Watie's Confederate Indians.* Norman, OK:
    University of Oklahoma Press, 1998. Military history of the Cherokee
    Rifles and Stand Watie.
Dale, Edward Evert. "Cherokees in the Confederacy." *The Journal of Southern
    History* 13, no. 2 (May 1947): 159–85. Scholarly essay on the role of
    Indians, especially Cherokee Indians, serving in the CSA.
Franks, Kenneth Arthur. *Stand Watie and the Agony of the Cherokee Nation.*
    Memphis State University Press, 1979. A biography of Stand Watie
    focusing on politics and government and also covers Watie's military
    career.
Harold, Keith. *Rifles for Watie.* New York: HarperCollins, 1957. A well-
    researched fictional account and winner of the Newbery medal.
Hauptman, Laurence M. *Between Two Fires: American Indians in the Civil War.*
    New York: Free Press, 1995. Covers both the southern and northern
    Indian participation in the war.
Josephy, Alvin M., Jr. *The Civil War in the American West.* New York: Vintage, 1993.
    Places the Indian Confederates into the larger context of the Civil War.
Waugh, John C. *Sam Bell Maxey and the Confederate Indians.* Abilene, TX:
    McWhiney Foundation Press, 1998. A military history of the
    Confederate Indians in the trans-Mississippi during the Civil War with

the central focus on General Sam Bell Maxey's relationship with his all-Indian command.

World Wide Web

"A Guide to Cherokee Confederate Military Units, 1861–1865." http://www .thepeoplespaths.net/history/CherConfed.htm. Detailed history with many images and detailed regimental information.

"Cherokee Stand Watie." http://www.historynet.com/cherokee-stand-watie.htm. Detailed summary of the controversies surrounding Watie's life.

Dwyer, John J. "Stand Watie and the Confederate Indians." http://www .lewrockwell.com/orig3/dwyer7.html. Short summary of Watie's career as a Confederate general.

"Stand Watie." http://www.civilwarhome.com/watiebio.htm. Short military biography that cites Watie's Civil War battles.

"Stand Watie." http://www.nativeamericans.com/StandWatie.htm. Covers Indian removal, the Cherokee factionalism, and Civil War histories of Watie with external links to relevant information.

"Stand Watie and Elias Boudinot Family Genealogy." http://www .paulridenour.com/swatie.htm. Includes many interesting photographs as well as images of autographed documents.

Multimedia Source

Indian Warriors: The Untold Story of the Civil War. Dir. Geoffrey Madjea. A&E, 2007. DVD. 50 minutes. Explores the role of Ely Parker, Stand Watie, and other Indians and their involvement in the U.S. Civil War.

45. Dakota Sioux Uprising (1862)

The Dakota Uprising (war or conflict) involved two Dakota tribes, the Mdewakantons and Wahpekutes, who lived along the Minnesota River in southwestern Minnesota, while Wahpetons and Sissetons stayed out of the fight. The causes of the uprising centered on corrupt Indian traders and agents, late annuity payments, and bitterness toward the land cession treaties of 1851 and 1858. Because the Dakota depended on annuities to purchase food and clothing, they began to suffer from starvation, and they demanded food held in agency warehouses to be distributed on credit. The traders, however, wanted cash on delivery: "If they are hungry, let them eat grass." After the traders made their sentiments clear, a series of unfortunate encounters between Dakotas and Whites led to the killing of White settlers. The killing of white settlers led to a full-scale frontier war, where bands of the two Dakota tribes attacked agencies, farms, towns, and forts, killing several hundred more White settlers and forcing some 2,000 refugees to flee to Mankato. Governor Alexander Ramsey dispatched Colonel Henry Sibley to squash the rebellion, which he accomplished by September, and he was able to force the hostile Dakota to surrender. Acting on unclear authority, Sibley immediately put the captured Dakota on trial for murder, and over a six-week period 393 cases were tried, with 323 Dakota convicted and 303 sentenced to death. President Abraham Lincoln reduced the number to 39, and 38 (with 1 reprieved) were hung on December 26 in Mankato, the largest mass execution in U.S. history. In 1863, Congress passed a removal bill, and all of the Dakota were forcibly removed west of the Mississippi.

TERM PAPER SUGGESTIONS

1. Explore the motivations and reasons for the Minnesota Dakota to rebel.
2. Unknown to the participants, the annuity payments arrived a couple of days too late to prevent the uprising. Investigate the outright refusal of the traders to release their goods to the Dakota when the U.S. government could have guaranteed payment.
3. In the historical record, white settlers have commented on the Dakota people. Write an essay examining their perspectives and views of this tribe of Indian people.
4. According to the U.S. Constitution and Indian treaty rights, discuss the rights of Indians and the right, or lack thereof, of Colonel Sibley to summarily put on trial captured Indian hostiles.
5. Why did President Lincoln reduce the number of executions, and why did he not reprieve them all?
6. Can Indians live side by side with White Americans? What prevents such a solution to this conflict? Explore the pro and cons of the system of reservations and separation between Indians and Whites in the Dakota Uprising example.

ALTERNATIVE TERM PAPER SUGGESTIONS

1. Write a newspaper account of the tragedies inflicted on Whites by Indians during the Dakota Uprising. Study the actual accounts for inspiration.

2. From the point of view of the Dakota, write an appeal for tolerance, reprieve, and forgiveness for the Dakota involved in the uprising, citing corruption and violated treaty rights as supporting evidence to justify such an appeal.

SUGGESTED SOURCES

Primary Sources

Anderson, Gary C., and Alan R. Woolworth. *Through Dakota Eyes: Narrative Accounts of the Minnesota Indian War of 1862.* St. Paul, MN: Minnesota Historical Society Press, 1988. Thirty-six primary source narratives from the Dakota point of view.

"Letter of Colonel Sibley Describing the Battle of Birch Cooley, Sept. 4, 1862." http://www.mnhs.org/library/tips/history_topics/94dakota _sibley01.html. Digital facsimile.

"Light and Shadows of a Long Episcopate." http://www.law.umkc.edu/faculty/ projects/ftrials/dakota/Light&Shadows.html. Pertinent and relevant excerpts from the 1902 book of the same name by Bishop B. Whipple.

"Recollections of the Sioux Massacre of 1862." http://www.wisconsinhistory.org/ dictionary/index.asp?action=view&term_id=10620&term_type_id=3 &term_type_text=Things&letter=S. Archival primary source article.

Secondary Sources

Anderson, Gary C. *Little Crow, Spokesman for the Sioux.* St. Paul, MN: Minnesota Historical Society Press, 1986. A detailed biography of the principal leader of the Dakota during the uprising of 1862.

Bergemann, Kurt D. *Brackett's Battalion: Minnesota Cavalry in the Civil War and Dakota War.* St. Paul, MN: Borealis Books, 2004. Describes the role of this cavalry regiment's suppression of raiding Dakota warriors into Minnesota in 1864.

Carley, Kenneth. *The Dakota War of 1862.* 2nd edition. St. Paul, MN: Minnesota Historical Society Press, 2001. Concise and readable account of the war.

Clodfelter, Michael. *The Dakota War: The United States Army Versus the Sioux, 1862.* Jefferson, NC: McFarland, 2006. Military history of the war (tactics and strategy).

Cox, Hank H. *Lincoln and the Sioux Uprising of 1862.* Cumberland House, 2005. Describes Lincoln's connection to the uprising but follows a tradition of savagism on the part of the author's portrayal of Indians.

Dakota War of 1862. (Dakota Conflict). http://www.mnhs.org/library/tips/ history_topics/94dakota.html. A bibliography page of primary and secondary source materials, with links to some primary source digital collections, including visual sources.

Gilman, Rhoda R. *Henry Hastings Sibley: Divided Heart.* St. Paul, MN: Minnesota Historical Society Press, 2004. Biography of the first governor of Minnesota.

Keenan, Jerry. *The Great Sioux Uprising: Rebellion on the Plains, August–September 1862.* Cambridge, MA: De Capo Press, 2003. Short narrative summary of the war.

Monjeau-Marz, Corinne L. *The Dakota Indian Internment at Fort Snelling, 1862–1864.* Champlin, MN: Prairie Smoke Press, 2005. Tells the story of the hundreds of Dakota who were imprisoned as a result of the uprising of 1862, whether they participated or not.

Nichols, David A. *Lincoln and the Indians: Civil War Policy and Politics.* Champaign, IL: University of Illinois Press, 1978. Reprint, 1999. Detailed treatise of Lincoln's Indian policies that covers the implications of giving the military carte blanche when dealing with hostile Indians.

Schultz, Duane. *Over the Earth I Come: The Great Sioux Uprising of 1862.* New York: St. Martin, 1992. Comprehensive examination of the war and its aftermath.

Swain, Gwenyth. *Little Crow: Leader of the Dakota.* St. Paul, MN: Minnesota Historical Society Press, 2004. Biography of the principal leader of the Dakota during the uprising of 1862, meant for young readers.

World Wide Web

"Dakota Conflict." http://www.rrcnet.org/~historic/. A links site organized within a time line; includes links to the treaties of 1851 and 1858 as well as to local museums and historic sites.

"Dakota (Sioux) Uprising." http://www.mnsu.edu/emuseum/history/ oldmankato/1852-1900/siouxuprising.html. Short summary of the conflict.

"1862 War Site Being Restored." http://news.minnesota.publicradio.org/ features/2003/09/25_steilm_slaughterslough/. A news report on the restoration of one of the major sites of the uprising.

Linder, Douglas. "The Dakota Conflict Trials." http://www.law.umkc.edu/ faculty/projects/ftrials/dakota/Dak_account.html. Thorough description of the Dakota uprising, subsequent trials, and executions.

Multimedia Source

The Dakota Conflict: The Great Sioux Uprising. Dir. Kristen Berg. Twin Cities
Public Television, 1993. VHS. 60 minutes. Radio host Garrison Keillor
and Floyd Red Crow Westerman give an account in English and Dakota,
respectively, from their cultural perspectives.

46. Long Walk of the Navajo (1863–1868)

In 1863, with the help of Kit Carson, famous American frontiersman and
Indian fighter, the U.S. government forcefully removed the Navajo from
their traditional homelands in the Four Corners, the only region in the
United States where four states (Arizona, Colorado, New Mexico, and
Utah) meet, and marched them to New Mexico territory near Fort
Sumner, to what some have described as a concentration camp at Bosque
Redondo. At least 200 Navajo died along the 300-mile trek, which took
18 days to traverse on foot. Eventually 10,000 Navajos were imprisoned
at Bosque Redondo for over five years, in a camp originally designed for
5,000. Conditions were not good for agriculture, and the Navajos suffered from malnutrition. Water and firewood were scarce. The reason
the United States removed the Navajo was due to their frequent raiding
of neighboring Indians, Mexicans, and Americans and because the United
States thought the Navajo were taking advantage of the Civil War to exert
their power. The Navajo were angry over the building of forts and the
additional U.S. acquisition of Navajo land via the Bonneville Treaty of
1858. Most of the Navajo were rounded up and marched to Bosque
Redondo, but those that escaped were hunted and captured by Kit Carson
and his New Mexico volunteers, who fought the escapees for almost a year
until they surrendered and were subsequently marched to Bosque
Redondo in 1864. The Treaty of Bosque Redondo of 1868 returned some
of the Navajo lands and recognized their tribal sovereignty, but only after
years of hardship.

TERM PAPER SUGGESTIONS

1. Explore the reasons and motivations for the United States to remove the
   Navajo from their lands. Was there enough justification for military action?

2. Investigate the invasion of the Confederacy of New Mexico and Arizona and its relation to the Navajo wars. Could the Long Walk have been part of a larger strategic and military plan?

3. Write on the role of Navajo tribal sovereignty. For American Indian tribes, is sovereignty limited?

4. Compare the camp at Bosque Redondo to other similar camps, like the Japanese internment camps of World War II, one of which was situated very close to a Navajo Indian reservation. To what extent can the camp be compared to the German concentration camps of World War II?

5. Explore President Lincoln's Indian policy. How does the Long Walk fit in? (See "Dakota Sioux Uprising [1862]").

6. Analyze the Treaty of Bosque Redondo of 1868 (also called "Treaty Between the United States and the Navajo Tribe") for the intent and purpose. Was it beneficial to the United States and/or the Navajo? Why?

ALTERNATIVE TERM PAPER SUGGESTIONS

1. Create and record a narrative account of the Long Walk from the perspective of a Navajo person and in the manner of Navajo storytelling.

2. Using available maps and images of the actual terrain, create a slide show presentation of the lands actually walked by the Navajos to demonstrate the extent of the forced march.

SUGGESTED SOURCES

Primary Sources

"Historic Documents Related to the U.S.–Navajo Treaty of 1868." http://reta.nmsu.edu/modules/longwalk/lesson/document/index.htm. Primary source links page to proceedings, letters, and the treaty.

Kelly, Lawrence. *Navajo Roundup: Selected Correspondence of Kit Carson's Campaign Against the Navajo, 1863–1865.* Boulder, CO: Pruett Publishing Co. 1970. Primary source collection of documents related to the Long Walk.

Walker, John G., and Oliver L. Shepard. *The Navajo Reconnaissance: A Military Exploration of the Navajo Country in 1859.* Tucson, AZ: Westernlore Press, 1964. A report on the important places and potential resources in the lands of the Navajo.

Secondary Sources

Bailey, Lynn R. *Bosque Redondo: An American Concentration Camp.* Pasadena, CA: Socio-Technical Books, 1970. Details the Long Walk, the wars with the Navajo, Kit Carson, and the squalid living conditions experienced by the Navajos at the camp at Bosque Redondo.

Bailey, Lynn R. *The Long Walk: A History of the Navajo Wars, 1846–1868.* Tucson, AZ: Westernlore Press, 1988. A more detailed scholarly history.

Buel, Crawford R. "The Navajo 'Long Walk': Recollections By Navajos." *The Changing Ways of Southwestern Indians: A Historic Perspective.* Al Schroeder, ed. Glorieta, NM: Rio Grande Press, 1973, 171–88. Navajo oral traditions and recounting of the Long Walk.

Denetdale, Jennifer. *The Long Walk: The Forced Navajo Exile.* New York: Chelsea House Publications, 2007. A short and concise history aimed at ages 9–12.

Dunlay, Thomas. *Kit Carson and the Indians.* Lincoln, NE: University of Nebraska Press, 2005. A balanced account of Carson's life that shows how he could be critical of Indian policy, which mellows his reputation as an ardent Indian hater.

Gordon-McCutchan, R. C., ed. *Kit Carson: Indian Fighter or Indian Killer.* Boulder, CO: University Press of Colorado, 1996. A collection of essays exploring the life of Kit Carson that tries to separate fact from fiction.

Iverson, Peter, and Monty Roessel. *Dine: A History of the Navajos.* Albuquerque, NM: University of New Mexico, 2002. A balanced general history of the Navajo that uses both Navajo oral traditions and archival source material to reveal the truth.

McNitt, Frank. *Navajo Wars: Military Campaigns, Slave Raids, and Reprisals.* Albuquerque, NM: University of New Mexico Press, 1972. A military history.

Roessel, Ruth, ed. *Navajo Stories of the Long Walk Period.* Tsaile, AZ: Navajo Community College Press, 1973. Original oral stories of the Navajo.

Thompson, Gerald. *The Army and the Navajo: The Bosque Redondo Reservation Experiment 1863–1868.* Tucson, AZ: The University of Arizona Press, 1976. Explores the largest Indian reservation ever created, its construction, and its abandonment after five years, as a learning experience for future Indian policymakers.

Trafzer, Clifford. *The Kit Carson Campaign: The Last Great Navajo War.* Norman, OK: University of Oklahoma Press, 1990. Relies on Navajo oral stories and perpetuates the Indian-hating mythology surrounding Kit Carson's life.

World Wide Web

Ackerly, Neal W. "A Navajo Diaspora: The Long Walk to Hwéeldi." http://members.tripod.com/~bloodhound/longwalk.htm. An online detailed digital scholarly essay with maps, statistics, and other relevant data.

"The Long Walk." http://reta.nmsu.edu/modules/longwalk/default.htm. Three-part lesson with interactive image tour, historic documents, and maps.

"The Long Walk of the Navajos: The Emigration of the Navajo Indian to Fort Sumner, New Mexico." http://www.logoi.com/notes/long_walk.html. A short summary accompanied by three short views on the Long Walk from the U.S. perspective.

The Navajo Long Walk: The True Stories of the Residents Inside Canyon De Chelly." http://www.canyondechelly.net/long_walk.html. A short summary followed by texts of oral Navajo history.

"Navajo Long Walk to Bosque Redondo." http://www.legendsofamerica.com/NA-NavajoLongWalk.html. A short description with links to visual images and data.

Sharp, Jay W. "Desert Trails: The Long Walk of the Navajos." http://www.desertusa.com/mag03/trails/trails09.html. Although meant as a travel guide, this essay summarizes the event very well and it includes a map, period photographs, and recent color photographs of prominent features.

Multimedia Source

Burnett, John. "The Navajo Nation's Own 'Trail of Tears.'" http://www.npr.org/templates/story/story.php?storyId=4703136. An *All Things Considered* radio report that describes the long walk to Bosque Redondo in 1866.

47. Ely S. Parker's U.S. Military Career and Role as Commissioner of Indian Affairs (1863–1871)

Born in 1828 on the Tonawanda Seneca Reservation of New York State, Ely S. Parker decided early in life to pursue a White man's education. He secured a professional career in the White man's world while serving and maintaining ties to the Seneca people, often helping his tribe as an interpreter and legal assistant. However, he soon learned that his Indian heritage could be a detriment, when in 1847 New York state law prevented him from practicing law because he was not a U.S. citizen. Undaunted, in 1849, he pursued a career in engineering and worked on the Genesee Valley Canal and the Erie Canal. In 1857, he received an appointment from the U.S. Treasury Department to construct a hospital and customhouse in Galena, Illinois; there he met Ulysses S. Grant. Meanwhile, in 1852, Parker had been made a Seneca chief and "Keeper of the Western Door," a title to a revered position in the Seneca tribe. At the outbreak of the Civil War and after some difficulties, he was commissioned as captain of engineers of the U.S. Army, and by 1863, he was appointed to General Grant's personal staff. He soon became Grant's personal secretary and eventually earned the rank of brigadier general. Not without some irony, on April 9, 1865, Parker penned the surrender terms given to General R. E. Lee at Appomattox Court House, bringing the end of the Civil War. After the war, in 1869, he became first American Indian appointed as the commissioner of Indian Affairs and was directly involved in Red Cloud's War of 1866–1868 and the Fort Laramie Treaty of 1868. After being exonerated from accusations of defrauding the government, Parker resigned in 1871.

TERM PAPER SUGGESTIONS

1. Explain how Parker's various professions (engineer, officer in the U.S. Army, and commissioner) exemplified the capacity of American Indians to adapt to the American way of life.

2. Show how Parker was able to assimilate but retain a loyal connection to his tribe.

3. Explore how racism played a role in Parker's life and careers.

4. Examine U.S. citizenship and how it has related to Indians. Parker was prevented from practicing law in New York State, and he could not vote in any local or national election because he was not a citizen.

5. Write an essay examining the importance of education for American Indian people in the nineteenth century, using Parker as an example.

6. Explore the relationships that Parker had with famous white men, like Lewis Henry Morgan, the father of anthropology, who wrote the *League of the Ho-de-no-sau-nee, or Iroquois* (1851), and Ulysses S. Grant, army general and president. For the former Parker served as an "informant," providing invaluable primary source material and insight into Iroquois history and culture, and for the later, he was a good friend and confidant.

ALTERNATIVE TERM PAPER SUGGESTIONS

1. From the perspective of a "civilized" Indian such as Parker, write a letter of recommendation to Red Cloud, the chief of the Oglala Sioux Indians, explaining what he should do to better his people and to prevent further hostilities with the citizens and army of the U.S. government.

2. From the perspective of Red Cloud, chief of the Oglala Sioux, write a letter to Parker, Seneca Indian and commissioner of Indian Affairs, telling him the position of the Lakota in terms of U.S. expansion and questioning Parker's loyalty to the United States when the Americans will not even make Parker a citizen.

SUGGESTED SOURCES

Primary Sources

"Grant's Personality." http://www.granthomepage.com/intparker.htm. Parker writes about his friend.

"Letter to General Ulysses S. Grant, January 24, 1864, from Ely S. Parker." *Great Documents in American Indian History.* Cambridge, MA: De Capo Press, 1995, 186–187. In this letter, Parker details a "plan for the establishment of a permanent peace . . . between the United States and the various Indian tribes."

"Parker to Delano, March 15th, 1871." http://www.csusm.edu/nadp/r871004.htm. Letter to Secretary of State Delano describing Indian issues from Wisconsin to California.

Secondary Sources

Armstrong, William H. *Warrior in Two Camps: Ely S. Parker, Union General and Seneca Chief.* Syracuse, NY: Syracuse University Press, 1978. Biography examining Parker's loyalty to the Seneca and to the United States.

Felton, Harold W. *Ely S. Parker, Spokesman for the Senecas.* New York: Dodd, Mead, 1973. Short, readable biography.

Fenton, William, ed. *Parker on the Iroquois.* Syracuse, NY: Syracuse University Press, 1968. Edited version of Arthur C. Parker's history of the Iroquois.

Hauptman, Lawrence. *The Iroquois in the Civil War: From Battlefields to Reservations.* Syracuse, NY: Syracuse University Press, 1993. Examines the service of Iroquois soldiers and their lives after the war.

Morgan, Lewis Henry, *League of the Ho-de-no-sau-nee, or Iroquois.* Rochester, NY: Sage and Company, 1851. Reprint, Whitefish, MT: Kessinger Publishing, 2006. The pivotal work of early American Indian ethnography, for which Parker was the primary source.

Olson, James C. *Red Cloud and the Sioux Problem.* Lincoln, NE: University of Nebraska Press, 1965. The role of Parker as commissioner is explored.

Parker, Arthur C. *The Life of Ely S. Parker: Last Grand Sachem of the Iroquois and General Grant's Military Secretary.* Vol. 23. Buffalo, NY: Publications of the Buffalo Historical Society, 1919. An insider's biography by Parker's nephew.

Wallace, A. F. *The Death and Rebirth of the Seneca.* New York: Vintage, 1972. A history of the revitalization of the Seneca inspired by the Seneca prophet Handsome Lake, a contemporary of the Treaty of Canandaigua, Cornplanter, and Red Jacket.

Waltmann, Henry G. "Ely Samuel Parker, 1869–71." *The Commissioners of Indian Affairs: 1824–1977.* Robert M. Kvasnicka and Herman J. Viola, eds. Lincoln, NE: University of Nebraska Press, 1979, 123–31. Short biography.

World Wide Web

"Ely Parker." http://www.buffaloah.com/h/parker/. Brief biography with visual data such as the painting of Lee's surrender and photographs of Parker and of his gravestone.

Ely Parker (Seneca): Warrior in Two Worlds. http://www.pbs.org/warrior/indexf.html. Comprehensive Web site source that includes a short biography, biographies of important friends, historian commentaries, and lesson plans.

"Ely S. Parker." http://www.answers.com/topic/samuel-parker. A general summary of Parker's life.

"General Ely Parker Dead." http://query.nytimes.com/gst/abstract.html?res=9806E5DE113DE433A25752C0A96F9C94649ED7CF. PDF download facsimile of Parker's obituary from the September 1, 1895 edition of the *New York Times.*

Gilmore, Gerry J. "Seneca Chief Fought Greed, Injustice." http://www.pentagon.gov/specials/nativeam02/injustice.html. Brief but comprehensive biography.

Gudzune, Jeffrey R. " 'We Are All Americans': Ely S. Parker—Two Worlds, One Man." http://nativeamericanfirstnationshistory.suite101.com/article.cfm/we_are_all_americans. Starting with Parker's famous quote, the author writes a comprehensive biographical sketch of Parker's life and contributions.

" 'We are all Americans,' Native Americans in the Civil War." http://www.nativeamericans.com/CivilWar.htm. A general history of American Indians serving on both sides in the Civil War.

Multimedia Sources

Ely Parker (Seneca): Warrior in Two Worlds. Dir. Ann Spurling. WXXXI Public Broadcasting, 2004. VHS. 52 minutes. Documentary study of Parker's life.

"General Grant's Staff, June 1864." http://www.sonofthesouth.net/ civil-war-pictures/photography/general-grant-staff.htm. A photograph that shows Colonel Ely S. Parker, General U.S. Grant's military secretary.

Indian Warriors: The Untold Story of the Civil War. Dir. Geoffrey Madjea. A&E, 2007. DVD. 50 minutes. Explores the role of Ely Parker, Stand Watie, and other Indians and their involvement in the U.S. Civil War.

48. Sand Creek and the Cheyenne Arapaho War (1864–1865)

On November 29, 1864, without congressional approval and of their own accord, Colonel John M. Chivington and 700 troopers of the Third Colorado Volunteer Cavalry Regiment attacked a Cheyenne and Arapaho village along Sand Creek in Colorado. The village's leader, Southern Cheyenne Chief Black Kettle, when warned of the impending attack, tried to stop it by waving a white flag of truce and peace. The attack killed over 150 Cheyenne and Arapaho, including women and children, and has gone down in history as a brutal massacre of innocents. However, some participants, politicians, and historians have tried to call Sand Creek a "battle" in an effort to downplay the atrocities that were witnessed and chronicled in many contemporary sources, including the *Congressional Record,* letters, testimonials, court records, and oral histories. The controversies that have been generated center on the brutal mutilations of the Indian victims, who were, reportedly, dismembered and violated, versus the claims of those who have said that such atrocities were and are the result of the brutal nature of war and battle. However, even in the midst of the Civil War, the bloodiest of all American wars to date, the public and Congress sought to find reasons for the brutality of this battle or massacre. What has resulted from the investigation and public inquiry has been a history of disputed facts and contending theories.

TERM PAPER SUGGESTIONS

1. Analyze the primary sources to determine whether the evidence supports definition of this event as a battle or massacre.

2. "Nits make lice," said Colonel John Chivington, in an 1864 speech delivered in Denver, where he called for the extermination of all Indians, including women and children. Research primary sources, for example, newspaper articles, for the role of racist rhetoric in fueling hostilities against the Cheyenne and Arapaho.

3. Study the Hotamitainio or Dog Soldier Society of the Cheyenne. Some historians have said their militant activities started the war, or, as others have said, "provided sufficient provocation" for Colonel Chivington to condemn all Cheyenne.

4. Write on the larger picture. According to some historians, readers of the event should understand the greater context of this Indian war by looking at the overall threat Indians posed to settlements, and/or readers should understand that valuable minerals such as gold and silver were discovered on Cheyenne lands.

5. Study the congressional investigation and the testimony of eyewitnesses. What do they reveal about the incident?

6. Show how the Sand Creek massacre united the Cheyenne and Arapaho to the southern Sioux, which sparked a yearlong war with all of these tribes.

ALTERNATIVE TERM PAPER SUGGESTIONS

1. Based on the Dog Soldiers of the Cheyenne, create your own male or female soldier society with rules of behavior and conduct, a decorative shield, and a colorful name. Be sure to emphasize the role of protecting and policing your own community as opposed to engaging in aggression toward outsiders.

2. Hold a mock trial where Colonel Chivington is charged with crimes against humanity, and record the trial using iMovie.

SUGGESTED SOURCES

Primary Sources

"Documents of the Sand Creek Massacre." http://www.pbs.org/weta/thewest/ resources/archives/four/sandcrk.htm. Three pertinent primary source documents: "Two Editorials from the Rocky Mountain News, 1864," "Congressional Testimony by John S. Smith, an Eyewitness to the Massacre, 1865," and the "Deposition by John M. Chivington, 1865."

"Sand Creek Papers, 1861–1864, Mf 0018." http://www.coloradocollege.edu/
library/specialcollections/Manuscript/SandCreek.html. A set of primary
source letters of significant personalities involved in the Sand Creek
affair.

Secondary Sources

Craig, Reginald S. *The Fighting Parson: The Biography of Colonel John M. Chivington.* Tucson, AZ: Westernlore Press, 1994. A biography that tries to
sanitize the brutalities of war.

Cutler, Bruce. *The Massacre at Sand Creek; Narrative Voices.* Norman, OK:
University of Oklahoma Press, 1995. This well-researched novel
attempts to view the incident from the perspective of the victims.

Greene, Jerome A., and Douglass D. Scott. *Finding Sand Creek: History,
Archeology, and the 1864 Massacre Site.* Norman, OK: University of
Oklahoma Press, 2004. Combines narrative history, investigative journalism, and archeological methodologies to tell the story and to find
the site of the Sand Creek massacre, which has resulted in the creation
of a national historic site.

Hatch, Thom. *Black Kettle: The Cheyenne Chief Who Sought Peace but Found
War.* Hoboken, NJ: John Wiley & Sons, 2004. Examines the peace and
assimilation efforts of Black Kettle that ended in ruin and death.

Hoig, Stan. *Sand Creek Massacre.* Norman, OK: University of Oklahoma Press,
1961. Reprint, 1974. Standard history of the event.

Mails, Thomas E. *Dog Soldiers, Bear Men and Buffalo Women: A Study of the Societies and Cults of the Plains Indians.* Englewood Cliffs, NJ: Prentice Hall,
1973. Detailed account of the warrior societies of the Cheyenne Dog
Soldiers, with colorful painting and pencil drawings/illustrations of
regalia and clothing.

Michno, Gregory. *Battle at Sand Creek: The Military Perspective.* El Segundo, CA:
Upton and Sons, 2004. A military history that changes the focus from
"massacre" to an expeditious military operation that responded to Indian
hostilities perpetrated by young Indian warriors that the elders could not
control.

Schultz, Duane P. *Month of the Freezing Moon.* New York, St. Martin's Press,
1990. Places the event into a large context but at the expense of down-
playing the brutality of the attack.

Scott, Robert. *Blood at Sand Creek: The Massacre Revisited.* Caldwell, ID:
Caxton Printers, 1994. Attempts to discredit the "massacre" label by
omission and by attacking the credibility of eyewitnesses, who were
mostly white.

Svaldi, David. *Sand Creek and the Rhetoric of Extermination: A Case Study in Indian-White Relations.* Lanham, MD: University Press of America, 1989. Examines the use of anti-Indian rhetoric in newspapers and by word of mouth to fuel an acceptance of Indian hating and killing.

World Wide Web

"Black Kettle." http://www.pbs.org/weta/thewest/people/a_c/blackkettle.htm. Short biography of the Cheyenne Indian chief.

"John M. Chivington." http://www.pbs.org/weta/thewest/people/a_c/chivington.htm. Short biography of the colonel of the Colorado Volunteers.

"Sand Creek Battle Summary." http://www.nps.gov/hps/abpp/battles/co001.htm. Short statistical summary of the massacre/battle.

"The Sand Creek Massacre Letters." http://rebelcherokee.labdiva.com/sandcrkltrs.html. Selected links page to secondary and primary sources.

"Sand Creek Massacre National Historic Site." http://www.nps.gov/sand/. Official site of the actual site, just recently established and opened in 2007.

Smiley, Brenda. "Sand Creek Massacre." http://www.archaeology.org/9911/newsbriefs/sand.html. Short "news brief" of the finds by archeological investigators of the Sand Creek battle site.

Multimedia Source

The West. Dir. Steven Ives and Ken Burns. Florentine Films, 1996. 4 DVDs. 537 minutes. "Episode 4" describes the Sand Creek battle and Black Kettle's actions as a result of the surprise attack.

49. Treaties of Medicine Lodge and Fort Laramie (1866–1869)

War started in 1866 between the U.S. government and the Oglala Lakota (Sioux) because Oglala Lakota (Sioux) Chief Red Cloud refused to sell the lands that comprised the Bozeman Trail, which led to the gold fields of Montana, near the lands of the Lakota, and Red Cloud warned he would kill any White man who used the trail. To protect the gold miners and others who intended to use the trail anyway, Colonel Henry B. Carrington began building three forts along the trail, when Red Cloud attacked to throw the U.S. Army on the defensive. Angered by the audacity of the Lakota, Captain William J. Fetterman, who said that with 80 troopers he could "ride through the entire Sioux nation," provoked a battle with them in December of 1866. The battle ended with his entire command of 80 troopers slaughtered by an ambush designed by the young Oglala warrior Crazy Horse. Then in the Hayfield Fight and the Wagon Box Fight, the Lakota were defeated with heavy casualties, but they refused to make peace. In 1867, General W. S. Hancock and Colonel George Armstrong Custer were dispatched to war against the Plains Indians, but their efforts ended in failure; this led to the signing of the Medicine Lodge Treaty of 1867 and the Fort Laramie Treaty of 1868. The first set aside reservations for the Cheyenne, Arapaho, Kiowa, Comanche, and Kiowa-Apache, and the second created the Great Sioux Indian Reservation, with the Black Hills at its center and which encompassed most of the Sioux lands. However, many Indians would not be confined to the small land bases of the reservations set aside for the non-Sioux, particularly the Dog Soldiers of the Cheyenne. In 1868, a third campaign of "total war" against the hostile Plains Indians was organized and led by General Philip Sheridan, who said at one time, "the only good Indian is a dead Indian." He and Custer launched attack after attack, pursuing Indians to their winter encampments and conducting military operations well into 1869.

TERM PAPER SUGGESTIONS

1. Examine the purpose of these wars against the Plains Indians. Were they wars to force the Indians to comply with U.S. demands of rights of passage, access to mineral wealth, and lands for settlement? Or were they wars to protect Americans settlers, miners, and immigrants?

2. Study and compare the military tactics and prowess of Carrington, Fetterman, Hancock, Sheridan, and Custer to Red Cloud, Crazy Horse, Roman Nose, Satanta, Black Kettle, and Tall Bull.

3. Compare the Treaty of Medicine Lodge to the Treaty of Fort Laramie.

4. Examine the diplomatic skills of Red Cloud and how he acted on behalf of his people rather than for personal gain. What were his ethics and his morals?

5. Explore the Plains Indians' perception of the increasing encroachments of Americans onto their lands and the American desire for gold and wealth. Treaties created reservations and were designed and intended to prevent further hostilities and encroachments. Did that plan work?

6. How did the wars escalate to "total war," winning at all cost? Use the Battle of Washita, where Custer killed 900 Indian ponies and defeated and killed Black Kettle, survivor of the Sand Creek massacre, as an example of "total war."

ALTERNATIVE TERM PAPER SUGGESTIONS

1. Organize a treaty conference with the express goal of creating a lasting peace between two warring parties. Write up a treaty with at least four articles that both sides agree should be included as important to bind the parties to honor the agreement.

2. Red Cloud never broke his promises and always honored the treaties he signed. However, once gold was discovered in the Black Hills, the United States broke their promise not to take more Sioux land and forced the Sioux onto smaller reservations. From the perspective of an Oglala elder, write a response to the U.S. government about the breaking of the Fort Laramie Treaty of 1868 and your refusal to accept money as compensation. Be sure to have sound reasons and supporting data to back up your stance.

SUGGESTED SOURCES

Primary Sources

Cozzens, Peter, ed. *The Long War for the Northern Plains (Eyewitnesses to the Indian Wars).* Mechanicsburg, PA: Stockpole Books, 2004. A collection of primary source accounts (letters, reports, newspaper articles, oral stories, and the like) of the battles and skirmishes. "Part Two: Red Cloud's War, 1866–68" is of particular interest.

Jones, Douglas C. *The Treaty of Medicine Lodge: The Story of the Great Treaty Council as Told by Eyewitnesses.* Norman, OK: University of Oklahoma Press, 1966. Nine professional journalists observed the treaty-making process and reported their findings to their respective newspapers. This work adds to that information a wealth of other primary source materials to create a text that takes you step by step through the arduous process of making a treaty with Indians.

"Medicine Lodge Treaty, 1867." http://digital.library.okstate.edu/encyclopedia/entries/M/ME005.html. Links page to the three treaties made at Medicine Lodge in 1867; provides a short introduction to their content.

Paul, R. Eli. *Autobiography of Red Cloud: War Leader of the Oglalas.* Helena, MT: Montana Historical Society Press, 1997. With a detailed introduction, this is an as-told-to story of the great chief that provides valuable insight into the life of the Oglala Lakota.

"Transcript of Treaty of Fort Laramie (1851)." http://www.canku-luta.org/PineRidge/laramie_treaty.html. Digital facsimile of the entire treaty, including a map of the reserved lands of the 1868 Fort Laramie Treaty (a hyperlink to the text of the treaty is to the left of the map) compared to the smaller lands of subsequent treaties and agreements. The Fort

Laramie Treaty of 1868 can also be found at http://digital
.library.okstate.edu/kappler/Vol2/treaties/sio0998.htm.

Secondary Sources

Brill, Charles J. *Custer, Black Kettle and the Fight on the Washita.* Norman, OK:
University of Oklahoma Press, 2002. A new history that takes into consideration Cheyenne and Arapaho accounts of the battle and campaign.

Brown, Dee. *The Fetterman Massacre.* Lincoln, NE: University of Nebraska Press,
1962. Detailed narrative history of Red Cloud's War that focuses on the
military campaign.

Greene, Jerome A. *Washita, The Southern Cheyenne and the U.S. Army.* Campaigns
and Commanders Series, vol. 3. Norman, OK: University of Oklahoma
Press, 2004. A complete history of the Southern Cheyenne from the seventeenth century until Black Kettle's death at the battle of the Washita.

Hatch, Thom. *Black Kettle: The Cheyenne Chief Who Sought Peace but Found
War.* Hoboken, NJ: Wiley & Sons, 2004. Examines the peace and
assimilation efforts of Black Kettle that ended in ruin and death.

Hebard, Grace Raymond, and Earl Alonzo Brininstool. *The Bozeman Trail.* Spo-
kane, WA: Arthur H. Clark Company, 1922. Google Books, 2008. A
copyright-free digital facsimile. http://books.google.com/books?id=Jc8-
BAAAAMAAJ. Historical accounts and history of the trail as well as the
"fights with Red Cloud's warriors."

Hoig, Stan. *The Battle of the Washita: The Sheridan-Custer Indian Campaign of
1867–69.* Lincoln, NE: University of Nebraska Press, 1980. A clear
and readable narrative of the campaign that is well documented.

Hyde, George E. *Red Cloud's Folk: A History of the Oglala Sioux Indians.* Norman,
OK: University of Oklahoma Press, 1984. Detailed and comprehensive
history of the Oglala from their earliest times to 1900 that provides deep
insight into the culture and life ways of the Oglala.

Keenan, Jerry. *The Wagon Box Fight: An Episode in Red Cloud's War.* Cambridge,
MA: De Capo Press, 2001. Narrowly focused military narrative of the
fight supported by primary source materials, including recent archeological evidence.

Larson, Robert W. *Red Cloud: Warrior-Statesman of the Lakota Sioux.* Norman,
OK: University of Oklahoma Press, 1999. A long biography of the great
chief that covers his diplomatic prowess.

Robinson, Charles M., III. *Satanta: The Life and Death of a War Chief.* Abilene,
TX: State House Press, 1997. A biography of the Kiowa Indian chief who
fought against Custer and who was present at Medicine Lodge. The book
describes Kiowa culture.

Viegas, Jennifer. *The Fort Laramie Treaty, 1868: A Primary Source Examination of the Treaty that Established a Sioux Reservation in the Black Hills of Dakota in 1868.* Rosen Central, 2005. An excellent, 64-page book designed for juveniles, with contextual narratives, visual materials, a glossary of words, time line, and controversies.

World Wide Web

Calitri, Shannon Smith. " 'Give Me Eighty Men': Shattering the Myth of the Fetterman Massacre." http://findarticles.com/p/articles/mi_qa3951/is_200410/ai_n9464906. A 17-page essay examining in detail the Fetterman Massacre and separating fact from fiction and myth.
Herman, Tawnya. "A Re-Telling of The Medicine Law Treaty." http://www.museumgreatplains.org/lawtoncentennial/medicinelodgetreaty.html. An oral story about the treaty with a link to a lesson plan.
"Medicine Lodge and Barber County, Kansas & Its History." http://www.cyberlodg.com/mlcity/. A community site with short summaries of historical personalities, including information on the Medicine Lodge Peace Treaty and the celebratory pageant held every three years in honor of that peace.
"Red Cloud." http://www.pbs.org/weta/thewest/people/i_r/redcloud.htm. Short biography with links to other relevant information.
"The Story of the Battle of the Washita." http://www.nps.gov/archive/waba/story.htm. Concise historical essay with a link to a battlefield map.

Multimedia Sources

"Red Cloud's War Shirt." http://www.nps.gov/history/museum/treasures/html/S/redcloud.htm. Digital photograph of the war shirt located at the Agate Fossil Beds National Monument museum.
The West. Dir. Steven Ives and Ken Burns. Florentine Films, 1996. 4 DVDs. 537 minutes. Expansive documentary treatment of the American West. "Episode 5" and "Episode 6" cover the period of the two treaties.

50. Indian Appropriation Act of 1871 and President Ulysses S. Grant's "Quaker" Peace Policy

On March 3, 1871, the Indian Appropriation Act was signed by President Ulysses S. Grant and enacted by Congress to abolish the treaty-making powers of Indian tribes and nations residing within the boundaries of the United States. Indian tribes would no longer be recognized as independent nations with the sovereign power to negotiate treaties. Congressional statutes and/or executive orders and the Congress would handle all future negotiations with Indians, and the congressional and executive branches of government would, in principle, exercise that power over Indians with discretion and with compassion. However, from that moment forward Indians became "wards of the state" where the individual Indian was more important than the tribe. This act was the start of President Grant's Peace Policy, a policy whose goal was ultimately to prepare the Indian for citizenship through a process of assimilation. This assimilation would occur through education and vocational training and would thereby shift the emphasis of Indian policies from war, or as Grant writes, "wars of extermination." Under Grant's initiatives, programs for education and for medical care for Indians were institutionalized within the Department of the Interior, and the age of humanitarian reform was begun. Another step was to replace the Indian agents, who were mostly military officers or Indian traders, with a new breed of Christian humanitarians, like the Quakers but not limited to them exclusively, in the hopes that they would be less corrupt and would pay more attention to the welfare and well-being of their Indian charges. Monies generated from the sale of Indian land would pay for the new programs and initiatives.

TERM PAPER SUGGESTIONS

1. Examine how the end to treaty making with American Indians severely damaged tribal sovereignty, and explore the adjustments Indian tribes made to accommodate this monumental change in policy.

2. Write an essay investigating how the federal government proceeded with the acquisition of Indian lands and the creation of new Indian reservations without the treaty-making process.

3. Why change the focus to the individual rather than the communal group? What does that refocus have to do with American ideals: freedom and the pursuit of happiness?

4. Write on the positive intentions of the Grant Peace Policy for the Indians' future. Would the programs adequately prepare Indians for "civilization"?

5. Write on the negative consequences of "reprogramming" Indian youth to western and Christian ways.

6. Investigate the many boarding schools created as a result of the new Peace Policy and the boarding school experience of American Indian children. Was this system of acculturation humanitarian by standards of the time period and/or by standards of today?

ALTERNATIVE TERM PAPER SUGGESTIONS

1. Imagine yourself as an Indian youth transported to an Indian boarding school for nine months. Based on your reading of Zitkala-Sa's experiences, how would you write about your experience? Create an oral presentation where you share your feelings.

2. From the point of view of a pacifist Quaker teacher, prepare a lesson plan for teaching Quaker values to a class of Indian students.

SUGGESTED SOURCES

Primary Sources

Butler, Josiah. "Pioneer School Teaching at the Comanche-Kiowa Agency School 1870–3: Being the Reminiscences of the First Teacher." http://digital.library.okstate.edu/chronicles/v006/v006p483.html. The experiences of a Quaker teacher and his efforts to Christianize and civilize the Indian, often at the expense of tribal identity.

"The Pertinent Rider Attached to the Indian Appropriation Act of 1871 (16 Stat. 566; Rev. Stat. § 2079, now contained in 25 U.S.C. § 71)." This rider makes it clear that Indian tribes will no longer be acknowledge or recognized as nations and treaties will no longer be made with them.

Zitkala-Sa (Gertrude Bonnin). "The School Days of an Indian Girl." http://www.facstaff.bucknell.edu/gcarr/19cUSWW/ZS/SDIG.html. Describes how the Quakers wanted to destroy Indian identity by cutting hair and forcing Indian students to submit to Christian discipline.

Secondary Sources

Bender, Norman J. *New Hope for the New Indians: The Grant Peace Policy and the Navajos in the 1870s*. University of New Mexico Press, 1989. Examines an area where the Peace Policy was implemented and much reported on at the time.

Deloria, Vine, Jr., and David E. Wilkins. *Tribes, Treaties, and Constitutional Tribulations*. Austin, TX: University of Texas Press, 2000. Explores the relationship between the U.S. Constitution and Indian tribes and the effect of the "no more treaties" rider of the Indian Appropriation Act.

Hoig, Stan, *White Man's Paper Trail: Grand Councils and Treaty-Making on the Central Plains.* University of Colorado Press, 2008. Examines treaty making on the Plains from the early 1800s to the last treaty made in 1871.

Keith, Murray, A. *American Protestantism and United States Indian Policy, 1869–82.* Lincoln, NE: University of Nebraska Press, 1983. Explores the role of members of Christian denominations other than Quakers who were involved in the "Americanization" of American Indians.

Kelsey, Rayner. *Friends and the Indians, 1655–1917.* Philadelphia, PA: Associated Executive Committee of Friends on Indian Affairs, 1917. Google Books, 2008. A copyright-free digital facsimile. http://books.google .com/books?id=SXTkJdhFhikC. A survey and history based on primary sources of the Quakers. Chapter VIII covers "Grant's Peace Policy," and other chapters are relevant as well.

Milner, Clyde A. *With Good Intentions: Quaker Work among the Pawnees, Otos and Omahas in the 1870s.* Lincoln, NE: University of Nebraska Press, 1982. Explores the failure of the Grant Peace Policy due to the lack of concern for preserving American Indian culture and identity to make Indians bicultural.

Prucha, Francis Paul. *American Indian Treaties: The History of a Political Anomaly.* Berkeley, CA: University of California Press, 1994. An overview of treaties, policies, and laws as they pertain to American Indians.

Prucha, Francis Paul. *The Great Father: The United States Government and the American Indians.* 2 vols. Lincoln, NE: University of Nebraska Press, 1984. General summary of federal Indian policy, including a long discussion of Grant's Peace Policy and the Indian Appropriation Act.

Tatum, Lawrie. *Our Red Brothers and the Peace Policy of President Ulysses S. Grant.* 1899. Reprint, Lincoln, NE: University of Nebraska Press, 1970. A standard study of the policy as it relates to the Indians involved.

Wilkins, David E. *American Indian Sovereignty and the U.S. Supreme Court: The Masking of Justice.* Austin, TX: University of Texas Press, 1997. Detailed analysis of 15 U.S. Supreme Court cases involving Native Americans.

Wilkins, David E. *Uneven Ground: American Indian Sovereignty and Federal Law.* Norman, OK: University of Oklahoma Press, 2001. A scholarly study of federal law and Supreme Court rulings, including a change in sovereignty caused by the Indian Appropriation Act.

World Wide Web

"General Indian Legislative History." http://users.sisqtel.net/armstrng/ Indlegis.htm. A chronology with links to other pertinent sites. Places the Indian Appropriation Act within a larger context of the erosion of tribal sovereignty and power (examined thoroughly by Deloria and Wilkins, listed in the Secondary Sources).

Giejer, Erik. "Quakers Participated in Cultural Genocide against Indians." http://geijer.nu/quakersandindians.shtml. Interesting essay from the point of view of a Swedish Quaker who has analyzed Quaker boarding schools on Indian reservations created to help the Indian, but he has found them lacking and racist.

"Indian Affairs: Result of the Peace Policy of the Indian Tribes in New Mexico, March 29, 1873." *New York Times.* http://query.nytimes.com/gst/abstract.html?res=9C03E3DB163-DE43BBC4151DFB5668388669FDE. Downloadable PDF file of a facsimile of the historical article reporting on effects of the Peace Policy.

"Indian Treaties." http://law.onecle.com/constitution/article-2/21-indian-treaties.html. A links page to pertinent legal cases, laws, and amendments as they apply to Indian treaties; has a very good definition of what an Indian treaty was and is.

Jones, Louis Thomas. "The Iowa Quakers and the American Indians." http://iagenweb.org/history/qoi/QOIPt4Chp2.htm. A short general overview of the relation between Quakers and Indians; also has a section on Grant's Peace Policy.

"Native Americans and Law." http://law.jrank.org/pages/12523/Native-Americans.html. A very good summary of tribal governance, tribal sovereignty, treaty-making before 1871, congressional control after 1871, and other Indian legal matters.

"The Savages: Results of the President's Peace Policy, July 22, 1873." *New York Times.* http://query.nytimes.com/gst/abstract.html?res=9D0CE5-DA1438E63ABC4A51DFB1668388669FDE. Downloadable PDF file of a facsimile of the historical article reporting on effects of the Peace Policy.

Multimedia Source

The West. Dir. Stephen Ives. Public Broadcasting Service, 1996. 4 DVDs. 750 minutes. "Episode 7" explores Grant's Peace Policy and the efforts at Americanization and assimilation.

51. Wars in the Pacific Northwest (1864–1878)

After the wars with Mexico, 1835–1848, and the great trek westward that followed (that is, the Oregon Trail), the desire for Indian land and resources stretched west of the Rocky Mountains to the shores of the Pacific Ocean, from the Pacific Northwest to California, and most have never heard of the Indians the American settlers encountered. The most famous are the ones who fought the Americans: the Bannocks, the Shoshones and Paiutes commonly known as the Snakes of the Columbian River basin, and the Modocs and Klamath of northern California and Oregon. The hundreds of other tribes, like the Miwok, Pomo, and Yurok, were often destroyed and subjugated without much historical notice or fighting. Even the "fighting" Indians of this region are not as well-known as their Plains Indian contemporaries. As was the case in most Indian wars, these followed a predictable pattern of breaking into full-scale war after the encroachment of Whites upon traditional Indian lands and when the Indians' way of life had became threatened. What was different about these wars was that the sizes of the opposing combatant groups were relatively small, and, except for the Snake War, 1864–1868, the wars were fought after the end of treaty making in 1871. This resulted in a policy of unconditional surrender and military management of Indians in the region. However, that did not stop two heroic defenders of Indian rights from surfacing to fight for justice and rights after the wars ended. In 1872–1873, Winema Riddle, a Modoc, and in the 1880s and 1890s, Sarah Winnemucca, a Shoshone, emerged to become leaders, activists, and fighters on a different battlefield and to perform heroic deeds that preserved Indian rights for future generations.

TERM PAPER SUGGESTIONS

1. Using one, two, or three examples from the Indian wars in the Pacific Northwest (1864–1878), write an essay on the justifications each side uses for starting a war in a cause-and-effect pattern of rhetorical investigation, being sure to follow all of links in the causal chain.

2. Study U.S. military strategy and tactics. For example, the Snake War was a concerted war of attrition, a strategy employed by General George Crook, who in the course of 49 small engagements eventually forced the Snakes to sue for peace.

3. Explore the relationships between the United States, the Modoc, and the Klamath in the Modoc War. Why could the Klamath reach an accommodation with the United States that avoided war but the Modoc could not?

4. Explore the reasons and motivations for brutality and atrocities on both sides of the Modoc War. The Modocs killed Peace Commissioner E. R. S. Canby,

and later the U.S. Army tried, convicted, and hanged Modoc leaders, including Captain Jack.

5. Write on the life and times of Winema Riddle in helping her people and bringing peace during the Modoc War.

6. Research and write on the life of Sarah Winnemucca, who not only served the army during the Bannock War of 1878 *but also* fought for Indian rights. In her book, the first ever written and published by an Indian woman, she writes: "For shame! For shame! You dare to cry out Liberty, when you hold us in places against our will, driving us from place to place as if we were beasts."

ALTERNATIVE TERM PAPER SUGGESTIONS

1. Create a debate presenting the reasons American settlers had a right and desire to live on the Lost River lands and the reasons the Modoc should not have been removed from the same lands. The goal is to understand why the Modoc would wage war and desire to return to their lands after being removed from them.

2. Craft an appeal for peace and justice from the perspective of an American Indian woman of the region and time period. What skills and techniques would an Indian woman employ that would be different from those of men?

SUGGESTED SOURCES

Primary Sources

Cozzens, Peter. *Eyewitnesses to the Indian Wars, 1865–1890: The Wars for the Pacific Northwest.* Mechanicsburg, PA: Stackpole Books, 2002. A collection of primary source accounts (letters, reports, newspaper articles, oral stories, and the like) of the battles and skirmishes. "Part One: The Snake-Paiute War and After, 1866–72" and "Part Two: The Modoc War, 1872–73" are of particular interest.

Odeneal, Thomas Benton. *The Modoc War: Statement of Its Origin and Causes; Containing an Account of the Treaty, Copies of Petitions and Official Correspondence.* Reprint, Whitefish, MT: Kessinger Publishing, 2007. First published in 1873, Odeneal writes a history close to when the Modoc War ended in 1873, and he includes as appendices many primary sources.

"Shoshone Bannock Treaty of 1868." http://www.ccrh.org/comm/river/treaties/shoban.htm. Standard peace and reservation treaty.

Winnemucca, Sarah. *Life among the Paiutes: Their Wrongs and Claims.* Boston, MA: Boston Stereotype Foundry, 1882. Reprint, Whitefish, MT:

Kessinger Publishing, 2007. Chapter three covers "Wars and Their Causes" and chapter seven covers "The Bannock War"; additionally, the book offers insight into Paiute culture and people from the first American Indian (Paiute) woman to write a book.

Secondary Sources

Brimlow, George Franci. *The Bannock Indian War of 1878.* Caldwell, ID: Caxton Printers, 1938. General history of the war with the Modoc and Nez Perce wars covered. Sarah Winnemucca is mentioned.

Glassley, Ray Hoard. *Pacific Northwest Indian Wars: The Cayuse War of 1848, the Rogue River Wars of the '50s, the Yakima War, 1853–56, the Coeur d'Alene War, 1857, the Modoc War, 1873, the Nez Perce War, 1877, the Bannock War, 1878, the Sheepeater's War of 1879.* Portland, OR: Binfords and Mort, 1953. Short narrative descriptions.

James, Cheewa. *Modoc: The Tribe That Wouldn't Die.* Happy Camp, CA: Naturegraph Publishers, 2008. An enrolled member of the Modoc Tribe of Oklahoma, James has written a comprehensive cultural and personal history of the Modoc that includes the Modoc War and, more importantly, what happened to the Modoc Indians after the war. Includes rare color and black and white photographs.

Knight, Oliver. *Following the Indian Wars: The Story of the Newspaper Correspondents among the Indian Campaigners.* Norman, OK: University of Oklahoma Press, 1960. An interesting 10-example history of journalists and their stories as they covered Indian wars of the west. Chapter four is entitled "Modocs Hold Off U.S. Army."

Michno, Gregory. *Deadliest Indian War in the West: The Snake Conflict, 1864–1868.* Caldwell, ID: Caxton Press, 2007. A micro study of the conflict from a military tactics perspective that is well documented and explained.

Murray, Keith A. *The Modocs and Their War.* Norman, OK: University of Oklahoma Press, 1959. Reprint, 1984. Military analysis of the war, major battles, and leaders.

Quinn, Arthur. *Hell with the Fire Out: A History of the Modoc War.* Boston, MA: Faber and Faber, 1998. A new history that attempts to show the willingness of the Modocs to live in peace if left alone or fight to death if not.

Riddle, Jeff C. *The Indian History of the Modoc War.* San Francisco, CA: Marnell and Co., 1914. Reprint, Mechanicsburg, PA: Stackpole Books, 2004. Written by the son of a white father and Modoc mother who was heavily involved in the conflict, Riddle's book tries to give a balanced narrative of the war and of Captain Jack.

Zanjani, Sally. *Sarah Winnemucca.* Lincoln, NE: Bison Books, 2004. Biography of Sarah Winnemucca (1844–1891), a Paiute who, among many adventures, was an interpreter and messenger for the U.S. Army during the Bannock War of 1878. More importantly, she was an activist for her people who criticized the Indian policy, particularly the reservation system. She was the first American Indian woman to write and publish a book in English.

World Wide Web

Bales, Rebecca. *Winema and the Modoc War: One Woman's Struggle for Peace.* http://www.archives.gov/publications/prologue/2005/spring/winema.html. A detailed essay on the role of Winema Riddle, mother of the author Jeff C. Riddle, listed in the Secondary Sources, who fought a war of peace and justice for her Modoc people. Rare photographs of the fighting augment the text.

"The Bannock War, June 4, 1878." http://query.nytimes.com/gst/abstract.html?res=9C02EFDB1E3FE63BBC4C53DFB0668383669FDE. Downloadable *New York Times* article on the war from 1878.

Beck, Warren A., and Ynez D. Hasse. "The Modoc War, 1872–1873." http://www.militarymuseum.org/Modoc1.html. General summary and map of the war.

"Sarah Winnemucca." http://memory.loc.gov/ammem/today/oct14.html. A detailed biographical sketch of the daughter of Chief Winnemucca.

"Sarah Winnemucca." http://www.greatwomen.org/women.php?action=viewone&id=172. Short biography and tribute.

"Snake War." http://www.enotes.com/salem-history/snake-war. Short article on the Snake War of 1866–1869 in PDF downloadable format.

Multimedia Sources

Drum Beat. Dir. Delmer Daves. Hollywood, CA: Jaguar Productions, 1954. DVD. 111 minutes. Based on the Modoc War and stars a young Charles Bronson as Captain Jack, the Modoc leader.

Google Images of Sarah Winnemucca. http://images.google.com/images?hl=en&q=Google+Images+of+Sarah+Winnemucca&btnG=Search+Images&gbv=2. One of the great women of American Indian history who sought to right the wrong perpetrated on her people.

52. Red River and Apache Wars (1874–1886)

After the assassination of Peace Commissioner and General E. R. S. Canby by the Modocs in 1873, President Ulysses S. Grant's Peace Policy, as it applied to hostile Indians, changed to coordinated military actions designed to force recalcitrant Indians to unconditional surrender through the destruction of their means to wage war. After American frontiersmen violated the Medicine Lodge Treaty of 1867 and as white hunters continued to kill buffalo at a frightening rate, Satanta and Big Tree led war bands of the Comanche, Southern Cheyenne, and Kiowa on a series of raids. Known as the Red River Campaign or War, the U.S. military responded with a large invasion army to force battle when possible but to ensure devastating victory by destroying Indian villages and provisions and killing Indian ponies. This forced the unconditional surrender of the war leaders and warriors by October of 1874.

Following on the heels of the Red River campaign, the Apache War, 1876–1886, broke out because federal officials abrogated four Apache reservations and tried to remove the Apache residents to a new, larger reservation in Arizona, at San Carlos. Led by Victorio and Geronimo, a diverse band of Apache warriors bolted and evaded capture. However, Victorio was killed at the Battle of Tres Castillos in 1880; in that same year an Apache prophet, Nakaidoklini, emerged with a message of Apache resurgence of power of the southwest, and his prophecy spread to all of the Apache tribes. When a U.S. trooper killed him, hostilities escalated and new leaders such as Naiche came forward and joined Geronimo. A series of battles destroyed their will to fight, but Geronimo held out until 1886, when he was forced to unconditionally surrender.

TERM PAPER SUGGESTIONS

1. Explore how the Peace Policy of President Grant changed to direct and decisive military action against hostile and recalcitrant Indian people.

2. Investigate the role that buffalo played in contributing to the Red River War.

3. Write on the military tactics employed to defeat the Indians in the Red River War and compare them to earlier wars with Indians, like the Pequot War of 1637 or King Philip's War of 1675. How are they different and how are they the same?

4. In the Apache War, investigate the role of the U.S. Army/Cavalry in forcing Indians to comply with federal Indian policy. How difficult was that task?

5. Compare the various leaders involved in the Red River and Apache wars. Individually, what were their roles and what were their motivations? In the Apache case, how could a spiritual leader be more powerful than a military one?

6. Look at the concept of "inevitability." Were the Indians doomed to defeat and subjugation? Were they destined to be confined to reservations despite their efforts to resist that outcome?

ALTERNATIVE TERM PAPER SUGGESTIONS

1. As though you were a literate Apache, write a five-day journal about being pursued by the U.S. Army. Study the primary source journals to get an idea of how to write journal entries of the time period, but write the entries within the imagination of a Apache warrior.

2. Write a military plan of war against a hostile group of Indians, such as the Comanche, Kiowa or Cheyenne, that would guarantee success. Are there any moral and/or ethical considerations?

SUGGESTED SOURCES

Primary Sources

Cozzens, Peter. *The Struggle for Apacheria: Eyewitnesses to the Indian Wars, 1865–1890.* Mechanicsburg, PA: Stackpole Books, 2001. Numerous firsthand accounts and primary sources collected under one cover, including documents describing the aftermath.

Kraft, Louis, ed. *Lt. Charles Gatewood & His Apache Wars Memoir.* Lincoln, NE: University of Nebraska Press, 2005. The officer in charge of the Apache Scouts relates his battlefield experiences and his chase and capture of Geronimo.

Marshall, J. T. *Miles Expedition of 1874–1875; an Eyewitness Account of the Red River War.* 1937. Lonnie J. White, ed. Irvine, CA: Reprint Services Corporation, 1991. Marshall's account includes 13 photographs of the soldiers, scouts, and Indian chiefs involved.

Turner, Frederick, and S. M. Barrett, eds. *Geronimo: His Own Story: The Autobiography of a Great Patriot Warrior.* 1906. Reprint, New York: Plume, 1996. A as-told-to account from the words of Geronimo that provides insight into the culture of the Apache and of the wars with the Americans and Mexicans. Includes editorial introductions.

Secondary Sources

Aleshire, Peter. *Reaping the Whirlwind: The Apache Wars.* New York: Facts on File, January 1998. A history meant for grades 7–12. Although a recommended introduction to the wars that is written in a short, to-the-point style, it nevertheless glosses over the causes and motivations of major participants.

Blazer, Almer N. *Santana: War Chief of the Mescalero Apache.* A. R. Pruitt, ed. Ranchoes de Taos, NM: Dog Soldier Press. 2000. Edited version of a history written by Almer Blazer, son of Joseph Blazer, friend and confidant of Santana.

Chalfant, William Y. *Cheyennes at Dark Water Creek: The Last Fight of the Red River War.* Norman, OK: University of Oklahoma Press, 1997. Detailed military history of the battle.

Cruse, J. Brett. *Battles of the Red River War: Archeological Perspectives on the Indian Campaign of 1874.* College Station, TX: Texas A&M Press, 2008. The findings of six archeological investigations of battlefield sites.

Haley, James L. *The Buffalo War: The History of the Red River Indian Uprising of 1874: The Final Campaign of the White Man Versus the Southern Plains Indians, Illustrated with 32 Pages of Rare Photographs.* Garden City, NY: Doubleday, 1976. Reprint, Abilene, TX: State House Press, 1998. Demonstrates how the killing of the buffalo, the main food and subsistence source, provoked Indians into rebelling and raiding.

Jauken, Arlene Feldmann. *The Moccasin Speaks: Living as Captives of the Dog Soldier Warriors, Red River War, 1874–1875.* Lincoln, NE: Dageforde Publishing, 1998. The author, a descendent of one of the captives, creates a narrative history based on family oral stories and primary/secondary source research.

Kraft, Louis. *Gatewood and Geronimo.* Albuquerque, NM: University of New Mexico Press, 2000. Explores the relationship, military and personal, of two "soldiers" on opposing sides.

Lummis, Charles, and Don Perceval, eds. *General Crook and the Apache Wars.* Flagstaff, AZ: Northland Publishing, 1985. A *Los Angeles Times* reporter's account of the Apache War in the spring of 1886, edited by Perceval.

Roberts, David, *Once They Moved Like the Wind: Cochise, Geronimo and the Apache Wars.* New York: Touchstone, 1994. Detailed and comprehensive character study that reveals much about Apache culture while not holding back about the violent nature of the Apache Wars.

Robinson, Charles M., III. *Satanta: The Life and Death of a War Chief.* Abilene, TX: State House Press, 1997. A biography of the Kiowa Indian chief who was a war chief in the Red River War. The book describes Kiowa culture.

World Wide Web

Connell, Michelle, and Silvia Moreno. "Victorio Fought to the Death for Homeland." http://www.epcc.edu/nwlibrary/borderlands/22_victorio.htm. An excellent short essay on the life and death of Victorio.

"Geronimo." http://www.legendsofamerica.com/NA-Geronimo.html. A fair and accurate summary of Geronimo's life with pictures and links to other relevant entries.

Hodge, Frederick. "Apache History Brief." http://www.manataka.org/page667. html. From the *Handbook of American Indians* (1906), the brief summary includes a section on Nakaidoklini as well as the Apache War.

"Red River War." http://www.mobeetie.com/pages/rrwar.htm. A short summary that has photos of U.S. leaders and a time line of the war.

"The Red River War." http://www.texasbeyondhistory.net/redriver/index.html. Comprehensive summary that includes teaching resources, photographs, maps of battles and reservations, and a Kiowa ledger drawing in color of a battle.

"The Red River War." http://www.tsl.state.tx.us/exhibits/indian/showdown/ page3.html. Includes primary sources (letters and reports) from the *Texas Indian Papers*.

Multimedia Source

Geronimo: An American Legend. Dir. Walter Hill. Hollywood, CA: Columbia Pictures, 1993. DVD. 115 minutes. An excellent docudrama of the relationship between Geronimo and Lt. Charles Gatewood. Shows the failure of Apache scouts to achieve some advantage and respect for cooperating with the U.S. military when they are thrown on the same prison train as Geronimo.

53. Lakota War for the Black Hills (1876–1877)

After the Fort Laramie Treaty of 1868, the Lakota living in the Great Sioux Reservation suffered from continued incursions into that reserved land by Americans, incursions that increased when Colonel George Armstrong Custer's military expedition into the Black Hills discovered gold. Because the Lakota revered the Black Hills as sacred and the center of their universe, they refused to sell or lease the land despite many attempts by federal authorities. At that point, due to the assassination of Peace Commissioner and General E. R. S. Canby by the Modocs in 1873, President Ulysses S. Grant's Peace Policy had been abandoned, and the military felt little obligation to continue negotiations with the Lakota.

In 1875, they ordered the Lakota to report by January 31, 1876, and be confined to near their designated agencies on a newly created and smaller Sioux Indian reservation east of the Black Hills, but not including the Black Hills, or else be hunted down and killed as recalcitrant hostiles. When many of the Lakota and their leaders (Sitting Bull, Crazy Horse, Gall, and Lame Deer to name a few) failed to report, Generals Phil Sheridan (commander), George Crook, and Alfred Howe Terry (including Custer) initiated a series of military campaigns against the Lakota. The spring campaign of 1876 resulted in the Battle of the Rosebud and the Battle of the Little Big Horn, where Custer and part of the Seventh Cavalry met their demise. After the Custer disaster, Congress authorized the militarization of the Lakota Indian agencies and an increase in military strength. General Nelson Miles commanded a U.S. force that defeated a few bands of Sioux and Cheyenne at the Battle of Wolf Mountain, Montana, on January 8, 1877, and another group of Sioux and Cheyennes at Muddy Creek, Montana, on May 7, 1877. These two battles and a few smaller ones triggered massive surrenders of the Sioux and Cheyenne and brought about the end of the Great Sioux War. Despite the pressures of continuous warfare, a few bands, like Sitting Bull's band, fled to Canada and held out until the summer of 1877 before surrendering. In that same year, Congress transferred the Black Hills to the United States and further reduced the Great Sioux Indian Reservation with the passage of the Black Hills Act of 1877.

TERM PAPER SUGGESTIONS

1. Write on the sacredness that the Lakota attribute to the Black Hills, the Devil's Tower, and Bear Butte to explain why the Lakota would not sell or lease that sacred land to the federal government.

2. Explore how the end of the Peace Policy led to military solutions to Indian "problems" and for enforcing Indian policy. How is the war for the Black Hills an exemplar of this change to military management of Indian affairs?

3. Investigate how Custer's fight at the Little Big Horn generated negative, if not racist, attitudes toward the Lakota and Indians in general. How does the word "massacre" play a role in generating ill feelings?

4. Aside from the Custer disaster, examine the strength and tactics of the U.S. military campaigns against the Lakota and Cheyenne. Was it inevitable that the United States would eventually win the war? If so, why did the Indians continue to fight, hold out, and resist confinement to reservations?

5. Compare the personalities, tactics, and strategies of the various Lakota, Cheyenne, and Arapaho chiefs. How did their cultural beliefs and worldview influence how they acted within the context of this war?

6. Study the ethics and morality surrounding the legality of treaties. Should the federal government enforce Indian treaty rights and therefore protect Indians from the incursions and encroachments of American citizens on Indian land? By what authority did the military act in changing the boundaries of Indian reservations created by solemn treaties, such as the Great Sioux Indian Reservation?

7. Write on the fight for the Black Hills that continues to this day, for example, the refusal of the Lakota to take a cash settlement when the taking of the Black Hills from the Lakota was ruled illegal by the United States in 1979.

ALTERNATIVE TERM PAPER SUGGESTIONS

1. Create a Microsoft PowerPoint slide show presentation or an iMovie to show how the Black Hills were and are sacred to the Lakota people and have served as their spiritual center. Use illustrations from Bad Heart Bull and other sources to make a powerful visual display.

2. Write a one-week journal as a U.S. soldier on campaign during the Great Sioux War.

SUGGESTED SOURCES

Primary Sources

Bad Heart Bull, Amos, and Helen H. Blish. *Pictographic History of the Oglala Sioux.* Lincoln, NE: University of Nebraska Press, 1967. Reprint, 1995. Not only are illustrations of the Battle of Little Big Horn included, but Bad Heart Bull provides a map of the Black Hills to show their religious significance and sacredness to the Oglala Lakota.

Cozzens, Peter, ed. *The Long War for the Northern Plains (Eyewitnesses to the Indian Wars).* Mechanicsburg, PA: Stackpole Books, 2004. A collection of primary source accounts (letters, reports, newspaper articles, oral stories, and the like).

Greene, Jerome A. *Lakota and Cheyenne: Indian Views of the Great Sioux War, 1876–1877.* Norman, OK: University of Oklahoma Press, 2000. A collection of oral histories of the war from American Indian warriors.

"Transcript of Treaty of Fort Laramie (1851)." http://www.canku-luta.org/Pine-Ridge/laramie_treaty.html. Digital facsimile of the entire treaty, including a map of the reserved lands of the 1868 Fort Laramie Treaty (a hyperlink to the text of the treaty is to the left of the map) compared to the smaller lands of subsequent treaties and agreements. The Fort Laramie Treaty of 1868 can also be found at http://digital. library.okstate.edu/kappler/Vol2/treaties/sio0998.htm.

"Western Reservations, 1875." http://www2.csusm.edu/nadp/map75.htm. Digital reproduction of a map produced in 1875 for the Office of Indian Affairs, showing the changes in the Great Sioux Reservations (and others) without the need for treaty negotiations.

Secondary Sources

Greene, Jerome A., ed. *Battles and Skirmishes of the Great Sioux War, 1876–1877.* Norman, OK: University of Oklahoma Press, 1996. Military history survey of the war with maps.

Greene, Jerome A. *Yellowstone Command: Colonel Nelson A. Miles and the Great Sioux War, 1876–1877.* Norman, OK: University of Oklahoma Press, 2006. Military history of the battles following Little Big Horn, which forced many of the combatant Indians to surrender and return to their respective
reservations.

Hatch, Thom. *Custer and the Battle of the Little Bighorn: An Encyclopedia of the People, Places, Event, Indian Culture and Customs, Information Sources, Art and Films.* Jefferson, NC: McFarland and Company, 2000. Very useful reference.

Hedren, Paul. *Traveler's Guide to the Great Sioux War: The Battlefields, Forts, and Related Sites of America's Greatest Indian War.* Helena, MT: Montana Historical Society Press, 1996. Though meant for tourist, this book is great resource not only because of the great maps but also the mini histories provided about each site.

Lazarus, Edward. *Black Hills, White Justice: The Sioux Nation Versus the United States: 1775–Present.* Lincoln, NE: University of Nebraska Press, 1999. A chronology of historical, military, and legal events that led the federal government to take the Black Hills from the Lakota, as well as the ways the Lakota have fought back.

Michno, Gregory. *The Indian Narrative of Custer's Defeat.* Missoula, MT: Mountain Press Publishing, 1997. Using Indian oral stories, Michno challenges most of the histories about Custer's last stand, and he shows how Custer was a capable and skilled military officer. He also shows how the military prowess of the Indian opposed to Custer was what was important, not overwhelming numbers, which he downgrades.

Petri, Hilda Neihardt, and Raymond J. DeMallie. *The Sixth Grandfather: Black Elk's Teachings Given to John G. Neihardt.* Lincoln, NE: Bison Books,

1985. Details the religion of the Oglala Lakota and the sacredness of the Black Hills.

Robinson, Charles M., III. *A Good Year to Die: The Story of the Great Sioux War.* Norman, OK: University of Oklahoma Press, 1996. Scholarly and military analysis that uses Indian sources and tries to describe Indian tactics and leadership.

Scott, Douglas D., et al. *Archaeological Perspectives on the Battle of Little Bighorn.* Norman, OK: University of Oklahoma Press, 2000. Demonstrates how the tactics used by the Indians, along with their firepower, overwhelmed Custer and his men.

Sundstrom, Linea. "The Sacred Black Hills: An Ethnohistorical Review." *American Indians.* Nancy Shoemaker, ed. Hoboken, NJ: Blackwell Publishing, 2001. In chapter five, entitled "Sacred Places," Sundstrom surveys the primary sources describing the sacredness the Oglala attribute to the Black Hills.

Walker, James R. *Lakota Myth.* 2nd edition. Elaine A. Jahner, ed. Lincoln, NE: Bison Books, 2006. Walker collected cultural information about the Oglala Lakota from 1896–1914, and this work allows readers access to the Lakota worldview and their belief in the sacredness of the Black Hills.

World Wide Web

"The Battle of Little Bighorn." http://www.pbs.org/weta/thewest/resources/archives/six/bighorn.htm. Text of an eyewitness account of Lakota Chief Red Horse, recorded in pictographs and oral story.

"The Battle of the Little Bighorn, 1876." http://www.eyewitnesstohistory.com/custer.htm. Short and concise summary of the battle with images and a map.

"The Black Hills: Documents for the Investigation." http://www.uic.edu/educ/bctpi/historyGIS/blackhills_1wk/bhdocuments.html. A comprehensive, all-in-one links page on the Lakota and the Black Hills, with biography links for major Indian and military officers, including a seven-part series entitled "Native American Culture and the Black Hills."

Corbin, Amy. "Black Hills." http://www.sacredland.org/historical_sites_pages/black_hills.html. An excellent history of the conflict over the Black Hills with hyperlinked references.

"Paha Sapa." http://www.geocities.com/crazyoglala/pahasapa.html. Black Hills historical time line since 1858, with a few links to other relevant entries.

Red Shirt, Delphine. "Cultural Heritage and Sacred Sites: When My Black Hills Money Comes in ... We Will Never Sell These Sacred

Hills." http://www.dialoguebetweennations.com/n2n/pfii/english/ DelphineRedShirt.htm. A personal view of the sacredness of the Black Hills.

White Face, Charmine. "The Black Hills are Still Sacred." http://westgate house.com/art113.html. Description of the religious significance of the Black Hills.

Multimedia Sources

Dying with Custer. Dir. Andrew Grace. Amalgamation Films, 2003. 59 minutes. A documentary of the annual spring reenactment of the Battle of Little Bighorn near Crow Agency in Montana that shows the popularity and fame of this Great Sioux War battle.

In the Light of the Reverence: Protecting American Sacred Lands. Dir. Christopher McLeod. La Honda, CA: Sacred Land Film Project, 2003. DVD. 72 minutes. A documentary that explores the sacredness of American places, including the Black Hills, and the efforts of some to protect and preserve them.

54. Nez Perce War (1877)

In the Wallowa Valley of Washington, the Nez Perce tribe was divided into "no new treaty" and "pro treaty" factions when the discovery of gold on reservation lands in 1863 caused the United States to desire a new treaty, one that would revise the boundaries of the reservation to exclude the mineral-rich lands. The Nez Perce living outside the new boundaries refused to sign, while those within did sign. Chief Joseph and Chief Joseph the Younger lived outside of the new reservation boundaries, and President Ulysses S. Grant, after the death of the senior Chief Joseph, supported their right by setting aside part of the valley as a reservation for them. Nevertheless, after the end of treaty making and due to increased pressure from American settlers and from orders by General Oliver Howard to move to the new reservation or be forced there, Chief Joseph the Younger and most of his people, in order to avoid hostilities, made preparations to move. At that point young warriors killed four racist Whites, and the fighting escalated to the killing of many more—this time peaceful—settlers. Chief Joseph tried to talk peace, but undisciplined civilian volunteers fired at his delegation. Then Chief Joseph and up to 800 Nez Perce fled, some say to join Sitting Bull in Canada. Thus began the epic 3-month, 1,700-mile chase led by Civil War veterans General

Howard, Colonel Samuel Sturgis and the Seventh Cavalry, and General Nelson Miles, interrupted by the Battle of Clearwater and many other skirmishes. Finally the Nez Perce were defeated at the Battle of Bear Paw Mountain, and the Nez Perce surrendered. At Bear Paw, Chief Joseph lamented: "Hear me, my Chiefs! I am tired; my heart is sick and sad. From where the sun now stands, I will fight no more forever."

TERM PAPER SUGGESTIONS

1. Show how the power relation of "treaties" shifted to the United States. Could the Nez Perce negotiate as equals?

2. How did the United States encourage the Nez Perce to sign a new treaty and encourage all Nez Perce to move onto a new reservation? What were the consequences if they did not?

3. Show how some of the actions of the military actually forced more of the Nez Perce, such as Looking Glass and his people, to join Chief Joseph's exodus.

4. Study the role of undisciplined white settlers in the conflict. Did they have a vested interest in starting a war between the U.S. military and the Nez Perce?

5. Was war necessary? Could it have been avoided? Study how Chief Joseph and his people attempted many times to avoid war. When killing did occur, how did Chief Joseph try to find a peaceful alternative to an increase in hostilities?

6. Study and write on the great speech of Chief Joseph. Why is it remembered by so many today?

ALTERNATIVE TERM PAPER SUGGESTIONS

1. From the perspective of a military officer, write a criticism of the behavior of certain local white citizens who provoked the Nez Perce to hostilities. Give at least two examples from the sources.

2. Starting with Chief Joseph's lament, quoted here, continue the speech retrospectively to explain why his heart was sick and tired and why he would fight no more forever.

SUGGESTED SOURCES

Primary Sources

Cozzens, Peter. *Eyewitnesses to the Indian Wars, 1865–1890: The Wars for the Pacific Northwest*. Mechanicsburg, PA: Stackpole Books, 2002. A collection of primary source accounts (letters, reports, newspaper articles, oral stories, and the like) of the battles and skirmishes. "Part Three: The Nez Perce Campaign, 1877" is of particular interest.

Howard, O. O. *Nez Perce Joseph.* Lee and Shepard, 1881. http://books.google.com/books?id=Ky3-06qjgtYC&printsec=titlepage. General O. O. Howard writes from his own perspective of the epic chase of Chief Joseph and the Nez Perce.

Joseph, Nez Perce Chief. *That All People May Be One People, Send Rain to Wash the Face of the Earth.* 1879. Reprint, Kooskia, ID: Mountain Meadow Press, 1995. The text of an interview with a reporter from the *North American Review* in 1879, where Chief Joseph recounts the Nez Perce War of 1877 and his people's dealings with local Whites.

Secondary Sources

Beal, Merrill D. *"I Will Fight No More Forever": Chief Joseph and the Nez Perce War.* Seattle, WA: University of Washington Press, 1966. An ethnohistorical and military study of the Nez Perce and the war.

Greene, Jerome A. *Nez Perce Summer, 1877: The U.S. Army and the Nee-Me-Poo.* Helena, MT: Montana Historical Society Press, 2000. A 14-chapter online book of the entire war with 16 battle maps, and 26 illustrations. Excellent analysis and a quick read.

Gulick, Bill. *Chief Joseph Country: Land of the Nez Perce.* Caldwell, ID: Caxton Printers, 1981. A detailed general history of the Nez Perce and the land they lived in, from the early times to Lewis and Clark to the War of 1877.

Hampton, Bruce. *Children of Grace: The Nez Perce War of 1877.* Lincoln, NE: Bison Books, 2002. Explores the relationship between Whites and the Nez Perce, along with the massacre of 18 settlers that started the war.

Lavender, David S. *Let Me Be Free: The Nez Perce Tragedy.* Norman, OK: University of Oklahoma Press, 1999. Looks at the tragedy of "friendly" Indians who were nevertheless subjected to the same treatment from Whites as other recalcitrant tribes.

Moeller, Bill, and Jan Moeller. *Chief Joseph and the Nez Perces: A Photographic History.* Missoula, MT: Mountain Press Publishing Company, 1995. A collection of photographs of the landscape, free of modern blemishes, that Chief Joseph and his people traveled through.

Moulton, Candy V. *Chief Joseph: Guardian of the People.* New York: A Forge Book: Published by Tom Doherty Associates, LLC. A readable and detailed biography aimed at young adults.

Nerburn, Kent. *Chief Joseph and the Flight of the Nez Perce: The Untold Story of an American Tragedy.* San Francisco, CA: Harper San Francisco, 2005. Questions the role of Chief Joseph as war leader of the Nez Perce and asserts that U.S. generals overemphasized Joseph's role to heighten their own.

Thompson, Scott M. *I Will Tell of My War Story: A Pictorial Account of the Nez Perce War*. Seattle, WA: University of Washington Press, 2000. Ledger drawings and illustration detailing the war from a Nez Perce perspective, with interpretive descriptions and essays.

World Wide Web

Beck, Jennifer. "Freedom Hero: Chief Joseph." http://myhero.com/myhero/hero.asp ?hero=c_joseph. A concise and readable biography written by a young adult.
"Chief Joseph Speaks: Selected Statements and Speeches." http://www.pbs.org/weta/ thewest/resources/archives/six/jospeak.htm. Interesting commentary on the changes Indians have had to make to live within the white man's world.
Greene, Jerome A. *Nez Perce Summer 1877: The U.S. Army and the Nee-Me-Poo Crisis*. http://www.nps.gov/archive/nepe/greene/contents.htm. A 14-chapter online book of the entire war with 16 battle maps and 26 illustrations. Excellent analysis and a quick read.
Kittelson, Adam. "Nez Perce." http://www.mnsu.edu/emuseum/cultural/ northamerica/nez_perce.html. Short description of the tribe.
"Nez Perce National Historic Trail." http://www.fs.fed.us/npnht/. Travel the actual trail the Nez Perce used on this comprehensive site of the National Historic Trail, which not only has a map of the epic chase but also has many short biographies of participants of the war.
Venn, George. "Soldier to Advocate: C. E. S. Wood's 1877 Diary of Alaska and the Nez Perce Conflict." http://www.historycooperative.org/journals/ ohq/106.1/venn.html. An essay by Venn followed by Wood's diary, which reveals C. E. S. Wood's views of the Nez Perce War of 1877.

Multimedia Source

I Will Fight No More Forever. Dir. Richard T. Heffron. Hollywood, CA: David Wolper Productions, 1975. DVD. 100 minutes. A sympathetic Hollywood version of the epic chase of Chief Joseph and the Nez Perce.

55. Women's National Indian Association Is Founded (1879)

Founded in Philadelphia in 1879 by Mary Bonney and Amelia Stone Quinton, the Women's National Indian Association (WNIA) advocated for American Indians' rights: the protection of their lands from further white encroachment and upholding of federal Indian treaties. However, the Christianization and assimilation of American Indians was their often-stated goal. Composed mostly of middle- to upper-class white Christian women, and with a membership that was never very large, they were nevertheless an influential and powerful lobby for Indian rights due their overall goal of Christianizing and civilizing Indians; they also believed the willful encroachments of land-hungry railroad men, settlers, and prospectors would make these goals more difficult. In 1880, they presented their first petition to President Rutherford B. Hayes, requesting that he and Congress "prevent the encroachments of white settlers upon Indian Territory, and to guard the Indians in the enjoyment of all the rights which have been guaranteed to them on the faith of the nation." By 1881 they changed their name to "Indian Treaty-Keeping and Protective Association." However, assimilation, the WNIA believed, was the answer to war and confinement to reservations. Assimilation required Indian people to shed communal land in favor of individual allotments and for Indian children to be provided an "industrial" education. Therefore, the WNIA urged for the dismantling of the reservations and the creation of schools to train and prepare Indians for civilization. This made them ardent advocates for the passage of the Allotment (Dawes) Act of 1887. They remained active until 1951.

TERM PAPER SUGGESTIONS

1. Examine the membership of WNIA and its leaders, Mary Bonney and Amelia Stone Quinton, and discuss the role of American women in the reform movements of the nineteenth century. Why was the plight of the Indian a worthy cause?

2. Write on the role of Christianity as well as the U.S. Constitution in the WNIA's ability to formulate an effective moral and ethical argument for Indian policy reform and the protection of Indian rights.

3. Look at the plans that were advocated by the WNIA for the development of schools designed to educate the Indian for civilization. What is an "industrial school" or a "manual labor training school"? Were the goals of training Indian men to be farmers and Indian women to be ideals of domesticity achievable goals?

4. Investigate the missionary activities of WNIA. How did they play to incorporate Christianization in their efforts to "save" the Indian?

5. Write on the idea of the WNIA to slowly dismantle the reservations system, breaking apart the communal land base into individual allotments, which saw fruition in the passage of the Allotment (Dawes) Act of 1887. What was the logic behind this idea to help Indians?

6. Explore the desire or lack of desire of Indians to participate in the civilizing and Christianizing efforts of the WNIA. Were they ever consulted?

ALTERNATIVE TERM PAPER SUGGESTIONS

1. Write an appeal to women in the manner of Mary Bonney on the plight of the American Indian at the end of the nineteenth century, with the goal of persuading your listeners/readers to action.

2. Organize an online convention of women Indian reformers by putting together slides of historic and fictional members of the WNIA with photographs, position statements, and short biographies to share as an overall report on the association, its purposes, goals, and accomplishments

SUGGESTED SOURCES

Primary Sources

"The Care of the Rev Men: Meeting of the Women's National Indian Association." http://query.nytimes.com/gst/abstract.html?res=9E0CE6DA1338E233A2575B-C0A9649D94639ED7CF. Downloadable PDF facsimile of the 1892 *New York Times* article covering the national meeting, "where about 200 delegates from nearly every state of the Union" were present.

"The Dawes Act, February 8, 1887." http://www.pbs.org/weta/thewest/resources/archives/eight/dawes.htm. Online facsimile of the Allotment Act of 1887.

Painter, C. C. *The Condition of Affairs in Indian Territory and California.* Philadelphia, PA: Indian Rights Association, 1888. Reprint, Brooklyn, NY: AMS Press, 1976. A report by a WNIA member.

Quinton, Amelia S. "The Woman's National Indian Association (1894)." http://digital.library.upenn.edu/women/eagle/congress/quinton.html. A detailed history in the words of one of its founders. Presented at the Congress of Women at the 1893 Columbian Exposition in Chicago.

Secondary Sources

Hagan, William T. *The Indian Rights Association: The Herbert Welsh Years, 1882–1904.* Tucson, AZ: The University of Arizona Press, 1985. A detailed history of the Indian Rights Association at the peak of its reform efforts.

Mathes, Valerie Sherer. "Nineteenth Century Women and Reform: The Women's National Indian Association." *American Indian Quarterly* 14, no. 1 (Winter 1990): 1–18. A scholarly essay and history of the association, its goals, accomplishments, and leaders.

Newman, Louise Michele. *White Women's Rights.* New York: Oxford University Press, 1999. Chapter one explores the activism of white women in Indian missions and their participation in WNIA as a forerunner of the suffrage and other women's rights movements.

Prucha, Francis P. *The Great Father: The United States Government and the American Indians.* Lincoln, NE: University of Nebraska Press, 1984. General reference to laws and acts concerning Indians and to Indian rights groups who opposed or advocated for them.

Tong, Benson. *Susan La Flesche Picotte, Md.: Omaha Indian Leader and Reformer.* Norman, OK: University of Oklahoma Press, 1999. A comprehensive biography of La Flesche Picotte that explores how Americanization does not necessarily mean that La Flesche loses her Omaha Indian identity.

World Wide Web

"Amelia Stone Quinton." http://www.awomanaweek.com/quinton.html. Explores the political activism of Quinton and her role with the WNIA.

"Dawes Act." http://www.bartleby.com/65/da/DawesAct.html. Short description of the act WNIA helped to get passed and enacted.

Green, Norma Kidd. "Susan La Flesche Picotte." Radcliffe College, 1971. http://www.awomanaweek.com/picotte.html. Through a program of financing professional training for talented Indians, the WNIA sponsored Susan La Flesche, from the Omaha Reservation, to attend the Woman's Medical College of Pennsylvania in Philadelphia. She became the first female Indian doctor when she graduated in 1889.

"People & Events: Mary Lucinda Bonney, 1816–1900." http://www.pbs.org/wgbh/amex/grant/peopleevents/p_bonney.html. Short biography of Bonney.

Multimedia Source

In the Whiteman's Image. Dir. Christine Lesiak. WGBH, 1992. DVD. 60 minutes. Season 4, Episode 13 of the television series *The American Experience* (1988), exploring the Indian boarding school experience, an educational goal of the Women's National Indian Association.

56. Richard Pratt and the Founding of the Carlisle Indian School (1879–1904)

During the 1860s and 1870s, Richard Pratt fought in the American Civil War. After the war he continued his military career in the Southern

Western Plains as captain of the 10th (Colored) Cavalry, the famous Buffalo Soldiers. In 1879 he founded the Carlisle Indian School after, as a jailor of 72 Indian prisoners at Fort Marion Prison, St. Augustine, Florida, Pratt developed an educational indoctrination program. The program was based on military training methods: cutting of hair, wearing of uniforms, learning a new language, marching in formation, and learning a trade. With help from Christian reformers who loathed federal Indian policies that were designed to exterminate the Indians, Pratt was able to convince the secretary of the interior and the war department to take his St. Augustine experiment to a larger scale and facility. Carlisle Barracks in central Pennsylvania became the home of Pratt's experimental Indian school. The larger plan was to recruit Indians from places such as the Dakotas and take them far away from their homes and separate them from their families, languages, and cultures. Carlisle was the first off-reservation boarding school, and over 12,000 Indians would eventually make the trip, with many of them never returning home. Once at Carlisle, the practice of "killing the Indian to save the man" (Pratt's most famous quotation) was put into action within a military and educational environment that assumed the inferiority of the Indian mind and the need to teach young Indian students, male and female, basic skills of industrial labor and domesticity as well as academic instruction. Although the school would eventually close in 1918, Carlisle would serve as the model of Indian boarding schools throughout the nation, well into the late 1980s.

TERM PAPER SUGGESTIONS

1. Write on the concept of total assimilation and Americanization that required the complete reeducation of an individual and that person's indoctrination and socialization into another culture and society.

2. Explore the reasoning behind the reformers like Pratt who believed assimilation was better than extermination.

3. The prevailing attitude toward Indian students and youth was that they were savages. Study the racial issues involved in the Indian education system and the methodology implemented and explain it in an essay.

4. Were Indians blank slates? Was the belief that nothing of Indian culture (language, art, craft, philosophy, oral tradition, and religion) was redeemable? Explore the impossibility of achieving "total" assimilation through boarding school methods.

5. Explore the boarding school experience at Carlisle from the words of the Indian students themselves. Some of their experiences were positive, and some the programs, like Pop Warner's football program, were legendary.

6. Investigate the way Indian students retained and celebrated their Indian identity regardless of the indoctrination process. Look at songs, art, and writings to determine whether any vestige of Indian identity remained.

ALTERNATIVE TERM PAPER SUGGESTIONS

1. Make an electronic photo gallery of famous Indians who attended Carlisle Indian School and who became successful professionals (for example, Jim Thorpe, Lone Star Dietz, Zitkala-Sa, Luther Standing Bear).

2. From the perspective of an Indian student spending one full year away from home, write letters to your parents describing your experiences (good and bad) during one nine-month school year and a summer working at a local Pennsylvania farm as part of Carlisle's "outing program."

SUGGESTED SOURCES

Primary Sources

Archuleta, Margaret L., et al., eds. *Away from Home: American Indian Boarding School Experiences.* Phoenix, AZ: Heard Museum, 2000. A collection of writing, poems, photographs, paintings, and illustrations by and about the American Indians forced to attend boarding schools, including Carlisle.

Pratt, Richard Henry. *Battlefield & Classroom: Four Decades with the American Indian, 1867–1904.* Robert M. Utley, ed. Yale University, 1964. Reprint, Norman, OK: University of Oklahoma Press, 2003. Memoirs of the famous Indian educator and policy maker.

U.S. Bureau of Education. *The Indian School at Carlisle Barracks.* U.S. Office of Education, 1880. http://books.google.com/books?id=iZwIAAAAQAAJ. Report of officials as they toured and inspected the schools, the lodgings, the shops, and the infirmary, as well as reports on the instruction and physical exercise of the Indian students.

Secondary Sources

Adams, David Wallace. *Education for Extinction: American Indians and the Boarding School Experience 1875–1928.* Lawrence, KS: University Press of Kansas, 1997. Thoroughly examines the government's Indian education plan to, as Pratt has stated, "kill the Indian to save the man." Indian culture was to be eradicated and replaced.

Benjey, Tom. *Keep A-Goin': The Life of Lone Star Dietz.* Carlisle, PA: Tuxedo Press, 2006. Biography of a the colorful life of this adopted Indian whose exploits included playing football at the Carlisle Indian School and evading military service in World War I due his non-Indian status.

Child, Brenda J. *Boarding School Seasons: American Indian Families, 1900–1940.* Lincoln, NE: University of Nebraska Press, 1998. Although focusing on the Red Lake Chippewa, the book covers the topic entirely (in about 150 pages), "From Reservation to Boarding School" to "Runaway Boys, Resistant Girls."

Eastman, Elaine Goodale. *Pratt, the Red Man's Moses.* Norman, OK: University of Oklahoma Press, 1935. Written by the wife of Charles Eastman, a Lakota and Americanization advocate and supporter of the Dawes Act, 1887. Praises Pratt for his idea and accomplishments.

Fear-Segal, Jacqueline. *White Man's Club: Schools, Race and the Struggle of Indian Acculturation.* Lincoln, NE: University of Nebraska Press, 2007. Examines all of the Indian boarding schools in terms of race relations and in the context of Indian inferiority.

Hoxie, Frederick E. *A Final Promise: The Campaign to Assimilate the Indian, 1880–1920.* Lincoln, NE: University of Nebraska, 2001. A scholarly examination of assimilation/Americanization Indian policies, including the creation of Indian schools.

Jenkins, Sally. *The Real All Americans: The Team That Changed a Game, a People, a Nation.* Garden City, NY: Doubleday, 2007. Covers the history and fame of "Pop" Warner, Jim Thorpe, and many others of the famous Carlisle football team. Jenkins argues that the Carlisle team invented and executed the forward pass.

Lomawaima, K. Tsianina, and Teresa L. McCarty. *To Remain an Indian: Lesson in Democracy from a Century of Native American Education.* New York: Teachers College Press, 2006. Places the Americanization and assimilation practices of Pratt into a larger context of Indian education, where mistakes or misguided policies are explored and where the ability of Indian students to maintain and perpetuate an Indian identity is celebrated. More importantly, the authors present the Indian student as a dynamic and capable learner and not as a blank slate that has to be reprogrammed.

Trafzer, Clifford E., et al. *Boarding School Blues.* Lincoln, NE: University of Nebraska Press, 2006. A collection of essays examining experiences, mostly negative, of American Indians from boarding schools across the nation, including Carlisle.

World Wide Web

Anderson, Stephanie. *On Sacred Ground: Commemorating Survival and Loss at Carlisle Indian School.* http://www.wordsasweapons.com/indianschool.htm. A short historical essay that ends with acknowledgement of the Indian students who died at Carlisle and were buried in the "Indian" cemetery.

"An Indian Boarding School Photo Gallery." http://www.english.uiuc.edu/maps/poets/a_f/erdrich/boarding/gallery.htm. Photographs of students from a variety of boarding schools in the late eighteenth and early nineteenth centuries.

"Carlisle Indian Industrial School, 1879–1918." http://home.epix.net/~landis/. Complete Web site resource with photographs, historical essays, and bibliographies for primary and secondary source materials. A good place to start any research project.

Davis, Julie. "American Indian Boarding School Experiences: Recent Studies from Native Perspectives." http://www.oah.org/pubs/magazine/deseg/davis.html. Survey of recent scholarship in the subject of Indian boarding school experiences.

"Let All That Is Indian Within You Die!" http://www.twofrog.com/rezsch.html. An excellent online resource with many links to primary source materials and a historical essay, "The Reservation Boarding School System in the United States, 1870–1928." Appended to this essay is the most complete list of links to this subject and the Carlisle Indian School.

"Photographs from Indian Boarding Schools." http://www.hanksville.org/sand/intellect/gof.html. Links page to photographic collections; includes several links to photos from Carlisle.

Rosa, Sonia M. "The Puerto Ricans at Carlisle Indian School." http://www.kacike.org/SoniaRosa.html. Reveals the presence of Hispanics sent to Carlisle.

Multimedia Sources

In the Whiteman's Image. Dir. Christine Lesiak. WGBH, 1992. DVD. 60 minutes. Season 4, Episode 13 of the television series *The American Experience* (1988), exploring the abuses of the Indian boarding school experience.

Jim Thorpe: All American (1951). Dir. Michael Curtiz. Warner Home Video, 2007. DVD. 105 minutes. This history of Jim Thorpe includes his college career, his Olympic story, and his baseball and basketball playing.

Teaching Indians to Be White. Dir. Brian Moser. Central Productions, 1993. VHS. 30 minutes. An excellent survey of the history of Indian boarding schools from Pratt to the present. Available from Films for the Humanities and Sciences, P.O. Box 2053, Princeton, NJ 08543; (800) 257–5126.

57. Courts of Indian Offenses (1883) and Indian Major Crimes Act (1885)

With the intention of moving Indians toward assimilation and Americanization, the Courts of Indian Offenses (1883) were established by the "Indian Office" on an Indian reservation with the judges (Indian) being appointed by Indian agents (white). Also, the Indian Major Crimes Act, 23 Stat. 385 was passed by Congress in 1885, making murder and other serious crimes committed by an Indian in Indian land to be federal offenses that would be tried in federal court. Rather than being fashioned on Indian notions of law and punishment, the Courts of Indian Offenses and the codes they administered were created in the image of the federal system, so from their very creation certain religious, ceremonial, and ritual practices, as well as plural marriage, were outlawed. Following this trend of eroding the power of traditional tribal governments and practice, the Major Crimes Act took the power of criminal law as it pertains to major crimes away from tribal authorities and placed it within the jurisdiction of the United States. The act was in direct conflict to the Supreme Court case of *Ex Parte Crow Dog,* 109 U.S. 566 (1883), which upheld the sovereign power of the tribe to oversee murder of one Indian by another and that federal courts did not have jurisdiction. The creation of the Indian courts and the passage of the Indian Major Crimes Act furthered the goal of Americanization, plus the goals of federalization of American Indians and American Indian tribal governments. They also set a juris-prudential foundation and precedent for the practice of U.S. Indian law in Indian country to this day.

TERM PAPER SUGGESTIONS

1. Write on the outlawing of Indian religious practices, such as the Sun Dance, Scalp Dance, and War Dance, and of plural marriage through the

establishment of the Courts of Indian Offenses as a component of the Americanization of American Indians.

2. Despite the acculturation and assimilation purposes behind the creation of Indian courts, examine the way that this action supported tribal sovereignty. Why were/are Indians the only racial minorities with governments and courts?

3. Write on the ways in which tribal courts have changed since 1883 and have been able to incorporate tribal traditions and practices within their own judicial system. Most tribal courts have Web sites and offices that will help researchers and students to investigate this topic.

4. Explore the implications in terms of sovereignty and tribal rights of the Supreme Court finding in *Ex Parte Crow Dog,* 109 U.S. 556 (1883).

5. Explain why the U.S. Congress passed the Indian Major Crimes Act in 1885 in direct opposition to *Ex Parte Crow Dog,* 109 U.S. 556 (1883).

6. Examine the jurisdictional and sovereignty implications of the Indian Major Crimes Act. On one hand, the Federal Bureau of Investigation is responsible for investigating major crimes and the federal courts system is responsible for trials; on the other hand, tribal governments are robbed of a substantial portion of their sovereign rights.

ALTERNATIVE TERM PAPER SUGGESTIONS

1. Create a pamphlet, using the many templates available in software applications, to describe the legal rights of American Indians living on reservations.

2. Create several scenarios where an Indian commits a major or minor crime against another Indian in a variety of locations (Indian country, county land, state land, and federal land, examples of federal land being a dam or military reserve). Have others determine who has jurisdiction: tribal, local, state, or federal courts.

SUGGESTED SOURCES

Primary Sources

Ex Parte Crow Dog, 109 U.S. 556 (1883). http://supreme.justia.com/us/109/556/case.html. Complete text and opinion of the Supreme Court case.

"Indian Major Crimes Act (18 S.S.C. § 1153)." http://www4.law.cornell.edu/uscode/uscode18/usc_sec_18_00001153———000-.html. The U.S. code as it reads today. Notice that the original 7 major offensives have been increased to 16.

Secondary Sources

Deloria, Vine, Jr., and David E. Wilkins. *Tribes, Treaties, and Constitutional Tribulations.* Austin, TX: University of Texas Press, 2000. Explores the relationship between the U.S. Constitution and the federal government and Indian tribes and their governments.

Haring, Sidney L. *Crow Dog's Case: American Indian Sovereignty, Tribal Law, and United States Law in the Nineteenth Century.* Cambridge, UK: Cambridge University Press, 1994. Describes how the Congress in its enforcement of "plenary" power circumvented the Supreme Court opinion that Indian governments had sole jurisdiction over crimes committed in Indian country.

Johansen, Bruce E., ed. *The Encyclopedia of Native American Legal Tradition.* Westport, CT: Greenwood Press, 1998. Page 340 starts a short history of the tribal courts.

Pevar, Stephen L. *The Rights of Indians and Tribes. The Authoritative ACLU Guide to Indian and Tribal Rights.* 3rd edition. New York: New York University Press, 2004. Provides a historical overview as well as answering many legal questions.

Rose, Jeffrey Ian, and Larry Gould, eds. *Native Americans and the Criminal Justice System.* Boulder, CO: Paradigm Publishers, 2006. A collection of essays that covers the full range of criminal and legal issues in Indian country, including tribal courts and major crimes.

Rosen, Lawrence. *American Indians and the Law.* Durham, NC: School of Law, Duke University, 1976. Reprint, Edison, NJ: Transaction Publishers, 1978. An older historical survey.

Wilkins, David E. *American Indian Sovereignty and the U.S. Supreme Court: The Masking of Justice.* Austin, TX: University of Texas Press, 1997. Detailed analysis of 15 U.S. Supreme Court cases involving Native Americans.

Wilkins, David E. *Uneven Ground: American Indian Sovereignty and Federal Law.* Norman, OK: University of Oklahoma Press, 2001. A scholarly study of federal law and Supreme Court rulings.

World Wide Web

Clark, M. Wesley. "Enforcing Criminal Law on Native American Lands." http://findarticles.com/p/articles/mi_m2194/is_4_74/ai_n13782082/pg_7. Describes the Major Crimes Act and amendments as well as the role of the Federal Bureau of Investigation and federal court jurisdiction on Indian lands.

"General Guide to Criminal Jurisdiction in Indian Country." http://www.tribal-institute.org/lists/jurisdiction.htm. A list with definitions of legal terms as they pertain to Indians, such as the question of "What is Indian Country?" Also has links to all official federal laws and acts.

Growe, Honorable Chief Tribal Judge Gary. http://www.ptla.org/wabanaki/court.htm. Growe writes: "This article is designed to provide a guide to any individual who has the occasion to appear in Tribal Court in connection to a Civil (any non-criminal) matter."

NiiSka, Clara. "Indian Courts: A Brief History." http://www.maquah.net/clara/Press-ON/01-06-08.html. A general history of the establishment of the Indian courts within a larger historical context, starting in 1868 with *Ex Parte Crow Dog*. Follow the links as she chronicles the relevant laws and cases to 1995.

Prygoski, Philip J. "From Marshall to Marshall: The Supreme Court's Changing Stance on Tribal Sovereignty." http://www.abanet.org/genpractice/magazine/1995/fall/marshall.html. Places the *Ex Parte Crow Dog* decision and the Major Crimes Act into a historical chronology of the erosion of tribal power and sovereignty.

"*United States v. Clapox*, 1888." http://www.ohs.org/education/oregonhistory/historical_records/dspDocument.cfm?doc_ID=0DF2E337-A7C5-5847-75179FF4F6689D3E. Places the courts of Indian offenses as "mere educational and disciplinary instrumentalities" to achieve the Americanization of Indians living on reservations.

Yazzie, Chief Justice (Emeritus). "History of the Courts of the Navajo Nation." http://www.navajocourts.org/history.htm. From a Navajo justice, a brief history of the largest and longest tribal court system in Indian country.

Multimedia Source

Tribal Nations: The Story of Federal Indian Law. Dir. Lisa Jaeger. Tanana Chiefs Conference Signature Media Production, 2006. DVD. 60 minutes. Documentary film examining the development of U.S. federal Indian law.

58. General Allotment Act (Dawes Act) (1887)

"Allotment" was a policy to divide lands held collectively by tribes into smaller sections for individuals, for the express purpose of advancing Americanization and assimilation and to save the Indian from "savagism" and extermination. Allotment advocates of the Christian humanitarian faction believed private ownership of property would lead to an easy conversion of Indians to Christianity and to American ways of life. On the other side, advocates such as land speculators, settlers, prospectors, and railroad men believed Indians (collectively) owned too much land. For this collection of biased Whites hungry for Indian land, the Allotment Act was a means to access Indian land for their own profitable purposes, and their desires led to the most egregious abuses of the allotment era. Over time, they were able to acquire more and more Indian land, and that would have never been possible without the benevolence and advocacy of the humanitarian reformers and the Allotment Act. Regardless, the Allotment Act was flawed for several more important if not insidious reasons: (1) Indians were not owners of the land allotted to them because, according to federal law and trust status, Indians, even individuals, could only use "Indian" land, but they could not sell it; (2) as long as they could not sell their land, Indians also could not give their land away, for instance, to a single descendant under the age-old custom of transferring land to a single offspring; (3) they could not instantaneously become farmers or ranchers; and (4) the best lands for agriculture or livestock were designated unscrupulously as "surplus" lands to be sold to non-Indians. The net result of the Allotment Act was another substantial loss of land for American Indians, from 138 million acres in 1887 to 48 million acres in 1934.

TERM PAPER SUGGESTIONS

1. Explore the reasons why the humanitarian reformers of Indian policy favored and advocated assimilation/Americanization. Was the extermination of Indians a real possibility?

2. Define and explain Indian "surplus" lands, the lands not allotted to Indians. Who bought the land? For what were the revenues generated from the sale of surplus land used?

3. Investigate how Indians were to be trained to "farm" the land that they were allotted. What if the land was not tillable?

4. Study how a select Indian reservation was allotted, for example, the Oglala Lakota's Pine Ridge Sioux Indian Reservation. Notice the checkerboard pattern of allotment. Note that the pre-allotment reservation boundaries are still present in many maps of reservations. What does this imply?

5. Write on the reactions of Indians to the allotment of their lands.

6. Study the inheritance issue. How were Indian lands further fragmented and divided due to this problem?

ALTERNATIVE TERM PAPER SUGGESTIONS

1. Create a pre-allotment and a post-allotment map of a single Indian reservation to show the loss of land and the pattern of land distribution.

2. Make another map that depicts county, reservation, and state boundaries to further show the complexities of land ownership and jurisdiction when "Indian country" becomes even harder to distinguish.

SUGGESTED SOURCES

Primary Sources

Prucha, Francis P. *Documents of United States Indian Policy.* Lincoln, NE: University of Nebraska Press, 2000. General primary source reference.

"Siletz Documents." http://www2.csusm.edu/nadp/dindex.htm. Toward the middle of the page under "Allotment" are five links to documents concerning the allotment on the Siletz Reservation.

"Summary of the General Allotment Act, Act of February 8, 1887 (24 Stat. 388, ch. 119, 25 USCA 331)." http://www.indianlandtenure.org/ILTFallotment/histlegis/GeneralAllotmentAct.htm. A summary of the pertinent sections of the act with a link to the full text in Kappler's *Indian Affairs Laws and Treaties.*

Secondary Sources

Carlson, Leonard A. *Indians, Bureaucrats, and Land: The Dawes Act and the Decline of Indian Farming.* Westport, CT: Greenwood Press, 1981. Using an economic analytical model, the author concludes that Indians would farm less rather than more after allotment.

Carter, Kent. *The Dawes Commission and the Allotment of the Five Civilized Tribes, 1893–1914.* Orem, UT: Ancestry Publishing, 1999. Examines the process of allotment, from enrollment to allotting the lands; to buying, selling, and renting; to the failure of the system.

Greenwald, Emily. *Reconfiguring the Reservation: The Nez Perces, Jicarilla Apaches, and the Dawes Act.* Albuquerque, NM: University of New Mexico, 2002. Demonstrates that Indians selected land and used that land for their own purposes rather than to farm and to become Americans.

Hoxie, Frederick E. *A Final Promise: The Campaign to Assimilate the Indians, 1880–1920.* Lincoln, NE: University of Nebraska Press, 1984. Reprint, 2001. Detailed historical treatment that traces the Indian Reform movement, the Dawes Act, and the tragic results of the assimilation policies.

Otis, Delos Sacket. *The Dawes Act and the Allotment of Indian Lands.* Norman, OK: University of Oklahoma Press, 1973. A general overview and history.

Prucha, Francis Paul, ed. *Americanizing the American Indian: Writings by the "Friends of the Indian" 1880–1900.* Cambridge, MA: Harvard University Press, 1973. Explores the humanitarian reformers and their efforts to Christianize and Americanize the Indian. Covers the Dawes Act in detail.

Prucha, Francis P. *The Great Father: The United States Government and the American Indians.* Lincoln, NE: University of Nebraska Press, 1984. General reference to laws and acts concerning Indians.

Washburn, Wilcomb E. *The Assault on Indian Tribalism: The General Allotment Law (Dawes Act) of 1887.* Philadelphia, PA: Lippincott, 1975. Shows that the reformers had good intentions but the effects of allotment were devastating to Indian people.

World Wide Web

"Allotment." http://www.indianlandtenure.org/ILTFallotment/allotindex/index.htm. A complete Web site with an introduction, Q&A, glossary, legislation (historic and recent), court cases, and tribal-specific information.

"Allotment Tables." http://www2.csusm.edu/nadp/atables.htm. Statistical tables showing the net reduction of tribal lands by year.

"Comparing Allotment to Homesteading, 1900–1915." http://www2.csusm.edu/nadp/acompare.htm. Analytical comparative essay.

"Dawes General Allotment Act, or Dawes Severalty Act (United States [1887])." http://original.britannica.com/eb/topic-152952/Dawes-General-Allotment-Act. Encyclopedia Britannica, 2008. A links page pointing to some very useful and relevant information.

"Dawes Severalty Act." http://www.answers.com/topic/dawes-act. Compilation of many Web sources on the subject.

"The Nez Perce and the Dawes Act." http://www.pbs.org/weta/thewest/lesson_plans/lesson03.htm. Comprehensive lesson plan that reveals the desire of the Nez Perce not to divide their lands.

"What Were the Results of Allotment?" http://www2.csusm.edu/nadp/asubject.htm. Traces the origin and effects of the act on Indian reservations.

Multimedia Sources

Bury My Heart at Wounded Knee. Dir. Yves Simoneau. HBO Films, 2007. DVD. 133 minutes. Though much criticized for inaccuracy and portrayal of characters, the movie does cover Senator Henry L. Dawes's efforts to get the Oglala Lakota to accept allotment.

500 Nations. Dir. Ack Leustig. 500 Nations Productions, 2005. 4 DVDs. 8 episodes (49 minutes per episode). "Episode 8: Attack on Culture" explores Americanization and Indian policy from 1887 to the present day.

59. Wovoka and the Ghost Dance Movement (1889)

Wovoka was born a Paiute Indian in western Nevada around 1856, and after his father died, David Wilson raised Wovoka (Jack Wilson) on his ranch. Wovoka learned English and, some claim, Christianity. In the late 1880s, during an eclipse of the sun, Wovoka had a vision, and he soon became a mystic and prophet. He prophesied that if Indian people prayed in the right manner, Whites would be swallowed into the earth, dead ancestors would come back to life, the buffalo would return, and the Indian people could enjoy a spiritual and immortal life. Praying was simple: Indians needed to dance in a large circle and make and sing songs in praise of the creator. In this way, Indian tribes could use the basic structure within their own language, dance, and song traditions, which appealed to the many diverse tribes of the west, for the Ghost Dance religion spread rapidly. In addition to ritual and communal prayer, Indians were also to live a moral and righteous life. "You must not fight. Do right always," Wovoka preached, and he stressed the importance of not making trouble with Whites. To some ethnographers and historians, Wovoka combined elements of Paiute mysticism and Christianity, because he did not hesitate to mention Jesus and used the term "Supreme Being" in his sermons. Regardless of the connection to Christianity, the federal authorities, especially the military, viewed the rise of the Ghost Dance movement as a prelude to an outbreak of hostilities, especially because many divergent groups of Indian tribes practiced the Ghost Dance. A general and unified Indian rebellion was feared, so the Ghost Dance was discouraged and outlawed by government officials. The movement ended with the slaughter of Big Foot's (Big Foot was a Minneconjou Lakota and religious leader) band of Ghost Dancer followers at Wounded Knee Creek in 1890, and Wovoka and his prophecies disappeared into obscurity.

TERM PAPER SUGGESTIONS

1. Examine the words of Wovoka's prophecies and his various "sermons" for their Christian references, and discuss the Ghost Dance within a context of multiculturalism.

2. Trace and examine the spread of the movement to Indian tribes of the west. How extensive was the movement? What language was used to spread the word?

3. Compare and link Wovoka and the Ghost Dance movement to other pan-Indian movements where messianic "prophets" played pivotal roles; for example, there was Neolin, the Delaware Prophet, and Tenskwatawa, the Shawnee Prophet.

4. Explain why Indian tribes, especially those that were recently defeated militarily by the U.S. Army, were very receptive to the Ghost Dance. What were the economic and social conditions that made Wovoka's message welcome?

5. Examine and write on the Ghost Dance Shirts made by the Lakota as a tribally specific interpretation of Wovoka's teachings. What were their purpose and why this creative addition? Did they work, and what did the army think about these shirts?

6. Define and discuss "pan-Indianism" and the role of the Ghost Dance as a forerunner of such pan-Indian activities as the Powwow, where songs and dances can be pan-Indian or intertribal.

ALTERNATIVE TERM PAPER SUGGESTIONS

1. Create your own Ghost Dance song based on your research of Mooney's text, and share as text or as music with others.

2. Make your own Ghost Dance Shirts based on research of the ones made by the Lakota. Use them in a discussion of the Lakota version of the Ghost Dance religion. Share them electronically or otherwise.

SUGGESTED SOURCES

Primary Sources

"The Messiah Letter." http://www.pbs.org/weta/thewest/resources/archives/eight/gdmessg.htm. Wovoka's Ghost Dance instructions recorded by a Cheyenne named Black Short Nose, who learned English at Carlisle Indian school and was able to transcribe Wovoka's speech into English. This letter appears in James Mooney's *The Ghost Dance Religion.*

Mooney, James. *The Ghost-Dance Religion and the Sioux Outbreak of 1890.* 1896. Reprint, Lincoln, NE: Bison Books, 1991. Very extensive coverage of

Wovoka and the Ghost Dance. His text is a wealth of primary source data: he recorded songs, oral histories, and reports. This Bison Books edition also has a photo gallery of Mooney's material collection showing an Arapaho Ghost Shirt, a drawing of a vision, a painting on buckskin of a Ghost Dance, and sacred objects from the Sioux Ghost Dance.

Parker, Mrs. Z. A. "The Ghost Dance among the Lakota." http://www.pbs.org/weta/thewest/resources/archives/eight/gddescrp.htm. Eyewitness description of a Ghost Dance observed on the Pine Ridge Indian Reservation, Dakota Territory, June 20, 1890.

Secondary Sources

Andersson, Rani-Henrik. *The Lakota Ghost Dance of 1890.* Lincoln, NE: University of Nebraska Press, 2008. Relying on Lakota language sources, the author builds a detailed study of the Ghost Dance from the Lakota perspective, but he does not ignore the many accounts of white Americans. Very dense book of 656 pages.

Barney, Garold D. *Mormons, Indians and the Ghost Dance Religion of 1890.* Lanham, MD: University Press of America, 1987. Argues that a connection exists between the Mormon religion and the Ghost Dance.

Hittman, Michael, and D. Lynch. *Wovoka and the Ghost Dance.* Expanded edition. Lincoln, NE: University of Nebraska Press, 1997. General and easy-to-read history.

Kehoe, Alice Beck. *The Ghost Dance: Ethnohistory and Revitalization.* 2nd edition. New Long Grove, IL: Waveland Press, 2006. Ethnohistorical case study of the Ghost Dance that covers the topic in 186 pages.

Maddra, Sam A. *Hostiles?: The Lakota Ghost Dance and Buffalo Bill's Wild West.* Norman, OK: University of Oklahoma Press, 2006. Explains how the Ghost Dance became a part of Buffalo Bill's famous Wild West show and how that preserved and perpetuated the Ghost Dance.

McLoughlin, William G. *The Cherokee Ghost Dance.* Macon, GA: Mercer University Press, 1984. Explores the Ghost Dance in the southern Plains.

Smoak, Gregory Ellis. *Ghost Dances and Identity: Prophetic Religion and American Indian Ethnogenesis in the Nineteenth Century.* Berkeley, CA: University of California Press, 2008. Shows how the Ghost Dance continued as a source of cultural revitalization and pan-"Indian" identity among the Shoshones and Bannock.

Thornton, Russell. *We Shall Live Again: The 1870 and 1890 Ghost Dance Movements as Demographic Revitalization.* Cambridge, UK: Cambridge University Press, 2006. A short monograph on the connection between a decline in population and the rise of the Ghost Dance.

Vander, Judith. *Shoshone Ghost Dance: Poetry Songs and Great Basin Context.* Champaign, IL: University of Illinois, 1997. Connects Shoshone music and song tradition to the 1890 Ghost Dance.

World Wide Web

"Ghost Dance." http://www.hanksville.org/daniel/lakota/Ghost_Dance.html. A very well-documented summary of the dance with numerous links to other relevant data. A good place to start research.

"The Ghost Dance." http://www.historyforkids.org/learn/northamerica/after1500/religion/ghostdance.htm. A short summary aimed at young children that includes a photograph of Wovoka and a Ghost Dance Shirt.

"The Indian Ghost Dance and War." http://www.pbs.org/weta/thewest/resources/archives/eight/wkballad.htm. Barracks ballad making fun of the Lakota and their Ghost Dance Shirts.

"Indian Ghost Dance History." http://www.accessgenealogy.com/native/tribes/history/indianghostdance.htm. A brief summary of the Ghost Dance that connects it to other Indian prophets. Links to other prophets such as Tenskwatawa, the Shawnee prophet, are provided.

"Wovoka/Jack Wilson." http://www.pbs.org/weta/thewest/people/s_z/wovoka.htm. A short biography with links to information about Big Foot and Wounded Knee Creek, 1890.

Multimedia Sources

Bury My Heart at Wounded Knee. Dir. Yves Simoneau. HBO Films, 2007. DVD. 133 minutes. Though much criticized for inaccuracy and portrayal of characters, the movie does cover the role of Wovoka and his influence on Indians west of the Mississippi in the 1880s.

Kavanagh, Thomas W. "Reading Photographs: Imaging and Imagining the Ghost Dance: James Mooney's Illustrations and Photographs, 1891–1893." http://php.indiana.edu/~tkavanag/visual5.html. Analysis of Mooney's data; includes many of Mooney's illustrations and photographs.

Native American Ghost Dancers. Global Journey, 2006. MP3. 4.08 minutes. A re-creation of a Ghost Dance song.

60. Wounded Knee (1890)

To label the 1890 Wounded Knee confrontation between Big Foot's band of Ghost Dancers and soldiers of the U.S. Seventh Cavalry on the Pine

Ridge Reservation in South Dakota as a "massacre" or a "battle" is a matter of word choice and rhetorical posturing. Was it a massacre, or was it a battle? The difference between the two words is dramatic and sensitive, depending on one's point of view. On that fateful day, conflict could have been entirely avoided, but while U.S. representatives were discussing surrender of arms and his return to the Cheyenne River Agency with Chief Big Foot and his comrades, a random gunshot from an unknown source threw the entire site into chaos. Those Lakota running for cover were caught in violent crossfire, and the shooting did not cease until 300 Lakota and at least two dozen U.S. soldiers were dead. The controversy over whether Wounded Knee was a battle or a massacre has two sides. On the side of "massacre" are the facts of the disparity of casualties and the use of rapid-fire cannons that certainly decimated human targets. On the side of "battle" is the fact that the U.S. Army was threatened by hostile combatants under a flag of truce, who had agreed to disarm but instead started shooting. What is not disputed is that the Indians, who were mostly women and children, were outnumbered and were tactically surrounded. When the fight was over, the overwhelming number of wounded, dying, and dead Lakota women, children, and men, in comparison to the relatively few wounded, dying, and dead (male) U.S. soldiers, was a hard fact to reconcile. Even so, the U.S. Army soldiers were awarded medals of honor and valor, and their regimental flag was decorated with a battle honor, which read: "Pine Ridge."

TERM PAPER SUGGESTIONS

1. Discuss the role of the Ghost Dance in the Wounded Knee conflict. Why did the Lakota convert to the Ghost Dance religion so readily and willingly? Why did federal officials ban the Ghost Dance? Why did the Lakota continue to hold dances?

2. Examine and write on the Ghost Dance Shirts made by the Lakota as a tribally specific interpretation of Wovoka's teachings. What was their purpose, and why this creative addition? Did they work, and what did the army think about these shirts?

3. Study the role of Lakota leaders (Big Foot, Red Cloud, Sitting Bull, Short Bull, and Kicking Bear) during the Ghost Dance outbreak from 1889 to 1890. Why was Sitting Bull killed? How was Red Cloud trying to alleviate the extent of hostilities and bring about peace? Why did Big Foot and his band leave the Cheyenne River Reservation? Why did Short Bull and Kicking

Bear advocate a more militant version of Wovoka's teachings that "You must not fight"?

4. Write on the role of Major Whitside and the infamous Seventh Cavalry and their role in the outbreak of fighting at Wounded Knee Creek. How could they claim they fought a battle?

5. Based on your research, would you call the actions at Wounded Knee Creek a battle or a massacre? Support your position with primary sources.

6. Write on the symbolism of Wounded Knee, 1890, as a massacre. How can the incident symbolize the destructive force of federal Indian policies?

ALTERNATIVE TERM PAPER SUGGESTIONS

1. In a black and white setting or conversion, create a photographic essay of an event, such as a dance, and have people interpret what is occurring in the photographs. Also create a slide show of images of the Ghost Dance and have people interpret what is happening in those photographs. Compare the results of each interpretive session and compare the interpretations to facts of what actually occurred.

2. Collect images of Wounded Knee, 1890, and create a slide show. The purpose is to show the tragedy of this event and to determine whether, by what is depicted in the photographs, the event could be called a massacre.

SUGGESTED SOURCES

Primary Sources

"General Nelson A. Miles on the 'Sioux Outbreak' of 1890." http://www.pbs.org/weta/thewest/resources/archives/eight/wkmiles.htm. From Mooney's text cited here. A series of reports and observations that the the outbreak was caused by a series of governmental failures.

"Lakota Accounts of the Massacre at Wounded Knee." http://www.pbs.org/weta/thewest/resources/archives/eight/wklakota.htm. Eyewitness testimony.

Mooney, James. *The Ghost-Dance Religion and the Sioux Outbreak of 1890.* 1896. Reprint, Lincoln, NE: Bison Books, 1991. Very extensive coverage of Big Foot and the incident at Wounded Knee Creek in 1890.

Parker, Mrs. Z. A. "The Ghost Dance among the Lakota." http://www.pbs.org/weta/thewest/resources/archives/eight/gddescrp.htm. Eyewitness description of a Ghost Dance observed on the Pine Ridge Indian Reservation, Dakota Territory, June 20, 1890.

Secondary Sources

Andersson, Rani-Henrik. *The Lakota Ghost Dance of 1890.* Lincoln, NE: University of Nebraska Press, 2008. Relying on Lakota language sources, the author builds a detailed study of the Ghost Dance from the Lakota perspective.

Brown, Dee. *Bury My Heart at Wounded Knee.* 1971. New York: Holt Paperbacks, 2007. A series of chapters covering the Indian wars in the west ending with chapter 18, "Dance of the Ghosts," and chapter 19, "Wounded Knee."

Coleman, William S. E. *Voices of Wounded Knee.* Lincoln, NE: University of Nebraska Press, 2001. The history makes use of substantial Lakota sources and firsthand accounts, which have been used to create a balanced presentation.

Di Silvestro, Roger. *In the Shadow of Wounded Knee: The Untold Final Story of the Indian Wars.* New York: Walker and Company, 2007. Compares two murder trials, one where a Lakota killed an army officer and another where a white rancher killed several Lakota, to argue that frontier justice has changed due to the massacre at Wounded Knee.

Jensen, Richard, et al. *Eyewitness at Wounded Knee.* Lincoln, NE: University of Nebraska Press, 1991. Reprint, Champaign, IL: University of Illinois Press, 1998. A collection of 150 photographs made before and immediately after the massacre, explanatory essays, and notes.

LeQuerrec, Guy. *On the Trail to Wounded Knee: The Big Foot Memorial Ride.* Guilford, CT: Lyons Press, 2002. At the 100th anniversary of the Wounded Knee massacre in 1990, a group of Lakota set on the trail from Cheyenne River Reservation to Wounded Knee, Big Foot's route, to commemorate and honor Big Foot and his people. This book is a photographic essay of the "memorial ride."

Viola, Herman J. *Trail to Wounded Knee: The Last Stand of the Plains Indians, 1860–1890.* National Geographic, 2004. An 8-chapter, 208-page survey of the Plains Indian wars from 1860 to 1890.

World Wide Web

"Big Foot." http://www.pbs.org/weta/thewest/people/a_c/bigfoot.htm. Short biography with a link to the Cheyenne River Reservation.

"The Indian Ghost Dance and War." http://www.pbs.org/weta/thewest/resources/archives/eight/wkballad.htm. Barracks ballad making fun of the Lakota and their Ghost Dance Shirts.

"The Massacre at Wounded Knee." http://www.hanksville.org/daniel/lakota/Wounded_Knee.html. A very well-documented summary of the Wounded Knee incident with numerous links to other relevant data.

"Massacre at Wounded Knee, 1890." http://www.eyewitnesstohistory.com/knee.htm. A good general description of the event that also includes an account by Philip Wells, a mixed-blood Sioux and U.S. Army interpreter.

"Wounded Knee Museum." http://www.woundedkneemuseum.org/index.htm. An interactive and beautiful site that presents exhibits and information for students and educators.

Multimedia Sources

Bury My Heart at Wounded Knee. Dir. Yves Simoneau. HBO Films, 2007. DVD. 133 minutes. Though much criticized for inaccuracy and portrayal of characters, the incident at Wounded Knee Creek is shown as a horrible massacre. Red Cloud visits the battlefield.

Ride to Wounded Knee. Dir. Robert Clapsadle. Ghost Dance, 1992. VHS. 90 minutes. Documentary of the memorial ride in 1990.

61. Indians and Buffalo Bill's Wild West Show (1893)

In the spring of 1893, Buffalo Bill's Wild West Show and Congress of Rough Riders of the World opened for business across from the entrance gates of the Chicago Columbian Exposition, to its largest grossing summer performance in its then-10-year history. The Wild West Show included numerous "real" Indian warriors, not examples of Americanization. Sitting Bull, before 1890, and Geronimo were "players" for a time. Most of the "real" Indian performers, however, notwithstanding an occasional appearance by Geronimo or Chief Joseph, were Plains Indians. And during performances, whatever their geographical or cultural origin, they often sported the Plains Indian war bonnet. Partially due to the success of the Wild West Show and the fact that the earliest films made depicted Buffalo Bill's Wild West, the Plains Indian war bonnet and the Plains Indian would become the most enduring symbol of the North American Indian, an iconic symbol of American heritage—an image of a fierce, proud warrior who protected animal life and "mother earth" with the same intensity that he protected his family and personal freedom. The Wild West Show contributed to the wholesale dissemination of this

Indian warrior image, and it contributed to the role of the Indian warrior as entertainment or as an icon to help sell commercial products. The selling of "Indian" trinkets as well as the selling of products that used an Indian warrior logo became very popular in the late 1800s; this popularity has hardly waned since. To this day, the entertainment value of sports teams such as the Cowboys, Redskins, Broncos, and Buffalo Bills, and the commercialism they are associated with, are evidence that the spirit of Buffalo Bill's Wild West and the spirit of the Indian warrior lives on.

TERM PAPER SUGGESTIONS

1. Write on the famous Indians who were performers at one time or another in Cody's Wild West Show. Why would somebody like Sitting Bull desire to be part of the Wild West Show?

2. Explore how the Indians of the Wild West Show (who were mostly Plains Indians) and their dress and their appearance became emblematic of the way Americans and the world understood and imagined Indians.

3. Study and write on the reason why the Wild West Show's climactic vignette was the reenactment of "Custer's Last Stand."

4. Examine the role of Indians in the idea and myth of the west. Why do heroes such as Buffalo Bill require Indians as part of their historic legacies?

5. Investigate the stereotypical Indian warrior and the use of that image on commercial products of the 1880s to 1900s. Compare images of Indians on commercial products to the images, logos, or mascots you might encounter in your own community. How are they the same and how are they different?

6. Examine the link between the Indians of the Wild West Show and Indians in Hollywood movies.

ALTERNATIVE TERM PAPER SUGGESTIONS

1. Stage a re-creation of the "Attack on the Deadwood Stagecoach by Indians and the Rescue by Buffalo Bill," or make an iMovie. Afterward, discuss the costumes you used for Indians as stereotypical representations that most people, including the audience, accept without comment.

2. From the perspective of a drama critic living in the modern world who has been transported back in time to watch a performance of the Wild West Show, write a review of the depiction of Indians.

SUGGESTED SOURCES

Primary Sources

Cody, Colonel William F. *Life and Adventures of "Buffalo Bill."* The West Film Project, 1917. http://www.pbs.org/weta/thewest/resources/archives/seven/w67bbauto/w67bb0.htm This is the entire online facsimile of the original text.

Delaney, Michelle. *Buffalo Bill's Wild West Warriors: A Photographic History by Gertrude Ksebier.* New York: HarperCollins, 2007. Shows many famous and not-so-famous Indian warriors- turned-actors who had an influence on how Indians would be perceived by the general public.

Secondary Sources

Aleiss, Angela. *Making the Whiteman's Indian: Native Americans and Hollywood Movies.* Westport, CT: Praeger Publishers, 2005. Examines the stereotypical representations of Indians in movies in a very accessible and readable manner.

Blackstone, Sarah J. *Buckskins, Bullets, and Business: A History of Buffalo Bill's Wild West.* Westport, CT: Greenwood Press, 1986. Though a book about logistics, the author does take the time to explore the treatment of Indians.

Bridger, Bobby. *Buffalo Bill and Sitting Bull: Inventing the Wild West.* Austin, TX: University of Texas Press, 2002. Anecdotal history of the two historical figures, the first stars of Cody's Wild West Show.

Burke, John M. *"Buffalo Bill," from Prairie to Palace.* New York: Rand, McNally and Company, 1893. http://books.google.com/books?id=yX4TAAAAYAAJ. Burke's biography makes Buffalo Bill famous as a sensational, Indian-fighting figure.

Kasson, Joy S. *Buffalo Bill's Wild West: Celebrity, Memory, and Popular History.* New York: Hill and Wang, 2000. Shows how historical figures can become celebrities with the right advertising, promotion, and act.

Kilpatrick, Jacquelyn. *Celluloid Indians: Native Americans and Film.* Lincoln, NE: University of Nebraska Press, 1999. Examines the role of Indians in film as foil for the American hero.

Maddra, Sam A. *Hostiles?: The Lakota Ghost Dance and Buffalo Bill's Wild West.* Norman, OK: University of Oklahoma Press, 2006. Explains how the Ghost Dance became a part of Buffalo Bill's famous show and how that preserved and perpetuated the Ghost Dance.

Mihesuah, Devon A. *American Indians: Stereotypes & Realities.* Atlanta, GA: Clarity Press, 1997. An excellent, straightforward examination of the preconceived ideas that perpetuate stereotypes about American Indians.

Walsh, Richard J. *The Making of Buffalo Bill: A Study in Heroics.* Indianapolis, IN: Bobbs-Merrill, 1928. On page 359, Walsh reports, Cody "died, in bed, and not in the arena as he had feared. In all except the literal sense he died with his boots on."

Warren, Louis S. *Buffalo Bill's America: William Cody and the Wild West Show.* New York: Alfred A. Knopf, 2005. Biography that tries to separate fact from fiction.

World Wide Web

"Buffalo Bill Cody & the Wild West Shows." http://photoswest.org/exhib/faves/ BBintro.htm. An informative photo gallery of images of the Wild West Show; has a photo of Buffalo Bill and Sitting Bull, Indians in European places, posters featuring Indians, and live shots of performances.

"Buffalo Bill Cody: Wild West Show." http://richgros.com/Cody/the_wild _west_show.html. A links site to many relevant and interesting source materials, including firsthand testimonies, artifacts, and photographs.

"Buffalo Bill's Wild West Show and Exhibition." http://www.bgsu.edu/ departments/acs/1890s/buffalobill/bbwildwestshow.html. General summary with images of posters and, most interestingly, a photograph of Black Elk, the famous Lakota spiritual leader.

"Buffalo Bill's Wild West Shows." http://www.americaslibrary.gov/cgi-bin/ page.cgi/aa/entertain/cody/show_2. This site has Thomas Edison's 25-second film "Sioux Ghost Dance," which was filmed September 24, 1894 by Edison's Black Maria Studio (RealVideo or MPEG format).

Fees, Paul. "Wild West Shows: Buffalo Bill's Wild West." http://www.bbhc.org/ edu/readyReference_02.cfm. A thorough summary of the history of Cody's Wild West shows and links to many other interesting and relevant sources offered by the center's online database.

"Images 7.17 to 7.27." http://www.pbs.org/weta/thewest/resources/archives/ seven/. Eight photographs of Cody, one with Sitting Bull, one with Indians after Wounded Knee, and one showing the "Death of Custer" as reenacted in the Wild West Show.

"William F. Cody: 'Buffalo Bill' (1846–1917)." http://www.pbs.org/weta/ thewest/people/a_c/buffalobill.htm. Short biography that mentions that the army called Cody back to service during the Ghost Dance period.

Multimedia Source

Buffalo Bill and the Indians, or Sitting Bull's History Lesson. Dir. Robert Altman. Dino De Laurentis, 1976. DVD. 123 minutes. Based on Arthur Kopit's play, *Indians,* the film explores how Americans do not understand the internal nature of the Indian but they do understand the role of the Indian in the development of a national heritage.

62. Curtis Act (1898)

The Curtis Act of 1898 was named after Kansas Congressman Charles Curtis, a Kansa (Kaw) tribal member and future vice president under Herbert Hoover. The Curtis Act, in order to take full federal control over the Five Civilized Tribes (Cherokee, Creek, Choctaw, Chickasaw, and Seminole) of the Indian Territory and to expedite the allotment of their lands, abolished tribal courts, nullified the power of Indian tribes to determine their own citizenship, and allowed the federal government via the Dawes Commission, appointed in 1893, to compile new tribal rolls for the purpose of allotting tribal lands to individual Indians without tribal interference or approval. The act also gave the Department of the Interior control over mineral leases in Indian Territory and the federal courts jurisdiction over Indian people living on Indian lands. Further, the act called for the incorporation of Indian towns in the Indian territories, so they could be surveyed and divided into lots for individuals, after which taxes could be levied to pay for public services and the building of schools. In 1898, the goal of the Curtis Act and the Dawes Commission was to terminate the tribal governments, sovereignty, and communal land base of the Five Civilized Tribes to hasten acculturation and assimilation. The result was the legal dismemberment of the tribes, the loss of almost all tribal land—even the allotted lands— through fraud and corruption, the fragmentation of tribes and families, and the destitution of Indian individuals. The Dawes Commission also introduced the concept of Degree of Indian Blood (or Blood Quantum) with the creation of "enrollment cards" for Indians.

TERM PAPER SUGGESTIONS

1. Study and write on the stated purpose of the Curtis Act to help Indians of the Five Civilized Tribes, who, under Section 8 of the General Allotment (Dawes) Act of 1887, were exempt from allotment, to allot the lands of the Five Civilized Tribes under the Curtis Act. Why was the imposition of allotment thought to help the Indians?

2. Examine the pertinent sections in Devlin's *Treaty Power* and write about the stated purpose of the Dawes Commission as opposed to its public and humanitarian purpose.

3. How did the desire to create the state of Oklahoma spur or accelerate the allotment of Indian lands?

4. Study and write on the allotment process. What was the mechanism? How many acres were Indian individuals promised? Was gender or age a factor? Why was the incorporation of towns a necessary component of the law?

5. Examine and write about the creation of tribal enrollment cards that stated the Degree of Indian Blood (or Blood Quantum) of each individual. What was the purpose of having these cards?

6. Why was it necessary to destroy the power and authority of the tribal governments in order to achieve the goals of the Curtis Act and of the Dawes Commission?

ALTERNATIVE TERM PAPER SUGGESTIONS

1. Make a map of Indian Territory after the Indian removal of the 1830s and a map of the same area every 10 years until 1910. Create a Microsoft PowerPoint slide show to show the disappearance of tribal lands.

2. Graph the loss of land in the Indian Territory from 1840 to 1920.

SUGGESTED SOURCES

Primary Sources

"Act of June 28, 1898, Curtis Act." http://www.accessgenealogy.com/native/laws/act_june_28_1898_curtis_act.htm. Full online text of the Curtis Act.

Devlin, Robert Thomas. *The Treaty Power under the Constitution of the United States.* San Francisco, CA: Bancroft-Whitney Company, 1908. Google Books, 2008. A copyright-free digital facsimile. In relation to Indian treaty rights, items 371–378, on pages 405–411, cover how the Dawes Commission manipulated treaties as they relate to American Indian tribes residing within the borders of the United States. Item 371 specifically states that the commission's purpose was to extinguish Indian title to land to make way for the creation of new states, not for the Americanization of Indians.

"U.S. Territorial Growth Maps." http://www.lib.utexas.edu/maps/histus.html. The 1830–1920 maps, center of page (or click button "Territorial Growth"), show the creation of several states in the Indian Territory and the shrinkage of Indian-owned lands to virtually nil by 1907, when Oklahoma becomes a state of the Union.

Secondary Sources

Carlson, Leonard A. *Indians, Bureaucrats, and Land: The Dawes Act and the Decline of Indian Farming.* Westport, CT: Greenwood Press, 1981. Using an economic analytical model, the author concludes that Indians would farm less rather than more after allotment.

Carter, Kent. *The Dawes Commission and the Allotment of the Five Civilized Tribes, 1893–1914.* Orem, UT: Ancestry Publishing, 1999. Examines the process of allotment, from enrollment to allotting the lands; to buying, selling, and renting; to the failure of the system.

Ewy, Marvin. *Charles Curtis of Kansas: Vice President of the United States, 1929– 1933.* Emporia, KS: Kansas State Teachers College, 1961. Biography.

Hoxie, Frederick E. *A Final Promise: The Campaign to Assimilate the Indians, 1880–1920.* Lincoln, NE: University of Nebraska Press, 1984. Reprint, 2001. Detailed historical treatment that traces the Indian Reform movement, the Dawes Act, and the tragic results of the assimilation policies.

Johnson, Troy R., ed. *Contemporary Native American Political Issues.* New York: AltaMira Press, 1999. Covers the long-term effects of the Curtis Act and the Dawes Commission.

Unaru, William E. *Mixed-Bloods and Tribal Dissolution: Charles Curtis and the Quest for Indian Identity.* Lawrence, KS: University Press of Kansas, 1989. Curtis's involvement in the debate over Indian policy during the late nineteenth and early twentieth centuries.

Washburn, Wilcomb E. *The Assault on Indian Tribalism: The General Allotment Law (Dawes Act) of 1887.* Philadelphia, PA: Lippincott, 1975. Shows that the reformers had good intentions, but the effects of allotment were devastating to Indian people.

Wilkins, David E. *American Indian Politics and the American Political System.* 2nd edition. New York: Rowman and Littlefield, 2006. Tribal governmental history, structure, and powers.

World Wide Web

Brown, Loren N. "The Dawes Commission." http://digital.library.okstate.edu/ Chronicles/v009/v009p071.html. An essay explaining the creation and purpose of the commission.

Chavez, Will. "Dawes Commission Defined CN Citizenship." http://www .cherokeephoenix.org/2489/Article.aspx. Short article explaining the authority of the Dawes Commission to determine who was Cherokee or who was not.

"Curtis Act (1898)." http://digital.library.okstate.edu/encyclopedia/entries/C/ CU006.html. Brief summary with bibliography.

"Curtis Act Brought Changes to Towns in Indian Territory." http://www
.muskogeephoenix.com/local/local_story_300234854.html. Essay
explaining how and why towns incorporated after the passage of the
Curtis Act.

"Enrollment Cards of the Five Civilized Tribes, 1898–1914." http://www.
kshs.org/genealogists/culture_ethnic/Native%20American/dawes.htm.
The enrollment cards are listed by lot, and a brief summary explains the
content of each card. Sample Freeman Documents are found in the next
entry and they are exactly the same kind of documents used for all
Cherokees.

"Sample Freeman Documents." http://www.african-nativeamerican.com/
7-docs.htm. Covers Cherokee Blacks who were allotted land as well. This
site has primary source documents of Land Allotment Records and
Blood Quantum (Enrollment) Cards.

"United States Vice-Presidents: Charles Curtis." http://www.juntosociety.com/
vp/curtis.html. Biography of the first American Indian vice president of
the United States.

Multimedia Source

Tribal Nations: The Story of Federal Indian Law. Dir. Lisa Jaeger. Tanana Chiefs
Conference Signature Media Production, 2006. DVD. 60 minutes.
Documentary film examining the development of U.S. federal
Indian law.

63. *Lone Wolf v. Hitchcock* (1903)

The decision of *Lone Wolf v. Hitchcock* (187 U.S. 533) held that the Medicine Lodge Treaty of 1867, between the Kiowa, Comanche, and Apache
(KCA) and the United States, did not "vest in the Indians either in their
individual or tribal capacity" land ownership and that Indians only
"occupied" the lands set aside in treaties for their exclusive use. Further,
the United States could nullify any part of a treaty to make use of the land
Indians occupied, and the United States could lease, sell, or take Indian land
and the tribes could not stop them. This was a major step in limiting and
reinterpreting Indian treaties, and the precedent set meant that the plenary
power of Congress and the executive branch was limitless. As was clearly
the intent, the opinion deprived Indian tribes and individual Indians property rights on reserved lands, and it left open the ability of the United States

to take as much land from Indians as it deemed necessary, even in direct violation of past solemn agreements and treaties. In the Kiowa and Comanche Treaty of 1868, three million acres had been set aside for these tribes' communal and exclusive use, and its Article 12 required a three-fourths vote of all adult male Indians to divide, sell, or even lease tribal lands. However, after the passage of the Allotment (Dawes) Act of 1887, federal authorities via the Jerome Commission pressured the KCA to sign an allotment agreement, and although by 1892 they had succeeded in obtaining signatures, they had not obtained the three-fourths required by the 1868 treaty. Despite the lack of signatures, the efforts of the Indian Rights Association, and even the opposition of Commissioner of Indian Affairs W. A. Jones, the "Jerome Agreement" became law in 1900, and the KCA Indian Reservation was to be allotted and the "surplus" land sold. Lone Wolf, a Kiowa chief who was vehemently opposed to the selling of Indian lands, along with others filed suit in opposition, and the Supreme Court heard and decided the case in 1903.

TERM PAPER SUGGESTIONS

1. Study "reserved" rights in the KCA 1868 treaty. What was the language that set land aside for Indians? Define "reservation." Why include the three-fourths vote?

2. Examine and write on the Jerome (Cherokee) Commission. What was it commissioned to do?

3. Define and explain the Jerome Agreement.

4. Explore and report on the actions of the Indian Rights Association and the commissioner of Indian Affairs to stop or amend the Jerome Agreement. Why were they opposed, and what were their proposed solutions?

5. Discuss the unanimous Supreme Court opinion on *Lone Wolf v. Hitchcock.* How did the decision change the definition of Indian land ownership? How did the decision change the sovereignty power and agreements set forth in the treaties with Indians?

6. Study and report on the aftermath of the decision. What happened to the KCA Reservation? How did the Indian people survive and in what condition?

ALTERNATIVE TERM PAPER SUGGESTIONS

1. Organize a formal debate on ethics, using the validity of the Jerome Agreement as the point of contention. Both sides of the argument should be

presented clearly to an audience. At the end of the debate, survey the audience for a decision. Follow this with an open discussion.

2. From the point of view of Lone Wolf, write an appeal to the public about the reason for Indians to hold land in common and why reservation land should be preserved.

SUGGESTED SOURCES

Primary Sources

Lone Wolf v. Hitchcock, 187 U.S. 553 (1903). http://caselaw.lp.findlaw.com/ scripts/getcase.pl?court=us&vol=187&invol=553. Complete text and opinion of the court delivered by Justice White, with links to cases citing this case.

"Medicine Lodge Treaty, 1867." http://digital.library.okstate.edu/encyclopedia/ entries/M/ME005.html. Links page to the three treaties made at Medicine Lodge in 1867 (KCA) and provides a short introduction to their content.

Secondary Sources

Clark, Blue. *Lone Wolf v. Hitchcock: Treaty Rights and Indian Law at the End of the Nineteenth Century.* Lincoln, NE: University of Nebraska Press, 1994. Explores the case and the how the case changed the lives of the Kiowa Indians. Photographs and maps included.

Deloria, Vine, Jr., ed. *American Indian Policy in the Twentieth Century.* Norman, OK: University of Oklahoma Press, 1992. A collection of essays exploring the impact of policy on American Indians. Deloria's contribution provides a brief history and overview of federal Indian policy making.

Deloria, Vine, Jr., and David E. Wilkins. *Tribes, Treaties, and Constitutional Tribulations.* Austin, TX: University of Texas Press, 2000. Explores the relationship between the U.S. Constitution and the federal government and Indian tribes and their governments.

Estin, Ann Laquer. "*Lone Wolf v. Hitchcock:* The Long Shadow." *The Aggressions of Civilization: Federal Indian Policy Since the 1880s.* Sandra L. Cadwalader and Vine Deloria Jr., eds. Philadelphia, PA: Temple University Press, 1984. Describes the methods used to get the Jerome Agreement passed through both houses of Congress.

Hagan, William T. *The Indian Rights Association: The Herbert Welsh Years, 1882– 1904.* Tucson, AZ: The University of Arizona Press, 1985. The Indian Rights Association worked to help the KCA in their lawsuits against the federal government.

Hagan, William T. *Taking Indian Lands: The Cherokee (Jerome) Commission, 1889–1893.* Norman, OK: University of Oklahoma Press. A thorough history of the activities of the Jerome Commission to reduce the reservations via allotment agreement so that Oklahoma could become a state.

Prucha, Francis Paul. *American Indian Treaties: The History of a Political Anomaly.* Berkeley, CA: University of California Press, 1994. An overview of treaties, policies, and laws as they pertain to American Indians.

Wildenthal, Bryan H. *Native American Sovereignty on Trial: A Handbook with Cases, Laws, and Documents.* Santa Barbara, CA: ABC-CLIO, 2003. A general reference on these complex issues meant for students and general readers that includes a section on *Lone Wolf v. Hitchcock.*

Wilkins, David E. *American Indian Sovereignty and the U.S. Supreme Court: The Masking of Justice.* Austin, TX: University of Texas Press, 1997. Examines the *Lone Wolf v. Hitchcock* case as a devastating step in abrogation of Indian treaty rights, especially concerning the ownership of Indian land.

Wilkins, David E. *Uneven Ground: American Indian Sovereignty and Federal Law.* Norman, OK: University of Oklahoma Press, 2001. Investigates the manner in which Indian sovereignty has eroded since the 1787 U.S. Constitution.

World Wide Web

"Native American Rights—Federal Power over Indians." http://law.jrank.org /pages/8749/Native-American-Rights-Federal-Power-over-Native-American-Rights.html. A detailed essay on federal power and explanation of the concept of "plenary power" derived from the "commerce clause" in Article I of the U.S. Constitution.

"Rebuilding a Nation." http://www.texasbeyondhistory.net/tejas/voices/ rebuilding.html. Discusses the activities of the Jerome Commission (nine-tenths down the page) on the Caddo and Wichita lands in Indian Territory in 1889. The site is valuable for its map at the top of the page showing Caddo and Wichita lands just north of the KCA lands, which are also shown.

Smith, Darrell. "Why Indians Are Second Class Citizens: Congress' Plenary Power, Tribal Sovereignty and Constitutional Rights." http://www .citizensalliance.org/CERA News/CERA News 2002 05/Why Indians are Second Class Citizens.htm. Short polemic on federal power over Indians.

Multimedia Source

Tribal Nations: The Story of Federal Indian Law. Dir. Lisa Jaeger. Tanana Chiefs Conference Signature Media Production, 2006. DVD. 60 minutes.

Documentary film examining the development of U.S. federal Indian law.

64. Burke Act (1906)

Section 6 of the General Allotment (Dawes) Act of 1887 provided for citizenship of American Indians after three conditions were met. Citizenship was given after all allotments had been made, after a 25-year trust period had elapsed to give Indians time to adjust to individual property ownership, and when Indians secured patents in fee-simple to replace their trust patents received at the time of allotment. (A "patent" is the federal title or deed transferred to people, and "fee-simple" is the form of land ownership by which the owner holds the title and controls the property.) When the Supreme Court decided in the *Matter of Heff* in 1905 that Indians were considered U.S. citizens at the beginning of the 25-year trust period, Congress passed the Burke Act (34 Stat. 182), which amended Section 6 of the Dawes Act of 1887 to control the rate of citizenship in defiance of the court's opinion. The Burke Act made clear that citizenship would only be bestowed at the end of the 25-year trust period, and it empowered the secretary of the interior to issue fee-simple patents to Indians that the secretary deemed competent in "managing their own affairs." Therefore under the trust period, Indians could be citizens in that they were subject to local, state, and federal law, but they also were considered dependent through their trust status. Further, an Indian could at any time be deemed competent and granted full citizenship and patent in fee-simple, or in contrast, the Indian might retain "not competent" status and have to wait out the 25-year trust period. In the latter case, full-blood Indians had to wait the longest for patents in fee-simple, while Indians of mixed blood sailed through the process.

TERM PAPER SUGGESTIONS

1. Connect at least three instances where the Supreme Court rendered a decision about a case and then the legislative and/or the executive branches of government either ignored the opinion or passed a law or executive order to in some way circumvent the court's ruling. The Burke Act is a case in point.

2. Citizenship was the hallmark of Americanization. Explore the role of land ownership in the Indian citizenship process.

3. The federal government acquired land from Indians via land cession treaties, and then the government transferred the land (mostly by sale) via patents to people who then owned the land in fee-simple thereafter. In the allotment system, even as amended by the Burke Act, Indians would hold individual allotments in trust for a period of time, maybe 25 years. Explain why the federal authorities thought this trust period was necessary.

4. Explore the relationship between mixed bloods and full bloods in the allotment and assimilation process. What were their respective views of allotment and/or citizenship? How did the mixed bloods influence decision making?

5. Investigate how the various secretaries of the interior determined the competency of Indians to manage "their own affairs." How was competency determined? Was the Degree of Indian Blood, or Blood Quantum, a factor?

6. If all Indians became citizens, then the tribe would cease to exist. Did this happen to even the most fragmented and allotted Indian reservations? Why do Indian tribes exist to this day?

ALTERNATIVE TERM PAPER SUGGESTIONS

1. As secretary of the interior you would have to develop logical standards to determine the competency of Indians to manage their own affairs on their individual allotments. Create a list of criteria with justification and explanation.

2. From the perspective of a tribal member who has been allotted an individual tract of land, write a story of how you will maintain your tribal identity despite the efforts of the federal government to civilize you.

SUGGESTED SOURCES

Primary Sources

"An Act to Amend Section Six . . . " http://www2.csusm.edu/nadp/a1906.htm. Full text of the Burke Act.

"In the Matter of the Application of Albert Heff, for a Writ of Habeas Corpus: *In Re Heff*, 197 U.S. 488, 25 S.Ct. 506, 49 L.Ed. 848 (1905)." http://www .utulsa.edu/law/classes/rice/ussct_cases/In_Re_Heff_197_488.htm. As a ward of the state, Indians could not sell or possess alcohol, but as U.S. citizens they could. The Supreme Court ruled that Indians holding trust allotments were citizens at the beginning of the 25-year trust period and, therefore, could sell or possess alcohol. This decision prompted the passage of the Burke Act.

"Summary of the Burke Act, Act of May 8, 1906 (34 Stat. 182)." Little Canada, MN: Indian Land Tenure Foundations, 2008. A summary of the pertinent sections of the act with a link to the full text in Kappler's *Indian Affairs Laws and Treaties,* http://www.indianlandtenure.org/ILTFallotment/histlegis/histlegis.htm.

"Summary of the General Allotment Act, Act of February 8, 1887 (24 Stat. 388, ch. 119, 25 USCA 331)." http://www.indianlandtenure.org/ILTFallotment/histlegis/GeneralAllotmentAct.htm. A summary of the pertinent sections of the act with a link to the full text in Kappler's *Indian Affairs Laws and Treaties.*

Secondary Sources

Cadwalader, Sandra L., and Vine Deloria Jr., eds. *The Aggressions of Civilization: Federal Indian Policy Since the 1880s.* Philadelphia, PA: Temple University Press, 1944. A collection of essays exploring the exponential increase of federal power over Indian tribes.

Carlson, Leonard A. *Indians, Bureaucrats, and Land: The Dawes Act and the Decline of Indian Farming.* Westport, CT: Greenwood Press, 1981. Using an economic analytical model the author concludes that Indians would farm less rather than more after allotment.

Carter, Kent. *The Dawes Commission and the Allotment of the Five Civilized Tribes, 1893–1914.* Orem, UT: Ancestry Publishing, 1999. Examines the process of allotment, from enrollment to allotting the lands; to buying, selling, and renting; to the failure of the system.

Greenwald, Emily. *Reconfiguring the Reservation: The Nez Perces, Jicarilla Apaches, and the Dawes Act.* Albuquerque, NM: University of New Mexico, 2002. Demonstrates that Indians selected land and used that land for their own purposes rather than to farm and to become Americans.

Hoxie, Frederick E. *A Final Promise: The Campaign to Assimilate the Indians, 1880–1920.* Lincoln, NE: University of Nebraska Press, 1984. Reprint, 2001. Detailed historical treatment that traces the Indian Reform movement, the Dawes Act, and the tragic results of the assimilation policies.

Olson, James S., and Raymond Wilson. *Native Americans in the Twentieth Century.* Champaign, IL: University of Illinois Press, 1984. Chapters four and five cover this era of reform and change, but the whole book is a short survey of the history of American Indians and tribal sovereignty in this volatile century.

Otis, Delos Sacket. *The Dawes Act and the Allotment of Indian Lands.* Norman, OK: University of Oklahoma Press, 1973. A general overview and history.

Prucha, Francis P. *The Great Father: The United States Government and the American Indians.* Lincoln, NE: University of Nebraska Press, 1984. General reference to laws and acts concerning Indians.

Washburn, Wilcomb E. *The Assault on Indian Tribalism: The General Allotment Law (Dawes Act) of 1887.* Philadelphia, PA: Lippincott, 1975. Shows that the reformers had good intentions but the effects of allotment were devastating to Indian people.

World Wide Web

"Burke Act." http://www.answers.com/topic/burke-act?cat=biz-fin. A brief introduction to the Burke Act.

"Glossary of Indian Land Tenure Terms." http://www.indianlandtenure.org/ILTFallotment/glossary/terms.htm. Defines "patent" and "fee simple" and other pertinent words and concepts concerning Indian land tenure.

Spilde, Kate. "Where Does Federal Indian Policy Really Come From?" http://www.indiangaming.org/library/articles/where-does-policy-come-from.shtml. This essay explores the concept of "mixed blood" as a racial standard of competency, which means any degree of "white" blood made an Indian competent. More entries discuss the "mixed blood" issue. The Burke Act of 1906 is the eighth entry down.

Tatro, M. Kaye. "Burke Act (1906)." http://digital.library.okstate.edu/encyclopedia/entries/B/BU010.html. A short, readable summary.

Multimedia Source

Tribal Nations: The Story of Federal Indian Law. Dir. Lisa Jaeger. Tanana Chiefs Conference Signature Media Production, 2006. DVD. 60 minutes. Documentary film examining the development of U.S. federal Indian law.

65. Winters Doctrine: *Winters v. United States,* 207 U.S. 564 (1908)

The concept of "reserved rights" derives from Indian treaties and agreements where the rights of Indians were preserved unless Indians, themselves, gave the rights away in a treaty and/or agreement. An Indian reservation created by treaty or agreement is "reserved" land set aside for the exclusive use of the tribe and is an "implied reservation" of Indian property rights. (Hunting and fishing on tribal lands are also reserved rights.) What about water rights? After the Fort Belknap Reservation in

Montana was established by Congress in 1888, Henry Winters, a Montana landowner, built a dam across the Milk River and blocked water from flowing into the reservation. Winters believed the tribe had no claim to the water, citing that the language of the agreement establishing the reservation did not mention water rights. However, the Supreme Court decided otherwise in a landmark opinion that recognized that Indian tribes have an "implied" right to water because they never implicitly gave their rights to water away. Therefore, tribal access to water became a "reserved right." To make another important point, the Supreme Court's opinion, written by Justice Joseph McKenna, reinforced the "rule of interpretation" that treaties and agreements should be interpreted by state and federal authorities, agencies, and courts as the Indians would have understood them. Even though the court recognized and made clear Indian reserved water rights, the opinion also recognized federal Indian assimilation policies by stating that formerly nomadic tribes required water to be agrarian and to pursue agriculture.

TERM PAPER SUGGESTIONS

1. Research and write on the doctrine of "reserved rights," a doctrine implicit in every Indian treaty or agreement. Use the Fort Belknap Reservation and *Winters v. United States* as an illustrative example.

2. Historically, hunting and fishing have been controversial reserved rights because, as with water rights, they place Indian tribes in direct competition with states and local citizens. Write a survey of those areas of the country where Indian hunting and fishing rights have generated conflict and controversy in the twentieth century, long after the last of the Indian wars.

3. Show how the Supreme Court ruling in *Winters v. United States* supported assimilation policies. Use Justice McKenna's four-point rationale, which discusses that the transformation of nomadic Indians to Indian farmers requires water, as the basis of the analysis.

4. Examine the "trust" relationship between the federal government and the Fort Belknap Indian Tribe. "Trust" is the federal responsibility to protect or enhance tribal assets through policies and management of Indian affairs (see Wilkins).

5. Why was it important for the Supreme Court to protect a tribe's right to and access to water? How did that decision help the plans of congressional Indian policy makers?

6. The "reserved rights" doctrine has been used to protect wildlife habitat, settling water disputes between states and reservations or among states themselves. Write a report detailing how the doctrine can be used in such a way.

ALTERNATIVE TERM PAPER SUGGESTIONS

1. Assume you are sent to an Indian reservation in Montana to help the Indians become farmers. Take a map of an Indian reservation in Montana and identify the water sources by marking them in blue, especially note the direction and flow of rivers into and out of the reservation. What are the difficulties of creating a plan of fair access to water that would allow water for the reservation (flowing in) that would not violate others' access to water (flowing out)?

2. An Indian hunter is arrested for hunting without a license on public trust lands near his reservation. Based on your understanding of "implied reserved rights," how would you decide the case? Provide at least four points of justification.

SUGGESTED SOURCES

Primary Sources

"Ad Hoc Group on Indian Water Rights." Denver, CO: Western Governors Association, 2004. Archive of the documents generated from a congressional briefing on April 24, 2001 on Indian water rights. Includes remarks and resolutions.

Winters v. United States, 207 U.S. 564 (1908). http://supreme.justia.com/us/207/564/. Full text of the argument (1907) and the decision (1908).

Secondary Sources

Burton, Lloyd. *American Indian Water Rights and the Limits of Law.* Lawrence, KS: University Press of Kansas, 1993. A critical study of the failure of the United States to live up to its "trust responsibilities" in the context of Indian water rights.

Colby, Bonnie G., et al. *Negotiating Tribal Water Rights: Fulfilling Promises in the Arid West.* Tucson, AZ: University of Arizona Press, 2005. Source book on Indian water rights and history of the problems encountered when tribes are confronted with competing interests in the same water.

McGuire, Thomas, et al. *Indian Water in the New West.* Tucson, AZ: University of Arizona Press, 1993. Examines rapid population growth in the west and the conflicts generated by claims of Indian water rights.

Nelson, Michael C. *The Winters Doctrine: Seventy Years of Application of Reserved Water Rights to Indian Reservations.* Tucson, AZ: University of

Arizona, 1977. The office of Arid Land Studies reports on the impact of *Winters.*

Shurts, John. *Indian Reserved Water Rights: The Winters Doctrine in Its Social and Legal Context.* Norman, OK: University of Oklahoma, 2003. Detailed historical study of the *Winters* case.

Sly, Peter W. *Reserved Water Rights Settlement Manual.* Washington, DC: Island Press, 1989. Shows how monuments, waterways, water disputes, wildlife habitats, and other lands that need protection may find the concept of "reserved rights" beneficial.

Thorson. John E., et al. *Tribal Water Rights: Essays in Contemporary Law, Policy and Economics.* Tucson, AZ: University of Arizona Press, 2006. Collection of essays examining contemporary issues generated by rapid growth and increasing demands for water.

Wildenthal, Bryan H. *Native American Sovereignty on Trial: A Handbook with Cases, Laws, and Documents.* Santa Barbara, CA: ABC-CLIO, 2003. A general reference on these complex issues such as water rights, meant for students and general readers.

Wilkins, David E. *American Indian Sovereignty and the U.S. Supreme Court: The Masking of Justice.* Austin, TX: University of Texas Press, 1997. Examines several Supreme Court opinions and their impact on tribal sovereignty and rights.

Wilkins, David E. *Uneven Ground: American Indian Sovereignty and Federal Law.* Norman, OK: University of Oklahoma Press, 2001. Provides clear definitions of "trust" and "reserved rights."

World Wide Web

"Federal Reserved Water Rights." http://www.blm.gov/nstc/WaterLaws/fedreservedwater.html. Brief but detailed article summarizing reserved rights and the concept of reserved water rights via the *Winters* decision.

"Federal Reserved Water Rights." http://www.humboldt.edu/~wrd1/reserved.html. Summary of four Supreme Court decisions (1908, 1963, 1976, and 1978) on the "reserved right" doctrine.

Lombardi, Lisa M. "American Indian Water Rights: Some Observations and Their Implications for Australia." http://www.austlii.edu.au/au/journals/ILB/2004/9.html. Outlines treaty-based reserved rights, water for beneficial use, and water rights to support treaty uses. Very succinct and informative for a short essay.

Pollack, Stanley. "Compact Conflicts & Navajo Water Rights." http://www.western.edu/water/ww28archives/Pollack.html. Excellent outline of the history of Navajo water rights, the problems they have encountered with other competing interests, and the compromises and compacts they have sought to find a resolution.

"Rights to Water." http://www.usgcrp.gov/usgcrp/nacc/education/native/ native-edu-5.htm. Looks at environmental, societal, and economic impacts of irrigation in Indian lands and the strategies for solutions to the impact on water resources. Includes a graph of the maximum acreage that could be irrigated on Indian lands according the *Winters* doctrine.

Williams, Susan M. "Overview of Indian Water Rights." http://www .ucowr.siu.edu/updates/pdf/V107_A1.pdf. PDF download of a brief survey of Indian water rights.

"*Winters v. United States,* Further Readings." http://law.jrank.org/pages/13674/ Winters-v-United-States.html. Converts the legal language of the case into an understandable point-by-point narrative.

Multimedia Source

"Treaty Rights: The Ultimate Habitat Protection Tool." Quinault Beach Resort, WA: Northwest Indian Fisheries Commission, 2008. http://www .habitatconference.org/2008/download.php?f=01-morisset-treaty_rights_and_habitat.pps. Microsoft PowerPoint presentation using *Winters v. United States* and the concept of "reserved rights" as a tool for habitat protection.

66. Society of American Indians Founded (1911)

Founded on Columbus Day in 1911, the Society of American Indians (SAI) was created "for the purpose of the protection and advancement" of Indian people due to the historic circumstance that had found the Indian "stripped of the greater portion of his possessions" and thrown into an alien world. From this heartfelt and knowing position, the SAI strongly advocated education and skill training for Indian youth to better prepare them for a new world. However, because SAI members had themselves experienced the methods of assimilation, they were highly critical of the Indian Affairs office and the policies it administered. Therefore, the members advocated for Indians to have a voice in policy making and in their own affairs, but the members' position of supporting assimilation remained paramount. In order to achieve their goals, they created two mechanisms for informing and educating the public that Indians were not savages and were capable of achieving success. One mechanism was a quarterly journal, and the other was an annual convention. The journal featured articles by members on critical issues, while the convention brought these issues to the public in a dramatic and well-publicized annual event. The members were mostly highly educated middle-class American Indian professionals: a few were Gertrude Bonnin (a Yankton Nakota and an author), Arthur C. Parker (a Seneca and an anthropologist), and Carlos Montezuma (a Yavapai Apache and a medical doctor). Members also were from a diversity of tribal backgrounds, and they formed the first pan-Indian organization where the English language and their shared experiences with the United States bound them together in unity and purpose. However, by the early 1920s, the SAI had broken apart over factional disputes.

TERM PAPER SUGGESTIONS

1. For the time period from 1911 to 1920, the involvement of women and men working together in a national organization was rare. Examine the role of Indian women in the SAI and their contributions to the goal and purpose of the society.

2. Unity of disparate Indian tribes or tribal members was hard due to the multitude of languages Indian people spoke and the differences in their cultures and social structures. Even Tecumseh, alluded to by the SAI, failed in his efforts to unify Indians for a single purpose. Write on the reasons that the SAI was successful for a time, while others in history were not.

3. Explore the purpose and goals of the SAI and how it was able to communicate these aspirations to people who could help.

4. Carlos Montezuma became critical of the federal administration of Indian reservations. Why? What were his major concerns?

5. Was total assimilation possible? The major bone of contention for some SAI members was that many Indian people retained a strong connection to their tribe and their culture.

6. The Native American Church and its use of peyote (a small spineless cactus found in southwestern Texas that has psychoactive alkaloids and is used by Indians for religious purposes) as a sacrament became an issue of debate in the SAI. Many called for the banning of this sacrament, while others supported its legitimacy. Write a report where this debate forms a contributing factor in the demise of the SAI as a viable organization for social and cultural change.

ALTERNATIVE TERM PAPER SUGGESTIONS

1. As a newspaper reporter in 1911 sent to cover the first annual convention of the SAI, write an informative article on this unique organization for its time with the intent of garnering support for the organization.

2. One of the goals of the SAI was to stop the use of stereotypical images of the American Indian, and they also discouraged the use of the words "buck" and "squaw" to describe Indian men and women. Find such stereotypical images and characterizations from popular magazines of the time and from commercial products labels and advertisements. From the perspective of an SAI member using modern technology, create a Microsoft PowerPoint slide show of these images and of this use of language to achieve the same SAI purpose.

SUGGESTED SOURCES

Primary Sources

"Holiday for Indians Urged on Nation (1916)." http://query.nytimes.com/gst/abstract.html?res=9F0CE3DC1439E233A25754C0A9639C9467 96D6CF. PDF download of a period article where the SAI advocates for the establishment of a national holiday for Indians, like Martin Luther King Day for African Americans.

Society of American Indians. *The American Indian Magazine.* Washington, DC: SAI (January 1916–August 1920). The first was called the *Quarterly Journal of the American Indian* (1913–1915) and was renamed *The American Indian Magazine* in 1915.

Society of American Indians. *The Papers of the Society of American Indians.* John W. Larner, ed. Wilmington, DE: Scholarly Resources, 1987. Ten reels of microfilm with a printed guide.

Society of American Indians. *Report of the Executive Council on the Proceedings of the First Annual Conference of the Society of American Indians.* Washington, DC: SAI, 1912. http://books.google.com/books?id=yUMBAAAAMAAJ. A detailed 188-page report on the goals and aspirations of the group as well as essays and photographs by and of SAI members.

Secondary Sources

Fitzgerald, Michael, ed. *The Essential Charles Eastman (Ohiyesa).* Bloomington, IN: World Wisdom, 2007. A selected representation of all of Eastman's writings.

Hertzberg, Hazel W. *The Search for an American Indian Identity: Modern Pan-Indian Movements.* Syracuse, NY: Syracuse University Press, 1971. Chapter one is a definitive history of the SAI.

Hoxie, Frederick E. *A Final Promise: The Campaign to Assimilate the Indians, 1880–1920.* Lincoln, NE: University of Nebraska Press, 1984. Reprint, 2001. Detailed historical treatment that traces the Indian Reform movement, including the SAI.

Iverson, Peter. *Carlos Montezuma and the Changing World of American Indians.* Albuquerque, NM: University of New Mexico Press, 1982. A comprehensive biography of Carlos Montezuma placed against a backdrop of dramatic cultural change and social disintegration of traditional tribal authority and autonomy.

Martinez, David. *Dakota Philosopher: Charles Eastman and American Indian Thought.* St. Paul, MN: Minnesota Historical Society Press, 2009. Examines Eastman from the perspective of his being an activist rather than a sellout.

Nabokov, Peter, ed. *Native American Testimony: A Chronicle of Indian-White Relations from Prophecy to the Present, 1492–2000.* New York: Penguin, 1999. Contains testimonials from the opening conference of the SAI in 1911.

Patterson, Michelle Wick. " 'Real' Indian Songs: the Society of American Indians and the Use of Native American Culture as a Means of Reform." *American Indian Quarterly* 26, no. 1 (2002): 44–66. The University of Nebraska Press. Very interesting examination of the use of traditional songs to advance the ideas of reform.

Porter, Joy. *To Be Indian: The Life of Iroquois-Seneca Arthur Caswell Parker.* Norman, OK: University of Oklahoma Press, 2001. Examines the life of Parker and touches on his role in the SAI.

Prucha, Francis P. *The Great Father: The United States Government and the American Indians.* Lincoln, NE: University of Nebraska Press, 1984. Overviews laws and acts concerning Indians and Indian rights groups who opposed or advocated for them.

Rappaport, Doreen. *The Flight of Red Bird: The Life of Zitkala-Sa.* New York: Puffin, 1999. Meant for grades 4–12. This is a readable and informative biography that adults will enjoy.

World Wide Web

"Arthur Caswell Parker." http://www.answers.com/topic/arthur-caswell-parker. A detailed but brief biography with links.

"Carlos Montezuma." http://www.answers.com/topic/montezuma-carlos. Two short biographies of the radical SAI member and founder of *Wassaja.*

"Charles Eastman (Ohiyesa, 1858–1939)." http://www.wsu.edu/~campbelld/amlit/eastman.htm. Links site with many complete downloadable texts written by Eastman.

"Dr. Carlos Montezuma." http://www.azmd.gov/Physicians_Interest/index.asp?profile=carlos_montezuma.inc. A brief biography that celebrates Montezuma's life as a medical doctor.

"Gertrude Simmons Bonnin (Zitkala-Sa) (1876–1938)." http://www.wsu.edu/~campbelld/amlit/zitkala.htm. Links page to online primary and secondary sources on Zitkala-Sa, including many of her writings.

Quinton, Amelia S. "The Woman's National Indian Association (1894)." http://digital.library.upenn.edu/women/eagle/congress/quinton.html. A detailed history in the words of one of its founders. Presented at the Congress of Women at the 1893 Columbian Exposition in Chicago. Quinton also was an associate (non-Indian) member of the SAI.

"Society of American Indians." http://www.answers.com/topic/society-of-american-indians. Two brief and concise summaries with a bibliography and links.

Multimedia Sources

"A Unique Writer, Activist and Person: Charles Eastman (Ohiyesa)." http://www.worldwisdom.com/public/slideshows/view.aspx?SlideShowID=3. World Wisdom, 2008. Online slide show of the famous Indian writer and Society of American Indians member.

Bury My Heart at Wounded Knee. Dir. Yves Simoneau. HBO Films, 2007. DVD. 133 minutes. Though much criticized for inaccuracy and portrayal of characters, the movie presents as the central character Charles Eastman, an SAI member.

67. Jim Thorpe and the 1912 Olympics

Athlete Jim Thorpe won the decathlon and pentathlon in the 1912 Summer Olympics in Stockholm, Sweden, but he had other triumphs and setbacks as well. Born in 1888 with the Sauk and Fox name "Wa-thohuck," or "Bright Path," Thorpe was raised in Oklahoma and attended Haskell Institute for Indians; at age 16, he enrolled in Carlisle Indian School, where he joined the track and football teams. During his stay at Carlisle he was twice named first-team All-American, and in 1912 he won two gold medals at the Stockholm Olympics, the first American

Indian to earn Olympic fame and popularity. But his Olympic fame was short-lived and soured when he was stripped of his Olympic medals for being paid to play baseball. Although many of his Olympic teammates played for pay, they did so under assumed names. Thorpe not only used his own name, he told the truth when questioned about the incident. After he returned his gold medals, Thorpe played professional baseball and football until the late 1920s. He was voted as the first president of the American Professional Football Association, the forerunner of the National Football League. In 1950 he was named the greatest football player and male athlete of the half-century, and in 1999 the U.S. Congress passes a resolution naming Thorpe America's Athlete of the Century. He died in 1953 never knowing that the International Olympic Committee decided to restore his Olympic records and his gold medals. The Olympic Committee returned the medals to his family in 1982.

TERM PAPER SUGGESTIONS

1. Thorpe was celebrated by educated American Indians of his time, especially by the members of the Society of American Indians, who also wrote about his athletic triumphs in the quarterly journal and magazine. Research and write on the society's reporting and its praise of Thorpe's achievements. What did Thorpe represent to them?

2. Carlisle Indian School's newspaper, *The Red Man,* also praised the accomplishment of Thorpe. Explore the paper's coverage, not only of the 1912 Olympics but also of his football career at Carlisle.

3. Write on Thorpe's football career. New histories claim that he was paid for his play at Carlisle, and others have claimed that the Carlisle Indians football team invented the forward pass. Test the validity of these assertions.

4. Examine the evidence for disqualifying Thorpe's achievements at the 1912 Olympics. Does the evidence hold up to the standards of the time? How does the evidence compare to doping or cheating in the Olympics of modern times?

5. Explore the significance of an Indian winning the decathlon and pentathlon (15 separate events for 2 medals). Not many athletes can claim such a feat. Is it comparable to Michael Phelps winning 8 gold medals in the Beijing Olympics in 2008?

6. Write an essay exploring the racism and prejudice that Thorpe encountered in his long career.

ALTERNATIVE TERM PAPER SUGGESTIONS

1. Imagine you are on the committee to decide whether to disqualify Thorpe for playing "professional" baseball and to strip him of his medals and records. Take a side and present your case, backed with facts and data, before the other committee members. The committee eventually restored his medals. Why?

2. Collect contemporary newspaper articles of Jim Thorp's Olympic triumph and look for and copy negative and positive comments about the Indian athlete. Create a poster collage or scanner collage where negatives comments are collected on the left side of a dividing line and positive comments are collected on the right side. The purpose is to demonstrate whether Thorpe generated much negative commentary as compared to positive in an era where the average Indian was depicted as downtrodden and defeated.

SUGGESTED SOURCES

Primary Sources

"Editorial Comment, Carlisle's Olympic Heroes." *The Red Man,* September 1912. http://home.epix.net/~landis/thorpe.html. Scroll down a bit and you find this facsimile of a tribute from the Carlisle Indian School newspaper written and published by Carlisle Indian students.

Sullivan, James Edward. *The Olympic Games, Stockholm, 1912.* American Sports Company, 1912. http://books.google.com/books?id=cwVIAAAAIAAJ &q=jim+thorpe. Describes the games, the participants, and the location.

Secondary Sources

Anderson, Lars. *Carlisle vs. Army: Jim Thorpe, Dwight Eisenhower, Pop Warner, and the Forgotten Story of Football's Greatest Battle.* New York: Random House, 2008. One football game and three great men of history, two from sports and one army.

Benjey, Tom. *Keep A-Goin': The Life of Lone Star Dietz.* Carlisle, PA: Tuxedo Press, 2006. Biography of the colorful life of this adopted Indian whose exploits included playing football at the Carlisle Indian School and evading military service in World War I due to his non-Indian status.

Bruchac, Joseph. *Jim Thorpe, Original All-American.* New York: Dial, 2006. A very well-written biography in first person by this famous Indian author. Aimed at young readers but still a good read.

Crawford, Bill. *All American: The Rise and Fall of Jim Thorpe.* Hoboken, NJ: Wiley, 2004. Explores the racism Thorpe encountered and the bad choices he sometimes made within the context of sports history.

Elfers, James E. *The Tour to End All Tours: The Story of Major League Baseball's 1913–1914 World Tour.* Lincoln, NE: University of Nebraska Press, 2003. Jim Thorpe's early baseball career is covered in this narrative adventure story and history of the New York Giants and Chicago White Sox and their trip around the world.

Jenkins, Sally. *The Real All Americans: The Team That Changed a Game, a People, a Nation.* Garden City, NY: Doubleday, 2007. Covers the history and fame of Pop Warner, Jim Thorpe, and many others of the famous Carlisle football team. Jenkins argues that the Carlisle team invented and executed the forward pass.

Lipsyte, Robert, and John Hite. *Jim Thorpe: 20th-Century Jock.* New York: HarperTrophy, 1993. A hard-hitting and straightforward examination of Thorpe's life meant for younger readers but which does not censor adult themes.

Newcombe, Jack. *Best of the Athletic Boys: The White Man's Impact on Jim Thorpe.* Garden City, NY: Doubleday, 1975. Discusses how Americanization could be harmful to American Indians.

Updyke, Rosemary Kissinger. *Jim Thorpe, the Legend Remembered.* Gretna, LA: Pelican Publishing Company, 1997. Aimed at younger readers, this biography serves as a short introduction to Thorpe's life.

Wheeler, Robert W. *Jim Thorpe: World's Greatest Athlete.* Norman, OK: University of Oklahoma Press, 1979. Popular biography of Thorpe. Easy-to-read.

World Wide Web

Jenkins, Sally. "The Team That Invented Football, April 23, 2007." http://vault.sportsillustrated.cnn.com/vault/article/magazine/MAG1116071/index.htm. A *Sports Illustrated* article that highlights the content of her book, listed in the Secondary Sources.

"Jim Thorpe, 1888–1953." http://www.the-surfs-up.com/sports/jimthorpe.html. An informative overview of Thorpe's up-and-down athletic career.

"Jim Thorpe: The 1912 Olympics." http://sports.jrank.org/pages/4840/Thorpe-Jim-1912-Olympics.html. Brief summary of Thorpe's life that includes an informative and complete chronology.

"Jim Thorpe: Athlete of the Century." http://home.epix.net/~landis/thorpe.html. An excellent biography, secondary comments, and also a links page to other pertinent information about Thorpe.

"Jim Thorpe, Biography." http://www.notablebiographies.com/St-Tr/Thorpe-Jim.html. Short biographical sketch.

McCallum, Jack. "The Regilding of a Legend, October 25, 1982." http://vault.sportsillustrated.cnn.com/vault/article/magazine/MAG1126038/index.htm. Online version of this detailed *Sports Illustrated* article on Thorpe's athletic career and the posthumous restoration of his gold medals.

Multimedia Sources

"Images of Jim Thorpe." http://images.google.com/images?q=jim+thorpe+olympic&ie=UTF-8&oe=utf-8&rls=org.mozilla:en-US:official&client=firefox-a&um=1&sa=X&oi=image_result_group&resnum=1&ct=title. Images of Jim Thorpe at the Olympics and in Olympic uniforms.

Jim Thorpe: All American (1951). Dir. Michael Curtiz. Warner Home Video, 2007. DVD. 105 minutes. This history of Jim Thorpe includes his college career, his Olympic story, and his baseball and basketball playing.

68. World War I and Indian Involvement (1917–1918)

Some Indians were drafted to serve in World War I, but most of the over 12,000 Indian participants volunteered for service during World War I and fought gallantly for this nation, even though many were not citizens and many were the sons of those warriors who fought against the United States in the latter half of the nineteenth century. For most, the service of Indians in World War I is not well known or understood. Indians have been allied with Americans since colonial times and have served as scouts on the military rolls since the Civil War. World War I, however, saw an exponential increase in voluntary enlistment, to the awe and surprise of the average American at the time. Indians volunteered for many reasons: they felt kinship and pride in the United States, they sought to demonstrate their loyalty and prowess, and they manifested Indian identity and warrior status, important to their traditional communities. On the opposite end of the spectrum, Americans sought to use the image of the Indian as a symbol of national pride and Americanism, not to mention as racist comparison to the "Hun," the stereotypical image of the German soldier. As printed in a *Stars and Stripes* published March 1, 1918, "You will meet enemy more savage than we were," an Indian father tells his son who is on his way to fight in World War I. The famous squadron of volunteer

American pilots fighting with the French, the Lafayette Escadrille, painted a head profile of an Indian warrior decked in war bonnet on the sides of their airplanes, an insignia named "the Wild Sioux." Thus started a U.S. tradition of using Indian names and stereotypical images to name units and weapons that still persists to this day (for example, the Apache/Black Hawk helicopters or Tomahawk missiles).

TERM PAPER SUGGESTIONS

1. Relying on primary source accounts of experiences of the Indians themselves, explain why Indians would volunteer for military service in World War I. Why would they serve if they were not U.S. citizens?

2. Some of the Indian World War I servicemen were drafted because they were citizens, which was made possible by the General Allotment (Dawes) Act of 1887 and/or the Burke Act of 1906. Some refused to serve because they could prove they were not citizens. Write an essay exploring cases of draft and exemption. Why would the United States attempt to draft non-citizen Indians anyway?

3. Look at the issues of segregation and integration. Were Indians placed within their own units, or were they integrated in the general army population? You should know that Blacks were segregated until after World War II.

4. As a basis for a report, examine Indian warrior "attributes" exploited and used by the U.S. military for combat purposes. For example, Indian languages were used as communication codes and Indians were thought to be good scouts. Were any of these warrior qualities stereotypical?

5. Examine and report on the November 6, 1919 Indian Citizenship Act, which allowed Indian World War I veterans to apply for citizenship.

6. Explore the use of Indian language, iconography, and stereotypical representation by the U.S. military and its servicemen during World War I.

ALTERNATIVE TERM PAPER SUGGESTIONS

1. Imagine you are an Indian serviceman who is fluent in your native language. Propose a simple code that you could use for military communication. Create at least 10 coded words.

2. Consider that you are antiwar, a pacifist, and a member of an Indian tribe, but you are also half white American and you have been living off the reservation for some time. You are drafted. How would you argue that your draft is illegal and that you therefore refuse to serve? Prepare a written defense of your actions and desires.

SUGGESTED SOURCES

Primary Sources

Krouse, Susan Applegate. *Native Americans in the Great War.* Lincoln, NE: University of Nebraska Press, 2007. From the data collected from Indian veterans by Joseph K. Dixon, this selected compilation allows American Indians to describe their own World War I experiences and aftermath. Pride in serving as well as frustration with the U.S. government are common themes.

Washburn, Wilcomb E. *The American Indian and the United States: A Documentary History.* Westport, CT: Greenwood Press, 1973. Contains primary source documents, laws, and other pertinent materials.

"World War 1." http://www.wpt.org/wayofthewarrior/ww1.cfm. Web site page for *Way of the Warrior* (see Multimedia Sources section) coverage of World War I, containing some primary source photographs and a photo of pages from a journal written by a WW I veteran.

"Yank Indian Was Heap Big Help in Winning War." *The Stars and Stripes,* May 30, 1919. http://www.oldmagazinearticles.com/pdf/big help.pdf. A PDF download article reflecting both the contribution of the American Indians in World War I, including Indian prowess and code talkers, and the use of stereotyping. Search this site for more interesting articles about Indians in World War I.

Secondary Sources

Barsh, Russell L. "American Indians in the Great War." *Ethnohistory* 38, no. 3 (Summer 1991): 276–303. A good general survey.

Britten, Thomas A. *American Indians in World War I: At Home and At War.* Albuquerque, NM: University of New Mexico Press, 1997. Examines the Indians as draftees, volunteers, combat soldiers, and stereotypes in the Great War. Also explores their experiences after the war.

Dempsey, James L. *Warriors of the King: Prairie Indians in World War I.* Regina, SK, Canada: Canadian Plains Research Center, University of Regina, 1999. A similar work to Britten's but covers the First Nations, or Canadian Indians.

Gaffen, Fred. *Forgotten Soldiers.* Penticton, BC, Canada: Two Trails Press, 1993. Explores the First Nations' (Canadian Indians') participation in World War I and World War II.

Langellier, Phillip J. *American Indians in the U.S. Armed Forces, 1866–1945.* Mechanicsburg, PA: Stackpole Books, 2000. General overview of Indian participation in U.S. armed forces.

Lynn-Sherow, Bonnie, and Susannah Ural Bruce. " 'How Cola' from Camp Funston: American Indians and the Great War." *Kansas History: A Journal of the Central Plains* 24, no. 2 (Summer 2001): 84–97. Examines the Lakota at Camp Funston and their motivation to volunteer for war as predicated on their personal desires and aspirations rather than for assimilation.

Prucha, Francis P. *The Great Father: The United States Government and the American Indians.* Lincoln, NE: University of Nebraska Press, 1984. General overview of laws and acts concerning Indians.

Starita, Joe. *The Dull Knifes of Pine Ridge: A Lakota Odyssey.* New York: G.P. Putnam's Sons, 1995. Reprint, Lincoln, NE: Bison Books, 2002. Follows the war history of one Lakota family, whose member Guy Dull Knife Sr. served in the army in World War I.

Tate, Michael L. "From Scout to Doughboy: The National Debate over Integrating American Indians into the Military, 1891–1918." *Western Historical Quarterly* 17, no. 4 (October 1986): 417–37. Explores the issue of segregated units versus integrated units.

World Wide Web

"An Indian Technique: Code Talkers: Use of the Native Indian Tongue for Secure Communications." http://www.defenselink.mil/specials/nativeamerican01/code.html. A short article honoring Indian code talkers of World War I and World War II.

Camurat, Diane. "The American Indian in the Great War: Real and Imagined." http://net.lib.byu.edu/estu/wwi/comment/Camurat1.html. An excellent general overview of Indians in the Great War with not only participation data but information on stereotypical representations of Indians in the Great War as well.

Lockard, Vicki. "Code Talkers." http://www.turtletrack.org/Issues00/Co06032000/CO_06032000_Codetalk.htm. Short history of the Choctaw, Comanche, and Navajo code talkers of World War I and World War II.

"Mathew B. Juan—Native American Hero of World War I." http://hubpages.com/hub/Mathew-B-Juan–Native-American-Hero-of-World-War-I. The first American Indian and first Arizona casualty of the World War I killed by the machine gun fire. The site includes his history and digital photos of his draft registration.

"Native Americans and the U.S. Military." http://www.history.navy.mil/faqs/faq61-1.htm. A general and brief survey of the participation of Indians in the U.S. armed services, including in World War I.

"World War 1 Code Talkers Instrumental in Ending War." http://www
.choctawnation.com/files/codetalkersact.pdf. One-page PDF article with
a photograph describing Choctaw code talkers of World War I.

"World War I and II: Choctaw Code Talkers." http://www.oklachahta.org/code
talkers.htm. Brief history with links.

Multimedia Sources

"Native Words, Native Warriors." http://www.nmai.si.edu/education/code-
talkers/. Very interesting slide show presentation. A code talker site with
Choctaw, Comanche, and Navajo words moving over a line from left to
right and translating into English (be patient). Also introduces via native
song and images other multimedia sources on code talkers. Includes text
version and lesson plan.

Way of the Warrior. Dir. Patty Loew. Wisconsin Public Television, 2007. DVD.
60 minutes. Survey of Indians serving in the U.S. armed services from
WW I to the Gulf War.

69. Native American Church Is Incorporated (1918)

Concerned that the U.S. government would ban the Peyote religion, the
Native American Church (NAC) was incorporated in 1918 to protect
the religious freedom of its practitioners, who ingest the peyote cactus as
a religious sacrament and as part of their religious observances.
Anthropologist James Mooney was allegedly responsible for drafting the
language of the first charter and for advocating a legal stance against
efforts to ban the practice. The use of peyote goes back thousands of years,
some say 10,000 years, but the practice of the NAC is a relatively recent
phenomenon due to its combining of Christian theology with American
Indian beliefs and ritual practices. The NAC stresses community, chanting and singing, and meditation and prayer for the sick and needy.
Furthermore, the NAC is pan-Indian: its membership draws from almost
every American Indian tribe of the nation. Starting with around
12,000 members in 1918, the NAC has grown to over 300,000 in
modern times. In the historical record, one interpretation is that the
NAC emerged out of the Ghost Dance religion of the late 1880s and early
1890s, which was a pan-Indian messianic tradition involving dancing,
chanting, singing, praying, and Christianity. The NAC also traces its

roots back to peyote use among ancient Aztecs and other Indians of the U.S. southwest and northwestern Mexico. Franciscans priests reported its use among Indians in the Southwest as early as 1560 and peyote found in archeological sites have been dated as 7, 000 years old. The federal government, despite many attempts by state and federal officials to illegalize peyote, has upheld the right of Indians to use peyote in several court cases and laws; additionally it has, in a 1994 amendment to the American Indian Religious Freedom Act, legalized peyote for religious purposes.

TERM PAPER SUGGESTIONS

1. Examine the life and vision of John Wilson (of Caddo, Delaware, and French ancestry), a famous Ghost Dance leader who, as the oral tradition says, originated many basic ritual practices of the NAC after ingesting peyote for 14 days.

2. Write on Quanah Parker, the famous Comanche, who was allegedly saved from death after drinking peyote tea. He converted to the Peyote religion and gave up violence and killing.

3. Examine the role of the famous ethnographer/anthropologist James Mooney as a defender of the religious freedom of American Indians. Why was he so passionate?

4. Explore the Christian elements in the NAC. The NAC was originally named the "Firstborn Church of Christ," and every member was a Christian, baptized at one time or another in a Christian church.

5. Study and report on the opposition's argument against the formation of the NAC. Does religious freedom extend to those people who use a "drug," as described by the opponents, as their central religious sacrament? What is the NAC's strongest evidence?

6. Trace the legal chronology of the successful defense of the NAC to protect its right to worship how its members please. How were (are) they successful in arguing the constitutional validity of their position?

ALTERNATIVE TERM PAPER SUGGESTIONS

1. Imagine that you have been assigned to write a document defending the right of Indians to practice the Sun Dance, a ritual involving the piercing of skin, or any other religious practice questioned by the common citizen as barbaric and pagan.

2. Create a Microsoft PowerPoint slide show of a representative selection of peyote religious art, artifacts, and paraphernalia to demonstrate the beauty

and seriousness in which the practitioners of the NAC regard their religious worship and practice.

SUGGESTED SOURCES

Primary Sources

"American Indian Religious Freedom Act." [Public Law 95-341 (96 Stat. 469)]. 95th Congress. Recognizes the religious freedom of American Indians.

"American Indian Religious Freedom Act Amendments of 1994." [Public Law 103-344 (108 stat. 3124)]. 103rd Congress. Makes peyote legal for Indians to use for ceremonial purposes.

"The Laws Protecting Authorized Participants." http://www.nativeamericanchurch .net/Legal/law.htm. Starts with the Bill of Rights and ends with *State of Utah v. Mooney, et al* of 2004, which extended use of peyote to Indians who are not part of any federally recognized tribe.

Radin, Paul. *The Peyote Cult.* 1925. Reprint, Charleston, SC: BiblioBazaar, 2008. Firsthand accounts of the religious practice, followed by analysis by the famous ethnographer.

Secondary Sources

Aberle, David F. *The Peyote Religion Among the Navaho.* Norman, OK: University of Oklahoma Press, 1966. Reprint, 1991. Explores the use of peyote and ritual among some tribal members and their way of adapting the practice to their particular cultural background.

Anderson, Edward F. *Peyote, the Divine Cactus.* 2nd edition. Tucson, AZ: University of Arizona Press, 1996. Scientific scrutiny of the peyote cactus accompanies a thorough and well-documented history of the religious uses of the plant.

Bruguir, Leonard R. *Peyote and the Yankton Sioux: The Life and Times of Sam Necklace.* Norman, OK: University of Oklahoma Press, 2005. Five-generational history of a family and the rise of the Native American Church among the Yankton. Includes maps, illustrations, and photographs.

La Barre, Weston. *The Peyote Cult.* 5th edition. Norman, OK: University of Oklahoma Press, 1989. Results of primary source research from the 1930s through the 1980s.

Long, Carolyn N. *Religious Freedom and Indian Rights: The Case of Oregon v. Smith.* Lawrence, KS: University Press of Kansas, 2000. Detailed analysis of this Supreme Court case and of the use of peyote in American Indian religious ceremonies.

Slotkin, James S. *The Peyote Religion: A Study in Indian-White Relations*. New York: Octagon Books, 1975. A classic study of the use of peyote by Indians and the efforts of others to prevent that use.

Smith, Huston, and Reuben Snake. *One Nation Under God: The Triumph of the Native American Church*. Sante Fe, NM: Clear Light Publishers, 1996. Focuses on the legal struggles of American Indians to enjoy "freedom of religion" while presenting a factual case for the legal use of peyote within religious ceremonies and practice.

Stewart, Omer C. *Peyote Religion: A History*. Norman, OK: University of Oklahoma Press, 1987. An exhaustive history of the NAC.

Swan, Daniel C. *Peyote Religious Art: Symbols of Faith and Belief.* Jackson, MS: University Press of Mississippi, 1999. A visual history of the NAC through the art and craft of the practitioners. Beautiful in its own right without an understanding of peyote.

Tsa Toke, Monroe. *The Peyote Ritual: Visions and Descriptions*. San Francisco, CA: The Grabhorn Press, 1957. A brief description of the basic ritual practice.

Vecsey, Christopher, ed. *Handbook of American Indian Religious Freedom*. New York: Crossroad, 1991. A collection of essays on the relevant areas of legal struggle for American Indians as they pertain to Indian religious freedom.

World Wide Web

Fikes, Jay. "A Brief History of the Native American Church." http://www.csp.org/communities/docs/fikes-nac_history.html. Historical narrative essay linking the modern peyote practices with Christian influences to those practices of the past.

Kunze, Rachel. "On the Native American Church and the Ritual Use of Peyote." http://www.drury.edu/multinl/story.cfm?ID=2527&NLID=166. Detailed look at the medicinal and psychological benefits of peyote for American Indians.

Kunzelman, Michael. "No Lingering Effects of Peyote Found." http://findarticles.com/p/articles/mi_qn4188/is_20051128/ai_n15873185. New report on findings by researchers and the dismissal of NAC members charged with felony drug offenses.

Michel, Karen Lincoln. "For Native American Church, Peyote is Sacred." http://www2.jsonline.com/news/editorials/dec99/michel19121799.asp. Story of Tommy Billy, a member of the Native American Church of the Navajo Nation, who opposes laws designed to illegalize the use of peyote.

Morgan, George. "Reflections of the Peyote Road." http://www.lectlaw.com/files/drg29.htm. First-account narrative and experience.

"Native American Church." http://www.answers.com/topic/native-american-church. Basic and general information on the church and religious practices.

"The Native American Church Art." http://nac-art.com/contents.htm. A site celebrating the art of peyote church members, with images of art and artifacts as well as narrative descriptions.

Multimedia Source

The Peyote Road. Dir. Phil Cousineau et al. Kifaru Productions, 1993. VHS. 59 minutes. Examines historical intolerance toward American Indian religious practices, documents the use of peyote over hundreds of years, and details the legal and political issues.

70. Indian Citizenship Act (1924)

Though Indians were able to become citizens via other legal means, all Indians born within the boundaries of the United States were granted citizenship following the passage of the Indian Citizenship Act of 1924 (43 Stat. 253, ante, 420); later amendments clarified that the act applied to Native Alaskans as well. The act made American Indians citizens of the United States while retaining their citizenship to their own tribe, according to the citizenship criteria of that tribe. In this sense, Indian members of the federally recognized tribes have had dual citizenship and also dual citizenship responsibilities. Conferring U.S. citizenship to Indians does not necessarily mean a blanket right to vote in local, state and national elections, however; because several states withheld and delayed or otherwise made difficult the right to vote, many Indian citizens have not exercised their right to vote outside of their respective tribal elections. In another matter, several Indian tribes (or more accurately, political factions of tribes) have rejected any federal authority over tribal sovereignty in an effort to protect their tribal status as nations, recognized in their treaty agreements with the U.S. government.

TERM PAPER SUGGESTIONS

1. Examine the various ways Indians could become citizens before the Indian Citizenship Act of 1924. Consider treaty provisions, the General Allotment

Act of 1887, the Burke Act of 1906, the case of the Indian veterans of World War I, and other ways.

2. The citizenship act did not "impair or otherwise affect the right of any Indian to tribal or other property" or their relation to their tribe. This meant that Indians had and have dual citizenship. Explore the implications and complications of dual status.

3. How have Indians themselves viewed their U.S. citizenship? Explore their views, sometimes published in newspapers, on their new status. Were all Indians of the same mind?

4. Several tribes, the Hopi of the southwest and the Onondaga (Iroquois) of the northwest, held at the time, and factions still continue to believe to this day, that the act had no power over them as an exertion of sovereignty. Explore why these tribes would make such proclamations of sovereignty and denial of federal authority.

5. Before 1924, Indians were considered "outside" the United States, yet within its borders. Examine the contradiction inherent in this legal status and how blanket citizenship solves many problems of definitions, legal and civil.

6. Implicit in the granting of citizenship is the right to vote. However, the right to vote resides within individual states. Study the right to vote in Indian communities since 1924. Have they always been able to vote in local, state, and federal elections? How could state governments prevent them from voting? (Compare to Jim Crow Laws.)

ALTERNATIVE TERM PAPER SUGGESTIONS

1. Imagine yourself an Indian who believes in assimilation and education. Write a statement reacting to the passage of the act.

2. Alternatively, assume you are a Hopi or Onondaga who opposes any law that challenges your tribe's independence and sovereignty. Write a statement of rejection of federal law and of assertion of tribal rights.

SUGGESTED SOURCES

Primary Sources

"Indian Citizenship." Kappler's *Indian Affairs: Laws and Treaties, 1927.* http://digital.library.okstate.edu/kappler/vol4/html_files/v4p1165.html. Complete act and associated laws relating to voting and amendments to the 1924 act.

Washburn, Wilcomb E. *The American Indian and the United States: A Documentary History.* Westport, CT: Greenwood Press, 1973. Contains primary source documents, laws, and other pertinent materials.

Secondary Sources

Champagne, Duane, ed. *The Native North American Almanac: A Reference Work on Native North Americans in the United States and Canada.* 2nd edition. Farmington Hills, MI: Gale, 2001. General reference that includes a chapter on legislation.

Deloria, Vine, Jr., ed. *American Indian Policy in the Twentieth Century.* Norman, OK: University of Oklahoma Press, 1992. A collection of essays exploring the impact of policy on American Indians. Deloria's contribution provides a brief history and overview of federal Indian policy making.

McCool, Daniel, et al. *Native Vote: American Indians, the Voting Rights Act and the Right to Vote.* New York: Cambridge University Press, 2007. Examines the history of voting rights of American Indians and the struggle for citizenship.

Pevar, Stephen L. *The Rights of Indians and Tribes. The Authoritative ACLU Guide to Indian and Tribal Rights.* 3rd edition. New York: NYU Press, 2004. Provides a historical overview as well as answering many legal questions.

Prucha, Francis P. *The Great Father: The United States Government and the American Indians.* Lincoln, NE: University of Nebraska Press, 1984. General overview of laws and acts concerning Indians.

Rosen, Lawrence. *American Indians and the Law.* Durham, NC: School of Law, Duke University, 1976. Reprint, Transaction Publishers, 1978. An older historical survey.

Thompson, William Norman. *Native American Issues: A Reference Handbook.* Santa Barbara, CA: ABC-CLIO, 1996. General annotated set of legal facts, court cases, laws, and statistics about the Indian.

World Wide Web

"A Separate People: Tribal People's Citizenship Within the U.S." http://www.cwis.org/fwdp/Americas/itsg-cit.txt. Essay on tribal and U.S. citizenship as they relate to tribal sovereignty.

"Citizenship Act 1924." http://www.nrcprograms.org/site/PageServer?pagename=swirc_hist_citizenshipact. Concise and brief descriptive history.

Gudzune, Jeffrey R. "Act of Will: The Fight for Native American Citizenship." http://nativeamericanfirstnationshistory.suite101.com/article.cfm/act_of_will. An essay surveying the laws pertaining to American Indian citizenship, from exclusion to inclusion.

"Indian Citizenship Act." http://memory.loc.gov/ammem/today/jun02.html. An excellent descriptive essay with annotated links to other important information.

"Native American Citizenship." http://www.nebraskastudies.org/0700/frameset
_reset.html?http://www.nebraskastudies.org/0700/stories/0701_0140.
html. Informative essay comparing the struggle of Native Americans for
citizenship to the struggles of women and African Americans.

"1924 Indian Citizenship Act." http://www.nebraskastudies.org/0700/frameset
_reset.html?http://www.nebraskastudies.org/0700/stories/0701_0146.
html. Short description. Also includes a photo of Calvin Coolidge and
four Osage Indians shortly after Coolidge signed the bill.

"Right of Citizenship Given to Indians." *The Real American News,* June 12,
1924. http://faculty.washington.edu/gregoryj/civilrights/display.cgi?
image=plummer/Real%20American%206-12-24.jpg. Seattle Indian
newspaper report.

Multimedia Source

Tribal Nations: The Story of Federal Indian Law. Dir. Lisa Jaeger. Tanana
Chiefs Conference Signature Media Production, 2006. DVD. 60 minutes.
Documentary film examining the development of U.S. federal
Indian law.

71. Indian Defense League of America (1926) and the Jay Treaty (1794)

The Indian Defense League of America (IDLA) was established
December 1, 1926 to protect the right of "unrestricted passage" for
American Indians, especially the crossing of the Canadian and U.S. border, which was challenged by the Immigration Act of 1924. Many
U.S. tribal members hold the position that the Indian Citizenship Act of
1924 violated tribal sovereignty and forced Indians to become citizens
without their consent. On the other side, the Canadian government
through the "Order in Council of September 17, 1923" abolished the
traditional Iroquois governments residing in Canada and passed their
own citizenship act in the same year. Two treaties between the United
States and England, the Jay Treaty of 1794 and the Treaty of Ghent of
1814, the treaty that ended the War of 1812, guaranteed Indians "freely
to pass by land, inland navigation, into . . . the Continent of America . . .
and to navigate all lakes, rivers thereof, and freely to carry on trade and
commerce . . ." (Jay Treaty); the Treaty of Ghent reaffirmed these rights.
The treaties also exempted importation taxes and any other tariffs on

the "goods belonging bona fide to Indians" (Jay Treaty). The recognition of these rights and privileges has been very important to Indians on the U.S.–Canadian borders: both sides of the St. Lawrence Seaway and from the Great Lakes to the Pacific. In times of increased "Homeland Security" and with the threat of terrorists crossing the U.S.–Canadian border, these rights are still a focus of contention and controversy.

TERM PAPER SUGGESTIONS

1. At present, the law allows the unrestricted crossing into the United States of Canadian Indians who can prove 50 percent blood quantum (Degree of Indian Blood). Examine whether Indians from the United States have the same rights as those from Canada. What legal basis does Canada cite to avoid the provisions of the Jay and Ghent treaties?

2. The law allowing Indians to cross the United States border from Canada also allows Canadian Indians to work or attend college with the same rights and privileges as Americans. Investigate and report on the procedures that Canadian Indians must follow and the evidence they must produce to attain these rights.

3. Explore why Indian tribes do not recognize the border that splits their tribal land holdings and communities between two nations.

4. Why would the United States and England of the period 1790–1815 agree to protect the rights of tribal members to cross and recross the border between the United States and Canada?

5. In current times, with the terrorist threat, can the right of Indians to cross the international border be detrimental to the security of either Canada or the United States? Explain and support your position.

6. Why does the IDLA conduct annual, public border crossings in defense of the Indian's right to do so, and why do they insist on its preservation?

ALTERNATIVE TERM PAPER SUGGESTIONS

1. Imagine you are a border crossing guard at a port of entry between the United States and Canada and you are required to prepare a set of questions to determine the right of an Indian to cross the border freely and without restrictions. How could you determine the validity of such a crossing?

2. Create an agreement between two nations that share a common border. Write a set of conditions and rights that would be agreeable to both parties while at the same time protecting the security of both.

SUGGESTED SOURCES

Primary Sources

McCandless, Commissioner of Immigration. v. United States ex rel. DIABO. March 9, 1928. http://www.uniset.ca/other/cs3/25F2d71.html. Upholds the right of a Six Nations tribal member to cross the border to work as a high steel laborer in New York City. Has links to other relevant court cases, like *U.S. v. Rickert* and *Elk v. Wilkins*.

"Treaty of Amity Commerce and Navigation, Between His Britannick Majesty; and the United States of America, by Their President, with the Advice and Consent of Their Senate [The Jay Treaty]." http://avalon.law.yale.edu/18th_century/jay.asp. Full facsimile text of the treaty.

"Treaty of Peace and Amity, Between His Britannic Majesty and the United States of America [The Treaty of Ghent]." http://memory.loc.gov/cgi-bin/ampage?collId=llsl&fileName=008/llsl008.db&recNum=231. Full facsimile text of the treaty.

Secondary Sources

Deloria, Vine, Jr., and David E. Wilkins. *Tribes, Treaties, and Constitutional Tribulations*. Austin, TX: University of Texas Press, 2000. Explores the relationship between the U.S. Constitution and Indian tribes.

Dutha, N. Bruce, and Colin Calloway. *American Indians and the Law*. New York: Viking, 2008. Defines and clarifies sovereignty as it applies to federally recognized tribes since 1787.

Jennings, Francis. *The Ambiguous Iroquois Empire*. New York: W.W. Norton, 1990. Details the manner in which the Iroquois gained and maintained power in the early period of colonization.

Johansen, Bruce E., ed. *Enduring Legacies: Native American Treaties and Contemporary Controversies*. Westport, CT: Praeger, 2004. Examines and explores treaties' rights and controversies, including the Treaty of Canandaigua.

Johansen, Bruce E., and Barbara Alice Mann, eds. *Encyclopedia of the Haudenosaunee (Iroquois Confederacy)*. Westport, CT: Greenwood Press, 2000. Comprehensively written volume of short essays covering the history and culture of the Six Nations of the Iroquois.

Johansen, Bruce Elliott, ed. *The Encyclopedia of Native American Legal Tradition*. Westport, CT: Greenwood Press, 1998. Among other relevant information is a short description of the Indian Defense League of America (pages 143–44).

Rickard, Clinton, ed. *Fighting Tuscarora: The Autobiography of Chief Clinton Rickard.* Syracuse, NY: Syracuse University Press, 1994. Covers the border-crossing issue in chapter six.

Sadowski-Smith, Claudia. *Globalization on the Line.* New York: Macmillan, 2002. Donald A. Grinde Jr.'s chapter "Iroquois Border Crossings" presents the legal, social, and economic history of border crossings defended by the Indian Defense League of America.

Williq, Timothy D. *Restoring the Chain of Friendship: British Policy of the Great Lakes, 1798–1815.* Lincoln, NE: University of Nebraska Press, 2008. Examines British policy affecting the border between the United States and Canada.

World Wide Web

"Border Crossing Rights Between the U.S. and Canada for Aboriginal People." http://www.danielnpaul.com/AmericanBritishJayTreaty-1794.html. A how-to manual for those Canadian Indians who wish to work in the United States while still residing in Canada.

"Deskaheh, Levi General: Iroquois Patriot's Fight for International Recognition." http://www.idloa.org/pages/deskaheh.html. Firsthand account of the difficulties of restricting border crossings.

"First Nations and Native Americans." http://www.amcits.com/first_nations _canada.asp. Instructions from the U.S. Embassy of how to cross the border into the United States.

"Indian Defense League of America." http://idloa.org/. Web site of the organization founded in 1925, including links to the pertinent treaties; to the words of the founder, Chief Clinton Rickard; and to information about the symbolic annual border crossings of 1928 to 2008 to advocate for the right guaranteed by the Jay Treaty.

Kanentiio, Doug George. "The Paul Diabo Case Affects Us All." http:// indiancountrynews.net/index.php?option=com_content&task=view &id=3208&Itemid=1. Brief review of the Diabo case and the origins of the Indian Defense League of America (IDLA).

Nickels, Bryan. "Native American Free Passage Rights under the 1794 Jay Treaty: Survival under United States Statutory Law and Canadian Common Law." http://www.bc.edu/bc_org/avp/law/lwsch/journals/bciclr/24_2/ 04_TXT.htm. Comprehensive essay that compares the United States and Canadian application of the law and treaty.

Multimedia Source

"Chief Clinton Rickard Statue." http://niagaradowntown.com/video/
   060311PG_ChiefR.html. Short online video file of Chief Rickard,
   founder of the Indian Defense League of America.

72. Meriam Report (1928)

In 1928, Secretary of the Interior Hubert Work instructed the Institute
for Government Research to form a commission to investigate the living
conditions on Indian reservations in 27 states. After many months of
research and site visits, Lewis Meriam, the team leader, issued a report
under the title *The Problem of Indian Administration.* His report documented the failure of Indian policies, specifically the General Allotment
(Dawes) Act of 1887, to improve the Indian through allotment, and it
detailed how past policies had caused inhumane health and living conditions for Indians living on reservations. Further, his report showed that
Indian land allotment was a complete failure in terms of providing
for the health and welfare of Indian family farmers, because the net
result was abject poverty, poor health, and crippling isolation. These
policies had the effect of destroying the culture and society of American
Indians more than enriching them with the fruits of American civilized
society through agricultural training and farming. The report recommended new polices, the repeal of old polices, especially the Allotment Act, and that immediate action be taken to improve the health of
American Indians, which also meant allowing traditional healers to
work side by side with medical doctors to help, at least psychologically,
the sick. Inherent in the report was this recognition of the importance of
traditional culture and the role of self-determination and self-
government. Policy changes made in response to the report caused Indian
land loss to stop, health and educational facilities to be built, and tribal
communities to flourish, and, as a result, the health and welfare of Indians
improved.

TERM PAPER SUGGESTIONS

1. Study the pressure from the public to motivate Secretary of the Interior
   Hubert Work to take some action about the squalid living conditions on
   Indian reservations.

2. Write on the health conditions that the Meriam Commission found on their site visits. What were the major health problems in Indian country, and how easy or difficult were they to treat or cure? Look at infant mortality, tuberculosis, trachoma, measles, and mental health.

3. Research and write on how the Meriam Report detailed the failure of the Allotment Act of 1887. Some claim that the failure was in the preparing of Indians for individual land ownership rather than the allotting of land itself. What does the Meriam Report say?

4. Discuss the evidence that the report provides on the poverty of American Indians. Poverty, according to the report, was the single most important problem to solve. Do you agree, disagree? Why?

5. In this transitional period, when Indians were moving from being self-sufficient hunters and gathers to relying on farming and what the government provided, American Indians' diet was changing. Discuss this change. Did government-issued foodstuffs contribute to the poor health and dietary practices of Indians?

6. Research and write on the educational experience of Indian children as reported by Meriam. Were the mission schools or missionaries any better than government-run schools?

ALTERNATIVE TERM PAPER SUGGESTIONS

1. Imagine you are a member of the Meriam Commission. Look at the photographic evidence that documents the poverty on Indian reservations and the poor conditions of health and educational facilities. Write a seven-day journal of what you might have encountered on site visits to reservations and reservation facilities.

2. Pick one reservation or one state. Create comparative graphs between Indian health and poverty statistics and those of the general U.S. population at the time of the Meriam Report, also including the latest, most up-to-date statistics. How much has changed?

SUGGESTED SOURCES

Primary Sources

Meriam, Lewis. *The Problem of Indian Administration.* Baltimore, MD: Johns Hopkins Press, 1928. The actual report.

"The Meriam Report (1928) Investigates Failed U.S. Indian Policy." http://www .wisconsinhistory.org/turningpoints/search.asp?id=952. Provides an introduction and a link to the full text of *The Problem of Indian Administration* as well as links to related topics.

Secondary Sources

Adams, David Wallace. *Education for Extinction: American Indians and the Boarding School Experience 1875–1928.* Lawrence, KS: University Press of Kansas, 1997. Thoroughly examines the government's Indian education plan to "kill the Indian to save the man," and ends with the Meriam Report.

Canby, William C., Jr., *American Indian Law in a Nutshell.* 1981. Reprint, St. Paul, MN: West Publishing Group, 2004. A book that answers simple questions like "What is an Indian Tribe?" A good basic set of definitions.

Critchlow, Donald T. "Lewis Meriam, Expertise, and Indian Reform." *Historian* 43, no. 3 (1981): 325–43. Explores the effect of the Meriam Report on Indian policy reform.

Johansen, Bruce E. *The Native Peoples of North America.* Piscataway, NJ: Rutgers University Press, 2006. Chapter eight covers the period of the Meriam Report and the Indian Reorganization Act. A good general overview of American Indian history.

Prucha, Francis Paul. *The Great Father: The United States Government and the American Indians.* 2 vols. Lincoln, NE: University of Nebraska Press, 1984. General summary of federal Indian policy.

Reyhner, Jon Allan, and Jeanne M. Oyawin Eder. *American Indian Education, a History.* Chapters five through eight detail the conditions of Indian education, often relying on the Meriam Report for statistical data.

Rhoades, Everett R., ed. *American Indian Health: Innovations in Health Care, Promotion, and Policy.* Baltimore, MD: The Johns Hopkins University Press, 2001. A collection of essays covering the history of Indian health and health care policy since early times. Includes data and statistics on major diseases affecting Indians and consideration of cultural and ethical issues.

Stefon, Frederick J. "Significance of the Meriam Report of 1928." *Indian Historian* 8, no. 3 (Summer 1974): 2–7, 46. Brief overview of the findings and recommendations of the report.

Wilkinson, Charles F. *Blood Struggle: The Rise of Modern Indian Nations.* New York: W.W. Norton, 2005. Celebrates the economic triumphs of Indian tribes since the Meriam Report and the Indian Reorganization Act.

World Wide Web

"A New Deal for Native Americans." http://www.digitalhistory.uh.edu/native _voices/voices_display.cfm?id=93. Brief descriptive excerpt from the report written by Lewis Meriam.

"Exhibit Case 5: Meriam Commission and Health Care Reform (1925–1945)." http://www.nlm.nih.gov/exhibition/if_you_knew/if_you_knew_07 .html. Presents the report of Lewis Meriam of the Canton Insane Asylum for Indians. Photographs with captions.

"Legacy of the Dawes Act." http://frankwarner.typepad.com/free_frank_warner/ 2006/10/legacy_of_the_d.html. Although this is an opinion/editorial, Frank Warner provides a list of accurate facts and assessments of the failure of the Dawes Act of 1887 and the condition of Indian tribes, then and now.

"The Meriam Report." http://spirittalknews.com/MeriamReport.htm. An article summarizing the major "problems": health, living, and economic conditions and causes of poverty.

"Meriam Report." http://www.answers.com/topic/meriam-report. Brief description with bibliography and external links.

Stahl, Wayne K. "The U.S. and Native American Education." http://jaie.asu.edu /v18/V18S3sur.html. A brief survey that places the Meriam Report in a chronology of Indian education policy and reform.

"Their Blood Cries Up From the Ground." http://www.hiawathadiary.com/ HiawathaAsylum.html. Visual exploration of the Hiawatha Asylum for Insane Indians, a place the Meriam Commission visited and reported on.

Multimedia Source

Tribal Nations: The Story of Federal Indian Law. Dir. Lisa Jaeger. Tanana Chiefs Conference Signature Media Production, 2006. DVD. 60 minutes. Documentary film examining the development of U.S. federal Indian law.

73. Indian Reorganization Act (1934)

The Indian Reorganization Act (IRA) of 1934 reversed the Allotment policies and slowed the rate of allotment of Indian lands to non-Indians. The act also returned land and other assets to Indian tribes but reaffirmed and continued federal trust status. More importantly, it established a mechanism for Indian self-government but under a federal template rather than tribal. It also allowed for self-determination and management powers, but under a business model rather than a traditional one. What was certain was that the IRA, as envisioned by Commissioner of Indian Affairs John Collier, halted and reversed assimilation policies and the sale of tribal lands that sought to obliterate Indian tribes and notions of communal property at the expense of their cultures and tribal communities. Through the IRA Collier stressed a renewed respect for the importance of Indian tribal governments and cultures, and for their preservation and perpetuation. He believed cultural survival and retention of tribal identity were necessary elements for a healthy growth of social and economic welfare on Indian reservations. The act advocated for the writing and adoption of a tribal constitution with conditions that allowed for legal council, that prohibited the sale or lease of tribal lands without approval of the tribe, and that made it possible for tribes to negotiate with local, state, and federal governments. The Indian Reorganization Act also revitalized Indian arts and crafts as respected and commercially viable forms of cultural preservation and expression. Though not a perfect system of reform, the IRA created tribal governments with more power and autonomy, albeit in nontraditional forms, than the Allotment Act (1887) and other assimilation laws that sought to break apart the power of tribes.

TERM PAPER SUGGESTIONS

1. Examine the role of the Meriam Report and the eventual passing of the IRA legislation. How was the Meriam Report useful to Collier's efforts to get the IRA through both houses of Congress?

2. Write on Collier and his crusade for Indian reform. Why was he so passionate and dedicated? What were his motivations?

3. Write on the arts and crafts as an element of Indian culture worth preserving. Were arts and crafts corrupted by commercialism, or was commercialism an argument that swayed people to consider the preservation of Indian culture that assimilation polices would have, theoretically, destroyed?

4. Examine the IRA governmental structure. How has it been a reflection of state and federal governments? How is it different?

5. As documented by Deloria and others, Indians from every part of the nation opposed the adoption of the IRA. Discuss why Indian tribes would oppose the IRA and Collier. At the same time, Collier ignored some states, like Michigan, whose tribes might have benefited from the IRA. How do you explain his selection of tribes to convince that the IRA was to their benefit and his ignoring of others?

6. Study and write on the non-Indian opponents that Collier faced. Why would Protestant missionaries, to name one of many opposition groups, oppose and work to stop Collier from his goal for Indian policy reform?

ALTERNATIVE TERM PAPER SUGGESTIONS

1. Create a collection of images of American Indian arts and crafts from the early to mid-1900s via World Wide Web search, in order to create a Microsoft PowerPoint slide show that demonstrates the beauty and complexities of Indian arts and crafts. Your goal: convince people that the preservation of Indian cultures is beneficial and desired and that the loss of such a cultural resource would be tragic.

2. Imagine you are a tribal member designated to create and write a constitution for your tribe, one that followed the rules of the IRA while at the same time preserving some semblance of your traditional tribal government. How would you accomplish this task?

SUGGESTED SOURCES

Primary Sources

"A Bill of Rights for Indians." http://historymatters.gmu.edu/d/5059. Full facsimile of an article by Collier published in the *Literary Digest* in 1934.

Deloria, Vine, Jr., ed. *The Indian Reorganization Act: Congresses and Bills.* Norman, OK: University of Oklahoma Press, 2002. Primary source collection of minutes, proceedings, and laws surrounding the act, its implementation, and its acceptance by Indian tribes.

"The Indian Reorganization Act, June 18, 1934." http://www.cskt.org/ documents/reorganizationact.pdf. Downloadable PDF of a facsimile of the full text of the act.

The Indian Reorganization Act, June 18, 1934. http://www.fcpotawatomi.com/ index.php/Treaties/Indian-Reorganization-Act.html. Full text of the act.

"John Collier Promises to Reform Indian Policy." http://historymatters.gmu.edu /d/5058/. An excerpt from his 1938 report as commissioner of Indian Affairs.

Secondary Sources

Biolsi, Thomas. *Organizing the Lakota: The Political Economy of the New Deal on the Pine Ridge and Rosebud Reservations.* Tucson, AZ: University of Arizona Press, 1998. A case study examination of how the Office of Indian Affairs organized the tribal governments of the Lakota using the federal model and how they retained power despite the outward appearance of "self-government."

Daily, David. *W. Battle for the BIA: G. E. E. Lindquist and the Missionary Crusade against John Collier.* Tucson, AZ: University of Arizona Press, 2004. Explicates the efforts of Gustavus E. E. Lindquist to preserve Protestant missionary influence over Indian affairs through his staunch opposition to Collier's reforms.

Deloria, Vine, Jr., and Clifford M. Lytle. *The Nations Within: The Past and Future of American Indian Sovereignty.* New York: Pantheon, 1984. Explains Collier's struggle with both the U.S. Congress and Indian tribes to implement a "New Deal" for Indians.

Hauptman, Laurence M. *The Iroquois and the New Deal.* Syracuse, NY: Syracuse University Press, 1976. Explores how the Indian Reorganization Act was put into practice with the Iroquois tribes of New York and Wisconsin.

Parman, Donald Lee. *The Navajos and the New Deal.* New Haven: Yale University Press, 1976. Explores the effort and failure of John Collier to ratify and implement the Indian Reorganization Act on the Navajo Nation.

Philp, Kenneth R. *John Collier's Crusade for Indian Reform, 1920–1954.* Tucson, AZ: University of Arizona Press, 1977. Full-length study of Commissioner of Indian Affairs Collier and his fight to reestablish Indian tribes through what became known as the Indian New Deal.

Prucha, Francis P. *The Great Father: The United States Government and the American Indians.* Lincoln, NE: University of Nebraska Press, 1984. General overview of laws and acts concerning Indians.

Rusco, Elmer R. *A Fateful Time: The Background and Legislative History of the Indian Reorganization Act.* Reno, NV: University of Nevada Press, 2000. Comprehensive and detailed history.

Schrader, Robert Fay. *The Indian Arts & Crafts Board: An Aspect of New Deal Indian Policy.* Albuquerque, NM: University of New Mexico Press, 1983. Explores the role of the development, protection, and preservation of Indian arts and crafts in the Indian New Deal era.

Taylor, Graham D. *The New Deal and American Indian Tribalism: The Administration of the Indian Reorganization Act, 1934–45.* Lincoln, NE: University of Nebraska Press, 1980. An easy-to-read and well-organized history of the Indian New Deal.

World Wide Web

"Indian Reorganization Act." http://www.answers.com/topic/indian-reorganization-act. Brief overviews from three sites, bibliographies, and internal and external links.

Kersey, Harry A., Jr. *The Florida Seminoles in the Depression and New Deal, 1933–1944.* http://fulltext10.fcla.edu/cgi/t/text/text-idx?type=title;c

=fhq;sort=dated;rgn=div1;sid=340e7ddf9aad5f94883f46f3acb70edf;
view=text;cc=fhq;idno=SN00154113_0065_002;
node=SN00154113_0065_002%3A5;a=45. Explores the programs
implemented to help the Seminoles during the Great Depression era.

"Wheeler-Howard Act (Indian Reorganization Act) Shifts U.S. Policy Toward
Native American Right to Self-Determination on June 18, 1934." http://
historyink.com/essays/output.cfm?file_id=2599. Brief and concise summary of the act.

Multimedia Sources

Tribal Nations: The Story of Federal Indian Law. Dir. Lisa Jaeger. Tanana Chiefs
Conference Signature Media Production, 2006. DVD. 60 minutes. Illustrated introductory-level documentary of how federal Indian policy has
developed in the United States.

"'We Have Got a Good Friend in John Collier': A Taos Pueblo Tries to Sell the
Indian New Deal." http://historymatters.gmu.edu/d/26. Verbatim transcript and audio recording of an American Indian commenting on the
Indian Reorganization Act. Three other oral histories ("It Didn't Pan
Out . . . ," "It Had a Lot of Advantages," and "It Set the Indian Aside as
a Problem") are available via links and cover the IRA from both sides of
the issue.

74. Indian Arts and Crafts Board Created (1935)

The Indian Arts and Crafts Board was an independent agency of the
federal government created, in part, to help Indians to profit from their
arts and crafts, an area of historic exploitation and corruption. The Indian
Arts and Crafts Act (1935) was "an Act to promote the development of
Indian arts and crafts and to create a board to assist therein, and for other
purposes." Through the establishment of the Indian Arts and Crafts
Board, a group of commissioners was charged to look after and manage
the economic welfare of Indian tribes and individual Indians engaged in
arts and crafts. The board was given powers to conduct market research,
to manage federal resources, to create guilds or groups, to promote arts
and crafts, to seek financial loans, to create federal trademarks of authenticity, and to negotiate contracts. In 1990, the Indian Arts and Crafts Act
was passed as "a truth-in-advertising law that prohibits misrepresentation

in marketing of Indian arts and crafts products within the United States," and it clarified the penalties for fraud: convicted counterfeiters can face $250,000 in fines and five years in prison terms, or both. These laws and clarifications became necessary as the Indian arts and crafts business grew into an annually multimillion-dollar industry. However, the economic growth has shifted Indian arts and crafts from cultural production to profit making, which, to some, has corrupted the meaning of Indian traditions. The board, until recently, has been a sinecure for non-Indians. Furthermore, the building of an "industry" has perpetuated a distorted definition of culture.

TERM PAPER SUGGESTIONS

1. Explore the economic ramifications of creating an Indian Arts and Crafts Board. How could Indians economically benefit from such an organization?
2. Explore fraud in Indian arts and crafts. How easy is it to counterfeit Indian arts and crafts? How do consumers know authentic Indian arts and crafts from fraudulent products?
3. Explain through research on government sources how Indian arts and crafts are defined and how they can be authenticated. Also state how an Indian artist and/or crafts person is defined.
4. Explore the history of the board members. Some have accused the board members of being non-Indian hobbyists and art buffs rather than Indian artisans. Would non-Indian members have a different agenda than Indians? How would you know? Has the composition of the board changed in recent times? Why?
5. Culture is hard to define and discuss. However, one definition of culture can be the arts and crafts created by a people. Does the commercialization of arts and crafts subvert the definition of culture? Simultaneously, can a people produce arts and crafts for profit and for cultural purposes, like ceremonies and traditions?
6. From 1935 to the present, explore the views of American Indian artists and crafts people on the board and its function and activities.

ALTERNATIVE TERM PAPER SUGGESTIONS

1. From internet sources, books from which representative examples can be scanned or photographed, and any other relevant places, gather images of authenticated Indian arts and crafts, and do the same for non-Indian-produced arts and crafts, even those you are unsure of. Create a comparative

Microsoft PowerPoint slide show to demonstrate the differences and similarities of the two forms of Indian arts and crafts and to raise the relevant issues of debate. The Boy Scouts of America and hobbyists often produce "authentic" Indian arts and crafts, but they do not try to sell or represent the items they make as "Indian made." What is the difference from those people who do?

2. Gather images of authenticated arts and crafts and artifacts that are of ceremonial/religious purposes and that have been bought and sold. From these images create a Microsoft PowerPoint slide show with captions questioning the commercialization of religious objects. Make sure you separate with a few telling examples arts and crafts meant for consumers from those that are not. The purpose is to show how the development of Indian arts and crafts intended for the general public can confuse the general public about what is not appropriate for them to buy and own.

SUGGESTED SOURCES

Primary Sources

"Guide to Records of the Indian Arts and Crafts Board." http://www
.archives.gov/research/guide-fed-records/groups/435.html. A guide to
records from 1935 to 1988. Although a guide, the site has summaries
that provide valuable information at the general level.

"The Indian Arts and Crafts Act of 1935." http://www.doi.gov/iacb/iaca35.html.
Many other links to laws, rulings, directories, current board commissioners, and the mission statement. Museum exhibitions and
publications.

"The Indian Arts and Crafts Act of 1990." http://www.doi.gov/iacb/act.html.
Describes P.L 101-644 as a truth-in-advertising law and describes
penalties for violations.

"Testimony of the Indian Arts and Crafts Association." http://indian.senate
.gov/2000hrgs/arts_0517/eriacho.pdf. PDF download of testimony
presented to the Oversight Hearing on the Implementation of the
1990 Act.

Secondary Sources

Berlo, Janet Catherine. *The Early Years of Native American Art History: The Politics of Scholarship and Collecting.* Seattle, WA: University of Washington
Press, 1992. An anthology exploring the manner in which collectors
understand Indians and how this influences academic scholarship. John
Collier, the architect of the Indian New Deal and of the Arts and Crafts

Board, suffered from the same cultural bias and misreading of Indian arts and crafts.

Indian Arts and Crafts Association. *Collecting Authentic Indian Arts and Crafts: Traditional Work of the Southwest.* Summertown, TN: Book Publishing Company, 1999. Explains the traditional arts and crafts of the Indians of the southwest.

Montgomery, David R. *Indian Crafts and Skills: An Illustrated Guide for Making Authentic Indian Clothing, Shelters and Ornaments.* Bountiful, UT: Horizon Publisher and Distributors, 2003. An excellent how-to book that with a bit of skill and practice can teach almost anyone to manufacture an item used by Indians or mountain men.

Mullin, Molly H. *Culture in the Marketplace: Gender, Art and Value in the American Southwest.* Durham, NC: Duke University Press, 2001. Explores how wealthy non-Indian women art buyers influenced the production of Indian art of the southwest and how the art influenced them.

Rushing, W. *Native American Art in the Twentieth Century: Makers, Meanings, Histories.* New York: Routledge, 1999. A collection of images as well as essays on American Indian art. This work discusses many complex and controversial issues while presenting the material in an interesting and beautiful way.

Scafidi, Susan. *Who Owns Culture?: Appropriation and Authenticity in American Law.* New Brunswick, NJ: Rutgers University Press, 2005. In terms of copyists and forgers, this book is essential to understanding the position of Indian artisans.

World Wide Web

"Act of 1990." http://www.artnatam.com/law.html. Legal definitions and summaries. The site answers many questions; for example, it clarifies the definition of "Indian."

Berry, Christina. "The Indian Arts and Crafts Act of 1990 and What It Means to You." http://www.allthingscherokee.com/articles_culture_events_020101 .html. Good answers to questions such as "Why is the law necessary?"

"Definitions of Indian Art." http://edocket.access.gpo.gov/cfr_2005/aprqtr/pdf/ 25cfr309.18.pdf. The site addresses questions such as "What are examples of beadwork?"

"How to Buy Genuine American Indian Arts and Crafts." http://www.ftc.gov/ bcp/edu/pubs/consumer/products/pro12.pdf. PDF pamphlet. Can be viewed as HTML.

"Indian Arts and Crafts." http://nativeamericanlawus.blogspot.com/. Click on the "2005" in the Blog Archive listed on the left-hand side of the page, then click on the "August" link to find the article: a blog written by an American Indian artisan who provides legal and personal information, views, and links.

McCarthy, Ellen. "From Homeland Security to Indian Arts and Crafts." http://www.washingtonpost.com/wp-dyn/content/article/2005/10/16/AR2005101600962.html. Interesting article on the importation of millions of dollars of fake Indian arts and crafts that need to be looked for and tracked.

Multimedia Source

"Indian Arts and Craft Board: Know the Law." http://www.doi.gov/iacb/. Wes Studi, Hollywood actor and Indian, presents a public service message on authentic Indian art for the U.S. Department of the Interior and the Indian Arts and Crafts Board.

75. World War II (1941–1945)

During World War II 25,000 American Indians served in the armed services, while on the home front thousands helped in the war effort, constituting a high level of patriotism within the Indian nations. For example, the first time they were allowed, 99 percent of all eligible American Indians registered for the draft, although most volunteered for active duty. An estimated $12.6 million in war bonds were purchased by Indians, and Indian women worked in factories supporting the war effort. Many of the tribes passed their own declarations of war against the axis powers: the Six Nations of the Iroquois declared war on Germany twice, once in World War I and again for World War II. The heroism of Indian soldiers is without question, as five Indians earned the Medal of Honor, including Ira Hayes, who helped raise the American flag on Mt. Suribachi at Iwo Jima, February 1945. The most famous exploit was the use of Indian languages (Navajo, Comanche, and Choctaw) and language speakers to create the only unbreakable code in modern times. World War II also saw the exodus of thousands of Indians from their reservations for the first time, and many of the survivors never returned, choosing to settle in the major cities, creating a new urban Indian population. Coming from many different tribal backgrounds, cultures, and languages, Indian soldiers also formed pan-Indian groups that created songs and activities that could be shared by any member of any tribe; thus they started an intertribal cultural celebration called the Indian powwow.

TERM PAPER SUGGESTIONS

1. Write on the home front contributions of American Indians to the war effort. How did the tribes and individuals contribute and help out?

2. Write a paper on Indian war heroes. The list of medal recipients is large. Give an idea of the diversity of the recipients and what they did to earn their medals. What is the significance of their heroism?

3. Write a report on the Indian "Code Talkers." Be sure to include the lesser-known code talkers and their contributions as well. The most famous were the Navajo who served in the Pacific theater. Did code talkers serve in Europe?

4. Ernie Pyle, a famous war reporter, documented a variety of war dances performed by Indian soldiers in World War II (see *Indians in the War*). Research and write about these reports. What is the significance of this cross-cultural phenomenon?

5. Legend has it that 50 World War II Indian soldiers went to war and only 49 returned. Those 49, all from different tribes, created a song style, in honor of the one who did not return, called the "forty-niner." Research and write on this pan-Indian phenomenon.

6. Write about Indian war experiences. Some of the secondary sources have very detailed personal accounts. Focus on the themes of cultural preservation and opposition to assimilation. For example, the Navajo code talkers preserved their language while at the same time working as productive members of American society.

ALTERNATIVE TERM PAPER SUGGESTIONS

1. Many photographs exist of the Indians and World War II. Create a collage of photos representing the total of Indian contributions, not just soldiering.

2. Create an annotated time line of Indian participation in both World War I and World War II. In the former, many Indians were not citizens, and in World War II, Indians were eligible for the draft. So, the time line has to include federal Indian policies as well as events.

SUGGESTED SOURCES

Primary Sources

Indians in the War. Office of Indian Affairs, 1945. http://www.history.navy.mil/ library/online/indians.htm. The primary source information and photographs contained in this online pamphlet were collected during the war and honor all Indians involved in the war effort, including Indian women.

Johnston, Broderick, ed. *Navajos and World War II.* Tsaile, AZ: Navajo Community College Press, 1977. A collection of first-person accounts by Navajo veterans and their relatives, gathered in the 1970s.

University of South Dakota Indian Oral History Collection. American Indian Research Project, Glen Rock, NJ: Microfilming Corporation of America, 1975. Part of the *New York Times* Oral History Program on microfilm. A collection of interviews with Plains Indians and those working with them. Some native veterans of the world wars discuss their experiences, including some Canadian military veterans. A guidebook is available.

Secondary Sources

Bernstein, Alison R. *American Indians and World War II: Toward a New Era in Indian Affairs.* Norman, OK: University of Oklahoma Press, 1991. Explores the way Indian participation in World War II not only led to increased assimilation but also a to new urban Indian experience.

Bixler, Margaret T. *Winds of Freedom: The Story of the Navajo Code Talkers of World War II.* Darien, CT: Two Bytes Publishing, 1995. Includes bibliographical references and index as well as a map on lining paper.

Deane, Durett. *Unsung Heroes of World War II: The Story of the Navajo Code Talkers.* New York: Facts on File, 1998. Describes a select group of Navajo Marines who developed a code based on their own native language.

Franco, Jere Bishop. *Crossing the Pond: The Native American Effort in World War II.* Denton, TX: University of North Texas Press, 1999. Appended with a useful bibliography of published and unpublished sources.

Gaffen, Fred. *Forgotten Soldiers.* Penticton, BC, Canada: Two Trails Press, 1993. Explores the First Nations' (Canadian Indians') participation in World War I and World War II.

Hauptman, Laurence. *The Iroquois Struggle for Survival: From World War II to Red Power.* Syracuse, NY: Syracuse University Press, 1986. Focuses on tribal histories told from the Six Nations' point of view.

Kawano, Kenji. *Warriors: Navajo Code Talkers.* Flagstaff, AZ: Northland Pub. Co., 1990. Includes many illustrations by the noted photographer.

Langellier, J. Phillip. *American Indians in the U.S. Armed Forces, 1866–1945.* Mechanicsburg, PA: Stackpole Books, 2000. General overview of Indian participation in U.S. armed forces, ending with WW II.

Meadows William C. *The Comanche Code Talkers of World War II.* Austin, TX: University of Texas Press, 2002. Drawing on interviews with all surviving members of the unit, the book tells the full story of the Comanche code talkers.

Townsend, Kenneth. *World War II and the American Indian.* Albuquerque, NM: University of New Mexico Press, 2000. Explores the military as a way of assimilation and acculturation.

World Wide Web

"American Indians in World War II." http://www.defenselink.mil/specials/nati-veamerican01/wwii.html. A detailed overview of Indian participation in World War II with a useful chronology attached at the end.

"An Indian Technique: Code Talkers: Use of the Native Indian Tongue for Secure Communications." http://www.defenselink.mil/specials/nativeameri-can01/code.html. A short article honoring Indian code talkers of World War I and World War II.

"Ernest Childers Obit." http://www.medalofhonor.com/ErnestChildersObit.htm. Obituary of one of five Indians to receive the Medal of Honor, with photographs and a newspaper article.

La Vere, David. "North Carolina's American Indians in World War II." http://www.ncmuseumofhistory.org/collateral/articles/f05.indians.wwii.pdf. PDF download. An essay from the *Tar Heel Junior Historian* that explores North Carolina's Indian participation in World War II.

Molnar, Alexander, Jr. "Navajo Code Talkers: World War II Fact Sheet." http://www.history.navy.mil/faqs/faq61-2.htm. Includes a list of American Medal of Honor winners, a bibliography, and a "Navajo Code Talker Dictionary."

"Native Americans and the U.S. Military." http://www.history.navy.mil/faqs/faq61-1.htm. A general and brief survey of the participation of Indians in the U.S. armed services, including during World War II.

"World War I and II: Choctaw Code Talkers." http://www.oklachahta.org/code talkers.htm. Brief descriptive history with a photograph and external links.

Multimedia Source

Navajo Code Talkers. A&E Television Networks, 1998. DVD. 50 minutes. Tells the story of the only unbroken code in modern military history, which was created from the Navajo language using Navajo U.S. Marines.

76. National Congress of American Indians Founded (1944)

As the first intertribal and all Indian-controlled national political organization, the National Congress of American Indians (NCAI) was founded in

1944 in response to U.S. assimilation and termination policies and to protect American Indian treaty rights and strengthen tribal sovereignty. Representatives of more than 50 tribes met in Denver, Colorado in 1944 to establish the NCAI, and it has grown to over 250 member tribes in modern times. Since its inception, the NCAI has worked for a unified voice of tribal governments for the purpose of informing the U.S. government and the public of the rights of American Indians. Historically, the NCAI fought to create the Indian Claims Commission to investigate and compensate Indians for past wrongs, and the NCAI defended and promoted the rights of Native Alaskans. The NCAI were staunch defenders of tribal governments, and they were opposed to termination policies. They also fought for greater representation and participation in the processes of creating new or amending old federal Indian policies. The NCAI also assisted tribes in the local, state, and federal courts and helped tribes to negotiate with federal Indian bureaucracies, such as the Bureau of Indian Affairs and the Indian Health Service. Their current activities and issues center on helping preserve the health and well-being of Indian people and Indian rights by helping to protect and enhance basic infrastructure of tribal communities, like education of children, affordable housing, economic development, and health care.

TERM PAPER SUGGESTIONS

1. Explore the advantages of Indian tribes forming a unified political organization, a lobby in many ways. Are there disadvantages?

2. One of the hallmarks of the NCAI was that Indian intellectuals or assimilationists did not dominate it, and although women were few in the early years, within a decade they would represent at least 50 percent of the organization. Write on the diversity and composition of the NCAI membership.

3. One of the goals of federal Indian policy for many years was to create Americans out of Indians and therefore terminate the need for tribal governments and communal land. Explore why the NCAI was strongly opposed to termination and why they stressed a strengthening of tribal sovereignty.

4. Compare the NCAI to other pan-Indian organizations like the Society of American Indians (1911), the Native American Youth Council (1961), or the American Indian Movement (1968). What sets the NCAI apart from these other organizations?

5. From the many important concerns of the NCAI, like health, education, and housing, explore why the NCAI would oppose Indian sports team mascots and logos. How does that opposition fit into the mission of the organization?

6. Examine the position of the NCAI on Indian gambling operations. How does Indian gaming fit into the overall goals and mission of the organization?

ALTERNATIVE TERM PAPER SUGGESTIONS

1. The position of the NCAI is that Indian logos and mascots perpetuate a false image of Indian people and that they are detrimental to Indian youth. Create an electronic collage using as many mascots and logos as you can find from local, state, and national sports teams, either professional or not, to support or refute the NCAI position.

2. Indian fishing rights are supported by a variety of NCAI initiatives. Survey and report on historical newspaper headlines and stories covering Indian fishing from 1944 to the present. Create a Microsoft PowerPoint slide show of these headlines in order to demonstrate the seriousness of this issue without taking sides.

SUGGESTED SOURCES

Primary Source

Washburn, Wilcomb E. *The American Indian and the United States: A Documentary History.* Westport, CT: Greenwood Press, 1973. Contains primary source documents, laws, and other pertinent materials, such as the Termination Policy.

Secondary Sources

Cowger, Thomas W. *The National Congress of American Indians: The Founding Years.* Lincoln, NE: University of Nebraska Press, 1999. A narrative and complete history of the NCAI.

Hertzberg, Hazel. *The Search for an American Indian Identity: Modern Pan-Indian Movements.* Syracuse, NY: Syracuse University Press, 1971. A general history of the development of modern-day pan-Indian movements and organizations, like the National Congress of American Indians (NCAI) and the American Indian Movement (AIM).

McNickle, D'Arcy. *The Surrounded.* Albuquerque, NM: University of New Mexico Press, 1978. Reprint of McNickle's novel that, although a fictional account, clearly presents the problems and issues in Indian country in a time of assimilation and Americanization.

Parker, Dorothy R. *Singing an Indian Song.* Lincoln, NE: University of Nebraska Press, 1994. Biography of D'Arcy McNickle, principle founder of the NCAI.

Philp, Kenneth. *Termination Revisited.* Lincoln, NE: University of Nebraska Press, 2002. Places the NCAI within the struggle to stop the termination of Indian tribes and governments.

Purdy, John L. *The Legacy of D'Arcy McNickle: Writer, Historian, Activist.* Norman, OK: University of Oklahoma Press, 1996. A critical analysis of McNickle's writing and his political activism.

Wilkinson, Charles F. *Blood Struggle: The Rise of Modern Indian Nations.* New York: W.W. Norton, 2005. Celebrates the economic triumphs of Indian tribes since the Meriam Report and the Indian Reorganization Act.

World Wide Web

"AOL Partners with NCAI." http://www.csrwire.com/PressRelease.php?id=143. An announcement describing AOL's grant to the NCAI to develop digital opportunities in Indian country.

"NCAI." http://www.aipc.osmre.gov/Notes from Native America/9_2001.htm. Links page to many relevant economic, educational, and legal sites that the NCAI supports.

"NCAI." http://www.answers.com/topic/national-congress-of-american-indians. Brief summary that includes links and bibliography.

"NCAI." http://www.ncai.org/. Home page of the national organization that provides current events and concerns of the organization.

"NCAI: Denouncement of the Use of Any American Indian Name or Artifice Associated with Team Mascots by Any Professional/Non-Professional Sports Teams." http://www.aistm.org/ncai1993.htm. Argues that any use of Indian imagery for profit is demeaning and racist.

"NCAI ANWR Resolution 2002." http://aitc.org/node/23. A resolution calling for the protection of Alaska Native fishing rights, an example of NCAI activities.

"National Congress of American Indians Reaffirms Opposition of University North Dakota 'Fighting Sioux' Mascot and Logo." http://www.und.nodak.edu/org/bridges/ncai.html. NCAI continues to update and reaffirm their opposition to logos and mascots that demean and stereotype Indians.

Multimedia Source

Tribal Nations: The Story of Federal Indian Law. Dir. Lisa Jaeger. Tanana Chiefs Conference Signature Media Production, 2006. DVD. 60 minutes. Documentary film examining the development of U.S. federal Indian law.

77. Indian Claims Commission Is Established (1946)

By an act of Congress, August 13, 1946, the Indian Claims Commission (ICC) was established. The ICC's purpose was to hear claims and grievances of "any Indian tribe, band, or other identifiable group of American Indians" against the United States prior to 1946, with a deadline of August 13, 1951, by which date 610 claims were filed—but the commission was extended many times until 1978. The claims were centered on the illegal or unfair taking of Indian land via treaties/agreements and other acts of fraud or deceit. The act empowered the ICC and the U.S. Court of Claims to hear and adjudicate the legitimate claims of Indian people; in claims they found in favor of Indians, they could call for compensation and recovery, which could include the return of tribal land but has been historically translated into money damages. Of the original 610 dockets, 118 were settled with money judgments, totaling over $408,800,000 in 1971. The tribes also claimed that besides failing to compensate tribes for land taken from them, the U.S. government also mismanaged trust funds and tribal natural resources (timber, oil, coal, and uranium, to name a few). Some Indian tribes, like the Lakota Nations and the Taos Pueblo, rejected the decisions of the ICC, because they wanted the land returned, not a dollar-for-acre settlement. Furthermore, non-Indian lawyers held out for large sums so that their fees would be greater: over $100 million had been paid to lawyers for fees well before the money was released to tribes. However, allowing tribes to sue the federal government for damages was an unusual if not problematic solution to right past wrongs.

TERM PAPER SUGGESTIONS

1. The ICC Act stated that Congress was to "settle once and for all every claim Indian Tribes could possibly have" and to complete this process within 10 years. Explore why Indian tribes still have claims to this day.

2. According to experts, scholars, and Indian tribes, the way the ICC decided cases has seemed narrow and arbitrary. Explore how the ICC made a decision and what that decision meant for the tribes. Remember many of the claims were ruled to be without merit, so only a percentage were actually heard and decided.

3. The United States had its own lawyers and defense strategy. Write on these defense strategies and the details of United States' defense case.

4. What was the role of "expert" testimonies? For the first time in history, Indian tribes used experts, such as anthropologists, to prove their cases. The United States presented experts as well.

5. In one notable case of the Black Hills, the Court of Claims, after the 1978 termination of the ICC, finished the work of the ICC and awarded some $110 million to the Lakota Nations, who rejected the settlement because no

land was to be returned and they believe that the Black Hills are sacred. Study and write on the history and current status of the Black Hills land case and the Lakota Nations.

6. Examine why Indian tribes win cases, although not to their satisfaction. Also, many tribes lose. Explore the wins and losses of the cases.

ALTERNATIVE TERM PAPER SUGGESTIONS

1. Create a mock trial around a land claim by Indians who have a treaty where some of the conditions of the treaty have not been met. In addition, the United States has also appropriated lands from the tribe without a treaty and without any kind of compensation, even monetary. The charge: the United States illegally acquired Indian land.

2. Using maps showing the loss of Indian-owned lands over a period of a hundred years, try to demonstrate the legitimacy of Indian land claims via a Microsoft PowerPoint presentation.

SUGGESTED SOURCES

Primary Sources

"ICC." http://www.indianclaims.ca/menu-en.asp. Home page of the organization containing a link to primary source publications, including annual reports. Newsletters, proceedings, facts on claims, definitions, and many other primary sources are available in PDF downloads or HTML-viewable formats.

"Indian Claims Commission Decisions." OSU Library Digitization, 2008. http://digital.library.okstate.edu/icc/index/iccindex.html. A compilation of decisions in PDF download format through March 1973.

Secondary Sources

Barker, Robert W., and Alice Ehrenfeld. *Legislative History of the Indian Claims Commission Act of 1946.* Broomfield, CO: Clearwater Publishing Company, 1976. Comprehensive and technical compilation of legislation concerning the ICC.

Cohen, Felix S., and Rennard Strickland. *Handbook of Federal Indian Law.* Indianapolis, IN: Bobbs-Merrill, 1982. Covers civil and criminal jurisdiction as well as laws affecting the relationship between tribes and the federal, state, and local governments.

Fixico, Donald. *Termination and Relocation: Federal Indian Policy, 1945–1960.* Albuquerque, NM: University of New Mexico Press, 1990. Covers the ICC's opposition to termination and relocation policies.

Le Duc, Thomas. "The Work of the Indian Claims Commission under the Act of 1946." *The Pacific Historical Review* 26, no. 1 (February 1957): 1–16. Places the ICC into a context of the right of Indians to sue the federal government, a right not necessarily open to all citizens.

Lurie, Nancy Oestreich. "The Indian Claims Commission." *Annals of the American Academy of Political and Social Science* 436 (March 1978): 97–110. Criticizes the slowness of the claims process and the narrowness of the settlements.

Lurie, Nancy Oestreich. "The Indian Claims Commission Act." *Annals of the American Academy of Political and Social Science* 311 (May 1957): 56–70. Explores the role of expert testimony by anthropologists and other experts.

Rosenthal, H. D. *Their Day in Court: A History of the Indian Claims Commission, 1946 to 1978.* New York: Garland Publishing, 1990. A legal history of the ICC, its functions, and its desire to streamline, if not simplify, the process to the detriment of Indian tribes.

White, John R. "Barmecide Revisited: The Gratuitous Offset in Indian Claims Cases." *Ethnohistory* 25 no. 2 (Spring 1978): 179–92. Challenges the methods of the commission and the court of claims to determine compensation and finds that their decisions could be as inequitable as the original claim.

Wilkins, David E. *American Indian Sovereignty and the U.S. Supreme Court: The Masking of Justice.* Austin, TX: University of Texas Press, 1997. Explores the ICC and its desire to convert land into dollars.

World Wide Web

"Indian Claims Commission." Answers.com, 2008. http://www.answers.com/topic/indian-claims-commission. Brief summaries with bibliography and links to other relevant entries.

"Indian Law Research." M. G. Gallagher Law Library, 2008. http://lib.law.washington.edu/ref/indian.html. Bibliography as well as a links site for Indian law research. Toward the end of the page you find valuable information on the ICC.

Newcomb, Steven. "Failure of the U.S. ICC to File a Report." Native Web, 2008. http://www.nativeweb.org/pages/legal/shoshone/ili-report.html. An essay exposing the failure of the ICC to file a report with Congress in a case brought by Western Shoshone.

Thompson, Randy V., and Brandon Thomas. "Fifty Years Past the Deadline: Why Are Indian Tribes Still Suing Over Ancient Treaties?" PERM, 1996. http://theresourcesentinel.com/files/Indian_Claims_CommissionAct.pdf. PDF download or HTML format. An essay exploring the current status of

Indian claims against the United States as of 1996 and the reason for the continuance. HTML: http://www.citizensalliance.org/links/pages/articles/50_years_past_the_deadline.htm.

Multimedia Source

American Indian Homelands: Matters of Truth, Honor and Dignity. Dir. Barry ZeVan. Inglewood, CA: Victory Multimedia, 2007. DVD. 78 minutes. Covers U.S. laws and Indian land loss.

78. Indian Urban Relocation Program (1948)

Although World War II saw thousands of Indians moving to cities to support the war effort as soldiers or workers, 92 percent of Indians still lived on reservations. The Indian Urban Relocation Program (URP), starting in 1948, enticed more Indians to move to urban areas than any war or other federal Indian program. Starting as a small program for Navajos and Hopis, over the next 12 years thousands of Indians relocated, with many thousands more following. By the 1980 census 50 percent and by the 2000 census almost 70 percent of all Indians living in the United States lived in cities, and most were part of the initial URP exodus or were their sons and daughters, although a fair number still migrated for other reasons. The incentives of the URP were well-paying jobs, monies to relocate, support (weekly stipends and job training) at the point of destination, and temporary housing. Chicago, Denver, Los Angeles, San Francisco, San Jose, St. Louis, Cincinnati, Cleveland, and Dallas became centers of Indian relocation, and Bureau of Indian Affairs people staffed them. Once the Indians arrived they often found the centers poorly run, under-staffed, and not adequately equipped to handle the problems of Indians relocating from diverse Indian communities, who spoke different languages and were of different cultural backgrounds. In addition, many of the incentives were not forthcoming, and the Indian "relocatees," as they were called, suffered. Some went home, but many endured to find jobs, though not necessarily well-paying ones. Within this urban milieu, however, a pan-Indian movement and identity emerged as Indians of many reservations comingled, married, and formed social/cultural associations and celebrations, like the urban Indian powwow.

TERM PAPER SUGGESTIONS

1. The URP was very effective in recruiting and enticing Indians and Indian families to relocate. Explore its methodologies and its incentive program to lure Indians to take the step to relocate.

2. Study and write on the employment and earnings statistics of Indians compared to other minorities and the average American in 1950, using the census data or other sources. Based on your findings, write a report of why Indians and Indian families might be self-motivated to relocate to urban areas, especially if programs existed to help them.

3. Over 50 percent of the relocatees returned to their homelands. Explain the many reasons why Indians would return home.

4. Despite the high return rate, the Indian populations in URP cities grew. Explain the reasons Indians would stay despite the hardship they may have encountered and had to endure.

5. Write on the Federal Relocation Assistance Program, which was the bureaucratic mechanism to relocate Indians. The Federal Relocation Assistance Program took up many of the day-to-day responsibilities of the URP by the end of the 1950s and fueled the URP with trained government workers, funds for offices, and short-term monies for relocated Indians to assist them to find housing. An alternative is to compare the program of the 1950s to the one under the same name that is at work in modern times for victims of major disasters.

6. Write on one of the positive outcomes of relocations: the development of a vibrant urban Indian community that celebrated pan-Indianism and created new forms of cultural expression, like urban Indian powwows and cultural centers that led to intertribal unity.

ALTERNATIVE TERM PAPER SUGGESTIONS

1. Create a poster from the perspective of the Bureau of Indian Affairs officials trying to sell the URP to Indians of a fictional reservation. The poster should include a slogan, an image or set of images that tell a story, and a list of positive outcomes.

2. Imagine you are a "relocatee" and you want to create a social group of other relocatees from many different reservations. Create a poster inviting relocatees to a meeting to discuss ideas for a pan-Indian social organization. The poster should include a slogan, an image or set of images that tell a story, and a list of positive outcomes.

SUGGESTED SOURCES

Primary Source

"Come to Denver." http://www.malakota.com/relocation.jpg. A period poster of an Indian Urban Relocation Program.

Secondary Sources

Cowger, Thomas W. *The National Congress of American Indians: The Founding Years.* Lincoln, NE: University of Nebraska Press, 1999. Covers the Urban Relocation Program (URP) and the NCAI's scrutiny of the program.

Fixico, Donald. *Termination and Relocation: Federal Indian Policy, 1945–1960.* Albuquerque, NM: University of New Mexico Press, 1990. Examines relocation as another component of the federal plan to assimilate Indians to the mainstream of American society by moving them from their reservations to cities such as Chicago and Los Angeles for employment.

Fixico, Donald. *Urban Indian Experience in America.* Albuquerque, NM: University of New Mexico Press, 2000. Examines the urban Indian experience in many of the URP cities.

Gundlach, James H., and Alden E. Roberts. "Native American Indian Migration and Relocation: Success or Failure." *The Pacific Sociological Review* 21, no. 1 (January 1978): 117–28. A good statistically-supported essay and set of measures on Indian relocation, which is a windfall due to the Bureau of Indian Affairs eliminating statistics on the program to stave off critics in 1958.

"Inventory of the Bureau of Indian Affairs Indian Relocation Records, 1936–1975." http://www.newberry.org/collections/FindingAids/relocation/Relocation.html. Although a description of the primary source records of the Chicago BIA field office housed in the closed stacks of the Newberry Library, this site does have a short essay on the history of the relocation program.

LaGrand, James B. *Indian Metropolis.* Champaign, IL: University of Illinois Press, 2002. Explores the emergence of the urban Indian population of Chicago, 1945–75.

Lobo, Susan, and Kurt Peters. *American Indians and the Urban Experience.* Lanham, MD: Rowman Altamira, 2001. Collection of poetry, prose, art, photography, graffiti, rap, and other cultural expressions of urban Indians.

Lobo, Susan. *Urban Voices: The Bay Area American Indian Community.* Tucson, AZ: The University of Arizona Press, 2002. The author explains the emergence of a "cooperative, multi-tribal community" as an outcome of the URP, a community whose center was the Intertribal Friendship House in Oakland, California.

Nagel, Joane. *American Indian Ethnic Renewal.* New York: Oxford University Press, 1997. Explores pan-Indian activism in urban areas from the time of the URP.

Neils, Elaine M. *Native American Indian Migration and Relocation: Success or Failure.* Chicago, IL: University of Chicago, Department of Geography, 1971. Explores Indian rural/reservation-to-urban migration under federal laws and incentives and the successes and failures of the programs.

Wilkins, David E. *American Indian Politics and the American Political System.* 2nd edition. New York: Rowman and Littlefield, 2006. A section on the relocation program is covered in chapter four.

World Wide Web

"American Indian Center, Chicago." http://www.aic-chicago.org/history.html. One of the few "Indian Centers" still viable and active that emerged out of the URP. The site tells the history of the center, as well as giving current events and links to other important sites.

Arrieta, R. M. "Serving the Urban Tribe: Native American Will Walk the 'Red Road to Recovery' in S.F. Friendship House." http://www.sfbg.com/39/29/news_native_americans.html. Explains two of the negative results of relocation: alcoholism and drug abuse. However, the rise of urban centers like the Friendship House provides a way for urban Indians to find recovery.

Indian Country Diaries, "The Urban Relocation Program." http://www.pbs.org/indiancountry/history/relocate.html. Provides a good overview with statistical data of the URP, as well as an interactive map of URP centers and the reservations the Indians came from.

Lobo, Susan. "Census-Taking and the Invisibility of Urban American Indians." http://www.prb.org/Articles/2002/CensusTakingandtheInvisibilityofUrbanAmericanIndians.aspx. Explores the accuracy of urban Indian census data in the Bay Area, data Lobo reports on in her book, *Urban Voices.*

"Relocation." http://www.ncuih.org/Relocation (2).pdf. A PDF color brochure with black and white photos and statistics of the health problems Indian relocatees faced historically and in modern times.

Wilson, Novaline D. "Tribal Consequences of Urban Indian Relocation." http://www.law.msu.edu/indigenous/papers/2007-04.pdf. Examines the URP and the Indian Child Welfare Act. The author includes statistical data and supporting citations regarding the URP.

Multimedia Source

Indian Country Diaries. Public Broadcasting Service, 2007. http://www.pbs.org/
indiancountry/challenges/identity2.html. Two parts, "A Seat at the
Drum" and "Spiral of Fire," explore Indian urban experiences, challenges,
and the future of Indians living on reservations and in U.S. cities. Part of
the story explores the impact of relocation from firsthand accounts.

79. Termination Policy (1953)

On August 1, 1953, House Concurrent Resolution 108 called for the
"termination" of the relationship between the federal government and Indian
tribes, which ended special status of Indians by extinguishing federal services
and the recognition of tribal governmental powers. Over the next 15 years,
acts of Congress terminated over 100 tribes, with Menominee and the
Klamath tribes being the largest. Although each act passed to terminate a
particular tribe had its own unique features, the common thread was that
tribal land would become privately owned and subject to state and local taxes
and that the federal trust protections would no longer apply. Second, jurisdiction over the tribe, tribal members, and tribal lands would be transferred from
federal to state authority. Third, all federal Indian services (for example, health
care, housing, and education) would end. The policy was designed to leave
tribes without land, without government, without tribal courts, and without
protection of the federal government. The goal was to sever the tribal relationship with the federal government so that the tribes ceased to exist. The result
was that individual tribal members were forced to assimilate into mainstream
America. The effects of termination were devastating: tribal members were
impoverished, health declined, and the "benefits" of termination never
materialized. Even though the larger tribes and a few of the smaller tribes were
able to restore their federal-tribal relationship, the loss of land and services had
permanent economic and social effects. Despite these hardships, many of the
tribes maintained their tribal existence through the hard work of tribal members and the fact that treaty rights were preserved.

TERM PAPER SUGGESTIONS

1. Many consider the Termination Policy to be a draconian method of forced
   assimilation. Study the government's intent. Why did the idea of termination
   have such popular appeal in both houses of Congress?

2. Write on the social and economic effects of termination. The Menominee of Wisconsin and the Klamath of Oregon are the largest tribes terminated and the easiest to find data and information about.

3. The only assets Indian tribes had were land and the natural resources on that land. Study and report on what happened to the land and natural resources of Indian tribes terminated and what happened to the money generated from these assets.

4. Legal scholars say that the tribes were not terminated; rather the relationship between the federal government and the tribes was terminated. What does that mean? Explore the semantics of meaning and the use of language. In a causal analysis, does the termination of the relationship lead to the termination of the tribe?

5. The termination of a relationship does not mean the termination of treaty rights. This means tribes can still maintain their existence but without the help and protection of the federal government. Write an essay on how Indian tribes whose relationship with the federal government was terminated maintained a tribal existence and exercised their treaty rights.

6. One of the heroes of the Menominee restoration, the reestablishment of the trust relationship between the Menominee and the federal government in 1973, has been Ada Deer. Write an essay on her efforts to restore her tribe's status as a federally recognized Indian tribe and to reestablish the trust relationship with the federal government. (The Klamath were restored in 1986.)

ALTERNATIVE TERM PAPER SUGGESTIONS

1. Imagine you are a tribal member whose tribe has had its trust relationship with the federal government terminated. Devise a plan to keep your tribe together as a functioning governmental entity. Look to the efforts of Ada Deer for help. She created the Determination of Rights and Unity for Menominee Shareholders (DRUMS) and the Menominee Restoration Committee.

2. Create a chart and graphs to show the sale of Indian land and natural resources of those tribes subjected to termination policies. Although some tribes have recovered land in recent years, many have not.

SUGGESTED SOURCES

Primary Sources

House Concurrent Resolution 108. http://www.digitalhistory.uh.edu/native_voices/voices_display.cfm?id=96. The initial congressional resolution calling for termination. However, each tribe had an act of Congress passed calling for termination before action was taken.

"Public Law 280." http://www.tribal-institute.org/lists/pl280.htm. A detailed explanation of termination and termination law and policies. Includes a Q&A, definitions, and links to eight scholarly essays and primary sources, such as a statement by President Dwight D. Eisenhower.

Secondary Sources

Deloria, Vine, Jr., ed. *American Indian Policy in the Twentieth Century.* Norman, OK: University of Oklahoma Press, 1992. A collection of essays exploring the impact of policy on American Indians. Deloria's contribution provides a brief history and overview of federal Indian policy making.

Deloria, Vine, Jr., and Clifford M. Lytle. *American Indians, American Justice.* Austin, TX: University of Texas Press, 2008. Calls Termination Policy one of the six major periods of federal Indian policy. Explains and defines the evolution of tribal governments and judicial systems and the federal responsibility and power over Indian affairs.

Fixico, Donald Lee. *Termination and Relocation: Federal Indian Policy, 1945–1960.* Albuquerque, NM: University of New Mexico Press, 1986. General history of two federal policies that sought to forcibly assimilate the Indians into mainstream America and the results and effects.

Metcalf, R. Warren. *Termination's Legacy: The Discarded Indian of Utah.* Lincoln, NE: University of Nebraska Press, 2002. Explains the irrevocable effects of Termination Policy on the Ute Indians of Utah.

Peroff, Nicholas C. *Menominee Drums: Tribal Termination and Restoration, 1954–1974.* Norman, OK: University of Oklahoma Press, 1982. Reprint, 2006. Explores the successful efforts of the Menominee to reverse termination policies through the DRUMS organizations.

Philp, Kenneth R. *Termination Revisited: American Indians on the Trail to Self-Determination, 1933–1953.* Lincoln, NE: University of Nebraska Press, 1999. Detailed history of Termination Policy that expands on Fixico's work.

World Wide Web

"A History of the American Indians in California, 1934–1980." http://www.nps.gov/history/history/online_books/5views/5views1f.htm. Many small tribes of California were subject to termination policies, and this short essay explains the effects.

Cow Creek. http://www.cowcreek.com/govt/index.html. Cow Creek Indian tribal Web site that explains these tribes' termination and their efforts to regain federal recognition. A story of one of the smaller tribes of Oregon that suffered Termination Policy.

"Menominee Termination and Restoration." http://www.mpm.edu/wirp/ICW-97.html. A very detailed explanation of termination policies and how those policies effected the Menominee.

"1900s Indian Policies." http://www.harborside.com/~indianed/history.htm. The last two paragraphs of this brief overview of Indian policies cover termination and restoration.

"Termination: An Oregon Experience." http://education.uoregon.edu/feature.htm?id=762. Describes the effects of termination policies, which, according to the author, "ravaged the Tribes of Western Oregon and has been likened to post traumatic stress syndrome."

"Termination Policy, 1953–1968." http://www.nrcprograms.org/site/PageServer?pagename=cin_hist_terminationpolicy. A good general description of termination policies.

Multimedia Source

California's "Lost" Tribes. Dir. Jed Riffe. Sony, 2005. DVD. 56 minutes. Short documentary on Indian gaming in California, gaming that emerged on lands restored to tribes that had suffered from termination policies.

80. Public Law 280 (1953)

Enacted during the termination era as another part of the plan, Public Law 280 (PL 280) extended states' full criminal and civil jurisdiction over Indians residing within state boundaries of Alaska (starting in 1958), California, Minnesota, Nebraska, Oregon, and Wisconsin. The reservations of Red Lake, Minnesota; Warm Springs, Oregon; and the Menominee, Wisconsin were exempted from this federal mandate. Public Law 280 made criminal acts occurring on Indian land within these states a local and state matter. Through an official congressional act or through a state constitutional amendment, any other state not listed in the original law could assume jurisdiction over Indian country as well. The goal was to diminish the power of tribal courts, to reduce the burden on federal agencies and courts, and to prepare for when tribes and tribal lands would cease to exist through assimilation policies such as the Termination Policy. Public Law 280 also whittled at the Supreme Court ruling over *Worcester v. Georgia* (1832), which recognized tribal land as sovereign territory within the state in which the state "can have no force." However, PL 280 did not terminate the federal trust relationship and did not allow states to tax or otherwise encumber Indian trust lands. Furthermore, the treaty rights of Indian tribes, like hunting and fishing, were not to be interfered with by the states, nor could states extend any of their other powers beyond criminal and civil jurisdiction within Indian country; this remained a federal right. Public Law 280 created more problems, complications, and animosity between tribes and local and state governments.

TERM PAPER SUGGESTIONS

1. Public Law 280 was in preparation for and in conjunction with Indians losing their special status as tribal members and as wards of the state, through assimilation programs like Termination (1953). Write on how PL 280 was designed to achieve that goal of making ordinary citizens out of tribal members.

2. Sort out and explain the various jurisdictions that exist, or can exist, on Indian land. For example, how can the FBI, the Bureau of Indian Affairs Police, tribal police, local police (such as county sheriffs and deputies), and the state police all have jurisdiction or conflicting jurisdictions on Indian land?

3. Public Law 280, if you consider the complexities of jurisdiction, tried to make the issue of jurisdiction less complicated by simply turning over federal authority to state governments. What was the success and/or failure of this policy?

4. Even if the transfer of jurisdiction over Indian tribes to state authorities is a good idea, the federal government limited that jurisdiction only to civil and criminal cases. Write an essay explaining why the state may not view these limitations as fair or beneficial.

5. The federal government prevented states or local governments from taxing Indian lands and property, so the states could not generate revenue to actually pay for law enforcement on Indian lands. Explore the level of policing and other law enforcement activities in PL 280 states on or near Indian reservations.

6. Write an essay on how PL 280 could lead to greater friction and hostilities between Indian tribes and local and state governments.

ALTERNATIVE TERM PAPER SUGGESTION

1. Take an Indian reservation in a state like Minnesota and create a map of boundaries, including cities, townships, counties, reservations, and the state itself. Using Adobe Photoshop and the layers feature, make each boundary a different color, leaving the state as the background color. By turning on each layer, you can simulate the various local, state, tribal, and federal jurisdictions and the complexities overlapping jurisdictions can create.

SUGGESTED SOURCES

Primary Sources

Prucha, Francis Paul. *Documents of United States Indian Policy.* 3rd edition. Lincoln, NE: University of Nebraska Press, 2000. A complete collection of primary source documents as they relate to U.S. Indian policies

Public Law 83-280 (18 U.S.C. § 1162, 28 U.S.C. § 1360). http://www.tribal-institute.org/lists/pl_280.htm. Complete coverage of the law and its tertiary and related amendments and clarifications.

Public Law 83-820. 2004. http://caicw.org/PublicLaw280.html#Top. This site offers the full text of the law and its relation to the Indian Child Welfare Act (1978).

Secondary Sources

Canby, William C., Jr. *American Indian Law in a Nutshell.* 1981. Reprint, St. Paul, MN: West, 2004. A book that answers simple questions, like "What is an Indian Tribe?" A good basic set of definitions.

Deloria, Vine, Jr., and David E. Wilkins. *Tribes, Treaties, and Constitutional Tribulations.* Austin, TX: University of Texas Press, 2000. Explores the relationship between the U.S. Constitution and the federal government and Indian tribes and their governments.

Duthu, N. Bruce. *American Indians and the Law.* New York: Viking, 2008. A general, readable survey that explains the complexities of tribal governments, land rights, legal issues, and sovereignty.

Goldberg-Ambrose, Carole. *Planting Tail Feathers: Tribal Survival and Public Law 280.* Los Angeles, CA: UCLA American Indian Studies Center, 1997. A complete examination of Public Law 280 with recommendations for rebuilding tribal governments in the wake of the damage PL 280 caused.

Pevar, Stephen L. *The Rights of Indians and Tribes: The Authoritative ACLU Guide to Indian and Tribal Rights.* 3rd edition. New York: NYU Press, 2004. Provides a historical overview as well as answering many legal questions. Commits parts of three chapters to the legalities of PL 280.

Prucha, Francis Paul. *American Indian Treaties: The History of a Political Anomaly.* Berkeley, CA: University of California Press, 1994. A general history of United States and Indian treaty relationships.

Wilkins, David E. *American Indian Sovereignty and the U.S. Supreme Court: The Masking of Justice.* Austin, TX: University of Texas Press, 1997. Detailed analysis of 15 U.S. Supreme Court cases involving Native Americans, including *Johnson v. M'Intosh.*

Wilkins, David E. *Uneven Ground: American Indian Sovereignty and Federal Law.* Norman, OK: University of Oklahoma Press, 2001. A scholarly study of federal law and Supreme Court rulings, including the discovery doctrine.

Wilkinson, Charles F. *American Indians, Time, and the Law.* New Haven, CT: Yale University Press, 1987. Examines the recognition of Indian governments as part of the federal system in 1959 (*Williams v. Lee*).

World Wide Web

Jimenez, Vanessa J., and Soo C. Song. "Concurrent Tribal and State Jurisdiction under Public Law 280." http://www.wcl.american.edu/journal/lawrev/47/pdf/jimenez.pdf?rd=1. Washington College of Law, 2008. PDF essay that examines the politics behind Public Law 280.

Melton, Ada Pecos, and Jerry Gardner. "Public Law 280: Issues and Concerns for Victims of Crime in Indian Country." http://www.aidainc.net/Publications/pl280.htm. A very complete and informative site with explanations, answers to questions, ramifications for victims, and footnotes for further information.

"Public Law 280 and Law Enforcement in Indian Country." http://www.ncjrs.gov/pdffiles1/nij/209839.pdf. A complete PDF brochure from the Department of Justice under Attorney General Alberto Gonzales. Interesting for findings on the research priorities.

"Tribal Crime and Justice: Public Law 280." http://www.ojp.usdoj.gov/nij/topics/tribal-justice/pl280.htm. Consequences, impact on crime, and ongoing research are briefly covered.

Multimedia Source

Tribal Nations: The Story of Federal Indian Law. Dir. Lisa Jaeger. Fairbanks, AK: Tanana Chiefs Conference and Signature Media Production, 2006. DVD. 60 minutes. Documentary film examining the development of U.S. federal Indian law.

81. Indian Health Services Mandate (1955)

On August 5, 1955, Public Law 568 transferred responsibility for Indian health from the Department of the Interior to the Public Health Service, under the title of Indian Health Services (IHS). Public Law 568 mandated that "all facilities transferred shall be available to meet the health needs of the Indians and that such health needs shall be given priority over that of the non-Indian population." The first task of the IHS was to determine the state of health in Indian country; their year-long survey resulted in a report with four conclusions:

1. A substantial Federal Indian health program will be required;
2. All community health resources should be developed in cooperation with Indian communities and done on a reservation-by-reservation basis;
3. Federal Indian health programs should be planned in each community and services made available to Indians under State and local programs;
4. Efforts should be made to recognize the obligations and responsibilities to Indian residents on a nondiscriminatory basis from the State and local communities.

This report became known as the "Gold Report" because the report was bound in gold-colored card stock and their annual reports since the first have been known as "Gold Reports." Although the U.S. government provided health care to Indians intermittently, a formal assumption of responsibility by the Department of the Interior did not occur until 1911, when funds were allocated for that purpose. The IHS was created due to the poor health conditions of American Indians and the failure of the Department of the Interior to improve the health and health care of Indians under their jurisdiction. In 1921, the Snyder Act authorized federal health services to Indian tribes, but the care was dismal. IHS was created to provide improved health care for Indians and to reach the goals they set in their own "Gold Reports." However, criticism has followed every action taken by the IHS, and every IHS facility has been scrutinized for any wrongdoing and failure to meet their stated goals.

TERM PAPER SUGGESTIONS

1. Statistics show that Indians have lower life expectancy and higher infant mortality rates and many more deaths from tuberculosis, diabetes, and alcoholism than any other U.S. minority or majority group. Explore the ways IHS tries to combat these major health problems.

2. Suicide among Indians is the highest in the nation. Explore whether IHS addresses this major mental health problem. What are its proactive prevention strategies? Do Indians themselves have any solution?

3. The IHS system itself has been criticized for poor facilities, cumbersome regulations, worn-out equipment, and the issue of the sterilization of American Indian women without their consent or knowledge. Research and report on the legitimacy and accuracy of these criticisms and accusations.

4. Write on the health care of urban Indians. Do IHS facilities exist in urban areas? Must urban Indians without any other option return to reservations for health care?

5. Study and report on the complex administrative and service structure of the IHS. Is the bureaucracy overburdened? Do Indian tribes receive the same level of care as other federally supported health care systems? What is the ratio of care providers (doctors, dentists, nurses, and pharmacists) to administrative personnel?

6. Write on the role of "self-determination," "self-government," and the transfer of health care to individual tribes. In some cases, tribes manage their own health care facilities and provide alternative options to health care. What are the results (positive and/or negative) of such a transfer?

ALTERNATIVE TERM PAPER SUGGESTIONS

1. Scan a map (or download one) of Indian reservations in 1955, 1980, and in the current year. On each map mark with a visible and colorful icon IHS facilities, area offices, and headquarters for the three periods. Scan these and create a Microsoft PowerPoint document to show the growth and distribution of IHS presence in Indian country and/or urban areas.

2. Assume you were assigned to the 1956 survey team who wrote the first Gold Report. Write a health assessment of an Indian reservation in 500 words. What health problem would you prioritize?

SUGGESTED SOURCES

Primary Sources

"IHS Fact Sheets." http://info.ihs.gov/. Detailed one-page sheets describing the issue, providing background, assessing the situation, and providing IHS's plan of action. Also has links to the 2005 Gold Book report, which reviews IHS's 50-year history and current challenges.

"Public Law 568—August 5, 1954." http://www.ihs.gov/adminmngrresources/legislativeaffairs/legislative_affairs_web_files/key_acts/pub_law_83-658_transfer_act.pdf. The complete text of Public Law 568.

Secondary Sources

DeJong, David H. *If You Knew the Conditions: A Chronicle of the Indian Medical Service and American Indian Health Care, 1908–1955.* Lanham, MD: Lexington Books, 2008. Examines the period before the IHS when the "Indian Medical Service" was under funded and suffered from federal indifference to well-being of Indian peoples.

Dixon, Mim. *Promises to Keep.* Washington, DC: American Public Health Association, 2001. Explains the strategies that have been initiated to promote the control of health care by Indian tribes.

Dixon, Mim. *Strategies for Cultural Competency in Indian Health Care.* Washington, DC: American Public Health Association, 2006. Explores the need and provides solutions for cross-cultural understanding of health care practices when it comes servicing the Indian population.

Duran, Eduardo. *Healing the Soul Wound.* New York: Teachers College Press, 2006. A psychologist shares his clinical experiences with and strategies for counseling American Indians.

Rhoades, Everett A., ed. *American Indian Health: Innovations in Health Care, Promotion and Policy.* Baltimore, MD: John Hopkins University Press, 2000. A complete examination of demographics, politics, administration, major diseases and health conditions, and special cultural and ethnic considerations.

Rhoades, Everett A. *Indian Health Service: Trends in Indian Health, 1989.* Washington, DC: Department of Health and Human Services, 1989. A complete history of the IHS with a pre-IHS historical survey, as well as a final chapter on the inclusion of American Indian health practices that have proved to augment and improve the health of Indians under traditional care.

Steeler, William C. *Improving American Indian Health Care: The Western Cherokee Experience.* Norman, OK: University of Oklahoma Press, 2001. Gary W. Shannon and Rashid L. Bashshur, eds. Written by a former executive of the IHS, this book explores alternative health care options and self-help that could augment traditional health care.

Stuart, Paul. *Nations Within a Nation: Historical Statistics of American Indians.* Westport, CT: Greenwood Press, 1998. Chapter seven covers health care statistics on American Indians.

Tusatoo, Robert, et al. "Case 7: Indian Health Service: Creating a Climate for Change." *Public Health Leadership and Management: Cases and Context.* Thousand Oaks, CA: Sage Publications, 2002, 265–84. Aimed at students to develop decision-making skills, Case 7 explores the complexities of the IHS and the management problems it imposes on leaders.

Weaver, Hilary N., and Priscilla A. Day, eds. *Health and the American Indian.* New York: Routledge, 1999. A collection of essays that explores the health and social conditions of Indian people in variety of settings, including an examination of the Indian Child Welfare Act and the social impact of gaming.

Witko, Tawa M., ed. *Mental Health Care for Urban Indians.* Washington, DC: American Psychological Association, 2006. A collection of essays from American Indian practitioners who explore mental health care from an Indian perspective.

World Wide Web

Grim, Charles W. "2008 Statement of the Indian Health Service." http://www .hhs.gov/asl/testify/2007/02/t20070215d.html. The director's statement to the Committee on Indian Affairs, U.S. Senate.

Healy, Bernadine. "The Shame of a Nation." http://health.usnews.com/usnews/ health/articles/041004/4healy.htm. A 2004 article reporting on the health of Indians that includes statistical data.

"Indian Health Service Today." http://www.nlm.nih.gov/exhibition/if_you _knew/if_you_knew_09.html. A collection of photographs and IHS publications, including a 1984 map of IHS facilities.

Kutz, Gregory D. "IHS: Mismanagement Led to Millions of Dollars in Lost or Stolen Property and Wasteful Spending." http://www.gao.gov/ new.items/d081069t.pdf. PDF. The report of the managing director of the Forensic Audits and Special Investigations to the Committee on Indian Affairs, U.S. Senate.

Lawrence, Jane. "The Indian Health Service and the Sterilization of Native American Women." http://muse.jhu.edu/demo/american_indian_quar- terly/v024/24.3lawrence.html. Demonstrates that IHS doctors per- formed sterilization procedures on American Indian women as a matter of policy in the 1960s and 1970s.

"Previous Directors of the Indian Health Service 1955–1933." http:// www.ihs.gov/PublicAffairs/Bios/index.cfm?module=bios_previous _directors. Photographs and biographies of former directors.

Vogel, Lucy. "Health Planning in the Indian Health Service: Trends and Issues: Part I." http://www.apha.org/membergroups/newsletters/sectionnewslet- ters/comm/winter07/vogelarticle.htm. Describes the administrative struc- ture and the numbers of facilities constructed between 1955 and 2005.

Multimedia Source

500 Nations. Dir. Ack Leustig. 500 Nations Productions, 2005. 4 DVDs. 8 epi- sodes (49 minutes per episode). "Episode 8: Attack on Culture" explores Americanization and Indian policy from 1887 to the present day.

82. American Indian Chicago Conference (AICC) (1961)

In June of 1961, American Indians from 65 different tribes met at the University of Chicago for a convention organized by anthropologist Sol

Tax to discuss the state of Indian affairs in urban as well as reservation Indian communities in the United States. In addition, the organizers of the event planned to document every aspect of the conference, from communications to meetings, discussions, findings, resolutions, and official declarations. All of these data were recorded, categorized, collated, and filed for future reference and deposited in the Smithsonian Institution, which agreed to accept the conference archive. In this way, the AICC was the most documented conference of its kind, and the AICC archive was an important symbol of pan-Indian self-determination, joint political activism, and tribal sovereignty. After meeting and discussing the state of Indian affairs for 8 days, the 400-plus participants hammered out a *Declaration of Indian Purpose,* which was a manifesto from the point of view of tribal members on U.S. Indian policies. The declaration called for "the responsibility of the United States toward the Indian people in terms of a positive national obligation to modify or remove the conditions which produce the poverty and lack of social justice, as these prevail as the outstanding attributes of Indian life today. . . . What we ask of America is not charity, not paternalism, even when benevolent. We ask that the nature of our situation be recognized and made the basis of policy and action." Representatives of the AICC presented the declaration to President John F. Kennedy in September 1962.

TERM PAPER SUGGESTIONS

1. The AICC generated a political activism that was more confrontational than earlier pan-Indian movements. Compare the political activism of the AICC to earlier organizations, like the Society of American Indians and the National Congress of American Indians.

2. *Declaration of Indian Purpose: The Voice of the American Indian* advocated for policy reform, but it also called for the reversal of the Menominee Termination. Indian activist Ada Deer and other Menominee were present at the AICC, and they made this a priority. Examine why other Indian representatives supported their actions.

3. Write on the role and achievements of three AICC Indian participants at the conference and beyond: D'Arcy McNickle, Vine Deloria Jr., and Ada Deer.

4. Write on the major concerns of the AICC participants. How did they prioritize?

5. Explore and report on the methods proposed and used, successfully or otherwise, to get their political message out to the U.S. public and federal, state, and local officials. How about to other Indians?

6. Non-Indian author Wilcomb Washburn criticized the role of other non-Indians, especially anthropologists, in the organization of the AICC and the production of written material. Investigate the validity of these charges. Do many Indians share this view about interfering anthropologists?

ALTERNATIVE TERM PAPER SUGGESTIONS

1. In an effort to learn about "declarations" and/or manifestos, study the Declaration of Independence and the *Declaration of Indian Purpose.* Write your own declaration from the perspective of a young person. Your audience can be parents, school officials, local, state, or federal governments, or the general public, or all.
2. If you were given the job of creating a modern poster to advertise and announce the American Indian Chicago Conference, what would you create, and how would you disseminate it? Create a poster and a plan of action.

SUGGESTED SOURCES

Primary Sources

American Indian Chicago Conference. *Declaration of Indian Purpose: The Voice of the American Indian.* Chicago, IL: University of Chicago Press, 1961. Reprint, Whitefish, MT: Kessinger Publishing, 2006. The full 49-page text of the declaration.

"American Indian Chicago Conference Records 1960–1966." http://siris-archives.si.edu/ipac20/ipac.jsp?uri=full=3100001~!319!0. Records held by the Smithsonian. Includes a brief history and description of the holdings. Most importantly, the site lists all of the contributors.

"Declaration of Indian Purpose." http://www.digitalhistory.uh.edu/native_voices/voices_display.cfm?id=98. One-page version of the 1961 declaration.

"Declaration of Indian Purpose." http://www.personal.utulsa.edu/~nathan-wilson/declaration.pdf. A PDF of a three-page excerpt from the declaration.

Lurie, Nancy Oestreich. "The Voice of the American Indian: Report on the American Indian Chicago Conference." *Current Anthropology* 2, no. 5 (December 1961): 478–500. A very detailed report on the conference with analysis, photographs, and many drafts of various primary source documents.

"The Voice of the American Indian." *Great Documents in American Indian History.* Cambridge, MA: De Capo Press, 1995, 337–45. Three-quarters of the "Declaration" is printed here, as well as the words of D'Arcy McNickle (in the next section).

Secondary Sources

Clarkin, Thomas. *Federal Indian Policy in the Kennedy and Johnson Administrations, 1961–1969.* Albuquerque, NM: University of New Mexico Press, 2001. Examines the impact of the "Declaration of Indian Purpose" and its condemnation of federal Termination Policy.

Cowger, Thomas W. *The National Congress of American Indians: The Founding Years.* Lincoln, NE: University of Nebraska Press, 1999. Many members of the National Congress of American Indians (NCAI) were participants at the American Indian Chicago Conference (AICC). See the chapter "The New Indian Trail."

Deloria, Vine, Jr. *Custer Died for Your Sins.* New York: Macmillan, 1969. Reprint, 1988. An Indian manifesto written by this AICC participant and famous Indian author/activist that details the relevant issues raised at the conference.

Hauptman, Laurence M., and Jack Campisi. "The Voice of Eastern Indians: The American Indian Chicago Conference of 1961 and the Movement for Federal Recognition." *Proceedings of the American Philosophical Society* 132, no. 4 (December 1988): 316–29. Explores the origins of tribes seeking federal recognition due to oversight of federal policies as a hallmark of the conference.

LaGrand, James B. *Indian Metropolis.* Champaign, IL: University of Illinois Press, 2002. Includes a narrative analysis of the AICC.

Parker, Dorothy R. *Singing an Indian Song.* Lincoln, NE: University of Nebraska Press, 1994. A biography of D'Arcy McNickle, founder of the NCAI and AICC participant.

Prucha, Francis Paul. *American Indian Treaties: The History of a Political Anomaly.* Berkeley, CA: University of California Press, 1994. Contains a section entitled "Early Activism," where the AICC is discussed and placed within a trend of Indian activism.

Straus, Terry, et al. "Anthropology, Ethics and the American Indian Chicago Conference." *American Ethnologist* 13, no. 4 (November 1986): 802–4. A critical review of Wilcomb Washburn's *Against the Anthropological Grain,* which explores the role of scholars and professionals at the conference and whether their role interfered or helped.

Washburn, Wilcomb E. *Against the Anthropological Grain.* Edison, NJ: Transaction Publishers, 1998. Challenges anthropology as a credible discipline and includes an analysis of several anthropologists and their participation in the AICC.

World Wide Web

Ablon, Joan. "The American Indian Chicago Conference." http://jaie.asu.edu/ v1/V1S2ame.htm. An article written by a participant and University of Chicago graduate student who describes the AICC.

Dorfman, Ron. "Proposal for a Pilot Project in American Indian Education." http://www.pbs.org/shattering/indian-ed.html. A proposal prepared for the dean of the College of the University of Chicago, July 1961, as a result of the AICC. Includes statistical data, a "modest proposal," and concluding remarks.

Golus, Carrie. "Native Americans to Celebrate Heritage." http://chronicle .uchicago.edu/010920/powwow.shtml. Brief article describing the 2001 Eschikagou Powwow as the 40th anniversary of the AICC's powwow that they held at the University of Chicago's Old Staff Field in June 1961.

Lurie, Nancy Oestreich. "Sol Tax and Tribal Sovereignty." http://findarticles.com/ p/articles/mi_qa3800/is_199904/ai_n8842482. Argues that the AICC was the first conference to articulate the idea of tribal sovereignty and was the first place that term was ever used.

Multimedia Source

American Indian Homelands: Matters of Truth, Honor and Dignity. Dir. Barry ZeVan. Victory Multimedia, 2007. DVD. 78 minutes. Covers U.S. laws and termination polices.

83. National Indian Youth Council (NIYC) Founded (1961)

Emerging from regional Indian Youth Councils and Indian college student organizations, young Indians in 1961 arrived in Chicago and formed a caucus of their own on federal Indian policy at the American Indian Chicago Conference (AICC) held that summer. Sparked by this experience, members of the AICC youth caucus met in Gallup, New Mexico in the fall to write bylaws, to officially create the NIYC, and to elect its officers and board of directors. Initially, their major purpose was to counter detrimental federal Indian polices, especially the Termination Policy. In the 1960s and early 1970s, they fought for Indian fishing rights in the northwest and participated in militant Indian political activism, such as the occupation of Alcatraz Island and the "Trail of Broken

Treaties," acts designed to bring public attention to Indian rights and issues. However, the NIYC soon turned from sporadic and short-lived media events to long-term and lasting programs that generated tangible and meaningful results. In the late 1970s and 1980s, the NIYC shifted to "leadership-training programs" and government internships for Indian students. The NIYC fought legal battles in areas of discrimination, affirmative action, and religious freedom. They fought to protect Indian lands from exploitation, destruction, and annexation and fought for tribal voting rights and the restoration of tribal constitutions. More importantly, in the 1980s and beyond, they have expanded to provide a variety of voting and election services for Indian people, and they have expanded their service area to include the indigenous peoples of Central and South America.

TERM PAPER SUGGESTIONS

1. Explore the activities of the Indian Youth Caucus at the American Indian Chicago Conference and how they led to the creation of the NIYC.

2. Indian fishing rights emerged as a volatile issue in the 1960s. Examine and report on the involvement of the NIYC in the various "fish-ins" and protest activities.

3. Some historians and oral historians claim that the notion of Red Power, a new radical approach to political action, emerged out of youth organizations like the NIYC and that Red Power activists were more militant than other organizations whose memberships were much older. Examine the legitimacy of such observations and assessments.

4. Write an essay comparing the NIYC to other non-Indian "youth" political activist organizations of the 1960s.

5. The NIYC shifted focus to long-term programs and adopted the strategies of other conservative Indian organizations. Write an essay about the long-term programs and how they benefited Indian people. How were these programs different from the actions taken by more-militant Indian activist organizations?

6. Explore the voting rights programs and initiatives that the NIYC has been involved in since the 1980s.

ALTERNATIVE TERM PAPER SUGGESTIONS

1. Imagine you are a young Indian college student who is assigned a task of petitioning the organizers of the American Indian Chicago Conference (AICC)

for a place to hold an Indian Youth Caucus and for the right to publish a youth statement. Write a 1,000-word petition and appeal for a place in the conference.

2. Organize a caucus to discuss the federal Indian policies in place in 1961 and to produce a group statement of action and solution of 500 words. Remember, the Indian Youth Caucus at the AICC was composed of several Indian youth, ages 17–21, who became major contributors.

SUGGESTED SOURCES

Primary Source

National Indian Youth Council. *ABC: Americans Before Columbus.* Denver, CO: National Indian Youth Council, 1963– . A quarterly newsletter started in 1963 that continues to be published to this day.

Secondary Sources

Cobb, Daniel M., ed. *Beyond Red Power.* Sante Fe, NM: School for Advanced Research Press, 2007. Collection of essays exploring Indian politics and activism since 1900 from a variety of efforts and perspectives; not necessarily militant.

Cowger, Thomas W. *The National Congress of American Indians: The Founding Years.* Lincoln, NE: University of Nebraska Press, 1999. The first, longest-lasting Indian national organization is the National Congress of American Indians, and the National Indian Youth Council (NIYC) is the second; this is acknowledged and covered in this text.

Fluharty, Sterling. " 'For a Greater Indian America': The Origins of the National Indian Youth Council." Master's thesis, University of Oklahoma, 2003. Included because this is the only complete history of the organization under one cover.

Johnson, Troy R. *The Occupation of Alcatraz Island.* Champaign, IL: University of Illinois Press, 1996. A thorough history of this historic event of Indian political activism where members of NIYC were major participants.

LaGrand, James B. *Indian Metropolis.* Champaign, IL: University of Illinois Press, 2002. Explores the Indian youth movement in Chicago as well as in the NIYC.

Shreve, Bradley Glenn. "Up Against Giants: The National Indian Youth Council, the Navajo Nation and Coal Gasification, 1974–77." *American Indian Culture and Research Journal* 30, no. 2 (2006): 17–34. Examines the petition drives and protests against multinational corporations and their desire to gasify coal in Indian country.

Smith, Paul Chaat, and Robert Allen Warrior. *Like a Hurricane: The Indian Movement from Alcatraz to Wounded Knee.* New York: The New Press, 1996. Two Indian scholars' narrative essay on Indian political activism from the 1960s to the present.

Steiner, Stan. *The New Indians.* New York: Harper and Row, 1968. The first book to mention the NIYC as an organization at the forefront of Indian activism.

Warrior, Robert Allen. *Tribal Secrets: Recovering American Indian Intellectual Traditions.* Minneapolis, MN: University of Minnesota Press, 1995. Examines and contextualizes Indian intellectuals like Vine Deloria Jr. and members of Indian activist organizations like the NIYC.

Wilkinson, Charles F. *Blood Struggle: The Rise of Modern Indian Nations.* New York: W.W. Norton, 2005. Celebrates the economic triumphs of Indian tribes since the Meriam Report and the Indian Reorganization Act.

Wilkinson, Charles F. *Messages from Frank's Landing: A Story of Salmon, Treaties and the Indian Way.* Seattle, WA: University of Washington Press, 2006. One of the first political goals of the NIYC was to guarantee Indian fishing rights.

World Wide Web

Cobb, Daniel M. "Clyde Meron Warrior (1939–1968)." http://www.ponca.com/warrior_memorial/warrior_memorial.html. Short biography of one of the founders of the NIYC, who tragically died at a young age.

Fluharty, Sterling. "National Indian Youth Council." http://www.newmexicohistory.org/filedetails.php?fileID=21303. An informative essay describing the origin and activities of the NIYC.

"National Indian Youth Council." http://www.answers.com/topic/national-indian-youth-council. Brief description, bibliography, and external links.

"NIYC, Inc." http://www.niyc-alb.org/. Official Web site of NIYC. Includes history, programs, and activities.

"Timeline for Indian Activism." http://www.geocities.com/aimasheville/AIMtimeline.htm. Places the NIYC within a large context of Indian activism.

Multimedia Sources

American Indian Homelands: Matters of Truth, Honor and Dignity. Dir. Barry ZeVan. Victory Multimedia, 2007. DVD. 78 minutes. Covers U.S. laws and termination polices.

Tribal Nations: The Story of Federal Indian Law. Dir. Lisa Jaeger. Tanana Chiefs, 2006. DVD. 60 minutes. Illustrated introductory-level documentary of how federal Indian policy has developed in the United States.

84. American Indian Movement Founded (1968)

During the summer of 1968, over 200 Indians met in Minneapolis, Minnesota to discuss the dismal state of Indian country and Indian affairs and what action could be taken to help Indian people. The first step was to create an organization that soon became known as the American Indian Movement, or AIM, because the acronym symbolized direct action and serious intent to make changes. Dennis Banks, Russell Means, Clyde Bellecourt, and many others then embarked on a journey of Indian political activism that still resonates to this day. From Indian urban centers to Indian reservations and communities, AIM's goals were to renew cultural pride for American Indians, to fight against racial discrimination, to improve the poor living conditions of Indians, and to seek restitution for the United States' failure to honor treaties between the United States and Indian tribes. AIM actively sought media attention and used publicity as an effective communication tool. AIM's more prominent activities included participation in the 1969 occupation of Alcatraz Island, the 1970 takeover of a *Mayflower* replica on the 350th anniversary of the ship's landing, a 1972 cross-country caravan to Washington, D.C. called the "Trail of Broken Treaties" and the subsequent takeover of the Bureau of Indian Affairs building, and the 71-day standoff at Wounded Knee in 1973. After several years of these militant and public protests, AIM founded the International Treaty Council, and they worked to end the racist treatment of Indians caused by sports mascots and logos through their National Coalition on Racism in Sports and Media.

TERM PAPER SUGGESTIONS

1. AIM protected the urban Indian community in Minneapolis from police harassment. Write an essay exploring the problems the Indians were having with local law enforcement.

2. Explore the major concerns urban Indians had in 1968. How did these concerns fuel the need for an American Indian Movement?

3. Research and report on the long-term programs that brought about positive change for Indians due to AIM's efforts and political activism.

4. Examine the militancy and confrontational tactics used by AIM and the reason militancy was an effective way of drawing media attention to Indian issues and concerns.

5. Examine the targeted sites of AIM's political activities (the *Mayflower,* Plymouth Rock, the Bureau of Indian Affairs, and Wounded Knee, South Dakota). Why are these sites important to the political message AIM sought to communicate? How are they symbolic?

6. By 1974, AIM had established 75 chapters in cities across the nation, and it had generated support from many sources, including Hollywood movie stars and rock bands. Explain the reason for such popularity. How did the leadership cope with a newfound fame?

ALTERNATIVE TERM PAPER SUGGESTIONS

1. Create an iMovie montage of the many images of AIM members and their activities from the countless short news clips and interviews found on the World Wide Web.

2. Host a mock trial of AIM members who desecrated a national monument like Plymouth Rock, which AIM members painted red. How would AIM fashion a defense, and how would a prosecutor approach the case? How would a jury rule?

SUGGESTED SOURCES

Primary Sources

"AIM and Wounded Knee Documents." http://www.aics.org/WK/index.html. Links page to primary source documents such as newsletters, photographs, position statements, and legal documents.

"Declassified Government Records/Documents of AIM." http://www .aimovement.org/csi/index.html. A links page to hundreds of primary and secondary source records.

Secondary Sources

Banks, Dennis, and Richard Erdoes. *Ojibwa Warrior: Dennis Banks and the Rise of the American Indian Movement.* Norman, OK: University of Oklahoma Press, 2005. Biography of one of the cofounders of AIM.

Cobb, Daniel M., ed. *Beyond Red Power.* Sante Fe, NM: School for Advanced Research Press, 2007. Collection of essays exploring Indian politics and activism since 1900 from a variety of efforts and perspectives; not necessarily militant.

Hertzberg, Hazel W. *The Search for an American Indian Identity: Modern Pan-Indian Movements.* Syracuse, NY: Syracuse University Press, 1971. Part One is a definitive history of the Society of American Indians (SAI) and Part Two details the rise of the American Indian Movement.

Johnson, Troy R., et al., eds. *American Indian Activism.* Champaign, IL: University of Illinois Press, 1997. A collection of essays focused on the Indian occupation of Alcatraz Island to protest and symbolize Indian political and land issues.

Matthiessen, Peter. *In the Spirit of Crazy Horse.* New York: Penguin, 1992. Narrative history of AIM. Chapter 2 covers the origins of the movement in Minneapolis in 1968.

Smith, Paul Chaat, and Robert Allen Warrior. *Like a Hurricane: The Indian Movement from Alcatraz to Wounded Knee.* New York: The New Press, 1996. Two Indian scholars' narrative essay on Indian political activism from the 1960s to the present.

Stern, Kenneth S. *Loud Hawk: The United States Versus the American Indian Movement.* Norman, OK: University of Oklahoma Press, 1994. Examines the 1975 arrest of activists Kenny Loud Hawk, Dennis Banks, Leonard Peltier, Annie Mae Pictou Aquash, Kamook Banks, and Russ Redner and the subsequent trials and appeals.

Trimbach, Joseph A. *American Indian Mafia.* Parker, CO: Outskirts Press, 2007. The most complete work on AIM. Documents the killing of FBI Special Agents Jack Coler and Ron Williams as a "mafia style" hit and brutal, cold-blooded murder; it disputes and counters most of the other texts listed in this bibliography.

Wilkinson, Charles F. *Blood Struggle: The Rise of Modern Indian Nations.* New York: W.W. Norton, 2005. Celebrates the economic triumphs of Indian tribes since the Meriam Report and the Indian Reorganization Act.

World Wide Web

"AIM: Grand Governing Council." http://www.aimovement.org/. The home page of the American Indian Movement. Includes Webcasts, a multimedia archive, songs, speeches, and more.

"AIM: MySpace." http://www.myspace.com/aimggc. The MySpace page of the American Indian Movement Grand Governing Council.

American Indian Mafia. http://www.americanindianmafia.com/. The Web site for the book *American Indian Mafia,* which documents the murders, murder investigation, and trials of AIM members involved in the murder of three FBI agents on the Pine Ridge Indian Reservation.

"American Indian Movement." http://www.mnhs.org/library/tips/history _topics/93aim.html. Educational site aimed at students. Provides a brief overview and a list of secondary and primary sources with call numbers.

Norrell, Brenda. "Gentle Rage: Clyde Bellecourt Remembers the Birth of the American Indian Movement." http://narcosphere.narconews.com/ notebook/brenda-norrell/2008/08/gentle-rage-clyde-bellecourt- remembers-birth-american-indian-movemen. Interview of the famous AIM cofounder posted August 13, 2008.

Schneider, Jeremy. "From Wounded Knee to Capitol Hill." http://www .dickshovel.com/aimhis.html. Brief history and description of the activities of AIM.

Wittstock, Laura Waterman, and Elaine J. Salinas. "A Brief History of the American Indian Movement." http://www.aimovement.org/ggc/ history.html. Includes the 20-Point Indian Manifesto of 1972 and a detailed time line.

Multimedia Source

"AIM Multimedia Archive, Video." http://www.streamreel.com/archives/aim/ aim_video.htm. Many short and long video clips, interviews, speeches, and news footage.

85. Indian Civil Rights Act (1968)

A civil right is a societal principle of justice created to protect an individual from government abuse; the Bill of Rights, the first 10 amendments to the U.S. Constitution (for example, the freedoms of speech, press, religion, and so on), is the foundation of U.S. civil rights from which all other laws derive. In 1968, Congress passed the Indian Civil Rights Act (ICRA) because federal authorities perceived that tribal courts did not necessarily protect the civil rights of tribal members within their jurisdictions. Since the 1832 *Worcester v. Georgia* opinion Indian tribes have had the power to govern themselves, and this meant that tribal courts decided disputes according to their own laws and practices. The ICRA was designed to remedy the possibility of a violation of an Indian person's civil rights by tribal governments or courts. The law was immediately controversial, because it gave federal courts the power to overrule decisions of tribal officials and to protect the constitutional rights of tribal citizens "from arbitrary and unjust actions of tribal governments." However, the

ICRA was tailored to meet the needs of tribes and tribal governments. This meant that the "separation of church and state," the "Establishment Clause," was not applicable because religion and spiritual leaders have always been a part of tribal governance. A more obvious conflict was the fifteenth constitutional amendment, which prohibits voter discrimination due to race, color, gender, or ethnicity. The ICRA does not force tribes to follow the fifteenth amendment, because it would allow voters who were/are not tribal members to vote in tribal elections.

TERM PAPER SUGGESTIONS

1. Over time, the federal government has limited tribal sovereignty. How does the ICRA fit into this trend of limiting the authority of tribal governments?
2. Some tribal officials find the ICRA controversial and consider it another federal imposition. Write an essay exploring their reasons for opposing such a law.
3. Tribal members brought this matter of civil rights violations to the attention of Congress. Explore their argument, their desires, and their motivations to seek federal intervention.
4. Write on the lack of an "Establishment Clause" in the ICRA. What has been the traditional role of religion and religious leaders in many Indian tribes and governments?
5. Argue for the necessity of allowing discrimination in voting rights for tribal elections.
6. One of the civil rights of American Indians is the freedom of religion. Study and report on the special laws passed by Congress concerning Indian religious freedom.

ALTERNATIVE TERM PAPER SUGGESTION

1. As a federal official, you are asked to prepare an ICRA standard-size brochure (8.5 inches by 11 inches with two folds) to help tribal Indians understand their civil rights in a simple, straightforward, and understandable manner.

SUGGESTED SOURCES

Primary Sources

American Indian Civil Rights Handbook. https://www.law.umaryland.edu/marshall/usccr/documents/cr11033.pdf. Photocopy PDF file of the handbook meant for American Indians.

Indian Civil Rights Act of 1968 (25 U.S.C. §§ 1301-03). http://www.tribal-institute.org/lists/icra1968.htm. Complete text of the act and associated amendments and clarifications.

Prucha, Francis Paul. *Documents of United States Indian Policy.* 3rd edition. Lincoln, NE: University of Nebraska Press, 2000. Collected primary sources, including the Indian Civil Rights Act.

Secondary Sources

Canby, William C., Jr., *American Indian Law in a Nutshell.* 1981. Reprint, St. Paul, MN: West, 2004. A book that answers simple questions, like "What is an Indian Tribe?" A good basic set of definitions.

Dutha, N. Bruce, and Colin Calloway. *American Indians and the Law.* New York: Viking, 2008. Defines and clarifies sovereignty as it applies to federally recognized tribes since 1787.

French, Laurence A. *Native American Justice.* Lanham, MD: Rowman and Littlefield, 2003. Covers the ICRA in the chapter on "Jurisdictions."

McCool, Daniel, et al. *Native Vote: American Indians, the Voting Rights Act and the Right to Vote.* New York: Cambridge University Press, 2007. Examines the history of voting rights of American Indians and the struggle for citizenship.

Prucha, Francis P. *The Great Father: The United States Government and the American Indians.* Lincoln, NE: University of Nebraska Press, 1984. General overview of laws and acts concerning Indians.

Rosen, Lawrence. *American Indians and the Law.* Durham, NC: School of Law, Duke University, 1976. Reprint, Transaction Publishers, 1978. An older historical survey.

Wilkins, David E. *American Indian Politics and the American Political System.* 2nd edition. New York: Rowman and Littlefield, 2006. Tribal governmental history, structure, and powers.

Wilkins, David E. *Uneven Ground: American Indian Sovereignty and Federal Law.* Norman, OK: University of Oklahoma Press, 2001. Investigate the manner in which Indian sovereignty has eroded since the 1787 U.S. Constitution.

Wunder, John R., ed., *The Indian Bill of Rights, 1968.* New York: Routledge, 1996. A collection of essays exploring the ramifications of the ICRA.

Wunder, John R. *"Retained by the People": A History of American Indians and the Bill of Rights.* New York: Oxford University Press, 1994. Explores the relationship between Indians and the Bill of Rights.

World Wide Web

Allen, William B. "Statement on the ICRA." https://www.msu.edu/~allenwi/reports/Indian_Civil_Rights_Act.htm. Opinion of a commission charge on the investigation and study of the ICRA.

"Constitutional Rights of Indians." http://www4.law.cornell.edu/uscode/25/ch15.html. Links page to five sub-chapters within the U.S. Code collection.

"Indian Civil Rights Act." http://www.answers.com/topic/indian-civil-rights-act. Includes a summary, the text of the act, and a bibliography.

"Indian Civil Rights Act." http://www.lawhelp.org/documents/1594719202.pdf?stateabbrev=/WA. Pamphlet in PDF format defining the ICRA in plain and simple language.

Johnstonbaugh, Laurie. "Indian Civil Rights Hearings." http://depts.washington.edu/civilr/CRcommission.htm. Essay exploring a hearing held October 1977, where the U.S. Civil Rights Commission sought to collect information on possible civil rights violations concerning American Indians in the Seattle area.

"1968 Indian Bill of Rights." http://news.minnesota.publicradio.org/projects/2001/04/brokentrust/history/history10.shtml. Brief definition of what the law means.

Multimedia Source

Tribal Nations: The Story of Federal Indian Law. Dir. Lisa Jaeger. Tanana Chiefs, 2006. DVD. 60 minutes. Illustrated introductory-level documentary of how federal Indian policy has developed in the United States.

86. Occupation of Alcatraz Island (1969)

From November 20, 1969 to June 11, 1971, almost 19 months, American Indians of the Bay Area, mostly young urban Indians and Indian college students, took possession of Alcatraz Island in the name of "Indians of All Tribes." They took over the island in the name of Indian treaty rights, particularly the rights that reserved lands for Indian use. They also demanded that the federal government provide basic services like health care and education in exchange for the millions of acres of Indian land taken in Indian land acquisition treaties. In the San Francisco Bay area, these promised services were not sufficient to meet the needs of the growing urban Indian population, a growth caused by federal Indian programs like the Indian Urban Relocation Program and the Termination Policy. The catalyst for occupation occurred shortly after the Indian Center in San Francisco burned down. It was one of the important centers for Indian relocatees, pan-Indian cultural activities, and urban Indian health care and job training. This incident, combined with general dissatisfaction caused by inefficient federal Indian policy, fueled the desire to occupy Alcatraz, in order to draw worldwide public attention to the concerns of Indians and Indian treaty rights. More importantly, the occupation served to heighten the political awareness of Indian youth across North America, which in itself instilled a new pride in "being" Indian. Over 5,000 Indians from across North America arrived to spend some time, a few hours or a few days, supporting the original protesters. Members of the National Indian Youth Council, the newly incarnated American Indian Movement, and many individual Indian youth would find inspiration and motivation to pursue their own forms of political activism to effectuate change after visiting Alcatraz Island.

TERM PAPER SUGGESTIONS

1. Research and write a report on the non-Indian support of the Indians occupying Alcatraz Island in 1969 and 1970. For example, rock band the Grateful Dead and movie actress Jane Fonda, are famous examples of people who supported the occupation.

2. Examine the causes in the Bay Area Indian community that led to the occupation of Alcatraz Island. What role did the Bureau of Indian Affairs play in the dissatisfaction of the Indian community?

3. Did the occupation of Alcatraz Island lead to any policy changes, especially in heath and education services?

4. Why would the Indian protesters claim the island of Alcatraz by "discovery laws" and offer to buy the island for $24 of glass beads? Write about the symbolic protest rhetoric and its effectiveness in making a dramatic point.

5. Study and report on the Indian people who occupied or visited the island who became leaders or activists themselves. Most of the other "occupations" of federal sites or property were orchestrated by Indian youth who at one time or another visited the island.

6. Write an essay that details the federal strategies for dealing with the occupation and the tactics used to end the occupation.

ALTERNATIVE TERM PAPER SUGGESTIONS

1. Examine the "Proclamation: To the Great White Father and All His People" and add whatever else might be important or symbolic of Indian concerns. Create an interactive Web site of the expanded document to serve as a hyper-linked list of Indian grievances and concerns. Of course, a healthy review of American Indian federal policy will be invaluable.

2. Design and create a poster commemorating the event using an eye-catching motif and/or logo and an inspirational slogan.

SUGGESTED SOURCES

Primary Sources

"The American Indian Occupation of Alcatraz Island." http://www.csulb.edu/~aisstudy/alcatraz/. Three sets of black and white photographs of the occupation.

Fortunate Eagle, Adam, et al. *Heart of the Rock*. Norman, OK: University of Oklahoma Press, 2008. The story of the Alcatraz occupation by people who were there and stayed for the duration and aftermath of this famous event.

Johnson, Troy. *Alcatraz: Indian Land Forever*. Los Angeles, CA: University of California American Indian Studies Program, 1995. Speeches, poetry, pronouncements, and other political statements from "Radio Free Alcatraz" broadcast programming during the occupation.

Johnson, Troy, ed. *You Are On Indian Land*. Los Angeles: University of California American Indian Studies Program, 1995. A collection of mostly black and white photographs are used to document the bleak and lonely occupation of the island for 19 months.

"Proclamation: To the Great White Father and All His People." http://www.cwis.org/fwdp/Americas/alcatraz.txt. Full text of the famous proclamation read by the original protesters.

Secondary Sources

Hertzberg, Hazel W. *The Search for an American Indian Identity: Modern Pan-Indian Movements*. Syracuse, NY: Syracuse University Press, 1971. Part One is a definitive history of the Society of American Indians (SAI) and Part Two details the rise of the American Indian Movement (AIM).

Johnson, Troy. *The American Indian Occupation of Alcatraz Island: Red Power and Self-Determination*. Lincoln, NE: University of Nebraska Press, 2008. A comprehensive exploration of the local Bay Area Indians' social and political reasons for the occupation and how the reasons shifted, wavered, and fluctuated away from that original intent.

Johnson, Troy R. *The Occupation of Alcatraz Island.* Champaign, IL: University of Illinois Press, 1996. A thorough history of this historic event of Indian political activism.

Johnson, Troy R., et al, eds. *American Indian Activism: Alcatraz to the Longest Walk.* Champaign, IL: University of Illinois Press, 1997. A collection of essays focused on the Indian occupation of Alcatraz Island to protest and symbolize Indian political and land issues.

Lobo, Susan. *Urban Voices: The Bay Area American Indian Community.* Tucson, AZ: The University of Arizona Press, 2002. As an outcome of the Indian Urban Relocation Program, the author explains the emergence of a "cooperative, multi-tribal community," whose center was the Intertribal Friendship House in Oakland, California.

Smith, Paul Chaat, and Robert Allen Warrior. *Like a Hurricane: The Indian Movement from Alcatraz to Wounded Knee.* New York: The New Press, 1996. Two Indian scholars' narrative essay on Indian political activism from the 1960s to the present.

Wilkinson, Charles F. *Blood Struggle: The Rise of Modern Indian Nations.* New York: W.W. Norton, 2005. Celebrates the economic triumphs of Indian tribes since the Meriam Report and the Indian Reorganization Act.

World Wide Web

"Alcatraz Island." http://www.npca.org/cultural_diversity/treasures/Alcatraz.html. Argues that the takeover had legitimacy and purpose beyond simple civil disobedience.

"Alcatraz Is Not an Island." http://www.pbs.org/itvs/alcatrazisnotanisland/index.html. Web site for the Public Broadcasting Service documentary that includes links to many interesting and relevant entries. Includes links to two lesson plans for teachers.

Johnson, Troy. "We Hold the Rock." http://www.nps.gov/alca/historyculture/we-hold-the-rock.htm. A brief but detailed history of the Indian occupation by the leading scholar of the incident. Includes photographs.

Senior, Stephanie Rosa. http://www.californiahistoricalsociety.org/programs/pdf/2003_winner.pdf. PDF essay describing this event of 1969–1970.

Winton, Ben. "Alcatraz, Indian Land." http://siouxme.com/lodge/alcatraz_np.html. In a 1999 30-year retrospective, the author revisits the occupation through interviews with "veterans" of the takeover, period photographs, and insightful commentary.

Multimedia Source

Alcatraz Is Not an Island. Dir. James M. Fortier. Diamond Island Productions, 2001. DVD or VHS. 57 minutes. A documentary of the 19-month occupation.

87. *State of Michigan v. William Jondreau* (1971)

In 1965, William Jondreau was arrested and cited by a Michigan state conservation officer for violating state fishing regulations because he caught several lake trout in his fishing nets. As a Keweenaw Bay Chippewa, Jondreau claimed that he did not have to honor state fishing laws; he explained that he was fishing for herring and caught the trout by mistake. Rather than throwing them away and wasting them, he decided to bring them ashore, which was when and where he was arrested. His treaty rights, which reserved the rights of the Keweenaw Chippewas to fish and hunt, he claimed, predated and superceded the laws of the state, so he had right to take and keep the fish. In the case *State of Michigan v. William Jondreau,* the Michigan Supreme Court affirmed his right and the right of the Keweenaw Bay Indian community members to fish in the Keweenaw Bay waters of Lake Superior without regard to Michigan fishing regulations. Jondreau's victory sparked a resurgence of "treaty-rights-fishing" in the entire Great Lakes region and beyond. For the first time in many years, Indians exerted their tribal sovereignty through the exercise of fishing and, in some cases, hunting and gathering rights. Hunting, fishing, and gathering are "reserved" in the land cession treaties the Great Lakes Indians signed, mostly in the 1830s, that transferred the enormous tracts of land that became the Great Lakes states. Akin to "reserved" lands set aside for the exclusive use of Indians, the reserved rights of hunting, fishing, and gathering were rights never given up or taken away by acts of Congress.

TERM PAPER SUGGESTIONS

1. The Michigan Indian treaties are land cession treaties for the most part. However, Michigan Indian people reserved many rights in the treaties they signed. Examine and report on the concept of "reserved rights" in Indian treaties.

2. "Non-ceded lands" and "public lands" are held in trust by the federal government. Waterways (rivers, lakes, and oceans) are public lands and cannot be privately or state owned. Examine the right of Indians to fish in rivers, lakes, and oceans as water open to them via treaties and agreements.

3. Why did the victory of Jondreau in the State Supreme Court spark a wave of Indians exercising their right to fish, even in other states like in Wisconsin and Minnesota?

4. Does the right to fish mean that tribal governments allow Indians to fish unregulated? Study and report on the licensing and regulations imposed on tribal members by their own tribal governments.

5. Look at the gathering of wild rice and the harvesting of maple sugar from maple trees, and explain how law and Indian treaties protect these activities of Great Lakes Indians.

6. Hunting of wild game has been harder for Indians to exercise as a right. Explore why this is so and why Indians in some regions can exercise this right and why others cannot.

ALTERNATIVE TERM PAPER SUGGESTIONS

1. Make a map of Indian treaties and the Michigan Indians they involve. Highlight the areas of the Keweenaw Bay Indian community.

2. Produce a Microsoft PowerPoint slide show that explains how water, like oceans, Great Lakes, seaways, rivers, and inland lakes are public property and not owned by individuals or states. Consider: although the lands surrounding an inland lake, for example, can be owned, a public access to that lake must always exist and be maintained.

SUGGESTED SOURCES

Primary Sources

"The Jondreau Decision Based on the Treaty of 1854." http://www .coppercountry.com/article_96.php. Text of the case.

"Native American Treaties: Their Ongoing Importance to Michigan Residents." http:// clarke.cmich.edu/nativeamericans/treatyrights/treatyintro.htm. Comprehensive primary source site with complete texts of Michigan Indian treaties as well as links to a very complete section on the Michigan fishing rights issue.

Secondary Sources

Cleland, Charles. *Rites of Conquest: The History and Culture of Michigan's Native Americans.* Ann Arbor, MI: University of Michigan Press, 1992. General and comprehensive history that includes a discussion of Indian fishing rights.

Doherty, Robert. "Old-Time Origins of Modern Sovereignty: State-Building among the Keweenaw Bay Ojibway, 1832–1854." *The American Indian Quarterly* 31, no. 1 (Winter 2007): 165–87. An essay that links the activities of Jondreau's elders to tribal sovereignty and reserved rights.

LeBeau, Patrick Russell. *Rethinking Michigan Indian History.* East Lansing, MI: Michigan State University Press, 2005. Maps and discussions of treaty rights, including fishing rights, explore the sovereignty of Michigan Indians.

Satz, Ronald N. *Chippewa Treaty Rights.* Madison, WI: Wisconsin Academy of Sciences, Arts, and Letters, 1991. A detailed history of the struggle of Chippewa people to exercise their treaty rights.

Wilkins, David E. *Uneven Ground: American Indian Sovereignty and Federal Law.* Norman, OK: University of Oklahoma Press, 2001. Investigates the manner in which Indian sovereignty has eroded since the 1787 U.S. Constitution.

Wilkinson, Charles F. *American Indians, Time, and the Law.* New Haven, CT: Yale University Press, 1987. Examines the recognition of Indian governments as part of the federal system in 1959 (*Williams v. Lee*) and how that recognition has reversed to an extent past wrongs.

Wilkinson, Charles F. *Blood Struggle: The Rise of Modern Indian Nations.* New York: W.W. Norton, 2005. Celebrates the economic triumphs of Indian tribes since the Meriam Report and the Indian Reorganization Act, which covers Jondreau.

Wilkinson, Charles F. *Messages from Frank's Landing: A Story of Salmon, Treaties and the Indian Way.* One of the first political goals of the National Indian Youth Council was to guarantee Indian fishing rights.

World Wide Web

"A Historical Review." http://fwcb.cfans.umn.edu/courses/enr3001/Indigenous/historvw.htm. Places Jondreau within a larger context of Indian treaties and fishing rights.

"The Great Lakes Indian Fish & Wildlife Commission." http://www.glifwc.org/. Up-to-date information, publications, and, most interestingly, maps of treaty rights zones for specific tribes.

"Indian Fishing and Hunting Rights." http://www.leg.state.mn.us/LRL/Issues/indian.asp. An up-to-date status of Indian fishing and hunting rights as of 2008 with a bibliography.

Kelley, Frank J. "Opinion No. 5714." http://www.ag.state.mi.us/opinion/datafiles/1980s/op05714.htm. Former State of Michigan attorney general renders a legal opinion concerning Indian fishing rights in the state, via definitions of rights to "submerged lands and waters of Great Lakes."

"Links Page." http://www.glifwc.org/links.html. Links to Great Lakes tribes engaged in fishing, as well as to other relevant and informational sites.

People v. LeBlanc, 1971. http://www.1836cora.org/pdf/peoplevsleblanctext.pdf. Full text of a case similar and related to the Jondreau case.

Rastetter, William. "1836 Treaty—Time Line Re: Reserved Usufruct Rights." http://turtletalk.files.wordpress.com/2007/09/1836-treaty-timeline-obh-current-version.pdf. Definitions and time line.

Multimedia Source

Lighting the Seventh Fire. Dir. Sandra Osawa. P.O.V., 1995. DVD. 48 minutes. Documents the treaty rights of Chippewa Indians in Wisconsin to spear fish in Lac De Flambeau and the racist backlash Indians suffered from local non-Indians.

88. Alaska Native Claims Settlement Act (1971)

When President Richard M. Nixon signed into law the Alaska Native Claims Settlement Act (ANCSA) on December 18, 1971, he was also resolving a complicated dispute with, as some say, an even more complicated settlement. The Alaska Natives (generally called Eskimos, Indians, and Aleuts in 1971), the state of Alaska, and the federal government each had to compromise in order for the Natives and the state to prosper and grow. The act shifted away from past polices of reservations (reserves) and allotments, by revoking existing trust lands of reserves and allotments in favor of transferring 40 million acres of land to Alaska Natives in fee-simple title; that is, a title to land without federal trust status attached. The Alaska Natives would also receive $965.2 million in compensation for the extinguishing of any further land claims. What was unique about this act was that it created "corporations," a business model, to manage Alaska Natives' affairs rather than doing so through traditional groupings of families, clans, or tribes. In this organizational scheme, each qualified and registered Alaska Native would become a stockholder of 100 shares of stock of a regional corporation nearest his/her permanent home, with 13 corporations planned. All of the land and half of the money from the Settlement Act would go to the business corporations, which were organized to make money, and through the corporations Alaska Natives earned a living and collected benefits and dividends. However, the business model posed problems for traditional Alaska Natives, who may have had a hard time learning that stockholder and corporation had replaced clan and village.

TERM PAPER SUGGESTIONS

1. Research and report on the numerous peoples living in Alaska, collectively called Native Alaskans, before the arrival of the Russians and the Americans.

2. Define and explain land ownership in Alaska in four cases: Alaskan Native (aboriginal title), Russia (laws of discovery), the United States (trust), and the state of Alaska (trust). How did Alaska Natives own land before the ANCSA? What did the Russians sell when they sold Alaska to the United States in 1867? What lands did the state own when it became a state in 1958?

3. If the ANCSA dissolved the land trust responsibilities of the federal government, did the act also extinguish hunting and fishing rights? This is important because hunting and fishing are not only traditional subsistences and economic activities; they also plays an important role in Natives' cultural practices.

4. Write an essay on the difficulties faced by Native Alaskans in understanding their new role as shareholders in corporations. How does the concept of private property mesh with age-old concepts of communal property? After nearly 40 years, have Alaska Natives adapted fully to this new form of community organization?

5. The corporations were designed to make money. Research and report on their successes and failures. What are their main products? What are the market resources? What do they invest in? How do they plan to make a profit? Could they simply buy stocks and bonds rather than engage in some sort of business?

6. What rights do Native Alaskans have to other federal programs designed for Indians, like Indian Health Services and education programs?

ALTERNATIVE TERM PAPER SUGGESTIONS

1. Create a Natives' claim to land based on audio recording of a story of tribal traditions, like hunting and fishing, and Alaska land. The oral story should be a legitimate counter to "discovery laws" and a written deed.

2. Form (and name) two hypothetical Native Alaskan corporations of at least four members, where each member has 25 percent share and each corporation has an imaginary $100,000. One corporation must choose and "purchase" a

single stock from the New York Stock Exchange to simulate a business investment, and the other must choose 10 stocks. Follow the investment for 10 days
and see what profits, if any, were made.

SUGGESTED SOURCES

Primary Source

Alaskool.org. http://www.alaskool.org/projects/ancsa/ancsaindx.htm. An all-in-
one site, complete with primary and secondary sources. Of particular
interest are the letters and newsletters from Alaska Natives in 1966, court
opinions, newspaper articles, and archival materials.

Secondary Sources

Berger, Thomas R. *Village Journey: The Report of the Alaska Native Review
Commission.* New York: Hill and Wang, 1985. Describes what an author
actually saw when visiting villages in Alaska and explains how the Settlement Act has changed the lives of Alaska Natives.

Berry, Mary Clay. *The Alaska Pipeline: The Policies of Oil and Native Land
Claims.* Bloomington, IN: Indiana University Press, 1975. Argues that
when Alaska became a state in 1958, native land claims had to be settled
so that natural resources could be exploited.

Borneman, Walter R. *Alaska: Saga of a Bold Land.* New York: HarperCollins,
2003. This history starts at the time of Russian fur traders and ends with
the fight over the Arctic National Wildlife Refuge (ANWR). The Alaska
Native Claims Settlement Act is covered in great detail as well.

Coates, Peter A. *The Trans-Alaska Pipeline Controversy: Technology, Conversation,
and the Frontier.* Bethlehem, PA: Lehigh University Press, 1991. Argues
that the discussion between Alaska Natives and the U.S. government over
the Trans-Alaska Pipeline led to the 1971 Settlement Act.

Colt, Stephen. *Alaska Native and the "New Harpoon": Economics Performance of
the ANCSA Regional Corporations.* Anchorage, AK: Institute of Social
and Economics Research, University of Alaska Anchorage, 2001.
Explains how the Alaska Native Claims Settlement Act is different from
all other U.S. Indian policies in terms of economics and sovereignty.

Corral, Roy. *Alaska Native Ways: What the Elders Have Taught Us.* Portland, OR:
Alaska Northwest Books, 2002. Explains how Alaska's American Indians
needed to survive via the 1971 Settlement Act and also how they
succeeded in sustaining their culture.

Mitchell, Donald C. *Sold American: The Story of Alaska Natives and Their Land,
1867–1959.* Hanover, NH: Dartmouth College, University Press of New

England, 1997. Examines Alaska Natives and land before statehood and the Settlement Act.

Mitchell, Donald C. *Take My Land, Take My Life: The Story of Congress's Historic Settlement of Alaska Native Land Claims, 1960–1971.* Fairbanks, AK: University of Alaska Press, 2001. A complete, nearly 700-page history of the 160 years of the federal government's relation with Alaska Natives and their land.

Skinner, Ramona Ellen. *Alaska Native Policy in the Twentieth Century.* New York: Garland, 1997. Focuses on the aftermath and consequences of the Settlement Act for Alaska Natives.

World Wide Web

"ANCSA at 30." http://www.litsite.org/index.cfm?section=History-and-Culture&page=ANCSA-at-30. A site with links to articles, events, interviews, and lectures on ANCSA 30 years later.

"ANCSA Curricula - Teaching about the Alaska Native Claims Settlement Act." http://www.alaskool.org/projects/ancsa/ancsacurric.htm. A list of five links to teacher resources and curricula covering and exploring ANCSA.

"The Annotated ANCSA." http://www.alaskool.org/projects/ancsa/annancsa.htm. Each section of the act is analyzed and explained point by point.

Arnold, Robert D., et al. *Alaska Native Land Claims.* http://www.alaskool.org/PROJECTS/ANCSA/landclaims/LandClaimsTOC.htm. Three online units from a larger text that covers 14 chapters of history, starting with a description of Alaska Natives, following with their land claims struggles, and ending with an introduction to the Settlement Act. Contains many primary sources, maps, charts, diagrams, and photographs.

"Art of Story Telling." http://www.litsite.org/index.cfm?section=History-and-Culture&page=Art-of-Storytelling. Many interesting Alaska Native oral stories at this site, including "Origin of the Tides."

Jones, Richard S. "Alaska Native Claims Settlement Act of 1971." http://www.alaskool.org/projects/ANCSA/reports/rsjones1981/ANCSA_History71.htm. Complete and detailed history and analysis by an American government analyst, first written in 1972 and revised in 1981.

"Why ANCSA for Elementary Students." http://www.alaskool.org/projects/ancsa/elem_ed/elem_ancsa.htm. Elementary curricula but useful in terms of the complexities of ANCSA and land claims history in Alaska.

Multimedia Source

"ANKN Audio & Video Resources." University of Alaska, 2008. http://www.ankn.uaf.edu/media/. Flash Video, QuickTime, and WMA audio and video resources from Alaska Native Knowledge Network, including information on the Alaska Native Claims Settlement Act. These resources are also available on DVD.

89. Trail of Broken Treaties (1972)

After the last several Indian protesters were escorted off Alcatraz Island in the spring of 1971, American Indian activism, or Red Power, emerged in a more militant, confrontational, and very public form, and the occupation of federal property became a new tactic of political protest. In the fall of 1972, a caravan of Indian activists, mostly American Indian Movement (AIM) members, departed from California headed to Washington, D.C. in time for the presidential elections. They called their journey "the Trail of Broken Treaties." Their goal was to deliver a "20-Point Proposal," which was a comprehensive list of reforms for federal Indian policy that were broad in scope, fair, easy to adopt, and philosophically sound. On the way to Washington, the caravan stopped at rural Indian reservations and urban Indian centers to increase its strength and to publicize its grievances. Once the group arrived in Washington, the now 800-person-strong caravan found the logistical planning flawed, and the Indian protesters, many of them children and older people, were left without housing. They seized the offices of the Bureau of Indian Affairs (BIA) and stayed a week. During the occupation, according to some historians, AIM protesters ransacked the building, and members absconded with important government records. Land allotment deed books and Indian claim records came up missing, each side blaming the other for the lost documents. To end the siege, President Richard Nixon is alleged to have paid AIM members $66,650 to leave the bureau premises and to help pay for the return trip.

TERM PAPER SUGGESTIONS

1. Write an essay on the "Trail of Broken Treaties," its purpose, and the outcome.
2. Study and respond to the "20-Point Proposal." What was its intent, and how feasible was the plan? Were the protesters looking for the plan to be adopted or for the public to become aware of Indian concerns, or both? How did the government respond to these demands?
3. What went wrong? Why the occupation of the BIA building? Was it planned, or was it a fortuitous accident?

4. The destruction of BIA property and the alleged theft of government documents caused some protesters to become disillusioned with AIM leadership and tactics. Why would these actions cause some to quit AIM and their militant actions?

5. Examine and write about negotiations with federal officials, particularly the office of the president. Did the presidential election that November influence the negotiations, the process, and the outcome?

6. Write on the symbolism of the "Trail of Broken Treaties." What historical event does it allude to and what does the title of protest imply? What about the term "Red Power"?

ALTERNATIVE TERM PAPER SUGGESTIONS

1. Create your own political slogans and phrases inspired by the ones found in the aftermath of the BIA occupation, protest literature, and the title, "Trail of Broken Treaties."

2. From the perspective of an elderly person on the caravan to Washington and the "Trail of Broken Treaties," write a two-week daily journal of your experiences.

SUGGESTED SOURCES

Primary Sources

Adams, Hank. "Trail of Broken Treaties: For Renewal of Contracts—Reconstruction of Indian Communities and Securing an Indian Future in America." http://www.cwis.org/fwdp/Americas/20points.html. The final draft of the so-called "20-Point Proposal" composed by Hank Adams from the accumulative efforts of caravan participants, Indian authors, tribal leaders, and others.

Burnette, Robert. *The Road to Wounded Knee.* New York: Bantam Books, 1974. A member of the National Council of American Indians and former chairman of the Rosebud Lakota details his experience on the "Trail of Broken Treaties."

"Declassified Government Records/Documents of AIM." http://www.aimovement.org/csi/index.html. A links page to hundreds of primary and secondary source records.

"Preamble to Trail of Broken Treaties." http://www.aimovement.org/ggc/trailofbrokentreaties.html. This version includes the preamble and other front matter along with the complete text of the "20-Point Position Paper."

"Trail of Broken Treaties 20-Point Position Paper." http://www.aimovement.org/ archives/index.html. The full text of the 1972 proposal as well as links to other pertinent sites.

Secondary Sources

Banks, Dennis, and Richard Erdoes. *Ojibwa Warrior: Dennis Banks and the Rise of the American Indian Movement.* Norman, OK: University of Oklahoma Press, 2005. Biography of one of the cofounders of AIM.

Deloria, Vine, Jr. *Behind the Trail of Broken Treaties: An Indian Declaration of Independence.* New York: Delacorte Press, 1974. Provides the background of the "Trail of Broken Treaties."

Johnson, Troy. *The American Indian Occupation of Alcatraz Island: Red Power and Self-Determination.* Lincoln, NE: University of Nebraska Press, 2008. A comprehensive exploration of the local, Bay Area, Indian social, and political reasons for the occupation.

Johnson, Troy R., et al, eds. *American Indian Activism.* Champaign, IL: University of Illinois Press, 1997. A collection of essays focused on the Indian occupation of Alcatraz Island to protest and symbolize Indian political and land issues.

Matthiessen, Peter. *In the Spirit of Crazy Horse.* New York: Penguin, 1992. Narrative history of AIM. The most famous account of AIM activities in the late 1960s through the 1970s.

Means, Russell. *Where White Men Fear to Tread: The Autobiography of Russell Means.* New York: St Marin's Griffin, 1996. The story of AIM through the words of one of its most famous and flamboyant leaders.

Nagel, Joane. *American Indian Ethnic Renewal: Red Power and the Resurgence of Identity and Culture.* New York: Oxford University Press, 1996. Traces the growth of the American Indian population over the past 40 years.

Smith, Paul Chaat, and Robert Allen Warrior. *Like a Hurricane: The Indian Movement from Alcatraz to Wounded Knee.* New York: The New Press, 1996. Two Indian scholars' narrative essay on Indian political activism from the 1960s to the present.

Trimbach, Joseph A. *American Indian Mafia.* Parker, CO: Outskirts Press, 2007. Condemns some of the leaders of AIM (not all leaders and not all AIM members) as exploitive and ruthless gangsters and criminals.

Wilkinson, Charles F. *Blood Struggle: The Rise of Modern Indian Nations.* New York: W.W. Norton, 2005. Celebrates the economic triumphs of Indian tribes since the Meriam Report and the Indian Reorganization Act.

World Wide Web

Lorenzen, Tony. "Trail of Broken Treaties." http://revtonylorenzen.com/ministersstudy/Sermons_files/trailofbrokentreaties.htm. A sermon preached before the First Parish Church about broken promises that contains references to the "Trail of Broken Treaties," a relevant and contemporary reading.

Potter, Maximillian. "Broken Treaties." http://www.5280.com/issues/2005/0510/feature.php?pageID=110. An article covering the Annie Mae Pictou Aquash murder and the "Trail of Broken Treaties" as part of the short journey of Aquash's life.

"Trail of Broken Treaties." http://www.answers.com/topic/trail-of-broken-treaties. Brief summary that includes a short bibliography.

"Trail of Broken Treaties Caravan." http://siouxme.com/lodge/treaties.html. An excellent brief essay describing the "Trail of Broken Treaties."

Trimble, Charles. "Trimble: Buy-Out on the Trail of Broken Treaties." http://www.indianz.com/News/2008/007157.asp. The transfer of money to AIM members is described by the person who actually signed and cashed the check, an Oglala Lakota and former executive director of the National Congress of American Indians; this is the man who brokered the deal between the federal government and AIM.

Multimedia Source

"Photo of the Trail of Broken Treaties, 1972." http://calmarezphoto.com/-/calmarezphoto/gallery.asp?cat=24043&pID=1&row=15&photoID=1577900&searchTerm=. Shows protesters taking the "20-Point Position Paper" to President Nixon.

90. Wounded Knee (1973)

On February 27, 1973, Wounded Knee, South Dakota, was taken over by armed members of the American Indian Movement (AIM), who seized the town to draw attention to broken treaties, the abuse of tribal governments who ignored their own people and cultural practices, and the failure of federal Indian policy. They wanted an end to the strip mining of Indian lands for uranium and coal; also, they demanded the honoring of Indian treaties and the return of the Black Hills to the Lakota. The place was symbolic because Wounded Knee was the site of the 1890 massacre of Big Foot's band of Ghost Dancers by elements of the Seventh Cavalry,

George Armstrong Custer's old regiment. The Indians who were killed at that massacre, including women and children, were buried in a mass grave near where the town of Wounded Knee would grow. When AIM members arrived in 1973, they seized the trading post and museum, the post office, and the Sacred Heart Catholic Church, among other buildings, and they prepared to resist until their demands were met or until they were killed. Soon, federal marshals, the FBI, and the National Guard arrived and surrounded Wounded Knee, and a 71-day standoff ensued. In the end, two Indians were killed and two federal agents were severely wounded, and the town of Wounded Knee was destroyed by the AIM protesters, never to be rebuilt. To this day, what actually took place is debated and disputed in print and in the media, and new evidence surfaces on a yearly basis to fan the flames of controversy and conspiracy.

TERM PAPER SUGGESTIONS

1. According to some experts, most of the militants were from tribes from all over the nation, and close to half of the participants were non-Indian. Investigate the validity of these claims and the significance of that demographic.

2. Investigate the AIM's allegations against Dick Wilson as a corrupt tribal chairman of the Oglala Sioux Nation. The major division was between assimilationists and traditionalists. Define and explain the differences between these two factions.

3. Study the militancy of the occupiers. Explore the power of activists who are willing to lay down their lives for their beliefs. How is this act of defiance an effective method of protest? Does a militant stand cause any long-term positive outcomes? Would it work today, after the declaration of war on terror?

4. Write an essay on the success of the takeover and the effect it had on the Indian youth of the day.

5. Explore the symbolism of the site, Wounded Knee, and the images of Indians with guns. Why would that spark the imagination of the worldwide public and generate serious consternation on the part of federal and state officials?

6. Explore the reactions and sentiments of the Wounded Knee townspeople to the takeover and the destruction of their homes and property.

ALTERNATIVE TERM PAPER SUGGESTIONS

1. By using Microsoft PowerPoint, create three multiple image scenes of Wounded Knee using data available on the World Wide Web in three time periods: Wounded Knee, 1890, Wounded Knee before the 1973 takeover, and Wounded Knee after the takeover.

2. Create a diagram and/or graph of the many Wounded Knee trials, where over a hundred cases were tried and most of the AIM defendants were not convicted. Show charges, dates, and convictions or dismissals in an effort to show the enormity of the legal issues involved in the aftermath of the takeover.

SUGGESTED SOURCES

Primary Sources

"AIM and Wounded Knee Documents." http://www.aics.org/WK/index.html. Links page to primary sources such as newsletters and other important internal documents.

"Declassified Government Records/Documents of AIM." http://www .aimovement.org/csi/index.html. A links page to hundreds of primary and secondary source records.

Secondary Sources

Banks, Dennis, and Richard Erdoes. *Ojibwa Warrior: Dennis Banks and the Rise of the American Indian Movement.* Norman, OK: University of Oklahoma Press, 2005. Biography of one of the cofounders of AIM.

Churchill, Ward, and Jim Vander Wall. *The COINTELPRO Papers: Documents from the FBI's Secret Wars against Dissent in the United States.* 2nd edition. Cambridge, MA: South End Press, 2001. Argues in part of the book that the federal government's Counter Intelligence Program, designed to investigate and disrupt dissident groups like the Black Panther Party, was used against AIM, though the government claims the program was disbanded in 1971.

Matthiessen, Peter. *In the Spirit of Crazy Horse.* New York: Penguin, 1992. Narrative history of AIM. The most famous account of AIM activities in the late 1960s through the 1970s.

Means, Russell. *Where White Men Fear to Tread: The Autobiography of Russell Means.* New York: St Marin's Griffin, 1996. The story of AIM through the words of one of its most famous and flamboyant leaders.

Milligan, Edward A. *Wounded Knee 1973 and the Fort Laramie Treaty of 1868.* Bottineau, ND: Published by the author, 1973. Indians of North America, 1973. Detailed explanation of Wounded Knee, 1973, in relation to the Fort Laramie Treaty of 1868.

Peltier, Leonard. *Prison Writings: My Life is My Sun Dance.* New York: St. Martin's Press, 1999. Writings from prison by the AIM leader convicted of killing Jack Coler and Ron Williams.

Reinhardt, Akim D. *Ruling Pine Ridge: Oglala Lakota Politics from the IRA to Wounded Knee.* Lubbock, TX: Texas Tech University Press, 2007. Explores the way Oglala tribal government operated and functioned under the Indian Reorganization Act and how the act diminished the power of traditional forms of government and culture.

Sayer, John W. *Ghost Dancing the Law: the Wounded Knee Trials.* Cambridge, MA: Harvard University Press, 2000. Examines in detail the Wounded Knee trials and demonstrates the impact that legal institutions and the media have on political dissent.

Smith, Paul Chaat, and Robert Allen Warrior. *Like a Hurricane: The Indian Movement from Alcatraz to Wounded Knee.* New York: The New Press, 1996. Two Indian scholars' narrative essay on the Indian political activism from the 1960s to the present.

Trimbach, Joseph A. *American Indian Mafia.* Parker, CO: Outskirts Press, 2007. A view from the FBI side of the takeover, which challenges most of the other books in this list as well as presenting a convincing, compelling counter argument.

Weyler, Rex. *Blood of the Land: The Government and Corporate War against the American Indian Movement.* New York: Everest House, 1982. Discusses the government's desire to destroy or neutralize the American Indian Movement.

World Wide Web

"AIM: Grand Governing Council." http://www.aimovement.org/. The home page of the American Indian Movement. Includes webcasts, multimedia archive, songs, speeches, and more.

American Indian Mafia. http://www.americanindianmafia.com/. The Web site for the book *American Indian Mafia,* which documents the murder of three FBI agents on the Pine Ridge Indian Reservation, the murder investigation, and the trials of AIM members involved.

"American Indian Movement." http://www.mnhs.org/library/tips/history_topics/93aim.html. Educational site aimed at students. Provides a brief overview and a list of secondary and primary sources with call numbers.

"Incident at Wounded Knee." http://www.usmarshals.gov/history/wounded-knee/index.html. Honors the service of U.S. Marshals at Wounded Knee and the experience they gained from that service.

Norrell, Brenda. "Gentle Rage: Clyde Bellecourt Remembers the Birth of the American Indian Movement." http://narcosphere.narconews.com/notebook/brenda-norrell/2008/08/gentle-rage-clyde-bellecourt-remembers-birth-american-indian-movemen. Interview of the famous AIM cofounder posted August 13, 2008.

Wittstock, Laura Waterman, and Elaine J. Salinas. "A Brief History of the American Indian Movement." http://www.aimovement.org/ggc/history.html. Self-explanatory.

"Wounded Knee Siege, 1973, AIM." http://siouxme.com/siege.html. Brief summary of the Wounded Knee occupation as well as an explanation of Oglala Indian concerns.

Multimedia Sources

"AIM Multimedia Archive, Video." http://www.streamreel.com/archives/aim/aim_video.htm. Many short and long video clips, interviews, speeches, and news footage.

Tattoo on My Heart: The Warriors of Wounded Knee 1973. Dir. Charles Abourezk and Brett Lawlor. Badlands Films, 2004. DVD. 59 minutes. A documentary that commemorates the 30th anniversary of the event from the perspective and words of the AIM members who participated in the occupation.

91. *United States v. Washington State* (Boldt Decision) (1974)

In 1974, the Washington State fish wars, as they were called, reached a climactic end when Judge George Hugo Boldt ruled that Indians of the state owned half of the harvestable salmon and that they should be co-managers of the state's fisheries. Before Boldt's decision, the state viewed Indian net fishing as lawless poaching and harmful to state-regulated sports and commercial fishing. The state challenged the right of Indians to fish and attempted to force them to follow state laws. In the 1960s and early 1970s, when the state outlawed net fishing and when the state government closed rivers running through Indian settlements to salmon fishing, the Indians began to exercise their right to fish in protests they called "fish-ins" in open defiance of state laws designed to destroy their fishery. The state responded with arrests and confiscation of boats, netting, and other fishing gear, and, if Indians resisted, with tear gas, handcuffs, and brute force. The 25 tribes of Washington remembered the 1854 treaties that took away most of their land, but they also knew that the treaties reserved the rights to fish and hunt, rights never relinquished in the land acquisition treaties. Indian protests were designed to publicize treaty rights and to force the federal authorities to intervene to protect Indian fishing in the state. The trial, *U.S. v. Washington State,* lasted three years, and after that time Judge Boldt reaffirmed Indian treaty rights. Boldt's decision, a decision upheld all the way to the Supreme Court, forced the state to recognize Indian fishing rights and mandated state cooperation.

TERM PAPER SUGGESTIONS

1. Explain Indian treaty fishing rights. Even in the relatively brief two-to-three-page treaties common to Washington, the right to fish was preserved. Why?
2. The key phrase in the treaty of Medicine Creek is: "Indians in common with all citizens of the Territory." Judge Boldt determined that "in common with" meant 50 percent for both sides. Explore how Judge Boldt came to his determination and interpretation and how they have fared as legal precedents.
3. Examine why Washington State wanted to regulate or even put an end to the tribal fishery.
4. Write an essay exploring the tactics of Washington Indians to exert their rights and force a trial. Some of the Indians, like Billy Frank, a Nisqually, were arrested. Frank was arrested 40 times and risked his life to stand up for his right to fish. What is a "fish-in"?
5. Washington state police and conservation personnel were accused of brutality and racism. Investigate the validity of these accusations.
6. Write a report on the current status of treaty fishing in the state of Washington. How have the tribes and the state worked together to solve and ameliorate past conflicts and disagreements? What are their joint plans to conserve and regulate the fisheries of the state?

ALTERNATIVE TERM PAPER SUGGESTIONS

1. Create a poster that celebrates the cooperation between Washington State and Indian tribes over the conservation and sustainability of the salmon fishery. Be sure to use a drawing or image of a salmon in the poster and be sure to write a catchy slogan.
2. Create an interactive map of the Columbian River basin to demonstrate the complexities of Indian fisheries that spill over into neighboring states and north into Canada.

SUGGESTED SOURCES

Primary Sources

"Boldt Decision." http://www.nwifc.org/aboutus/documents/BoldtDecision8.5x11layoutforweb.pdf. PDF version of the Boldt Decision: 11 chapters covering the background, the case, the treaties, and the final decision of Judge Boldt.

"Document: Boldt Decision." http://www.ccrh.org/comm/river/legal/boldt.htm. The online version of the decision; the site also has links on the left side of the page to other important primary source documents, most notably, a map of the "Columbian Basin Native Fishery."

"The Treaty of Medicine Creek." http://www.nwifc.org/tribes/documents/TreatyofMedicineCreek.pdf. PDF text of the Medicine Creek Treaty (three pages) that Judge Boldt used to make his decision.

Secondary Sources

Brown, Jovana J. "Treaty Rights: Twenty Years after the Boldt Decision." *Wicazo Sa Review* 10, no. 2 (Autumn 1994): 1–16. Explores the environmental decision making that tribes bring to fishing policy in the state of Washington.

Canby, William C., Jr. *American Indian Law in a Nutshell.* 1981. Reprint, St. Paul, MN: West, 2004. A book that answers simple questions, like "What is an Indian Tribe?" A good basic set of definitions.

Cohen, Fay G. *Treaties on Trial: The Continuing Controversy over Northwest Indian Fishing Rights.* Seattle, WA: University of Washington Press, 1986. Explores the ongoing struggle to enforce Indian treaty rights and the continual court battles challenging Indian treaty rights.

Dutha, N. Bruce, and Colin Calloway. *American Indians and the Law.* New York: Viking, 2008. Defines and clarifies sovereignty as it has applied to federally recognized tribes since 1787.

Hunn, Eugene. *Nch'i-Wāna, "the Big River": Mid-Columbian Indians and Their Land.* Seattle, WA: University of Washington, 1990. Documents the relation that Indians of the Columbian basin have with the land and the salmon.

Kruckeberg, Arthur R. *The Natural History of Puget Sound Country.* Seattle, WA: University of Washington Press, 1995. A history of Puget Sound Country and, partially, of Indian fishing rights. Includes many beautiful photographs and interesting historical facts.

Smith, Courtland L. *Salmon Fishers of the Columbia.* Corvallis, OR: Oregon State University Press, 1979. History of the fishery of the Columbia River that comments on the Indian fishery as well.

Wilkins, David E. *American Indian Politics and the American Political System.* 2nd edition. New York: Rowman and Littlefield, 2006. Tribal governmental history, structure, and powers.

Wilkins, David E. *Uneven Ground: American Indian Sovereignty and Federal Law.* Norman, OK: University of Oklahoma Press, 2001. Investigates the manner in which Indian sovereignty has eroded since the 1787 U.S. Constitution.

Wilkinson, Charles F. *Messages from Frank's Landing: A Story of Salmon, Treaties and the Indian Way.* One of the first complete works on Indian fishing rights in the state of Washington.

World Wide Web

Dodge, John. "Years after the Boldt Decision." http://www.citizenreviewonline.org/feb2004/years.htm. Examines how the Boldt Decision made friends out of enemies and built on their mutual desire to manage the Great Lakes fishery for the benefit of all.

"Federal Judge George Boldt Issues Historic Ruling Affirming Native American Treaty Fishing Rights on February 12, 1974." http://www.historylink.org/essays/output.cfm?file_id=5282. Brief summary of the Boldt Decision.

Kamb, Lewis. "Boldt Decision: 'Very Much Alive' 30 Years Later." http://seattlepi.nwsource.com/local/160345_boldt12.html. Summary of the issues, with photographs; has a very good summary of the Boldt Decision at the end of the essay.

"Northwest Indian Fisheries Commission." http://www.nwifc.org/swf/slideshow.asp. NWIFC serves the Treaty Indian Tribes in western Washington. Many articles and up-to-date issues on the tribes, salmon, and management.

Thompson, Lorrine. "Tribes Play Key Role in County's History." http://news.theolympian.com/specialsections/ThurstonCountySesqui/20020112/166882.shtml. *The Olympian,* 2002. Short history of the Indians of South Sound, Washington.

Tizon, Alex. "25 Years after the Boldt Decision: The Fish Tale that Changed History." http://kohary.com/env/bill_020799.html. The story of Billy Frank Nisqually Jr., who has been arrested 40 times in 30 years for exercising his right to fish guaranteed by treaty.

Woods, Fronda. "Who's in Charge of Fishing." http://www.historycooperative.org/journals/ohq/106.3/woods.html. An essay examining Indian fishing in the northwest from 1854 to 2005. Includes photographs and citations.

Multimedia Source

Lighting the Seventh Fire. Dir. Sandra Osawa. P.O.V., 1995. DVD. 48 minutes. Documents the treaty rights of Chippewa Indians in Wisconsin to spear fish in Lac De Flambeau and the racist backlash Indians suffered from local non-Indians.

92. Leonard Peltier and RESMURS (1975)

Of the hundreds of murders and murder convictions that occurred in the 1970s on the Pine Ridge Indian Reservation, South Dakota, the murders of Federal Bureau of Investigation (FBI) Special Agents Jack Coler and Ron Williams, and the subsequent conviction of American Indian Movement (AIM) member Leonard Peltier for those murders, will endure as the most famous. The murders of Special Agents Coler and Williams are often referenced as "RESMURS," which means "Reservation Murder Scene" but has become a dignified way of referring to the murders and subsequent investigation without mentioning the agents' names. To serve a warrant on an Indian named Jimmy Eagle, the two agents drove into the Jumping Bull Compound on Pine Ridge and immediately came under long-range rifle fire. They were soon wounded, and because they were armed with service revolvers with limited range, they fired only a few rounds in defense while taking hundreds. After they were wounded, forensic evidence shows they were executed at point-blank range. Peltier was later convicted of their murders, and despite evidence linking him to their murders, RESMURS and the following trials have made Peltier an international folk hero and political prisoner. Peltier and others claim that at the Jumping Bull shootout they were acting in self-defense and that they feared that they would all be killed by federal authorities and/or paramilitary units sent out to destroy AIM. Due to hundreds of years of historical precedence of such actions in U.S. history, the United States and the international public did not easily dismiss such claims as trivial or beyond the scope of federal action against dissident and recalcitrant Indian groups or tribes. Because of this history, Peltier has garnered a huge national and international following and support system that has financially helped his defense and appeals to this very day.

TERM PAPER SUGGESTIONS

1. Examine the militancy of AIM at the time of the shooting at the Jumping Bull Compound. Why did they have so many weapons? Were their intentions simply defensive?

2. Carefully examine and report on the forensic evidence offered by the federal authorities. What is the difference between firing pins and shell ejection mechanisms in the determination that a shell originated from one gun or another?

3. Examine how Peltier was able to build a following of people who were and are convinced of his innocence and believe he was wrongfully convicted. How did Peltier and his defense team manipulate the press and the sentiments of the public?

4. What is the defense case? Most of the histories, polemical writings, and newspaper coverage, to about 2005, presented a condemnation of the prosecution's case because they believed it to be flawed, biased, and possibly rigged. Even so, how do they justify the murder of two FBI special agents?

5. What is the prosecution's case? Why has their case prevailed through more appeals than any other conviction in the history of U.S. jurisprudence?

6. Many of the secondary sources are pro-Peltier. Examine why that stance is changing and shifting since President Bill Clinton considered and then denied a presidential pardon for Peltier? What new evidence, if any, has emerged and what has changed due to the Annie Mae murder investigation?

ALTERNATIVE TERM PAPER SUGGESTIONS

1. Create a hearing where pro and con supporters of Peltier have to present a 1,000-word argument urging the president of the United States to pardon or not to pardon him. As a group, discuss the merits of each case.

2. From a pro and/or con perspective create a poster advocating your position(s). Use bandwagon, authority, and emotional appeals in your use of slogans and images to convince an audience of the legitimacy of your stance.

SUGGESTED SOURCES

Primary Sources

"Declassified Government Records/Documents of AIM." http://www .aimovement.org/csi/index.html. A links page to hundreds of primary and secondary source records.

"Leonard Peltier Exposed—NIFIC Files/Articles." http://indiancountrynews.net /index.php?option=com_content&task=category&sectionid=10&id =29&Itemid=70. Indian country's number one newspaper has compiled photographs, court transcripts, interviews, articles, a time line, and hundreds of other primary and secondary sources on the Peltier story. On the left-hand side of the page are links to Annie Mae Pictou Aquash and Ray Robinson files that are pertinent to the entire scope of the Peltier case.

Secondary Sources

Banks, Dennis, and Richard Erdoes. *Ojibwa Warrior: Dennis Banks and the Rise of the American Indian Movement.* Norman, OK: University of Oklahoma Press, 2005. Biography of one of the cofounders of AIM.

Churchill, Ward, and Jim Vander Wall. *The COINTELPRO Papers: Documents from the FBI's Secret Wars against Dissent in the United States.* 2nd edition. Cambridge, MA: South End Press, 2001. Argues in part of the book that the federal government's Counter Intelligence Program, designed to investigate and disrupt dissident groups like the Black Panther Party, was used against AIM, though the government claims the program was disbanded in 1971.

Matthiessen, Peter. *In the Spirit of Crazy Horse.* New York: Penguin, 1992. Narrative history of AIM. The most famous account of AIM activities in the late 1960s through the 1970s and of the shootout at Jumping Bull.

Means, Russell. *Where White Men Fear to Tread: The Autobiography of Russell Means.* New York: St Marin's Griffin, 1996. The story of AIM through the words of one of its most famous and flamboyant leaders.

Messerschmidt, James W. *The Trial of Leonard Peltier.* Boston, MA: South End Press, 1983. This book describes the circumstances surrounding the arrest of the American Indian political activist Peltier, for the murders of two FBI agents, and discusses Peltier's trial and conviction.

Peltier, Leonard. *Prison Writings: My Life is My Sun Dance.* New York: St. Martin's Press, 1999. Writings from prison by the AIM leader convicted of killing Jack Coler and Ron Williams.

Sayer, John W. *Ghost Dancing the Law: The Wounded Knee Trials.* Cambridge, MA: Harvard University Press, 2000. Studies the Wounded Knee trials and demonstrates the impact that legal institutions and the media have on political dissent.

Smith, Paul Chaat, and Robert Allen Warrior. *Like a Hurricane: The Indian Movement from Alcatraz to Wounded Knee.* New York: The New Press, 1996. Two Indian scholars' narrative essay on the Indian political activism from the 1960s to the present.

Stern, Kenneth S. *Loud Hawk: The United States Versus the American Indian Movement.* Norman, OK: University of Oklahoma Press, 1994. Examines the 1975 arrest of Kenny Loud Hawk, Dennis Banks, Leonard Peltier, Annie Mae Pictou Aquash, Kamook Banks, and Russ Redner, as well as the following trials and appeals.

Trimbach, Joseph A. *American Indian Mafia.* Parker, CO: Outskirts Press, 2007. Documents the killing of Jack Coler and Ron Williams as a "mafia style" hit and a brutal, cold-blooded murder; disputes and counters most of the other texts listed in this bibliography.

Weyler, Rex. *Blood of the Land: The Government and Corporate War against the American Indian Movement.* New York: Everest House, 1982. The government's desire to destroy or neutralize the American Indian movement.

World Wide Web

"CNN Interview with Peltier." http://www.aics.org/LP/transcript.html. Text of a broadcast interview; has links to other sites. This source can be compared to a compilation of Peltier interviews found at the "No Parole Peltier" site listed below.

"Leonard Peltier Case Chronology." http://users.skynet.be/kola/lpchrono.htm. Chronology of Peltier's life before and during his incarceration.

"Leonard Peltier Defense Committee." http://www.leonardpeltier.net/. Defense site for Peltier that continues to proclaim that he is innocent and that he is a political prisoner.

"The Leonard Peltier Trial," *Famous Trials.* http://www.law.umkc.edu/faculty/projects/ftrials/peltier/peltiermaps.html. A complete site exploring both sides of the Peltier trial and controversy. Includes maps, chronology, and links to primary source materials and bibliography.

"No Parole Peltier Association." http://www.noparolepeltier.com/movie.html. A site collecting evidence to demonstrate that Peltier should not be paroled and that he was involved in the murder of Jack Coler and Ron Williams. The site contains video, audio, and other primary and secondary sources supporting their position.

"RESMURS Case, Minneapolis Division of the FBI." http://minneapolis.fbi.gov/history_peltier.htm. Presents facts and evidence, including photographs, compiled by FBI investigators.

Multimedia Source

Incident at Oglala. Dir. Michael Apted. Miramax Films, 1991. VHS. 90 minutes. Documentary of the defense side of the story, strongly disputed by the prosecution side (see Trimbach's book for balance).

93. Indian Self-Determination Act (1975)

To decrease the federal domination of Indian programs and to further the goal of tribal independence, Congress passed the Indian

Self-Determination and Education Assistance Act (ISDA) in 1975. In the congressional declaration of policy, the act recognizes: (1) the obligation of the United States to allow "maximum Indian participation" in federal services; (2) the commitment of the United States to maintain and continue its trust responsibility to Indian people and tribes; and (3) the need to ensure that the United States provides "the quantity and quality of educational services and opportunities" to Indian children. Indian self-determination in federal services, self-determination in planning and administration of those services, self-determination in tribal governance, and self-determination in Indian educational services mean a transfer of federal dominance to Indian tribal dominance in all matters of Indian affairs. Self-determination from the tribal perspective can be seen to entail self-rule, economic development, and cultural preservation. The ISDA and the goals of Indian tribes demanded greater Indian administration of Indian affairs and programs without destroying the trust relationship with the federal government and without tribes being terminated. Further, the logic of Indians running Indian affairs is that they would know how to tailor programs and services to meet the needs of their own people. However, the ISDA requires the approval of the secretary of the interior and other Indian bureaucracies for requests of Indian tribes to assume control of any federal service or program, which has often made the transition a difficult and complicated process.

TERM PAPER SUGGESTIONS

1. Study and report on the role of President Richard M. Nixon and the development of the ISDA. How did he initiate the policy by executive acts and statements?

2. Explain why Indians and Indian tribes need to be part of the development of policies designed to help them and why Indians need to staff, administer, and control those programs and services, like health care and economic development programs.

3. Although this is contradictory and at times in defiance of U.S. law, bureaucracies like the Bureau of Indian Affairs and the Indian Health Service have a preferential hiring policy to make sure that Indians are hired for all employment levels and categories. The ISDA made this a mandate. Why? How is this fair?

4. Explore the successful tactics and strategies that Indian tribes have used to take control of their own tribal governments through the laws enacted via the ISDA. What are the unsuccessful strategies?

5. A good example of Indian self-determination is in the area of Indian education. Here the needs of the Indian community have been to educate Indian

children without destroying their connection to their culture and traditions. How have tribes accomplished this goal? How have they failed?

6. Examine the economic activities of tribes that have enabled some of them to become economically self-sufficient.

ALTERNATIVE TERM PAPER SUGGESTIONS

1. As an Indian educator, design a history lesson of the First Thanksgiving where the culture of the Indians is respected and not stereotyped.

2. As an Indian educator, prepare a short pamphlet on the manner in which any teacher should approach Indian learners in their classrooms. One example from the sources is never to make an Indian student in your classroom an expert on all Indian historical, cultural, or social experiences. Provide reasons for such cautions.

SUGGESTED SOURCES

Primary Sources

"Presidential Policies on Indian Self-Determination and Self-Government." http://www.oneidaindiannation.com/about/sovereignty/26287779. html. Interesting collection of presidential comments, statements, and speeches on the Indian Self-Determination and Education Assistance Act.

"US Code: Title 25, Subchapter II—Indian Self-Determination and Education Assistance." http://www.law.cornell.edu/uscode/html/uscode25/usc_sup_01_25_10_14_20_II.html. Full text of the law with appendices.

Secondary Sources

Anderson, Terry, et al. *Self-Determination: The Other Path for Native Americans.* Stanford, CA: Stanford University Press, 2006. A collection of essays exploring property rights and economics as a "path" to self-determination.

Castile, George Pierre. *Taking Charge: Native American Self-Determination and Federal Indian Policy, 1975–1993.* Tucson, AZ: University of Arizona Press, 2006. An examination of the efforts or lack thereof of Presidents Carter, Reagan, and Bush to continue the policies of the ISDA enacted during President Nixon's term in office.

Harvard Project on American Indian Economic Development. *The State of the Native Nations: Conditions under U.S. Policies of Self-Determination.* New York: Oxford University Press, 2008. Comprehensive collection of essays examining the current state of Indian nations and their efforts at self-determination, despite the continuance of dominant U.S. policies.

Lyons, Oren. *Rebuilding Native Nations: Strategies for Governance and Development.* Tucson, AZ: University of Arizona Press, 2007. An anthology of reports, analyses, tactics, and strategies of how tribes have worked to rebuild their nations without destroying their cultures.

Oppelt, Norman T. *The Tribally Controlled Indian Colleges: The Beginnings of Self-Determination in American Indian Education.* Tsaile, AZ: Navajo Community College Press, 1990. Examines the rise of tribally administered colleges and universities.

Senese, Guy B. *Self-Determination and the Social Education of Native Americans.* New York: Praeger, 1991. A discussion of the strategies tribes have used to take control of the economic, governing, educational, and social infrastructure of Indian communities.

Szasz, Margaret. *Education and the American Indian: The Road to Self-Determination, 1928–1973.* Albuquerque, NM: University of New Mexico Press, 1974. A complete history of federal Indian policy from the Meriam Report to the eve of the passage of the ISDA.

Wilkins, David E. *American Indian Politics and the American Political System.* 2nd edition. New York: Rowman and Littlefield, 2006. Tribal governmental history, structure, and powers.

Wilkins, David E. *Uneven Ground: American Indian Sovereignty and Federal Law.* Norman, OK: University of Oklahoma Press, 2001. Places the ISDA within a larger context of struggle for sovereignty under the restriction imposed by federal law.

Wilkinson, Charles F. *Blood Struggle: The Rise of Modern Indian Nations.* New York: W.W. Norton & Company, 2005. Celebrates the economic triumphs of Indian tribes since the Meriam Report, the Indian Reorganization Act, and the rise of Indian self-determination.

World Wide Web

Adams, David. "A Case Study: Self-Determination and Indian Education." http://jaie.asu.edu/v13/V13S2sel.html. Argues for more Indian control of the education of Indians to reflect traditional cultural values and to be responsive to the needs of the Indian community.

"American Indian Education." http://jan.ucc.nau.edu/~jar/IndianLinks.html. A links page to all manner of educational issues as they pertains to Indian youth and the teaching of Indian youth, a major component of the ISDA.

Cook, Samuel R. "What Is Indian Self-Determination?" http://faculty.smu.edu/twalker/samrcook.htm. Argues that the ISDA is a tool to achieve greater sovereignty by Indian tribes and that tribes should be more influential in all stages of policy making, the writing as well as the implementation.

"Indian Self-Determination Assistance." http://www.fedmoney.com/grants/ su0134.htm. Gives a good idea of the federal moneys available to Indian tribes pursuing self-determination.

"Self-Determination and Self-Governance Practice." http://www.sonosky.com/ practice-profile-14.html. A law firm's explanation of the ISDA and its practice within the Indian community.

Multimedia Source

Tribal Nations: The Story of Federal Indian Law. Dir. Lisa Jaeger. Tanana Chiefs, 2006. DVD. 60 minutes. Illustrated introductory-level documentary of how federal Indian policy has developed in the United States.

94. Murder of Annie Mae Pictou Aquash (1976)

The most disturbing news to emerge from Indian country was the murder of Indian activist Annie Mae Pictou Aquash in 1976. Aquash was a Mi'kmaq from Nova Scotia, born in 1945 in a small Indian village. After many years working as an activist in Boston, she joined the American Indian Movement (AIM) and participated in many protest activities, like the "Trail of Broken Treaties." On February 24, 1976, Aquash was discovered dead on the Pine Ridge Reservation in South Dakota. Because her frozen body was found weeks after her death, the initial autopsy report concluded that she died from exposure, while another, more careful examination discovered evidence of homicide. This discrepancy generated theories of a government cover-up and involvement in her death. On March 20, 2003, almost 30 years after her murder, Arlo Looking Cloud and John Graham were indicted. Looking Cloud was found guilty of first-degree murder and was sentenced to life in prison. After an intense legal battle, the Supreme Court of British Columbia ordered the extradition, and Graham stood trial in the fall of 2008. On August 28, 2008, a third man, Dick Marshall, was indicted in connection with Aquash's murder. Surprising to many was that all three men were active AIM members and that they killed Aquash, allegedly, at the orders of prominent AIM leaders because they believed her to be an FBI informant. Witnesses at the Looking Cloud trial testified that Graham shot Aquash in the head as she was praying and begging for her life.

TERM PAPER SUGGESTIONS

1. Write a report on the positive outcomes of Aquash's political activism. What were her goals and aspirations? What did she hope to accomplish? What did she accomplish? Was she a militant, and if so, why?

2. Explore how people have exploited the murder of Aquash as a way of supporting political, emotional, or even economical agendas.

3. Examine the role of women in AIM. Many have claimed that the movement was male-dominated and abusive toward women. In light of new evidence of her murder that has hinted that she may have been bound and raped before AIM soldiers murdered her, these allegations need explication.

4. Most people know that AIM as a whole has accomplished many positive reforms for Indian reservations and urban Indian centers. Do these accomplishments mean that the horrific murder of Aquash or the negative underbelly of AIM should be ignored in favor of their positive contributions?

5. Examine and report on the trials of those accused of murder or conspiracy to murder Aquash. How has AIM responded to the trials? When called to testify, what have its members said?

6. Write an essay on the efforts of many, including Aquash's two daughters, to seek justice for Aquash and to reveal to others the truth of her murder.

ALTERNATIVE TERM PAPER SUGGESTIONS

1. Write a poem about Aquash where you attempt to capture her strength and enthusiasm, not to mention her ability to move others to action.

2. Imagine you are Annie Mae and record a statement you would believe she would like a jury to hear.

SUGGESTED SOURCES

Primary Sources

"Aquash—NIFIC Files/Articles." http://indiancountrynews.net/index.php? option=com_content&task=view&id=14&Itemid=58. Indian country's number one newspaper has compiled photographs, court transcripts, interviews, articles, a time line, and hundreds of other primary and secondary sources on the murder.

"Look Here." http://www.jfamr.org/doc/. This site tries to include as much information as possible about the Annie Mae murder investigation and trials. Interviews and court testimonies are included.

Secondary Sources

Banks, Dennis, and Richard Erdoes. *Ojibwa Warrior: Dennis Banks and the Rise of the American Indian Movement.* Norman, OK: University of Oklahoma Press. 2005. Biography of one of the cofounders of AIM who denies involvement in the Aquash murder.

Brand, Johanna. *The Life and Death of Anna Mae Aquash.* Toronto, ON, Canada: James Lorimer and Company, 1978. Reprint, 1993. Early account of the activities and murder of Aquash that suggests the FBI had something to do with her murder.

Claypole, Antoinette Nora. *Who Would Unbraid Her Hair: The Legend of Annie Mae.* Ashland, OR: Anam Press West, 1999. Fictional account of Aquash told from a mixed-genre format of poetry, story, and first-person narrative.

Matthiessen, Peter. *In the Spirit of Crazy Horse.* New York: Penguin, 1992. Narrative history of AIM. The most famous account of AIM activities in the late 1960s through the 1970s. Covers Aquash and her murder as an FBI cover-up and conspiracy.

Means, Russell. *Where White Men Fear to Tread: The Autobiography of Russell Means.* New York: St. Marin's Griffin, 1996. The story of AIM through the words of one of its most famous and flamboyant leaders.

Nolan, Yvette. *Annie Mae's Movement.* Toronto: Playwrights Canada Press, 2007. A play that tells Aquash's story from her perspective as a woman in the male-dominated AIM.

Peltier, Leonard. *Prison Writings: My Life is My Sun Dance.* New York: St. Martin's Press, 1999. Writings from prison by the AIM leader convicted of killing Jack Coler and Ron Williams.

Stern, Kenneth S. *Loud Hawk: The United States Versus the American Indian Movement.* Norman, OK: University of Oklahoma Press, 1994. Examines the 1975 arrest of Indian activists Kenny Loud Hawk, Dennis Banks, Leonard Peltier, Annie Mae Pictou Aquash, Kamook Banks, and Russ Redner, as well as the following trials and appeals.

Trimbach, Joseph A. *American Indian Mafia.* Parker, CO: Outskirts Press, 2007. Thoroughly examines Aquash's murder as a cold-blooded assassination carried out by AIM members at the orders of AIM leadership.

Weyler, Rex. *Blood of the Land: The Government and Corporate War against the American Indian Movement.* New York: Everest House, 1982. The government's desire to destroy or neutralize the American Indian Movement.

World Wide Web

Giago, Tim. "AIM Responsible for Anna Mae's Death." http://www.discoverthenetworks.org/Articles/AIM%20Responsible%20for%20Anna%20Maes%20Death.html. A report from one of Indian country's most famous newspaper editors and journalists on the connection between AIM and the murder of Annie Mae Aquash.

"Indigenous Women for Justice" http://indigenouswomenforjustice.org/. An Aquash support site with many links to primary sources that demand justice for Indian women, as well as a site that reveals that the male-dominated American Indian Movement had little regard or respect for native women.

"Justice for Anna Mae and Ray." http://www.jfamr.org/. A site with links to primary and secondary source material on the murders of Aquash and Ray Robinson Jr., a black civil rights worker believed to have been killed at Wounded Knee in 1973.

"Our Freedom." http://ourfreedom.wordpress.com/. An up-to-date "defense" blog for John Graham, Arlo Looking Cloud, and Leonard Peltier.

Potter, Maximillian. "Broken Treaties." http://www.5280.com/issues/2005/0510/feature.php?pageID=110. A 2004 article detailing the role of Arlo Looking Cloud in the murder of Aquash.

Walker, Carson. "3rd Charged in '75 American Indian Movement Death." http://www.newsvine.com/_news/2008/08/26/1788917-3rd-charged-in-75-american-indian-movement-death. On August 28, 2008, a third man, Dick Marshall, was indicted in connection with Aquash's murder.

Multimedia Sources

Joy Harjo and Poetic Justice. "For Anna Mae Pictou Aquash." *Letter from the End of the Twentieth Century.* Mekko Productions, 1997. MP3. 4:12 minutes. Poetic song about the life and death of Aquash.

The Spirit of Annie Mae. Dir. Catherine Anne Martin. NFB, 2002. DVD. 72 minutes. A biography of the life and death of Aquash.

95. American Indian Religious Freedom Act (AIRFA) (1978)

In 1978, President Jimmy Carter signed into law the American Indian Religious Freedom Act (AIRFA), a joint resolution of Congress. In part, the act proclaims:

> Henceforth it shall be the policy of the United States to protect and preserve for American Indians their inherent right of freedom to believe, express, and exercise the traditional religions of the American Indian, Eskimo, Aleut, and Native Hawaiians, including but not limited to access to sites, use and

possession of sacred objects, and the freedom to worship through ceremonials and traditional rites.

The Congress further admitted that the United States and the Constitution had not protected the religious freedom of American Indians, and they acknowledged that federal assimilation and Americanization policies of the 1880s to the 1930s outlawed and attempted to eradicate American Indian religions and religious practices such as the Lakota Sun Dance. Despite these federal efforts, American Indian religions survived, and the AIRFA was designed to not only remedy the historic suppression of Indian religion but to protect the Indians' right of religious freedom that the U.S. Constitution failed to protect. Overall, the AIRFA has helped the resurgence and rekindling of American Indian rituals and practices throughout the nation, but problems have surfaced and continue to plague Indian religious freedoms. One area was the American Indian use of peyote (a small spineless cactus found in southwestern Texas that has psychoactive alkaloids and is used by Indians for religious purposes), and a special amendment to the AIRFA was passed in 1994 to remedy that challenge. In the early 2000s, the concern has been the failure of AIRFA to protect sacred sites and access by Indians to those sacred sites for religious purposes.

TERM PAPER SUGGESTIONS

1. From 1880 to well into the 1900s, Indian cultural practices, such as the long hair of males, were suppressed. Explore historic policies that suppressed the Indians' religious and cultural practices.
2. Certain practices, like the Lakota Sun Dance, required the piercing of skin, fasting, and going without water for several days. Why would federal authorities outlaw such practices? Why would they imprison Indians for practicing their religion? What effect would that have on the future generations?
3. Write an essay on how the outlawing of religious practices, like the use of peyote and fasting, is counter to rights and privileges protected by the U.S. Constitution and the Bill of Rights.
4. Examine the traditional religious practices that have not returned, such as certain Indian funereal practices. Compare them to what has returned, especially the return of some of the Indian women's religious practices.
5. Write an essay on the right to use "sacred objects" like buffalo skulls, or other natural and sacred objects, like plant material.
6. Examine the issues of sacred sites and the AIRFA. Some people complain that the AIRFA does not protect their access to sacred lands.

ALTERNATIVE TERM PAPER SUGGESTIONS

1. Using Google Earth, identify and mark at least seven Indian sacred sites in the United States and share them with supporting data of why these particular sites are sacred.

2. Create a photo album of Indian sacred objects found in museums. Many can be found via visits to museum Web sites and browsing their online galleries or by Google search. The goal of compiling a Microsoft PowerPoint or other software album of such images is to ask who owns Indian culture and religious artifacts.

SUGGESTED SOURCES

Primary Sources

"American Indian Religious Freedom Act." [Public Law 95-341 (96 Stat. 469)]. 95th Congress. PDF found at http://www.cr.nps.gov/local-law/FHPL _IndianRelFreAct.pdf. An online version of the act is found at http://www .dlncoalition.org/related_issues/religious_issues.htm. Recognizes the religious freedom of American Indians.

"American Indian Religious Freedom Act Amendments of 1994." [Public Law 103-344 (108 Stat. 3124)]. 103rd Congress. http://www.lectlaw.com/ files/drg25.htm. Makes peyote legal for Indians to use for ceremonial purposes.

Cousineau, Phil, ed. *A Seat at the Table: Hudson Smith in Conversation on Religious Freedom.* Berkeley, CA: University of California Press, 2006. Text of interviews with 11 American Indian religious leaders and scholars on American Indian religious freedoms.

"President Jimmy Carter's Statement on AIRFA." http://www.presidency.ucsb.edu/ ws/index.php?pid=31173. Brief presidential comment on the signing of the American Indian Religious Freedom Act into law.

Secondary Sources

Brown, Brian Edward. *Religion, Law and the Land: Native Americans and the Judicial Interpretation of Sacred Land.* Westport, CT: Greenwood Press, 1999. Examines five court cases involving sacred Indian lands, with arguments, responses, decisions, and appeals.

Deloria, Vine, Jr. *God is Red.* New York: Grosset and Dunlap, 1973. Reprint, 30th anniversary edition, Golden, CO: Fulcrum, 2003. General book on Indian religions and the struggle of Indians to practice their traditional religions.

Echo-Hawk, Walter, et al. "Issues in the Implementation of the American Indian Religious Freedom Act." *Wicazo Sa Review* 19, no. 2 (Autumn 2004): 153–67. A panel discussion from a variety of American Indian perspectives.

Gulliford, Andrew. *Sacred Objects and Sacred Places: Preserving Tribal Traditions.* Boulder, CO: University Press of Colorado, 2000. A combination of oral stories, photographs, drawings, and case studies exploring the right of Indians to practice religion with certain objects and in specific places.

Harjo, Suzan Shown. "American Indian Religious Freedom Act after Twenty-Five Years." *Wicazo Sa Review* 19, no. 2 (Autumn 2004): 129–36. Analyzes the successes and the areas in need of improvement concerning the AIRFA.

Long, Carolyn N. *Religious Freedom and Indian Rights: The Case of Oregon v. Smith.* Lawrence, KS: University Press of Kansas, 2000. Detailed analysis of the Supreme Court case and the use of peyote in American Indian religious ceremonies.

Markstrom, Carol A. *Empowerment of North American Indian Girls: Ritual Expressions at Puberty.* Lincoln, NE: University of Nebraska Press, 2008. An anthropological examination of ritual practices reemerging and being reinstituted in Indian communities due, in part, to the AIRFA.

Michaelsen, Robert S. "The Significance of the American Indian Religious Freedom Act of 1978." *Journal of the American Academy of Religion* 52, no. 1 (March 1984): 93–115. Explores the significance of the AIRFA of 1978, with special attention to its implications and legal complexities.

Nabokov, Peter. *Where the Lightning Strikes: The Lives of American Indian Sacred Places.* New York: Viking Adult, 2006. Descriptive narrative of 16 sacred places and why they are sacred to American Indians.

Vecsey, Christopher, ed. *Handbook of American Indian Religious Freedom.* New York: Crossroad, 1991. A collection of essays on areas of legal struggle for American Indians as they pertain to Indian religious freedom.

Wunder, John R, ed. *Native American Cultural and Religious Freedoms.* New York: Routledge, 1996. An anthology of essays covering traditional hairstyles, the bald eagle, the sacred use of public lands, and general essays on American Indian religious rights.

World Wide Web

"American Indian Religious Freedom Act." http://www.answers.com/topic/american-indian-religious-freedom-act. General description of the law, effects, and criticisms.

"Environmental Justice Case Study: The Struggle for Religious Freedom in Bear Butte State Park, South Dakota." http://www.umich.edu/~snre492/perrin.html. A site demanding unlimited access of Lakota Indians to Bear Butte for religious uses and practices.

"Indian Religious Freedom, to Litigate or Legislate?" http://www.loc.gov/today/
cyberlc/feature_wdesc.php?rec=4245. Sixty-five-minute law panel web-
cast discussion of Indian religious freedom, especially in the debate over
the protection of American Indian sacred sites.

McNally, Michael D. "Native American Religious and Cultural Freedom: An
Introductory Essay." http://www.pluralism.org/research/profiles/
display.php?profile=73332. A complete overview of AIRFA that reviews
the history of American Indian religious freedoms. Includes a time line
and a list of pertinent court cases.

"Protecting Religious Freedom and Sacred Sites." http://www.fcnl.org/issues/
item.php?item_id=1475&issue_id=96. Reviews legal protection of religious practices of American Indians and discusses the vulnerability of
American Indian sacred sites.

Ruvolo, David. "A Summary of Native American Religions." http://
are.as.wvu.edu/ruvolo.htm. Reviews the religious belief system and religious practices of American Indians.

Multimedia Sources

In the Light of the Reverence: Protecting American Sacred Lands. Dir. Christopher
McLeod. Sacred Land Film Project, 2003. DVD. 72 minutes. A docu-
mentary that explores the sacredness of American places, including the
Black Hills, and the efforts of some to protect and preserve them.

The Peyote Road. Dir. Phil Cousineau et al. Kifaru Productions, 1993. VHS.
59 minutes. Examines historical intolerance toward American Indian
religious practices, documents the use of peyote over hundreds of years,
and details the legal and political issues.

96. Indian Child Welfare Act (1978)

Because state agencies were frequently and improperly removing children
from Indian families due to misunderstanding or prejudice against Indian
culture and family practices, the Indian Child Welfare Act (ICWA) was
passed in 1978 to return to tribal authority the adoption or placement
in foster care of Indian children. By 1978, the rate of children being
removed by state agencies was so detrimental to the stability and longevity
of Indian families that a law that took precedence over state and local
adoption laws became necessary. The act recognizes that Indian tribes
have a vested interest in considering the importance of tribal culture and

heritage as a part of the decision to place children into foster care, which is in stark contrast to removing children from Indian families to be raised in non-Indian communities. The ICWA gives Indian tribes the right to control adoptions that involve tribal members, the children of tribal members, and individuals who could become tribal members. The ICWA regulates "placement proceedings" that apply to any child in a protective case, an adoption, a guardianship, a termination of parental rights, a runaway or truancy matter, or voluntary placement to be heard in tribal courts if possible or to be represented by ICWA authorities if not. ICWA has not solved the complexities of adoption and placement but has worked to shift the emphasis to tribal authority. However, in several court rulings Indian children were removed despite tribal intervention and objections because the tribe intervened "too late," which limits the authority of the ICWA in certain situations.

TERM PAPER SUGGESTIONS

1. Examine the economic incentives of state agencies and agents to be involved in Indian adoption and placement, a major bone of contention between states and tribes.

2. Explore the history of assimilation and Americanization policies that promoted the separation of Indian children from tribal communities and families.

3. Write a report on the reasons state authorities would remove Indian children from Indian families and communities. What was the justification for their actions?

4. Write an analysis of the successes of the ICWA. Has the act met its goals and intent?

5. Explore the shortcomings of the act and the setbacks that recent court rulings have had on the effectiveness and power of the act.

6. Investigate and report on the stories of Indian people about the effectiveness of the ICWA. How do ordinary Indian people assess the effectiveness of the act?

ALTERNATIVE TERM PAPER SUGGESTIONS

1. Create a newsletter that explains the ICWA to Indian people in a concise but easy-to-understand manner. The newsletter should be a one-page, colorful, and appealing informational package.

2. From the perspective of an Indian tribe, create an interactive time line of the inappropriate taking of Indian children from your tribe as a way of convincing the federal government to return authority to your tribal government over adoption and placement of Indian children.

SUGGESTED SOURCES

Primary Sources

"Indian Child Welfare Act of 1978" (25 U.S.C. §§ 1901–63). http://www.tribal-institute.org/lists/chapter21_icwa.htm. Full text of the act.

National Indian Child Welfare Association. http://www.nicwa.org/law/. A links page for all "existing law" pertaining to the act as well as the full text of the act in PDF format.

Secondary Sources

A Practical Guide to the Indian Child Welfare Act. Boulder, CO: Native American Rights Fund, 2007. Rules, laws, and procedures for child welfare workers.

Babb, L. Anne. *Ethics in American Adoptions.* Westport, CT: Bergin and Gravey, 1999. A general discussion of ethics and adoptions that covers the Indian Child Welfare Act.

Dutha, N. Bruce, and Colin Calloway. *American Indians and the Law.* New York: Viking, 2008. Defines and clarifies sovereignty as it applies to federally recognized tribes since 1787, with a section on the Indian Child Welfare Act.

Garner, Suzanne. "The Indian Child Welfare Act: A Review." *Wicazo Sa Review* 9, no. 1 (Spring 1993): 47–51. A retrospective of the impact of the ICWA on Indian communities and children.

Johnson, Troy R. *Indian Child Welfare Act.* Los Angeles, CA: American Indian Studies Center, 1993. Conference proceedings.

Jones, B. J. *The Indian Child Welfare Act Handbook: A Legal Guide to the Custody and Adoption of Native American Children.* 2nd edition. Chicago, IL: American Bar Association, 2008. An hands-on guide that is very useful to researchers.

Wilkins, David E. *American Indian Politics and the American Political System.* 2nd edition. New York: Rowman and Littlefield, 2006. Tribal governmental history, structure, and powers.

Wilkinson, Charles F. *Blood Struggle: The Rise of Modern Indian Nations.* New York: W.W. Norton & Company, 2005. Celebrates the economic triumphs of Indian tribes since the Meriam Report and the Indian Reorganization Act.

World Wide Web

ICWA. http://www.answers.com/topic/indian-child-welfare-act-1. Brief overview and simple summary of the act.

"Implementing the Indian Child Welfare Act of 1978." http://ssw.unc.edu/fcrp/ Cspn/vol11_no2/icwa.htm. An article from 2006 that is a how-to manual for implementing the ICWA. Contains a list of "10 Tips for Collaborating with Tribes," which is very informative of the perspective of a state agency.

"The Indian Child Welfare Act Fact Sheet." http://www.oregon.gov/DHS/ children/icwa.shtml. A bulleted list of facts about the ICWA as they apply to the state of Oregon.

Jones, B. J. "The Indian Child Welfare Act: The Need for a Separate Law." http://www.abanet.org/genpractice/magazine/1995/fall/ indianchildwelfareact.html. A detailed essay explaining the complexities of the ICWA.

Thoma, Rick. "Under Siege: The Indian Child Welfare Act." http://www .liftingtheveil.org/icwa.htm. A 2006 essay that argues that the ICWA is not as powerful a law as once thought.

"The Voices of Zak's Aunt and Uncle." http://ssw.unc.edu/fcrp/Cspn/ vol11_no2/zak.htm. Firsthand account of an Indian family experiencing the ICWA process.

Wilkins, Andrea. "The Indian Child Welfare Act and the States." http://www .ncsl.org/programs/statetribe/icwa.htm. A 2004 essay surveying the ICWA and enforcement problems in particular states.

Multimedia Source

Self-Esteem for Native American Students. Tell Me Why Sales Co., 1998. VHS. 20 minutes. Tells the story of how important cultural traditions and connection to ancestry are to the self-esteem of American Indian children.

97. *United States v. Michigan* (Fox Decision) (1979)

In the 1836 treaty of Washington, Michigan claimed that Indian tribes relinquished their rights to hunt and fish outside of state regulations, and therefore Michigan contested the rights of Indians to fish the Great Lakes. Beginning in the early 1970s and by citing the 1836 Treaty of Washington between the United States and Michigan Indians, the state of Michigan claimed that Michigan Indian tribes had, by signing the treaty, relinquished their rights to hunt and fish outside of state regulations. The state contested the rights of Michigan Indians to fish the Great

Lakes and the Michigan Indians fought back by filing a lawsuit against the state. The court found that Indians "have continuously exercised Indian fishing rights since the 1836 Treaty without abandonment" and that the reserved rights of fishing are guaranteed by this and other treaties. More significantly, Judge Noel Fox emphasized that a "treaty was not a grant of rights to the Indians, but a grant of rights from them," which is a very important distinction to the understanding that Indians retained fishing and hunting rights, rights that were not given but kept. This has become a key definition of "reserved rights." Further, Indians had engaged in commercial fishing in terms of trade and certainly in their sale of fish to the American Fur Company before 1830, which predated the treaties of the 1830s and after. This became an important point of contention for Michigan, which argued that Indian traditional practices were void of "commercial" interests beyond subsistence. Despite the state's contentions, Judge Fox ruled that the treaty of 1836 did not in any way relinquish Indian fishing rights and that in fact Indians "reserved" this right so as to sustain and perpetuate their tribe and culture.

TERM PAPER SUGGESTIONS

1. Judge Fox examines carefully the history of the aboriginal rights of Indians of Michigan in his thorough and detailed review of the history of American Indian law. Why must he be so complete and thorough? How does his completeness prevent criticism and reversal?

2. Examine and report on the concept of "reserved rights." What were Judge Fox's unique findings that have become very important precedents for future cases?

3. Write an essay explicating the case presented by the state of Michigan. Why would Michigan want to limit and/or eradicate Indian rights, treaty or otherwise, within the state?

4. Michigan wanted to outlaw the use of gill nets by Indians, even though other states, like Wisconsin, allowed their own licensed fishermen to use gill nets. Why the challenge? What purpose would it serve?

5. Explore the racism involved when the rights of Indians to hunt and fish outside state regulations become publicized. Examine the effect that slogans such as "Spear an Indian, Save a Fish," which even appeared on bumper stickers, would have on Indian children.

6. Do all Indians within a state have the right to fish? Do Indian tribes have their own licensing laws and regulations? Do Indians overfish or deplete the lakes of

fish more than other fishing activities, commercial and sport? Use answers to these questions as a foundation for countering stereotypes and misinformation about Indian fishing in the state.

ALTERNATIVE TERM PAPER SUGGESTIONS

1. Using maps of the Great Lakes and Adobe Photoshop or other software, color-code the zones of the Michigan Indian fisheries of the Great Lakes.
2. Using photographs available from the sources and/or books, create a slide show of the fish Michigan Indians catch as their main "cash crop."

SUGGESTED SOURCES

Primary Sources

"Native American Treaties: Their Ongoing Importance to Michigan Residents." http://clarke.cmich.edu/nativeamericans/treatyrights/treatyintro.htm. Comprehensive primary source site with complete texts of Michigan Indian treaties, as well as links to a very complete section on the Michigan fishing rights issue.

"Treaty of Washington, 1836." http://clarke.cmich.edu/nativeamericans/treatyrights/washington1836.htm. Provides all articles of the Treaty of Washington.

"*U.S. v. Michigan,* 1979." http://www.1836cora.org/pdf/usvmichiganfox1979.pdf. PDF of the entire text of Judge Fox's decision. Includes a historical foundation for his opinion and many interesting supporting explanatory details.

Secondary Sources

Cleland, Charles. *Rites of Conquest: The History and Culture of Michigan's Native Americans.* Ann Arbor, MI: University of Michigan Press, 1992. General and comprehensive history that includes a discussion of Indian fishing rights.

Connors, Paul, G. *Michigan Indian Fishing Rights Controversy.* Lansing: Michigan Legislative Research Division, 1999. This is a research report about Michigan Indian fishing rights.

Doherty, Robert. "Old-Time Origins of Modern Sovereignty: State-Building among the Keweenaw Bay Ojibway, 1832–1854." *The American Indian Quarterly* 31, no. 1 (Winter 2007): 165–87. An essay that links the activities of Jondreau's elders to tribal sovereignty and reserved rights.

LeBeau, Patrick Russell. *Rethinking Michigan Indian History.* East Lansing, MI: Michigan State University Press, 2005. Maps and discussions of treaty rights, including fishing rights, explore the sovereignty of Michigan Indians.

McClurken, James, and Charles Cleland, eds. *Fish in the Lakes, Wild Rice, and Game in Abundance: Testimony on Behalf of Mille Lacs Ojibwe Hunting and Fishing Rights.* East Lansing, MI: Michigan State University Press, 2000. Six scholars' expert testimony on Indian fishing and hunting rights in the Great Lakes region.

Pittman, Philip M., and George M. Covington. *Don't Blame the Treaties: Native American Rights and the Michigan Indian Treaties.* West Bloomfield, MI: Northmont, 1992. Full account of Michigan Indian treaty rights with maps.

Satz, Ronald N. *Chippewa Treaty Rights.* Madison, WI: Wisconsin Academy of Sciences, Arts, and Letters, 1991. A detailed history of the struggle of Chippewa people to exercise their treaty rights.

Wilkins, David E. *Uneven Ground: American Indian Sovereignty and Federal Law.* Norman, OK: University of Oklahoma Press, 2001. Investigates the manner in which Indian sovereignty has eroded since the 1787 U.S. Constitution.

Wilkinson, Charles F. *Messages from Frank's Landing: A Story of Salmon, Treaties and the Indian Way.* One of the first political goals of the National Indian Youth Council was to guarantee Indian fishing rights.

World Wide Web

"The Chippewas Want Their Rights." http://www.time.com/time/magazine/article/0,9171,946398,00.html. A 1979 *Time* article that describes Judge Fox's decision on Indian fishing rights in Michigan. It explores Indian militancy as well as white racism.

"Defending Our Treaty Rights: Historical Timeline." http://www.saulttribe.com/index.php?option=com_content&task=view&id=414&Itemid=2. Can be downloaded as PDF. Short summary and detailed annotated time line.

"The Great Lakes Indian Fish & Wildlife Commission." http://www.glifwc.org/. Up-to-date information, publications, and, most interestingly, maps of treaty rights zones for specific tribes.

"Native American Right - Hunting and Fishing Rights." http://law.jrank.org/pages/8750/Native-American-Rights-Hunting-Fishing-Rights.html. A general overview of reserved Indian hunting and fishing rights.

"State, Tribes Approve Historic Inland Hunting and Fishing Rights Agreement." http://www.michigan.gov/dnr/0,1607,7-153–181563–,00.html. A 2007 agreement that is an attempt to halt any more dispute over Indian fishing and hunting rights.

"Tribal Fishery." http://www.1836cora.org/tribalfishery.html. Brief overview of
    Indian fishing in the Great Lakes with photographs.
"Tribal Issues and Perspectives." http://www.glrc.us/documents/strategy/
    GLRC-Tribal-Briefing-Paper.pdf. PDF that provides information on
    Indian tribal sovereignty, fishing and hunting rights, and basic informa-
    tion about the Indians of the Great Lakes.

Multimedia Source

Lighting the Seventh Fire. Dir. Sandra Osawa. P.O.V., 1995. DVD. 48 minutes.
    Documents the treaty rights of Chippewa Indians in Wisconsin to spear
    fish in Lac De Flambeau and the racist backlash Indians suffered from
    local non-Indians.

98. *California v. Cabazon Band of Mission Indians* (1987)

For some time California tried to regulate or prevent Indian gambling
operations in the state, and it brought the Cabazon band to court to settle
the matter. After many years of litigation, the Supreme Court, in
California v. Cabazon, 1987, upheld the right of the Cabazon band of
Indians to operate casinos or other gambling activities free of state regulations and laws. After the "Cabazon Decision," a wave of Indian gaming
operations opened across the nation, accounting for billions of dollars of
revenue each year by the 2000s. This flood of economic opportunity led
to the passage of the Indian Gaming Regulatory Act of 1988, which
required states and Indian tribes to enter into "compacts" in order to
regulate Indian gaming in any particular state. These compacts made
partners of states and tribes when it comes to Indian gaming enterprises,
and Indian tribes cannot operate without them, especially after the case
of *Seminole Tribe v. Florida,* which ruled that states were immune to suits
brought by Indian tribes. For the most part, Indian gaming has been a
boon for Indian reservations and surrounding communities, especially
those reservations located near large metropolitan areas, but the overall
benefit to most Indian tribes has been minimal. Most tribal members
and their tribes are not rich from Indian gaming; nevertheless, a very
few extremely wealthy tribes have led many to believe this stereotype.
At this point, as most studies show the benefits outweigh the detriments,
the negative impact of Indian gaming has not been adequately analyzed.

TERM PAPER SUGGESTIONS

1. Examine the issue of sovereignty in the ability of Indian tribes to own and operate gambling enterprises. How is gambling an exercise of tribal sovereignty, and how is it comparable to state-sanctioned gambling operations like Las Vegas, Nevada?

2. Examine how the sovereignty of states was protected by the Supreme Court's decision in *Seminole Tribe v. Florida*. How did that decision weaken tribal sovereignty and authority within a state? Why must Indian tribes form compacts with states in order to open and operate a gambling enterprise?

3. Study the wealthiest Indian casino tribes and provide reasons why they may be so successful.

4. The vast majority of Indian gambling operations do not make the tribe or tribal members wealthy. Why? However, the tribes benefit to some extent. How?

5. Write an essay on the negative impact of Indian casinos on the tribe and surrounding community. Do they outweigh the benefits? Are they enough to prevent the building of new Indian casinos?

6. Study and report on the negative press and the generation of negative stereotypes about Indians and casinos. Some people have a very negative view of Indians and Indian casinos.

ALTERNATIVE TERM PAPER SUGGESTIONS

1. Look for Indian gambling stereotypes in cartoons and television shows, like *Family Guy*, and, using iMovie or other software and a scanner to capture images, create a short film of the numerous stereotypical images found in visual media. "The Facts About Indian Gaming" (http://www.bluecorncomics.com/) is a good starting place.

2. Make an electronic map of Indian casinos on an ordinary U.S. map using an image or photograph of a slot machine as a symbol so that the slot machine icon can be turned on or off. The sources list Indian casinos nationwide and the dates they came into operation. You can probably add planned casinos. In this way you can show the rapid growth of Indian casinos across the land by activating the icon by year.

SUGGESTED SOURCES

Primary Sources

California v. Cabazon Band of Mission Indians, 480 U.S. 202 (1987). http://www.oyez.org/cases/1980-1989/1986/1986_85_1708/. Full text of the decision with audio oral argument, opinion announcement, and written opinion.

Indian Gaming Regulatory Act (Public Law 100-497-OCT. 17, 1988 100th Congress, Sec. 2701). http://www.nigc.gov/LawsRegulations/ IndianGamingRegulatoryAct/tabid/605/Default.aspx. Complete text of the act.

Rand, Kathryn R. L., and Steven Andrew Light. *Indian Gaming Law: Cases and Materials.* Durham, NC: Carolina Academic Press, 2007. Supplements their 2006 texts with primary source documents from over 400 tribal casinos in 30 states.

Rice, William G. *Tribal Governmental Gaming Law: Cases and Materials.* Durham, NC: Carolina Academic Press, 2007. This is a law school casebook and compilation of primary source materials.

Seminole Tribe v. Florida, 517 U.S. 44 (1996). http://www.oyez.org/cases/1990-1999/1995/1995_94_12/. Full text with audio oral argument and written opinion.

Secondary Sources

Eadington, William R., and Judy Cornelius, eds. *Indian Gaming and the Law.* Reno, NV: University of Nevada, 1998. Anthology of essays on positives and negatives of Indian gaming.

Eisler, Kim Issac. *Revenge of the Pequots: How a Small Native American Tribe Created the World's Most Profitable Casino.* New York: Simon and Schuster, 2001. A detailed history of the Mashantucket Pequots' quest for economic development through the exercise of Indian treaty rights and federal trust responsibilities.

Fromson, Brett Duval. *Hitting the Jackpot: The Inside Story of the Richest Indian Tribe in History.* New York: Atlantic Monthly Press, 2003. Narrative description of the rise the Mashantucket Pequots' casino operation in Connecticut. Very critical of Indians and Indian gaming.

Kallen, Stuart A., ed. *Indian Gaming.* Detroit, MI: Greenhaven Press, 2006. Debate book: one side of the collection explores the negative effects of Indian gaming, focusing on the economy of non-gaming tribes, while the other essays explore the positive side of Indian gaming.

Lane, Ambrose I. *Return of the Buffalo: The Story Behind America's Indian Gaming Explosion.* Westport, CT: Bergin and Garvey, 1995. A case study of the Cabazon litigation, court cases, and appeals leading up to the famous 1987 decision.

Mason, W. Dale. *Indian Gaming: Tribal Sovereignty and American Politics.* Norman, OK: University of Oklahoma Press, 2000. Shows the political conflicts between Americans Indians, casinos, and private firms. Presents the points of view of private firms and why they oppose Indian gaming.

Mullis, Angela, and David Kamper. *Indian Gaming: Who Wins?* Los Angeles, CA: American Indian Studies Center, 2000. A collection of articles examining Indian gaming history, law, and literature.

Pommersheim, Frank. *Braid of Feathers: American Indian Law and Contemporary Tribal Life.* Berkeley, CA: University of California Press, 1995. Examines the eroding of sovereignty through federal laws and courts and advocates a strengthening of sovereignty through a return to traditional tribal practices.

Rand, Kathryn R. L., and Steven Andrew Light. *Indian Gaming Law and Policy.* Durham, NC: Carolina Academic Press, 2006. Explains the complicated political issues of American Indian gaming on Indian lands and within states.

Rand, Kathryn R. L., and Steven Andrew Light. *Indian Gaming and Tribal Sovereignty: The Casino Compromise.* Lawrence, KS: University Press of Kansas, 2005. Argues that Indian gaming is an exercise of tribal sovereignty.

World Wide Web

"The Facts about Indian Gaming." http://www.bluecorncomics.com/gaming.htm. Links pages to many primary and secondary sources, and below this list are many articles on the positive and negative impacts of Indian gaming. Keep going for more interesting information, including the Indian casino in *Family Guy* and other stereotypes.

"Indian Gaming in California." http://igs.berkeley.edu/library/htIndianGaming.htm. Online essay published in 2005 by the Institute of Governmental Studies, University of California. Has a list of selected Web sites and background reading and essays.

"Indian Gaming Regulatory Act of 1988." http://www.answers.com/topic/indian-gaming-regulatory-act. Brief summary of the act with external links.

Nash, Douglas Roger. "Indian Gaming." http://library.findlaw.com/1999/Jan/1/241489.html. A brief 1999 article summarizing the history and laws of Indian gaming.

National Indian Gaming Association. http://www.indiangaming.org/info/alerts/index.shtml. This is a links page maintained by the association to the most current laws and legislation on Indian gaming, which are given in PDF form. For example, this site has a PDF report on "The Economic Impact of Indian Gaming in 2006."

National Indian Gaming Commission. http://www.nigc.gov/. The Gaming Commission is charged with regulating gaming activities on Indian lands; the site has a wealth of information.

"*Seminole Tribe v. Florida.*" http://www.answers.com/topic/seminole-tribe-v-florida. Brief summary of the Supreme Court opinion with external links.

Multimedia Source

Tribal Nations: The Story of Federal Indian Law. Dir. Lisa Jaeger. Tanana Chiefs, 2006. DVD. 60 minutes. Introductory-level documentary of how federal Indian law has developed in the United States.

99. Native American Graves Protection and Repatriation Act (1990)

The passage of the Native American Graves Protection and Repatriation Act (NAGPRA) in 1990 required museums and any federal agency in possession of Indian human remains, funerary objects, sacred objects, and objects of cultural patrimony (important communally-owned objects) to inventory the items, to affiliate the remains/objects to a modern tribe, and to repatriate them (send them back to their homelands). Plus, any human remains and cultural objects located on tribal and federal lands would be protected under NAGPRA. The act clarifies the ownership rights of American Indians over human remains and cultural objects identified as originating from their tribe. The act imposes criminal penalties for "sale, purchase, or transport" of human remains and cultural artifacts without a legal right of possession. The clarification and criminal penalties are important because, in the past, U.S. museums, universities, agencies, and individuals who have obtained these objects from a variety of methods, some by grave robbing, have claimed ownership of items despite efforts of tribes to get them returned. However, a six-year dispute over the ownership of the Kennewick Man, a 9,000-year-old skeleton found near the Columbia River in Washington State, has complicated the definition of ownership. The case was decided in favor of the scientists, which, to many tribes, erodes the protective value of the act. Also causing contention is the power of museum experts and archeologists to make decisions on affiliation, which means they have the power to determine whether remains or objects belong to any particular tribe existing today, without necessarily obtaining any input from the tribes making a claim.

TERM PAPER SUGGESTIONS

1. Historically, Indian human remains and cultural objects have been the focus of scientific study and collector admiration. Write on the racist implications and disrespect of the dead these practices of possession imply.

2. Collectors of Indian artifacts have often acquired their possessions via nefarious and illegal means, even before the passage of NAGPRA. Examine the many cases where NAGPRA has been an important deterrent to the grave robbing practices seen in the past.

3. Write a statistical report on the volume of human remains and cultural objects that museums and others have in their possession. What percentage has actually been repatriated?

4. Discuss the issue of affiliation. Experts must determine whether remains or objects belong to a particular tribe of Indians living today. What are the problems and controversies surrounding affiliation? Why would Indians challenge expert opinions and assessments?

5. Examine the Kennewick Man controversy, which is another issue of affiliation. Why did the court rule in favor of the scientists?

6. Investigate the various sacred objects and cultural objects, like totem poles, that have been returned to Indian tribes. In some cases, the theft of sacred objects actually put an end to certain ceremonies until their return.

ALTERNATIVE TERM PAPER SUGGESTIONS

1. Make a slide show of images of Indian artifacts collected from online museum exhibits. How many of them are sacred or of cultural significance? How many of them are the property of the museum, given permission by tribes to exhibit the artifacts, and what is the number of those items that are not affiliated with any particular tribe?

2. Create a Web site that shows famously looted areas on Indian lands with a cautionary slogan warning of the illegality of taking Indian artifacts from Indian lands.

SUGGESTED SOURCES

Primary Source

Native American Graves Protection and Repatriation Act, Public Law 101-601—NOV. 16, 1990. http://www.nps.gov/history/nagpra/MANDATES/25USC3001etseq.htm. Full text of the law passed by the 101st Congress on November 16, 1990.

Secondary Sources

Bray, Tamara. *The Future of the Past: Archaeologists, Native Americans and Repatriation.* New York: Garland Publishing, 2001. An anthology exploring repatriation from many different perspectives.

Brown, Michael. *Who Owns Native Culture.* Cambridge, MA: Harvard University Press, 2003. Through a series of cases studies, the author examines the efforts of American Indians to reclaim legal ownership to artifacts, places, and practices.

Ferguson, T. J., et al. "Repatriation at the Pueblo of Zuni: Diverse Solutions to Complex Problems." *American Indian Quarterly* 20, no. 2 (Spring 1996): 251–73. Explores the long history of the Zunis' efforts to repatriate cultural property and human remains, which started in the 1970s, long before NAGPRA.

Fine-Dare, Kathleen S. *Grave Injustice: The American Indian Repatriation Movement and NAGPRA.* Lincoln, NE: University of Nebraska Press, 2002. Details the efforts of Indians to recover objects and remains appropriated by a variety of institutions and people.

Gulliford, Andrew. "Bones of Contention: The Repatriation of Native American Human Remains." *The Public Historian* 18, no. 4 (Autumn 1996): 119–43. A good general introduction to the issues and complexities involved in reclaiming and repatriating Indian human remains.

Jones, P. *Respect for the Ancestors: American Indian Cultural Affiliation in the American West.* Boulder, CO: Bäuu Press, 2005. A scholarly study, sparked by the discovery of Kennewick Man, of the connection of Indians of the northwest to their ancient ancestors and the role of NAGPRA as a guideline for inquiry.

Milesuah, Devon A., ed. *Repatriation Reader: Who Owns American Indian Remains?* Lincoln, NE: University of Nebraska Press, 2000. A collection of essays from scholars and others exploring key issues surrounding NAGPRA.

Price, H. Marcus, III. *Disputing the Dead: U.S. Law on Aboriginal Remains and Grave Goods.* Columbia, MO: University of Missouri Press, 1991. A detailed analysis of the conflicting views of the legal and proper way to handle Indian grave goods.

Riding In, James. "Repatriation: A Pawnee's Perspective."*American Indian Quarterly* 20, no. 2 (Spring 1996): 238–50. Argues for Indian participation in the definition and identification of human remains and cultural artifacts rather than *only* relying on expert opinion.

Thomas, David Hurst. *Skull Wars: Kennewick Man, Archeology and the Battle for Native American Identity.* New York: Basic Books, 2001. A sweeping analysis, survey, and history of American archeology and American Indians, ending with the impact that NAGPRA has had on changing the way archeologists study and define American Indians.

World Wide Web

The ABCs of NAGPRA. http://bss.sfsu.edu/nagpra/defs.htm. A good site that breaks down the law into easily understandable parts. Includes a glossary of terms and words such as "Rights of Possession."

American Indian Ritual Object Repatriation Foundation. http://www
.repatriationfoundation.org/. An excellent resource site on ritual, sacred,
and cultural objects.

"Kennewick Man." http://www.pbs.org/newshour/bb/science/kennewick/.
Chronicles a six-year dispute over an 8,400-year-old skeleton found in
Washington State, the oldest bones found in North America. Scientists
want to study the bones, while Indians want to rebury them immediately.

Kinzer, Stephen. "Homecoming for Totem Poles." http://www.unesco.org/
courier/2001_04/uk/doss23.htm. News story of the return of artifacts
found in the American Museum of Natural History in New York to their
rightful owners, the Tlingit Indians of Alaska.

NAGPRA. http://www.answers.com/topic/native-american-graves-protection-
and-repatriation-act. Brief summary with a bibliography and external
links to relevant information.

"Update of Compilation of State Repatriation, Reburial and Grave Protection
Laws (July 1997)." http://www.arrowheads.com/burials.htm. A links
page to state repatriation, reburial, and grave protection laws; the page
includes an overview and summary of the NAGPRA with a link to the
full text of the act.

National NAGPRA. http://www.nps.gov/history/nagpra/. Official federal Web site
of NAGPRA, loaded with laws, regulations, documents, and publications.

Multimedia Sources

Kennewick Man: An Epic Drama of the West. Dir. Kyle Carver and Ryan Purcell.
2002. DVD. 86 minutes. Documentary exploring the NAGPRA and
rights of scientists to examine and to conduct tests on bones of ancient
North American origin.

Mystery of the First Americans. Dir. Mark J. Davis. WGBH, 2000. VHS.
60 Minutes. A PBS documentary examining the legal debate over the
"ownership" of Kennewick Man, the 9,000-year-old Indian skeleton
found in Washington State.

100. Native American Languages Act of 1990

Of the many reforms that have reversed the assimilation/Americanization
policies of the late 1800s and early 1900s, the Native American Languages
Act (NALA), PL 101–477 (October 30, 1990), has been the most important

to Indian tribes in terms of their efforts at language preservation, despite the fact that no new programs, services, or funding were authorized. Because of Indian religious ceremonies and rituals, oral histories and stories, and other cultural and societal identifiers, language preservation has been equated with cultural preservation. The 10-point findings of Section 102 of the act recognizes this link as well as past policies that have tried to break that link between language and culture. For example, Item 5 reads: "there is a lack of clear, comprehensive, and consistent Federal policy on treatment of Native American languages which has often resulted in acts of suppression and extermination of Native American languages and cultures." The "Declaration of Policy" calls for the United States to "preserve, protect, and promote the rights and freedom of Native Americans to use, practice, and develop Native American Languages." From 1880 to well into the 1980s, many Indian schools discouraged students from speaking their tribal languages, and well into the 1950s corporal punishment was commonly administered if they did. In many tribes across the nation, tribal languages have almost become extinct, and in others, the languages have been severely crippled as the number fluent speakers has shrunk over time. With the NALA and the outlawing of the suppression and eradication of Indian languages, the hope of many Indian tribes is that this trend will reverse.

TERM PAPER SUGGESTIONS

1. Write on the history of federal Indian education and policy that discouraged, punished, and eradicated the speaking of American Indian languages in schools.

2. Explore the connection of language suppression and eradication in the goals of reformers and federal agencies to civilize and Americanize the Indian.

3. Explore the most recent U.S. census statistical records of the number of Indians still speaking their native language and the number of children under five learning tribal language in homes and local communities.

4. When you consider that the NALA does not offer any funding or create any new Indian services or programs, why do you think Indians have been enthusiastic about it becoming a law?

5. Research the numbers and success of Indian language revitalization and recovery programs in the United States since 1990. How has NALA helped?

6. Report on the use of the World Wide Web as a tool for Indian language revitalization and recovery. What is the significance of so many language resources on the WWW?

ALTERNATIVE TERM PAPER SUGGESTIONS

1. Create an interactive time line graph of Indian language decline and perhaps extinction. Link to scanned maps of Indian language regions and U.S. census records (number of speakers, number of speakers under five years of age, and the overall Indian population). Does the graph line ever make an upward trend?

2. Study Plains Indian sign language in its simplest form and share your knowledge with a group. Use a Microsoft PowerPoint slide show to teach listeners basic shapes and gestures.

SUGGESTED SOURCES

Primary Sources

Native American Languages Act of 1990 (NALA), P.L. 101-477 (October 30, 1990). http://ourworld.compuserve.com/homepages/jWCRAWFORD/nala.htm. The complete text of the act. PDF version is available here: http://www.nabe.org/documents/policy_legislation/NALanguagesActs.pdf.

U.S. Census Bureau. "Characteristics of American Indians and Alaska Natives by Tribe and Language: 2000." Washington, DC: U.S. Government Printing Office, 2003. Statistical information from the latest U.S. census.

Secondary Sources

Bruchac, Joseph. *Lasting Echoes: An Oral History of Native American People.* New York: Silver Whistle, 1997. Illustrated (oral) history told from the perspective of American Indians, demonstrating the power of oral tradition as a powerful cultural form linked to tribal languages.

Kroskrity, Paul V., and Margaret C. Field, eds. *Native Language Ideologies.* Tucson, AZ: University of Arizona Press, 2009. A collection of essays that samples the language ideologies of Indian tribes of the Americas.

Leap, William L. "Pathways and Barriers to Indian Language Literacy-Building on the Northern Ute Reservation." *Anthropology & Education Quarterly* 22, no. 1 (March 1991): 21–41. Explores the difficulties of the tribe's efforts to introduce a written form of the tribal language as a way of promoting a return to tribal language literacy.

Mallery, Garrich. *Sign Language among North American Indians.* Mineola, NY: Dover Publications, 2001. Illustrated and expertly described sign-words and body movements for phrases and sentences of Indian tribes, an almost extinct language art form.

Morgan, Mindy J. "Redefining the Ojibwe Classroom: Indigenous Language Programs within Larch Research Universities." *Anthropology & Education*

Quarterly 36, no. 1 (March 2005): 96–103. Explores the problems of language immersion instruction and of bringing the Indian community into large educational institutions.

Reyhner, Jon. *Education and Language Restoration.* New York: Chelsea House, 2006. Brief history of Indian education from board school experiences to the present day. In this 158-page book, Reyhner covers language and culture revitalization, language policies, and education goals.

Reyhner, Jon, et al., eds. *Nurturing Native Languages.* Flagstaff, AZ: Northern Arizona University Press, 2003. Examines immersion language teaching methods, use of technology in language revitalization, and efforts of Indian tribes to reclaim linguistic/cultural heritages.

Reyhner, Jon, and Jeanne M. Oyawin Eder. *American Indian Education, a History.* Norman, OK: University of Oklahoma Press, 2004. Examines the 180-year history of the United States' efforts to assimilate Indian children by destroying their culture languages.

Silver, Shirley, and Wick R. Miller. *American Indian Languages.* Tucson, AZ: University of Arizona Press, 2000. A comprehensive survey of the diversity and complexities of American Indian languages within cultural and social context.

Sims, Christine P. "Tribal Languages and the Challenges of Revitalization." *Anthropology & Education Quarterly* 36, no. 1 (March 2005): 104–6. Compares language revitalization within academic institutional settings to language revitalization within families and communities.

White Hat, Albert, Sr. *Reading and Writing the Lakota Language: Lakota Iyapi Un Wowapi Nahan Yawapi.* Jael Kampfe, ed. Salt Lake City, UT: University of Utah Press, 1999. Fifteen units with lessons in Lakota vocabulary and grammar as well as in pronunciation. Lakota philosophy and world-view are also addressed.

World Wide Web

"General Language Resources." http://www.hanksville.org/NAresources/indices/ NAlanguage.html. A comprehensive links site to numerous general and specific Indian language resources.

Kipp, Darrell Robes. "American Indian Millennium: Renewing Our Ways for Future Generations." http://www.pieganinstitute.org/renewingways .html. Personal reflection on the loss of language in the Blackfeet Tribe of Montana and the recovery of that language since 1990.

"Links to Native American Language Resources." http://www-rcf.usc.edu/ ~cmmr/Native_American.html—language resources. Appearing below the links to specific tribes is an index of full-text articles and resources, with many interesting resources for teachers and students.

Littlejohn, Jim. "Impact of the Native American Language Act on Public School Curriculum." http://findarticles.com/p/articles/mi_qa3994/is_200010/ai_n8926958. An article from 2000 exploring the origins and impact of bilingual education in public schools since 1990.

Reyhner, Jon. "Native American Language Renewal." http://www.tribalcollegejournal.org/themag/backissues/spring2000/spring2000 resources.html. Brief and informative introduction to an annotated bibliography for Indian language resources.

The Society for the Study of the Indigenous Languages of the Americas. http://www.ssila.org/. Links to learning aids and numerous Internet resources.

Multimedia Source

Transitions: Death of a Mother Tongue. Dir. and prod. Darrell Robes Kipp and Joe Fisher. Browning, MT: The Piegan Institute, 1991. VHS. 30 minutes. Chronicles the disappearance of the Blackfeet language (and other Indian languages) during the 1890–1990 period. Information available from 406–338–3518.

Index

Mi'kmaq Tribe, 32, 338
Mineral rights, 223, 323
Minnesota removal, 159–60
M'Intosh, William, 125
Miwok Tribe, 182
Modoc Tribe, 182, 186, 189
Mohawk Tribe, 32, 79–80, 83, 103
Montana, 190, 233–34
Montezuma, Carlos, 238
Mooney, James, 1, 249
Moraviantown, Canada, 114–15
Mortality rates, 292
Mourt's Relation: A Journal of the Pilgrims at Plymouth, 1622, Part I, 22
Murder, 331, 338
Murray, John (Lord Dunmore), 76–77
Museums and Indian artifacts, 356
Mystic, Connecticut, 29

NAC (Native American Church), 238, 249–50
NAGPRA (Native American Graves Protection and Repatriation Act), 356
Naiche, 186
Nakaidoklini, 186
Nakota Tribe, 238
NALA (Native American Languages Act), 359–60
Narragansett Tribe, 29, 36
Natchez Massacre, 50–51
Natchez Tribe, 50–51
National Coalition on Racism in Sports and Media, 303
National Congress of American Indians (NCAI), 274–75, 301
National Indian Youth Council (NIYC), 299–300, 301, 310
Native Alaskans, 253, 275, 316–17

Native American Church (NAC), 238, 249–50
Native American Graves Protection and Repatriation Act (NAGPRA), 356
Native American Languages Act (NALA), 359–60
Native American Youth Council, 275
Native Hawaiians, 341
Navajo Tribe, 163, 271, 281
NCAI (National Congress of American Indians), 274–75, 301
Nebraska removal, 136
Neolin (Delaware Prophet), 66, 68–69, 111
New Bern, North Carolina, 47
New Echota, 144, 150, 156
New Hampshire Indians, 43
New Mexico, 5, 9, 39, 40, 163
Newspapers: Indian, 132–33, 242; World War I, 245
Nez Perce War, 194–95
Nixon, Richard, 320
NIYC (National Indian Youth Council), 299–300, 301, 310
North Carolina, 9, 46–47
Northwest Ordinance of 1787, 89–90, 91
Northwest Territory, 86, 90

Oglala Lakota Sioux Tribe, 173–74
Ohio, 65, 73–74; Dunmore's War, 76–77; Indian resistance, 86–87
Oklahoma, removal to, 135, 156
Old World diseases, 1–3, 5, 36, 39
Olympic athletes, 241–42
Oñate, Juan de, 9–10, 11, 12, 39
Oneida Tribe, 32, 83, 103
Onondaga Tribe, 32, 54, 83, 103, 254
Opechancanough (chief), 17, 25
Osceola (chief), 153

About the Author

PATRICK RUSSELL LEBEAU, Ph.D., is professor of Writing, Rhetoric, and American Cultures and former director of American Indian Studies at Michigan State University. He has published two books: *Stands Alone, Faces and Other Poems* (1999) and *Rethinking Michigan Indian History* (2005). He is an enrolled member of the Cheyenne River Sioux Indian Reservation of South Dakota (his father's home). His mother is from Turtle Mountain Chippewa Indian Reservation of North Dakota.